ASCENT
CENTER FOR TECHNICAL KNOWLEDGE

AutoCAD®/AutoCAD LT® 2018 Fundamentals Part 2

Student Guide

Metric - 1st Edition

AUTODESK.
Authorized Publisher

CONTINUING EDUCATION AIA

ASCENT - Center for Technical Knowledge®
AutoCAD®/AutoCAD LT® 2018
Fundamentals - Part 2
Metric - 1st Edition

Prepared and produced by:

ASCENT Center for Technical Knowledge
630 Peter Jefferson Parkway, Suite 175
Charlottesville, VA 22911

866-527-2368
www.ASCENTed.com

Lead Contributor: Renu Muthoo

ASCENT - Center for Technical Knowledge is a division of Rand Worldwide, Inc., providing custom developed knowledge products and services for leading engineering software applications. ASCENT is focused on specializing in the creation of education programs that incorporate the best of classroom learning and technology-based training offerings.

We welcome any comments you may have regarding this student guide, or any of our products. To contact us please email: feedback@ASCENTed.com.

AS-ACD1801-FND1MT-SG2 // IS-ACD1801-FND1MT-SG2

Contents Part 1

Contents Part 2

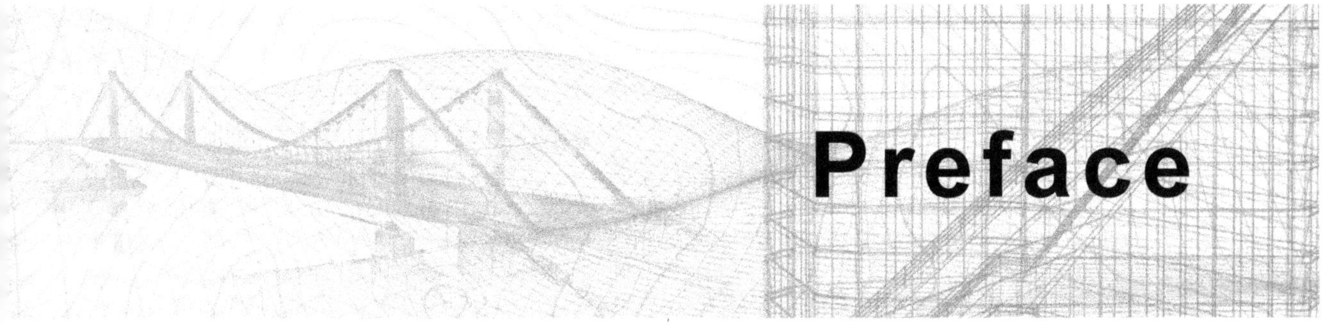

Preface

The *AutoCAD®/AutoCAD LT® 2018: Fundamentals* student guide is designed for those using AutoCAD® or AutoCAD LT® 2018 with a Windows operating system. This student guide is not designed for the AutoCAD for Mac software.

The objective of *AutoCAD/AutoCAD LT 2018: Fundamentals* is to enable students to create a basic 2D drawing in the AutoCAD software.

Part 1 (chapters 1 to 20) covers the essential core topics for working with the AutoCAD software. The teaching strategy is to start with a few basic tools that enable the student to create and edit a simple drawing, and then continue to develop those tools. More advanced tools are introduced throughout the student guide. Not every command or option is covered, because the intent is to show the most *essential* tools and concepts, such as:

- Understanding the AutoCAD workspace and user interface.
- Using basic drawing, editing, and viewing tools.
- Organizing drawing objects on layers.
- Inserting reusable symbols (blocks).
- Preparing a layout to be plotted.
- Adding text, hatching, and dimensions.

Part 2 (chapters 21 to 32) continues with more sophisticated techniques that extend your mastery of the software. For example, here you go beyond the basic skill of inserting a block to learning how to create blocks, and beyond the basic skill of using a template to understand the process of setting up a template. You learn skills such as:

- Using more advanced editing and construction techniques.
- Adding parametric constraints to objects.
- Creating local and global blocks.
- Setting up layers, styles, and templates.
- Using advanced plotting and publishing options.

This student guide refers to both the AutoCAD and AutoCAD LT software as the AutoCAD software. All topics, including features and commands, relate to both the AutoCAD and AutoCAD LT software unless specifically noted otherwise.

Note on Software Setup

This student guide assumes a standard installation of the software using the default preferences during installation. Lectures and practices use the standard software templates and default options for the Content Libraries.

Students and Educators can Access Free Autodesk Software and Resources

Autodesk challenges you to get started with free educational licenses for professional software and creativity apps used by millions of architects, engineers, designers, and hobbyists today. Bring Autodesk software into your classroom, studio, or workshop to learn, teach, and explore real-world design challenges the way professionals do.

Get started today - register at the Autodesk Education Community and download one of the many Autodesk software applications available.

Visit www.autodesk.com/joinedu/

Note: Free products are subject to the terms and conditions of the end-user license and services agreement that accompanies the software. The software is for personal use for education purposes and is not intended for classroom or lab use.

Lead Contributor: Renu Muthoo

Renu uses her instructional design training to develop courseware for AutoCAD and AutoCAD vertical products, Autodesk 3ds Max, Autodesk Showcase and various other Autodesk software products. She has worked with Autodesk products for the past 20 years with a main focus on design visualization software.

Renu holds a bachelor's degree in Computer Engineering and started her career as a Instructional Designer/Author where she co-authored a number of Autodesk 3ds Max and AutoCAD books, some of which were translated into other languages for a wide audience reach. In her next role as a Technical Specialist at a 3D visualization company, Renu used 3ds Max in real-world scenarios on a daily basis. There, she developed customized 3D web planner solutions to create specialized 3D models with photorealistic texturing and lighting to produce high quality renderings.

Renu Muthoo has been the Lead Contributor for *AutoCAD®/AutoCAD LT® Fundamentals* since 2015.

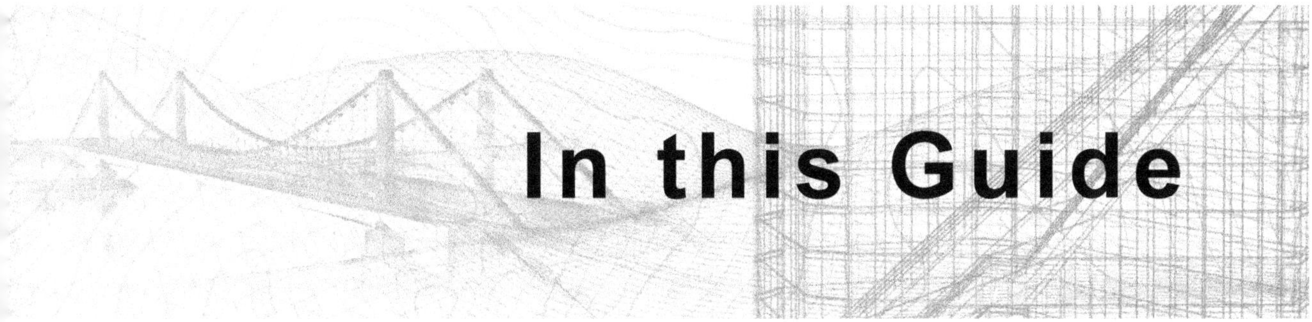

In this Guide

The following images highlight some of the features that can be found in this Student Guide.

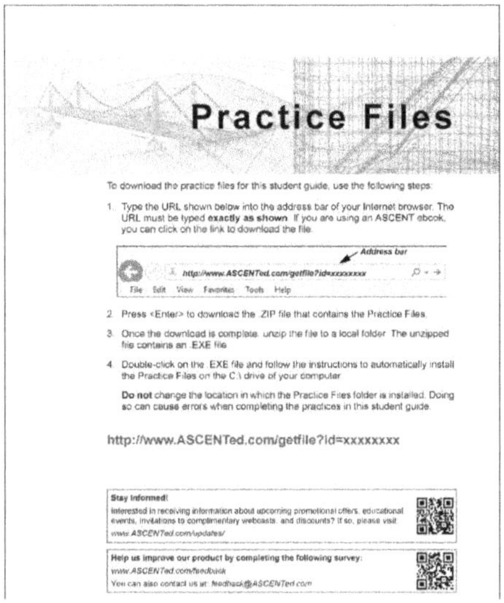

Practice Files

To download the practice files for this student guide, use the following steps:

1. Type the URL shown below into the address bar of your Internet browser. The URL must be typed **exactly as shown**. If you are using an ASCENT ebook, you can click on the link to download the file.

   Address bar
   http://www.ASCENTed.com/getfile?id=xxxxxxxx
   File Edit View Favorites Tools Help

2. Press <Enter> to download the .ZIP file that contains the Practice Files.
3. Once the download is complete, unzip the file to a local folder. The unzipped file contains an .EXE file.
4. Double-click on the .EXE file and follow the instructions to automatically install the Practice Files on the C:\ drive of your computer.

   Do not change the location in which the Practice Files folder is installed. Doing so can cause errors when completing the practices in this student guide.

http://www.ASCENTed.com/getfile?id=xxxxxxxx

Stay Informed!
Interested in receiving information about upcoming promotional offers, educational events, invitations to complimentary webcasts, and discounts? If so, please visit: *www.ASCENTed.com/updates/*

Help us improve our product by completing the following survey:
www.ASCENTed.com/feedback
You can also contact us at: *feedback@ASCENTed.com*

FTP link for practice files

Practice Files

The Practice Files page tells you how to download and install the practice files that are provided with this student guide.

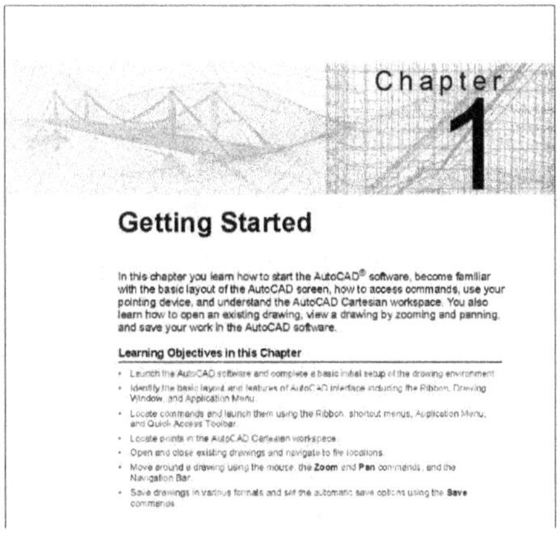

Chapter 1

Getting Started

In this chapter you learn how to start the AutoCAD® software, become familiar with the basic layout of the AutoCAD screen, how to access commands, use your pointing device, and understand the AutoCAD Cartesian workspace. You also learn how to open an existing drawing, view a drawing by zooming and panning, and save your work in the AutoCAD software.

Learning Objectives in this Chapter

- Launch the AutoCAD software and complete a basic initial setup of the drawing environment.
- Identify the basic layout and features of AutoCAD interface including the Ribbon, Drawing Window, and Application Menu.
- Locate commands and launch them using the Ribbon, shortcut menus, Application Menu, and Quick Access Toolbar.
- Locate points in the AutoCAD Cartesian workspace.
- Open and close existing drawings and navigate to file locations.
- Move around a drawing using the mouse, the **Zoom** and **Pan** commands, and the Navigation Bar.
- Save drawings in various formats and set the automatic save options using the **Save** commands.

Learning Objectives for the chapter

Chapters

Each chapter begins with a brief introduction and a list of the chapter's Learning Objectives.

Side notes

Side notes are hints or additional information for the current topic.

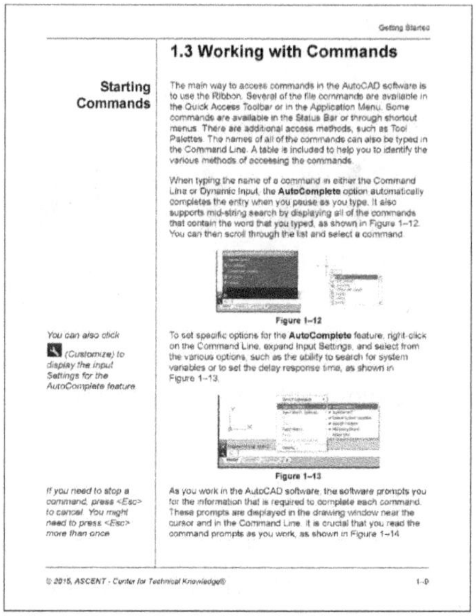

Getting Started

1.3 Working with Commands

Starting Commands

The main way to access commands in the AutoCAD software is to use the Ribbon. Several of the file commands are available in the Quick Access Toolbar or in the Application Menu. Some commands are available in the Status Bar or through shortcut menus. There are additional access methods, such as Tool Palettes. The names of all of the commands can also be typed in the Command Line. A table is included to help you to identify the various methods of accessing the commands.

When typing the name of a command in either the Command Line or Dynamic Input, the **AutoComplete** option automatically completes the entry when you pause as you type. It also supports mid-string search by displaying all of the commands that contain the word that you typed, as shown in Figure 1–12. You can then scroll through the list and select a command.

Figure 1–12

You can also click (Customize) to display the input Settings for the AutoComplete feature.

To set specific options for the **AutoComplete** feature, right-click on the Command Line, expand Input Settings, and select from the various options, such as the ability to search for system variables or to set the delay response time, as shown in Figure 1–13.

Figure 1–13

If you need to stop a command, press <Esc> to cancel. You might need to press <Esc> more than once.

As you work in the AutoCAD software, the software prompts you for the information that is required to complete each command. These prompts are displayed in the drawing window near the cursor and in the Command Line. It is crucial that you read the command prompts as you work, as shown in Figure 1–14.

© 2015, ASCENT - Center for Technical Knowledge® 1–9

Instructional Content

Each chapter is split into a series of sections of instructional content on specific topics. These lectures include the descriptions, step-by-step procedures, figures, hints, and information you need to achieve the chapter's Learning Objectives.

Practice Objectives

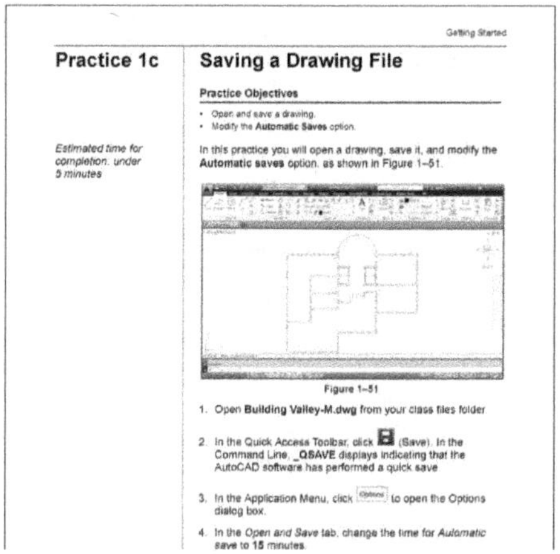

Getting Started

Practice 1c **Saving a Drawing File**

Practice Objectives

- Open and save a drawing.
- Modify the **Automatic Saves** option.

Estimated time for completion: under 5 minutes

In this practice you will open a drawing, save it, and modify the **Automatic saves** option, as shown in Figure 1–51.

Figure 1–51

1. Open **Building Valley-M.dwg** from your class files folder.
2. In the Quick Access Toolbar, click (Save). In the Command Line, **_QSAVE** displays indicating that the AutoCAD software has performed a quick save.
3. In the Application Menu, click Options to open the Options dialog box.
4. In the *Open and Save* tab, change the time for *Automatic save* to **15** minutes.

Practices

Practices enable you to use the software to perform a hands-on review of a topic.

Some practices require you to use prepared practice files, which can be downloaded from the link found on the Practice Files page.

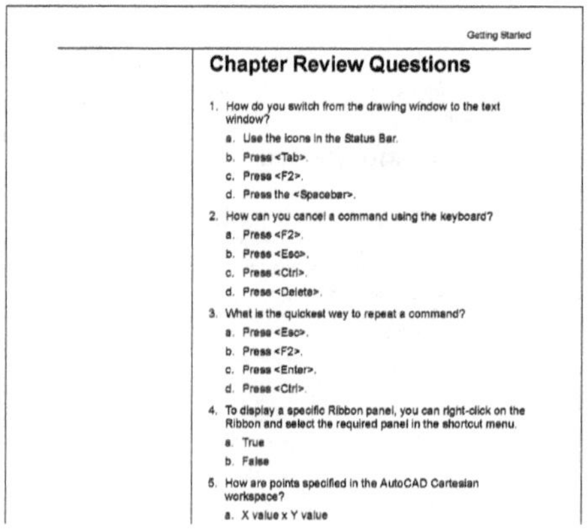

Getting Started

Chapter Review Questions

1. How do you switch from the drawing window to the text window?
   a. Use the icons in the Status Bar.
   b. Press <Tab>.
   c. Press <F2>.
   d. Press the <Spacebar>.
2. How can you cancel a command using the keyboard?
   a. Press <F2>.
   b. Press <Esc>.
   c. Press <Ctrl>.
   d. Press <Delete>.
3. What is the quickest way to repeat a command?
   a. Press <Esc>.
   b. Press <F2>.
   c. Press <Enter>.
   d. Press <Ctrl>.
4. To display a specific Ribbon panel, you can right-click on the Ribbon and select the required panel in the shortcut menu.
   a. True
   b. False
5. How are points specified in the AutoCAD Cartesian workspace?
   a. X value x Y value

Chapter Review Questions

Chapter review questions, located at the end of each chapter, enable you to review the key concepts and learning objectives of the chapter.

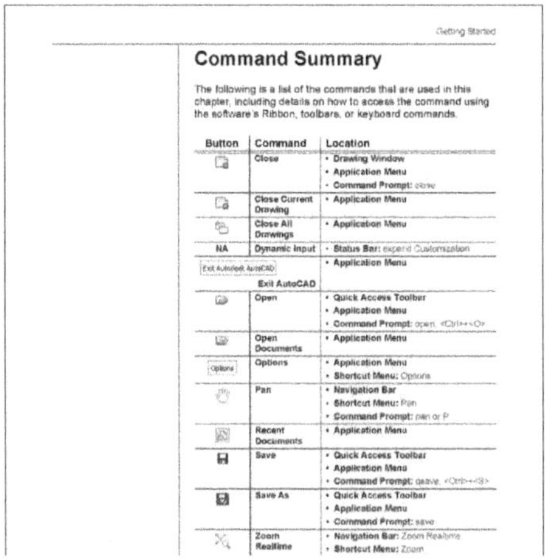

Command Summary

The Command Summary is located at the end of each chapter. It contains a list of the software commands that are used throughout the chapter, and provides information on where the command is found in the software.

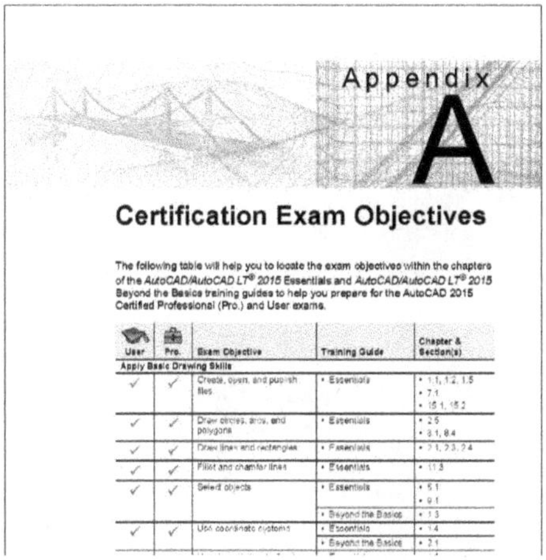

Autodesk Certification Exam Appendix

This appendix includes a list of the topics and objectives for the Autodesk Certification exams, and the chapter and section in which the relevant content can be found.

Icons in this Student Guide

The following icons are used to help you quickly and easily find helpful information.

New in **2018**	Indicates items that are new in the AutoCAD 2018 software.
Enhanced in **2018**	Indicates items that have been enhanced in the AutoCAD 2018 software.

Practice Files

To download the practice files for this student guide, use the following steps:

1. Type the URL shown below into the address bar of your Internet browser. The URL must be typed **exactly as shown**. If you are using an ASCENT ebook, you can click on the link to download the file.

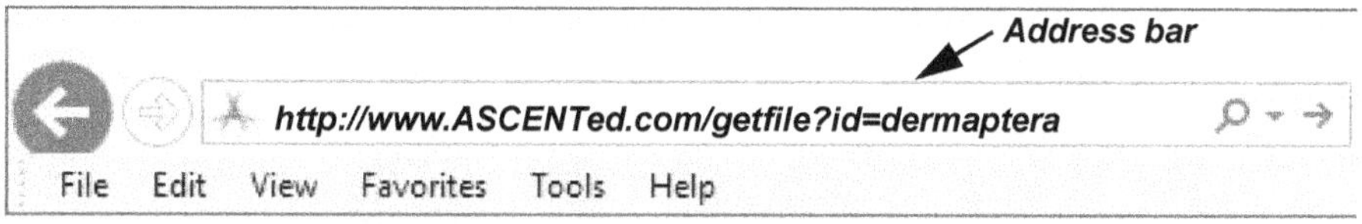

2. Press <Enter> to download the .ZIP file that contains the Practice Files.

3. Once the download is complete, unzip the file to a local folder. The unzipped file contains an .EXE file.

4. Double-click on the .EXE file and follow the instructions to automatically install the Practice Files on the C:\ drive of your computer.

   Do not change the location in which the Practice Files folder is installed. Doing so can cause errors when completing the practices in this student guide.

http://www.ASCENTed.com/getfile?id=dermaptera

Stay Informed!

Interested in receiving information about upcoming promotional offers, educational events, invitations to complimentary webcasts, and discounts? If so, please visit:

www.ASCENTed.com/updates/

Help us improve our product by completing the following survey:

www.ASCENTed.com/feedback

You can also contact us at: *feedback@ASCENTed.com*

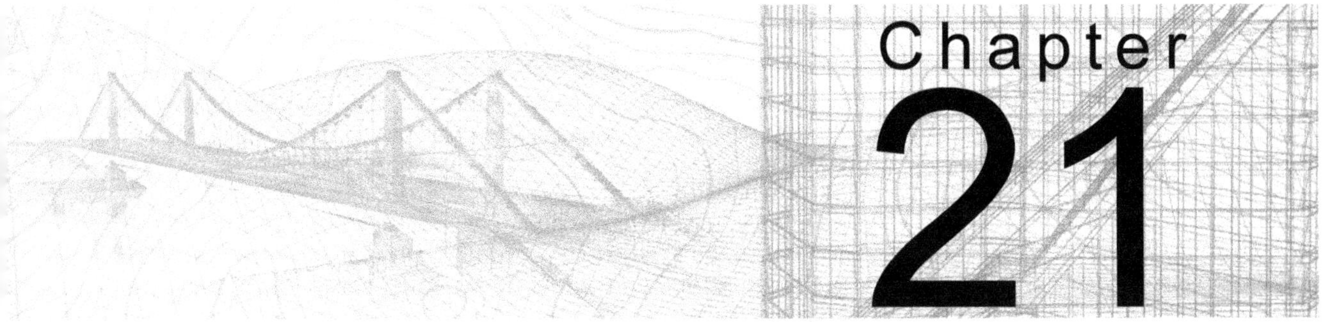

Working Effectively with AutoCAD

In this chapter you learn how to work with the ribbon and Workspaces, work with keyboard shortcuts, use copy and paste methods to duplicate information between drawings, edit objects with advanced grip techniques, and use additional layer tools.

Learning Objectives in this Chapter

- Create and save a custom workspace.
- Set up the ribbon to dock and hide palettes.
- Start commands using various methods.
- Create new objects of the same type and properties as a selected object.
- Cycle through overlapping objects and select one.
- Control the transparency and visibility of objects in a drawing.
- Switch between multiple open drawings using various interface components and commands.
- Copy, move, and paste information from one drawing to another.
- Modify layers and objects using grips.

21.1 Creating a Custom Workspace

As you learn the various ways of working with the AutoCAD® software, you need to set up your personal workspace. You can specify how the ribbon tabs and panels display, which tool palettes you want open, and how you want them to be organized, as shown in the example in Figure 21–1. When you are finished, you can create a new workspace to save the arrangement.

To maximize the drawing window, you can temporarily toggle off the ribbon and all of the tool palettes in the Status Bar by clicking (Clean screen). The Quick Access Toolbar, Command Line, and Status Bar are still displayed.

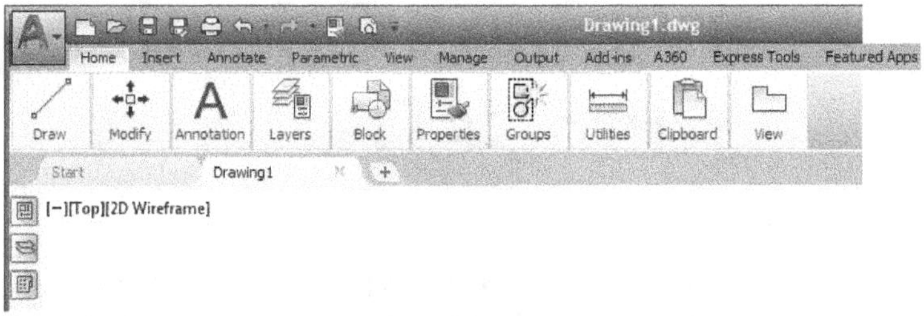

Figure 21–1

- (Workspaces) controls the display of ribbon tabs and panels, tool palettes and other palettes, and even the Command Line. You can select from the default workspaces, as shown in Figure 21–2, or create a custom version.

In the AutoCAD LT® software, the 3D Basics and 3D Modeling workspaces are not available.

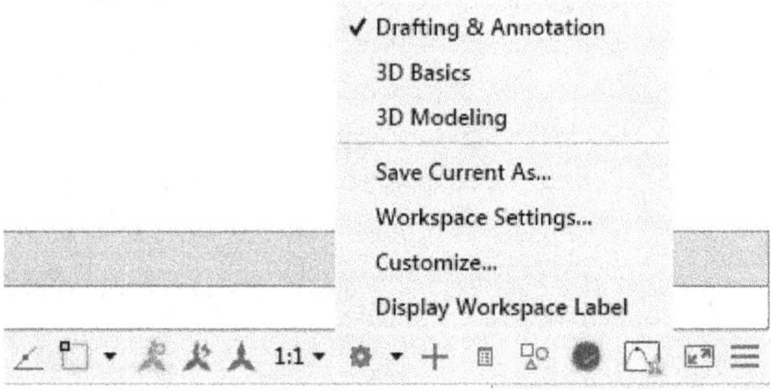

Figure 21–2

- The **Drafting & Annotation** workspace is the default. When you set it to be current, the default ribbon tabs and panels display. Any palettes and toolbars that you have displayed are closed and the Design Feed palette displays. Most of the tools you need can be found in the ribbon.

How To: Create a Custom Workspace

1. Set up the ribbon as you want it to be displayed.
2. Open the tool palettes that you want to include in the workspace, close any that you do not want to display, and arrange them in the drawing window.
3. In the Status Bar, expand the Workspace drop-down list, and select **Save Current As...**
4. In the Save Workspace dialog box, type a name for the new workspace and click **Save**, as shown in Figure 21–3.

Figure 21–3

- The new workspace becomes the current workspace.

- Selecting **Workspace Settings** opens a dialog box in which you can control the display and order of the workspaces in the list and add separator lines between names in the list, as shown in Figure 21–4. You also have the option of saving or not saving any changes to the workspace.

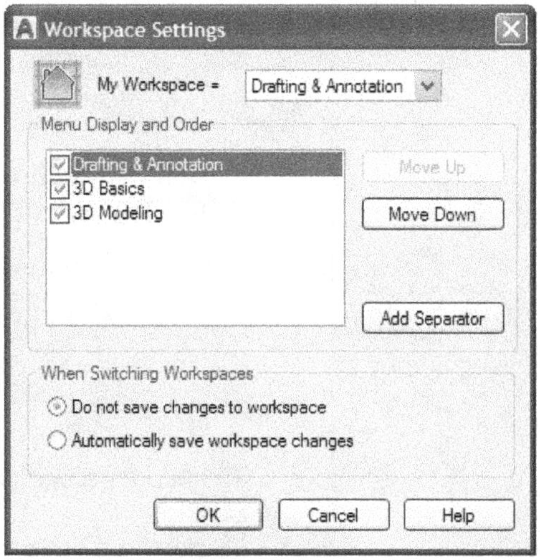

Figure 21–4

Docking and Hiding Palettes

Allow Docking ***should be selected for*** ***Anchor Left <*** *and* ***Anchor Right >*** *to be available.*

Many floating windows and palettes, such as Properties, DesignCenter, and Tool Palettes, can remain open at all times. You can dock and hide or anchor them to one side of the drawing window.

To dock a palette, select the title bar and drag it to one side of the drawing window until it docks. Alternatively, you can right-click on the title bar and select **Anchor Left <** or **Anchor Right >**.

- To hide the docked palette, click to minimize it, as shown in Figure 21–5.

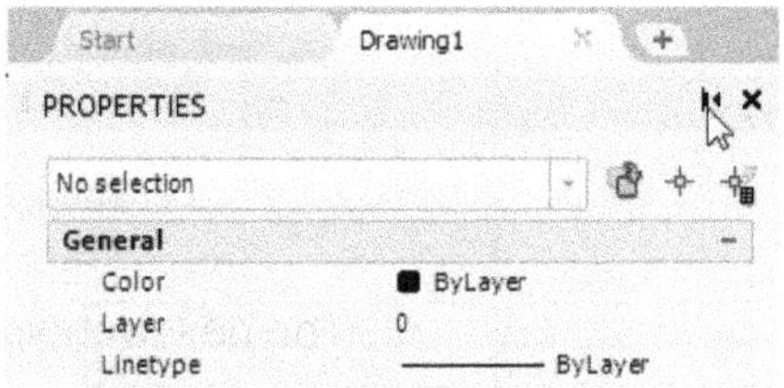

Figure 21–5

- When palettes are hidden, you can display either **Text only** or **Icons only**, as shown in Figure 21–6.

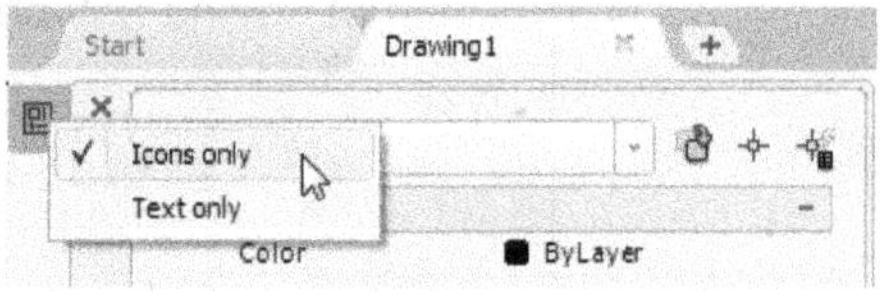

Figure 21–6

- When the palette is hidden, hover the cursor over the title bar or icon to display the full palette, as shown in Figure 21–7.

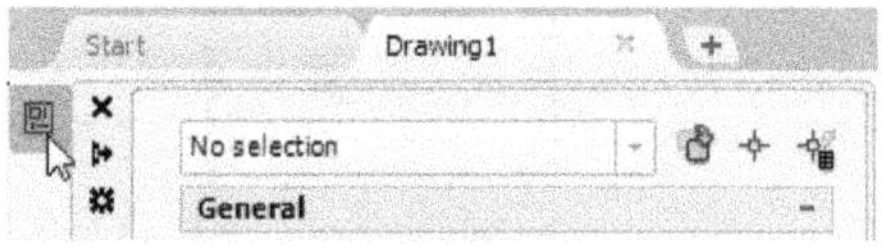

Figure 21–7

- To keep a palette open, click (Auto-hide).

- To close a palette, click (Close).

- All of the palettes in the AutoCAD software are grouped together in the *View* tab>Palettes panel, as shown in Figure 21–8.

Open palettes are highlighted in blue.

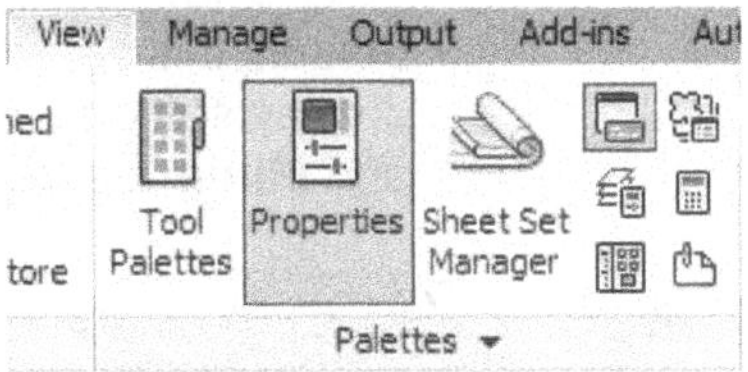

Figure 21–8

Setting Up the Ribbon

The ribbon is the primary place for starting commands. The ribbon can be docked to the top or side of the drawing window, or be kept floating. You can control how much of the ribbon displays, and you can drag and drop the ribbon panels to the drawing window or in a ribbon tab.

- Some of the panels contain extra tools. Click ▼ to expand the panel and display them. Click (Pin) to keep the expanded panel displayed in the drawing window, as shown in Figure 21–9.

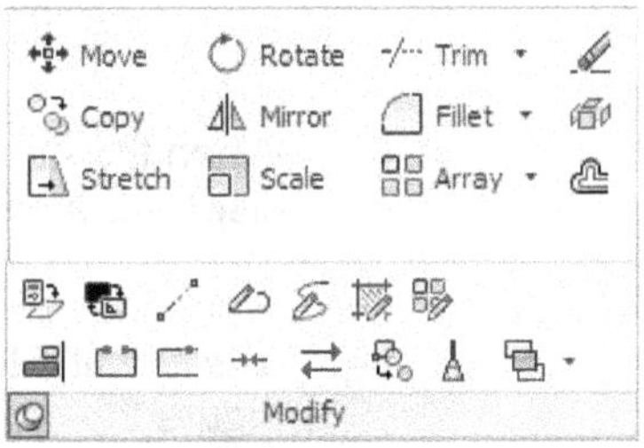

Figure 21–9

- Some of the ribbon panels display in their bottom right corners, which enables you to open a related dialog box.

Displaying the Ribbon

You can also expand [button] and select the required minimize option.

When the ribbon is docked at the top of the interface, you can control how it displays by clicking [button] to the right of the tabs. By default, it is set to **Cycle through All,** which cycles through the display settings of **Minimize to Tabs**, **Minimize to Panel Titles**, and **Minimize to Panel Buttons**, as shown in Figure 21–10.

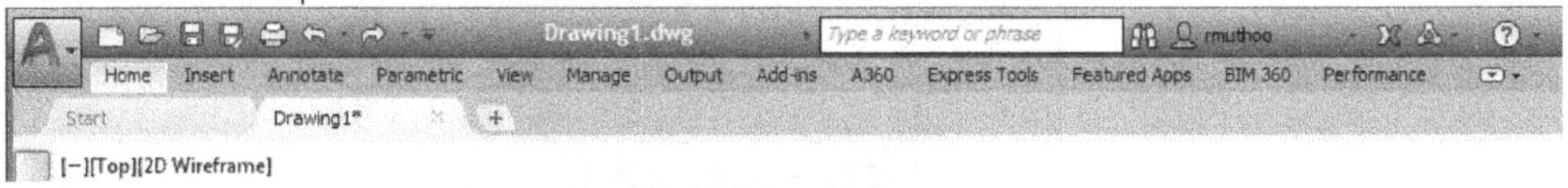

Minimize to Tabs

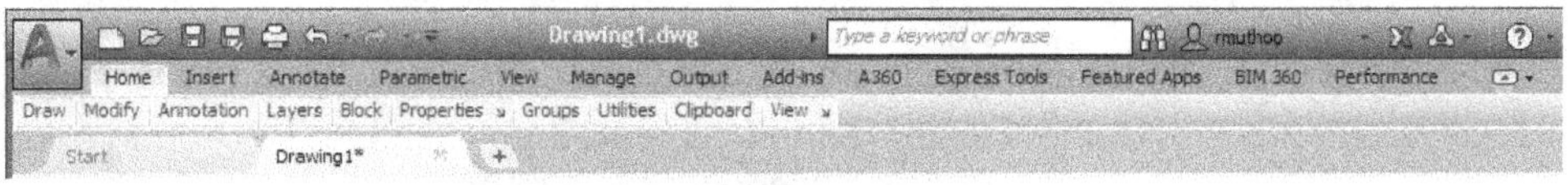

Minimize to Panel Titles

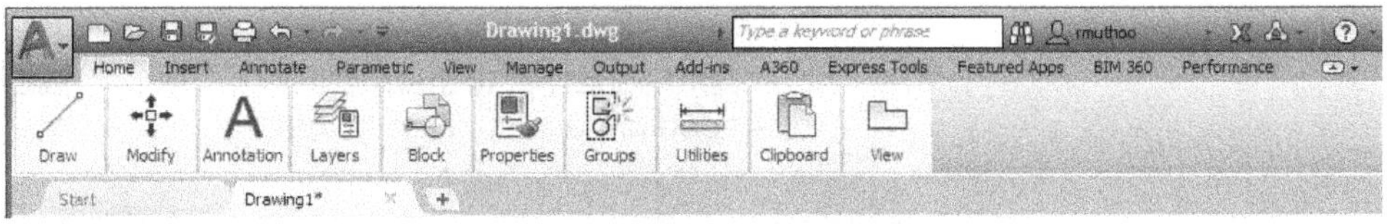

Minimize to Panel Buttons

Figure 21–10

- When the ribbon is minimized to tabs, select the tab to display the panels.
- When the ribbon is minimized to panel titles, hover the cursor over the title to display the commands, as shown in Figure 21–11.

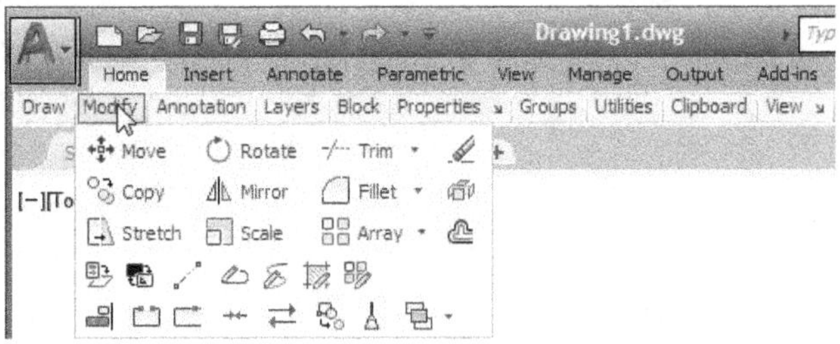

Figure 21–11

Relocating Individual Panels

Ribbon panels can be moved around. You can drag and drop panels to reorder them in a specific ribbon tab (but not between tabs). You can also float an individual panel in the drawing window, as shown in Figure 21–12.

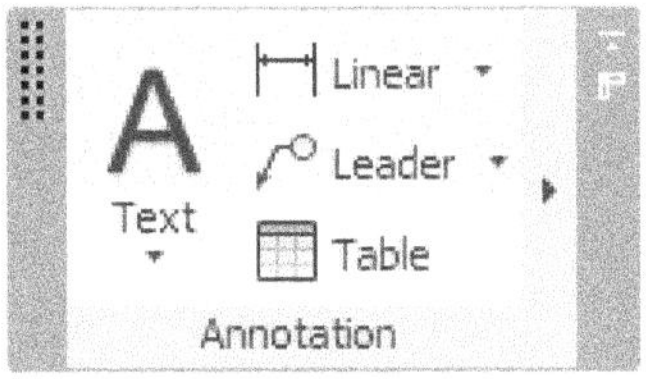

Figure 21–12

- To float an individual panel, drag and drop it on the drawing window. To re-dock the panel, drag it back to the ribbon.
- If you have a dual-monitor setup, individual panels can be moved to the second monitor and left open.

Docking the Ribbon to One Side

If you prefer to work with the ribbon floating or on one side of the drawing window, you can undock it from the top and then dock it to one side, as shown in Figure 21–13. The ribbon then becomes like other palettes that you can hide and display.

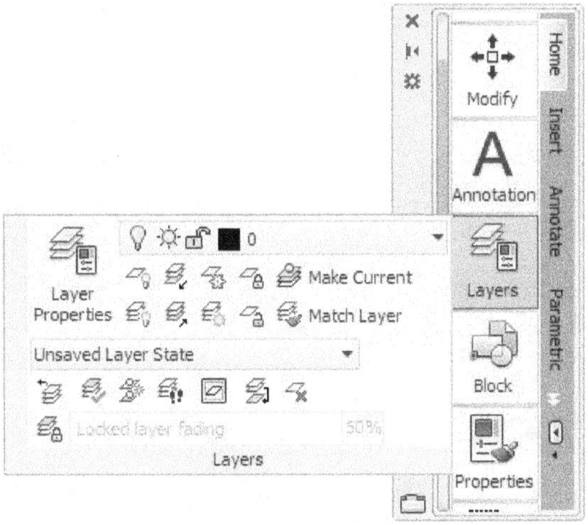

Figure 21–13

How To: Float and Dock the Entire Ribbon

1. Right-click in an empty space in the ribbon and select **Undock**, as shown in Figure 21–14.

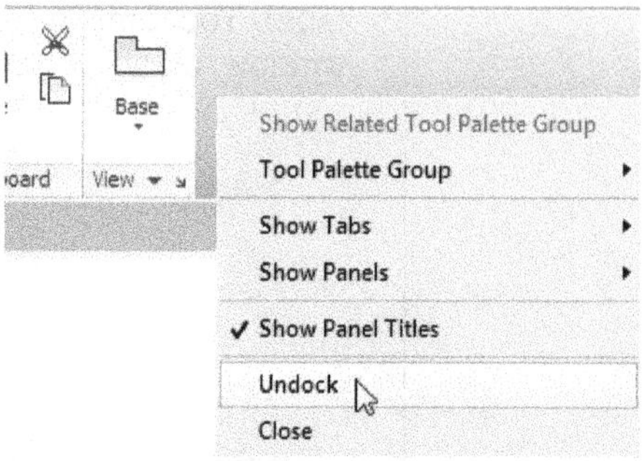

Figure 21–14

*Alternatively, you can right-click on the title bar and select **Anchor Left <** or **Anchor Right >**.*

2. The ribbon floats in the drawing window. If you want the ribbon to be docked to the side, click and hold on the ribbon title and drag it to the side of the drawing window.

   - When the ribbon is docked, you can click ⏮ (as shown in Figure 21–15) to hide the palette.

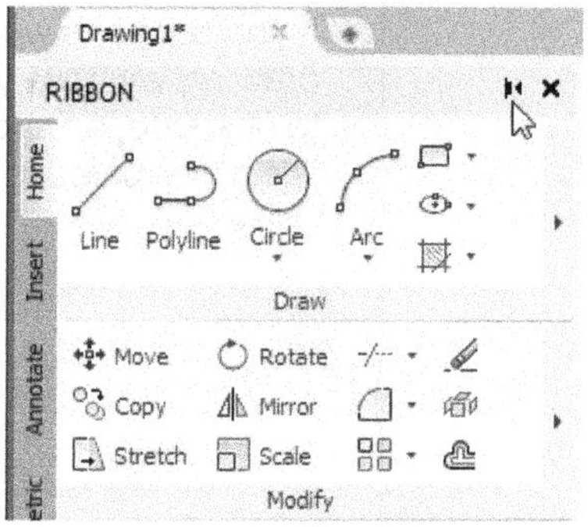

Figure 21–15

Hint: Tool Palette Groups

You can associate a tool palette group with a tab, so that when you right-click on the tab and select **Show Related Tool Palette Group**, the tool palette group automatically opens. You can select from existing groups, as shown in Figure 21–16. This makes it easy to open the tool palettes you want to use.

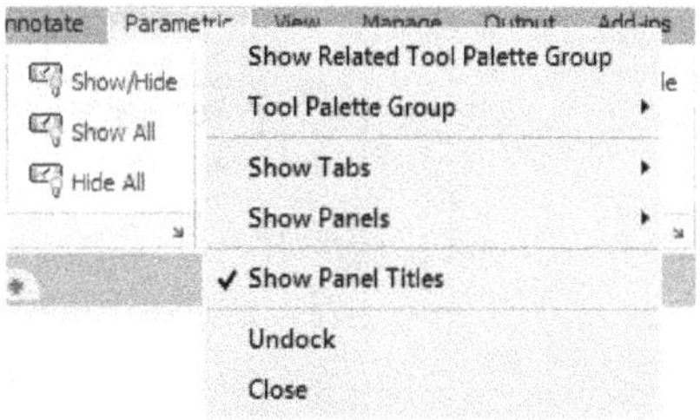

Figure 21–16

- If a tab does not have a related tool palette group, the **Show Related Tool Palette Group** option is grayed out in the shortcut menu.
- When you select **Show Related Tool Palette Group**, it opens the Tool Palette window, if it was not already open.

Practice 21a Setting Up Workspaces

Practice Objective

- Create a custom workspace and switch between workspaces.

Estimated time for completion: 5 minutes

In this practice, you will create a custom workspace, as shown in Figure 21–17, and note the effects of switching workspaces.

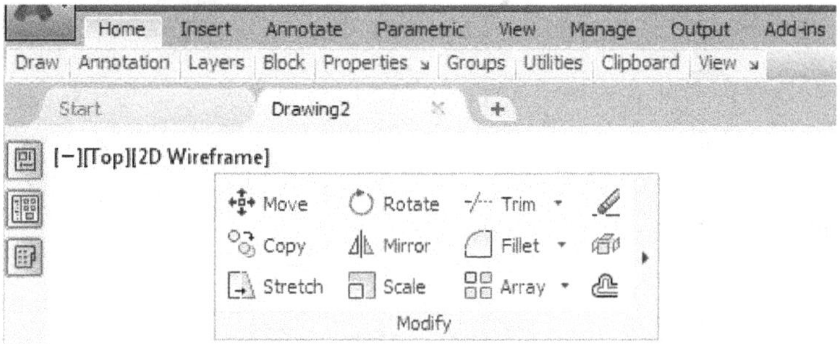

Figure 21–17

1. Start a new drawing based on the default AutoCAD template.

*In the AutoCAD LT software, switch to the **AutoCAD LT Classic** workspace.*

2. In the Status Bar, expand (Workspaces) and select **3D Modeling**. Note all the tabs and panels.
3. Change back to the **Drafting & Annotation** workspace. What are the differences?
4. Open the Properties palette (*View* tab>Palettes panel or press <Ctrl>+<1>). Right-click on the title bar and select **Allow Docking** and **Anchor Left <** to dock it to the left side of the drawing window.
5. If the palette is in the maximize position, hover the cursor on the title bar near the top of the docked palette and click to minimize the palette.
6. Right-click on the palette title bar and select **Icons only**.
7. Open DesignCenter (press <Ctrl>+<2>) and Tool Palettes (press <Ctrl>+<3>). Dock and minimize them to the same side of the drawing window as the Properties palette.
8. In any ribbon tab, click on the panel bar (for example, the Modify panel in the *Home* tab) and drag it onto the drawing window.

Cycle through the different options using .

9. Set the ribbon to **Minimize to Panel Titles** by using .

10. In the Status Bar, expand (Workspaces) and select **Save Current As...**.

11. In the Save Workspace dialog box, type **My 2D Workspace** and click **Save**. In the Status Bar, expand (Workspaces) and note that the new workspace is listed there and is made active.

12. Switch to the **Drafting & Annotation** workspace. What are the differences? Finish by selecting the workspace you want to work with.

13. Close the file. Do not save it. Your workspace is still available to use in other drawing files.

21.2 Using the Keyboard Effectively

The Command Line and Dynamic Input use information typed on the keyboard, as shown in Figure 21–18. For example, you can start the **Line** command by typing the command name (**line**) or shortcut (**L**). When you press <Enter> to start the command its options display in the Command Line. To use one of the options, you can type the capitalized letter(s) of the option or select it in the Command Line.

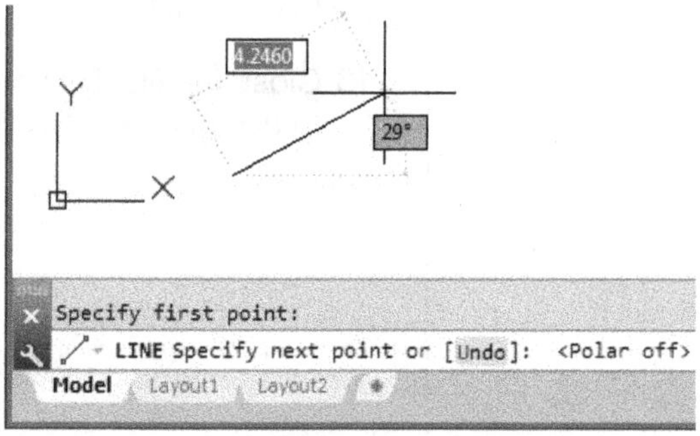

Figure 21–18

- All AutoCAD command can be typed in the Command Line or Dynamic Input. Using commands is one of the fastest ways to work in the software.
- To use typed commands, you must know the exact command name and spelling. For example, the command to draw polylines is **pline**, not **polyline**.
- You can start typing the first letters of a command name and then select the command in the **AutoComplete** list.
- You can quickly search for additional information about a command or system variable in the AutoComplete suggestion list. Hover the cursor over the required item in the list. A tooltip displays, providing a description of the command's functions, as shown in Figure 21–19. The Autocomplete list in the Command line also provides the **Search in Help** or **Search on Internet** icons, as shown in Figure 21–19.

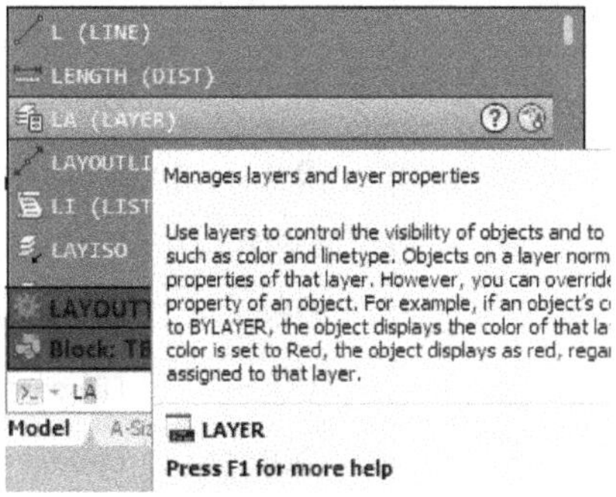

Figure 21–19

- You can easily reuse any command or number that you have typed. Press <Up Arrow> or <Down Arrow> to scroll through your typed input, and press <Enter> when you reach the command that you want to reuse. Press <Right Arrow> and <Left Arrow> to you to move the cursor along the text. You can also backspace, delete, or retype the text.
- You can quickly select from a list of the most recent commands by expanding in the Command Line.
- You can also copy and paste information from the Text Window to the Command Line. Highlight the text, right-click, and select **Paste to Cmdline**.

Command Aliases

Click (Command Aliases) in the Express Tools tab>Tools panel to define or modify command aliases in the file ***acad.pgp****.*

In the AutoCAD LT software, the ***Command Aliases*** *command is not available.*

Rather than typing the entire command name, you can use abbreviations called *command aliases*. The following aliases are some of the standard ones in the AutoCAD software.

- To locate most commands, try typing the first character of the command, then try the first two, and then try the first three. Other commands use various letters.

Alias	Command	Alias	Command
A	Arc	LT	Linetype
AA	Area	M	Move
AR	Array	MI	Mirror
B	Block	MS	Mspace
BR	Break	O	Offset
C	Circle	OS	Osnap
CHA	Chamfer	PE	Pedit (Polyline Edit)

CO, CP	Copy	PL	Pline (Polyline)
D	Dimstyle	PR	Properties
DAL	Dimaligned	PS	Pspace
DAN	Dimangular	PU	Purge
DBA	Dimbaseline	R	Redraw
DCO	Dimcontinue	RA	Redrawall
DDI	Dimdiameter	RE	Regen
DI	Distance	REC	Rectang (Rectangle)
DIV	Divide	REN	Rename
DLI	Dimlinear	RO	Rotate
DRA	Dimradius	S	Stretch
E	Erase	SC	Scale
ED	Textedit (ddedit)	SP	Spell
EX	Extend	T, MT	Mtext (Multiline Text)
F	Fillet	TR	Trim
H	Hatch	U	Undo
HE	Hatchedit	V	View
I	Insert	W	Wblock
L	Line	X	Explode
LA	Layer	Z	Zoom

Shortcut Keys

Another quick way to launch commands or change settings is to use the *shortcut keys* (also called *accelerator keys*). Many of these keystrokes follow the Microsoft Office standard.

To use the default shortcut keys, press <Ctrl> and a letter or number. You can also define customized key combinations in the Customize dialog box.

+<A>	Select All	**+<N>**	New drawing
+<B>	Snap on/off	**+<O>**	Open drawing
+<C>	Copy to the Clipboard	**+<P>**	Plot
+<D>	Dynamic UCS on/off	**+<R>**	Cycles layout viewports

+<E>	Toggle Isometric plane	+<S>	Save
+<F>	Object Snap on/off	+<T>	Tablet on/off
+<G>	Grid on/off	+<U>	Polar on/off
+<J>	Executes last command	+<V>	Paste from the clipboard
+<K>	Create Hyperlink	+<W>	Selection cycling on/off
+<L>	Ortho on/off	+<X>	Cut to clipboard

+<1>	Properties palette on/off	+<7>	Markup Set Manager on/off
+<2>	DesignCenter on/off	+<8>	QuickCalc on/off
+<3>	Tool Palettes on/off	+<9>	Command Line on/off
+<4>	Sheet Sets on/off	+<0>	(zero) Cleanscreen on/off

Function Keys

Function keys control most of the toggles for the drafting settings and several other features.

<F1>	Help	<F7>	Grid on/off
<F2>	Text Screen	<F8>	Ortho on/off
<F3>	Osnap on/off	<F9>	Snap on/off
<F4>	3DOsnap on/off	<F10>	Polar on/off
<F5>	Isoplane switch	<F11>	Osnap Tracking on/off
<F6>	Dynamic UCS on/off	<F12>	Dynamic Input on/off

Practice 21b Using the Keyboard Effectively

Estimated time for completion: 5 minutes

Practice Objectives

- Draw objects using keyboard commands.
- Use various techniques for entering information.

In this practice, you will draw lines, circles, and trim objects (as shown in Figure 21–20) using keyboard commands. You will select commands in the AutoComplete list using partial keyboard commands. You will also be able to toggle Command Line on and off using keyboard commands.

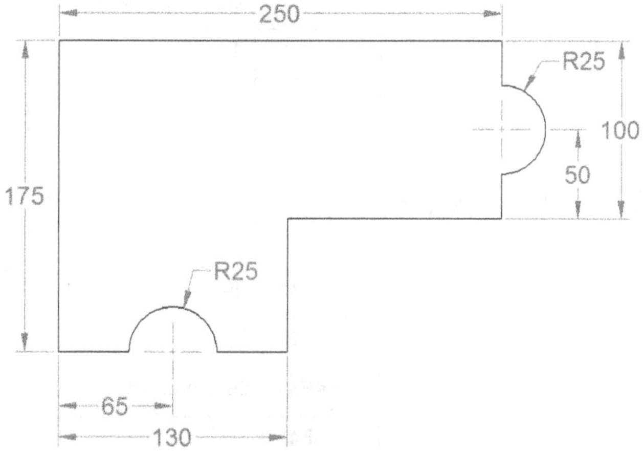

Figure 21–20

1. Start a new drawing based on **Mech-Millimeters.dwt**, which is located in your practice files folder.
2. Draw the objects shown in Figure 21–20. Use the command aliases **L (Line)**, **C (Circle)**, and **TR (Trim)** to start the required commands. Type the distances using Polar Tracking and Dynamic Input.

Verify that  *(Dynamic Input) is toggled on so that command prompts display at the crosshairs.*

3. To test the AutoComplete list of command names, type **D** and select **DIM** (the shortcut for **Dimension** command) in the list. This starts the command. Dimension the objects. If the Select Annotation Scale dialog box opens, set the *Scale* to **1:1** and click **OK**.
4. Save the drawing as **Jig.dwg** and close it.

21.3 Object Creation, Selection, and Visibility

Object Creation

You can use **Add Selected** to create new objects of the same type and properties as the selected object. Select an object, right-click, and select **Add Selected** as shown in Figure 21–21. The AutoCAD software launches the command that was used to create the selected object and sets some of the properties (such as the layer or color) to be the same as the original object.

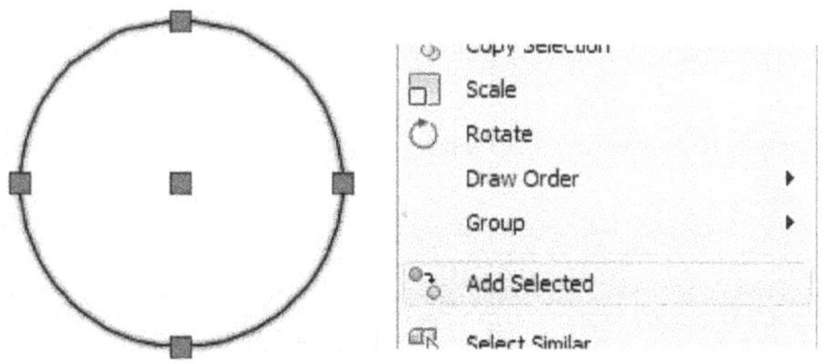

Figure 21–21

Selecting Similar Objects

You can use **Select Similar** to select an object and automatically select other objects of the same type and properties at the same time. For example, if you select a red rectangle on the layer **Walls**, all of the other red rectangles on the layer **Walls** are also selected.

How To: Select Similar Objects

1. Select an object.
2. Right-click and select **Select Similar**. All of the other objects that match the settings are selected.

- If you select more than one object and then use **Select Similar**, all of the objects that match the properties of all of the selected objects are selected.

How To: Modify Select Similar Settings

1. Without any object selected, at the Command Line, type or dynamically input **selectsimilar**.
2. At the Select objects prompt, press <Down arrow> and select **SEttings**.

3. In the Select Similar Settings dialog box (shown in Figure 21–22), select the property types by which you want to filter the selection set.

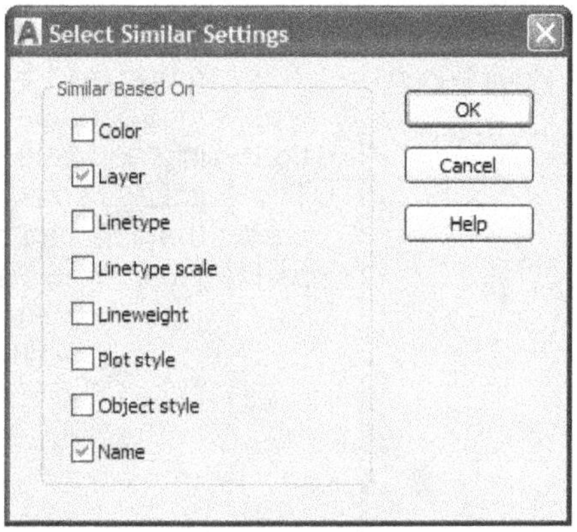

Figure 21–22

- The properties that are set in the dialog box are used to filter the selection process. The objects that are selected have the same properties.
- If you clear the **Name** option in the dialog box, the command looks for all of the objects that match the properties no matter what type they are.

Object Selection Cycling

If you need to select an object in a location in which many objects overlap, you can use **Object Selection Cycling**. When it is toggled on, and you hover the cursor over some overlapping objects, displays, indicating that more than one object can be selected. The Selection dialog box opens when you click on the objects, enabling you to select an object from the list, as shown in Figure 21–23.

In the Status Bar, (Selection Cycling) must be toggled on for this to work.

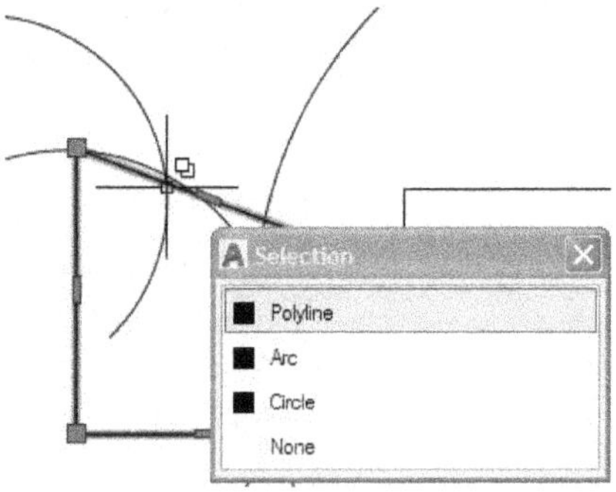

Figure 21–23

How To: Use Object Selection Cycling

1. In the Status Bar, toggle on (Selection Cycling).
2. Hover the cursor over some overlapping objects close to where the objects intersect. displays, indicating that there are overlapping objects.
3. Click to open the Selection dialog box.
4. Select the object that you want to use.

Object Visibility

You can control whether objects are displayed or hidden in the drawing. The **Isolate Objects**, **Hide Objects**, and **End Object Isolation** commands control this display.

Isolate Objects	Select the objects that you want to isolate, right-click, and select **Isolate>Isolate Objects**. The selected objects display and all other objects are hidden.
Hide Objects	Select the objects that you want to hide, right-click, and select **Isolate>Hide Objects**. The selected objects are hidden.
End Object Isolation	Right-click anywhere in the drawing window and select **Isolate>End Object Isolation**. All hidden objects display.

- If a drawing contains hidden or isolated objects, (Unisolate Objects) displays in the Status Bar.
- If a drawing does not contain hidden objects, (Isolate Objects) displays in the Status Bar.

How To: Isolate or Hide Objects

You can also use (Isolate/Hide /Unisolate) in the Status Bar.

1. Right-click and select **Isolate>Isolate Objects** or **Hide Objects**, as shown in Figure 21–24.

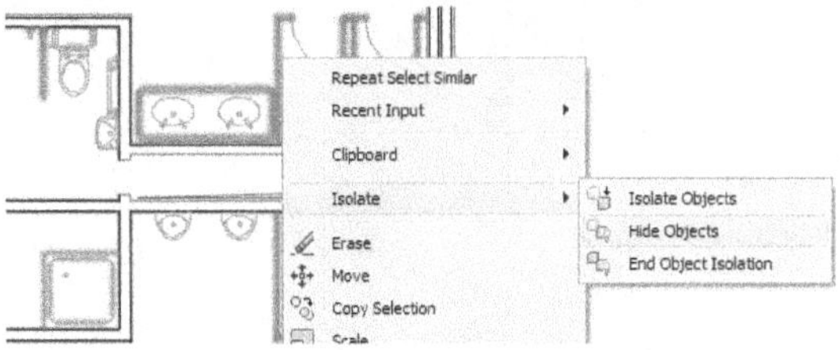

Figure 21–24

2. If you selected objects before starting the command, the objects are hidden or isolated. If you did not select objects, you are prompted to select them.

3. To display the isolated or hidden objects, right-click and select **Isolate>End Object Isolation**.

- If objects are already hidden or isolated, you can add additional objects to the isolated selection set.

Setting Transparency

Transparency can be applied to objects similar to applying other properties (such as Layer, Color, or Linetype). It can be set individually, ByLayer, or ByBlock. It is very useful when displaying hatches, as shown in Figure 21–25.

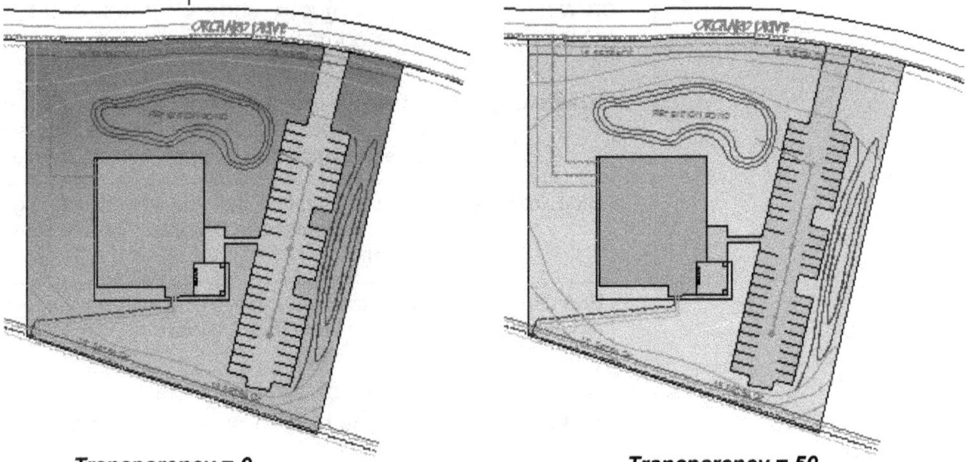

Transparency = 0 ***Transparency = 50***

Figure 21–25

- Transparency values vary from **0** (least transparent) to **90** (most transparent).

- When you are creating or editing objects, you can set the transparency in the *Home* tab>expanded Properties panel. You can also expand the Transparency drop-down list and select one of the options shown in Figure 21–26.

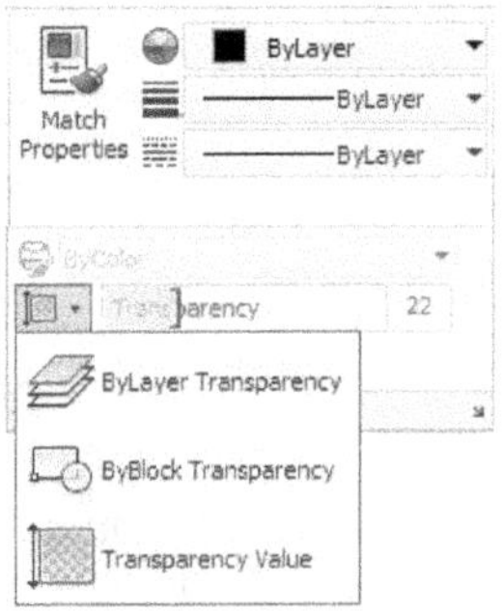

Figure 21–26

- Transparency is also available in the Properties palette when objects have been selected.

- You can toggle  (Transparency) on and off in the Status Bar.

- Transparency can be set in the Layer Properties Manager, as shown in Figure 21–27. It can also be modified by layer in a viewport.

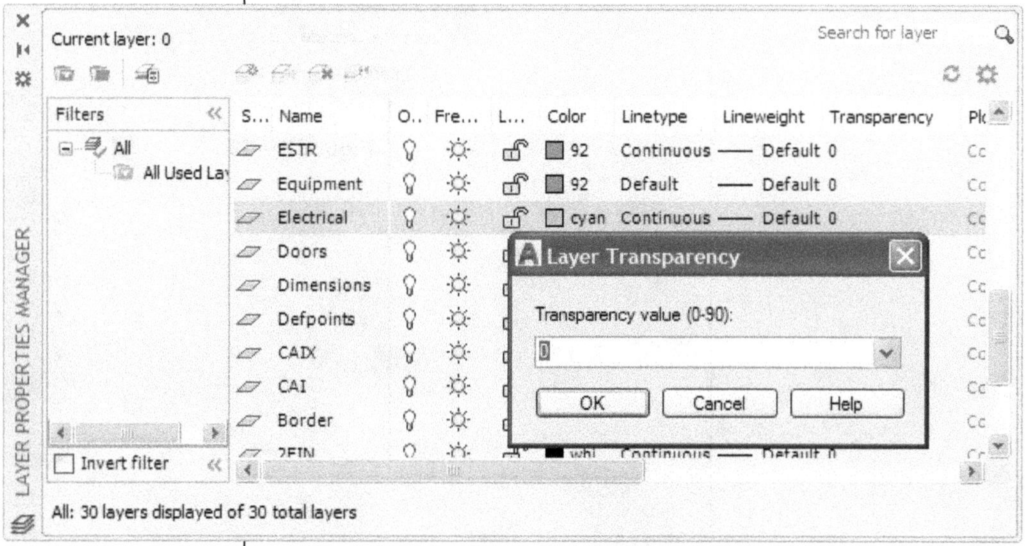

Figure 21–27

- Transparency can be set for **Match Properties**, as shown in Figure 21–28, and for **Quick Select** and **Filter**.

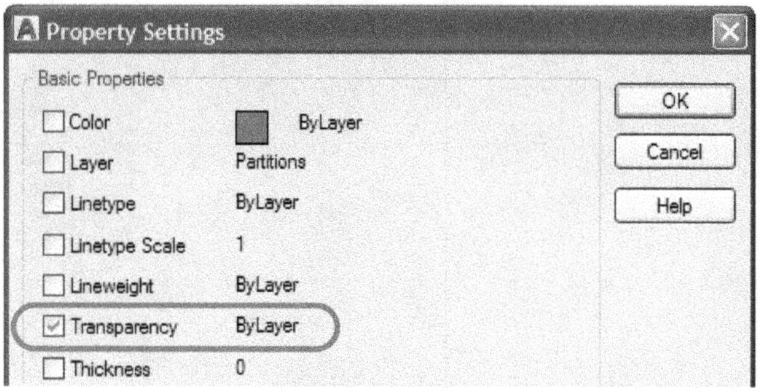

Figure 21–28

- To plot transparent objects, select the **Plot transparency** option shown in Figure 21–29, in either the Plot dialog box or Page Setup. This is toggled off by default because the file must be converted into raster for the transparency to plot.

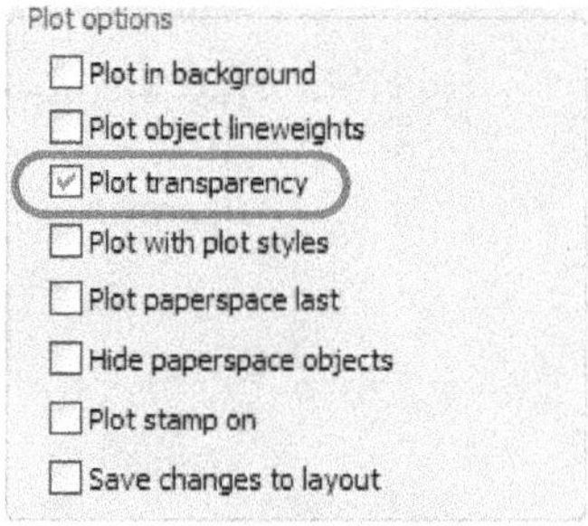

Figure 21–29

Practice 21c Object Creation, Selection, and Visibility

Practice Objective

- Modify the display of objects using various commands and options.

Estimated time for completion: 5 minutes

In this practice, you will modify the way objects display in a drawing using **Select Similar**, **Hide Objects**, and **Isolate Objects**. You will also modify the display of objects using the **Transparency** option.

Task 1 - Use selection and visibility tools.

1. Open **Office-Plan1-AM.dwg** from your practice files folder.
2. Select one of the double sided corner desks on the layer Cubicles.

*Some of the objects you will be selecting throughout this task might not be blocks, but instead consist of lines, circles, etc. Therefore, you might need to perform the **Select Similar** command several times.*

3. Right-click and select **Select Similar**. All of the double sided corner desks are selected, as shown in Figure 21–30.

Figure 21–30

4. Select one of the red desks and one of the red chairs and use **Select Similar**. All of the chairs are selected along with a few desks.

5. Right-click and select **Isolate>Hide Objects**.

6. Use **Select Similar** to select the rest of the furniture (red colored objects). Hide them as well.

7. How would you make it easier to select all of the furniture in the drawing?

8. Right-click and select **Isolate>End Object Isolation** to unhide the objects.

Task 2 - Modify object transparency.

1. Toggle on the layer **Hatching**.

2. Select one of the hatches.

3. In the *Hatch Editor* contextual tab>Properties panel, next to the **Transparency** option, use the slider bar to lighten the transparency of the hatch.

4. Open the Layer Properties Manager.

5. In the *Hatching* row, set the *Transparency* value to **50**, as shown in Figure 21–31.

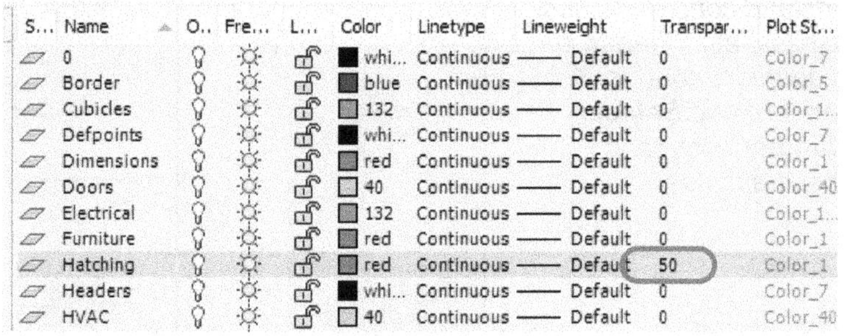

S...	Name	O..	Fre...	L...	Color	Linetype	Lineweight	Transpar...	Plot St...
	0				whi...	Continuous	Default	0	Color_7
	Border				blue	Continuous	Default	0	Color_5
	Cubicles				132	Continuous	Default	0	Color_1...
	Defpoints				whi...	Continuous	Default	0	Color_7
	Dimensions				red	Continuous	Default	0	Color_1
	Doors				40	Continuous	Default	0	Color_40
	Electrical				132	Continuous	Default	0	Color_1...
	Furniture				red	Continuous	Default	0	Color_1
	Hatching				red	Continuous	Default	50	Color_1
	Headers				whi...	Continuous	Default	0	Color_7
	HVAC				40	Continuous	Default	0	Color_40

Figure 21–31

6. All of the other hatches are lightened because they are all on the same layer, and each of their *Transparency* options is set to **ByLayer**.

7. Save and close the drawing.

21.4 Working in Multiple Drawings

You can open multiple drawings in the same session of the AutoCAD software, as shown in Figure 21–32. This can make it easier to copy information across drawings.

Having many complex drawings open can affect system performance.

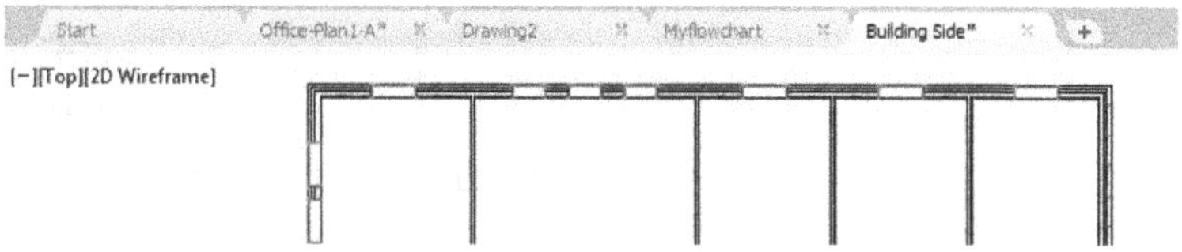

Figure 21–32

By default, the *Start* tab always displays as the first active tab and clicking it will display the initial Start window. The Start window contains tools to create new drawings, open existing ones, open the recently used files, and many other file and help related options.

File Tabs

The *File* tabs along the top of the drawing window are an easy way to switch between open drawing files and the initial Start window.

Switching Windows

The *File* tabs along the top of the drawing window display the names of the open drawings.

- The names of all of the open drawings display as tabs in the *File Tabs* bar. The currently active drawing tab displays with a white background.
- They display in the order in which they are opened, but you can change their order by dragging and moving the tabs.
- You can cycle between the drawings by pressing <Ctrl>+<Tab> or by selecting the required file tab in the *File Tabs* bar. The selected drawing tab opens the drawing and makes it active.

- You can also open and make another drawing active by clicking (Switch Windows) in the *View* tab>Interface panel, as shown in Figure 21–33, and then selecting the drawing from the list.

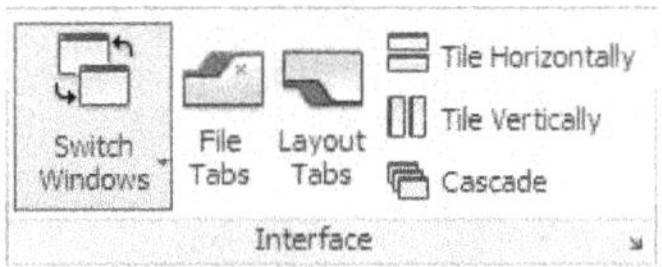

Figure 21–33

- If you want all of the open drawings to display, click (Tile Horizontally), (Tile Vertically), or (Cascade).
- When there are too many open drawing files and not enough room for all of the *File* tabs to fit along the top, displays at the end of the *File* tabs. Click to display a complete list of open files, as shown in Figure 21–34 and select the required filename to switch to that open drawing file.

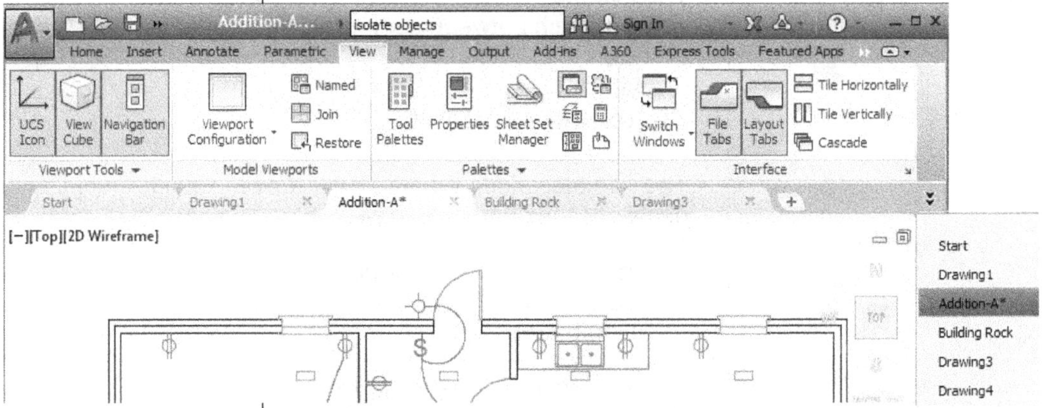

Figure 21–34

Appearance and Preview

The *File* tabs include some visual tools.

- A drawing file that is open as read-only is indicated by a lock on its tab.
- A drawing file that has been modified since its last save is indicated by an asterisk on its tab.

- To display a preview image of the model tab and layouts of any other open drawing, hover the cursor over its filename tab. Then hover the cursor over one of the previews to highlight it and temporarily display it in the drawing window, as shown in Figure 21–35. Select the preview to switch to that model or layout.

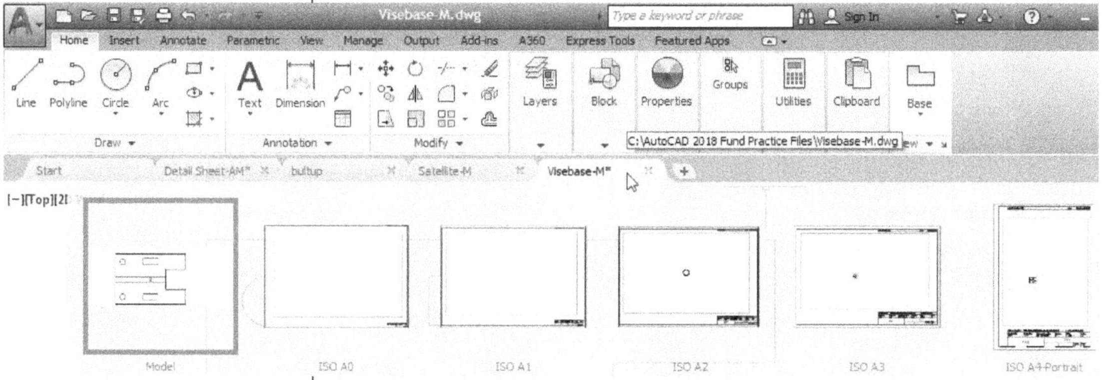

Figure 21–35

- When a preview image is highlighted, the icons at the top of the preview enable you to  (Plot) or  (Publish) it.

Shortcut Menu

You can right-click on the *File* tabs to display a menu (shown in Figure 21–36), which includes options to create, open, save, and close files.

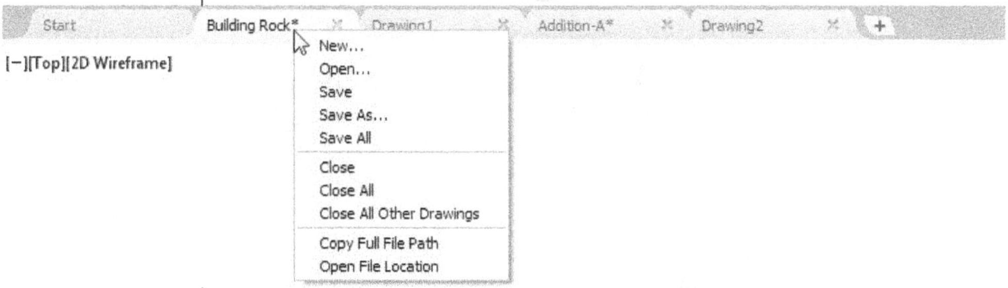

Figure 21–36

The Start tab always persists in the Tab bar and never closes.

- You can use **Close All** to close all of the drawings except the *Start* tab, or select **Close All Other Drawings** to close all of the drawings except the *Start* tab and the drawing where you opened the shortcut menu from.

- Other options include copying the full file path to the clipboard and opening the file location in Windows Explorer.

Toggle File Tabs On/Off

By default, the *File Tabs* bar displays along the top of the drawing window. However, when maximum screen real estate is more important, you can hide the *File Tabs* bar by toggling the (File Tabs) off in the *View* tab>Interface panel, as shown in Figure 21–37.

*When **File Tabs** is toggled off, you can use **Switch Windows** to switch between open drawing files.*

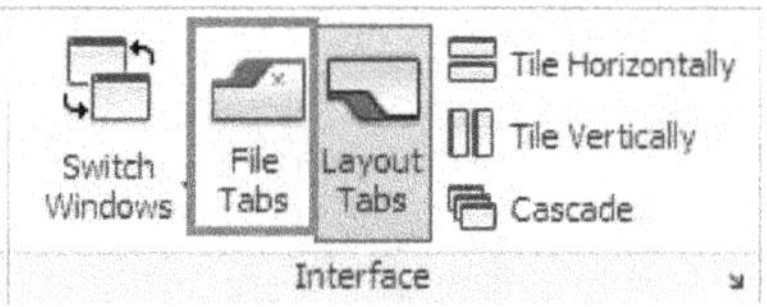

Figure 21–37

Selecting Drawings in the Application Menu

The Application Menu provides access to all of the already saved open drawings and recently used drawings, as shown in Figure 21–38.

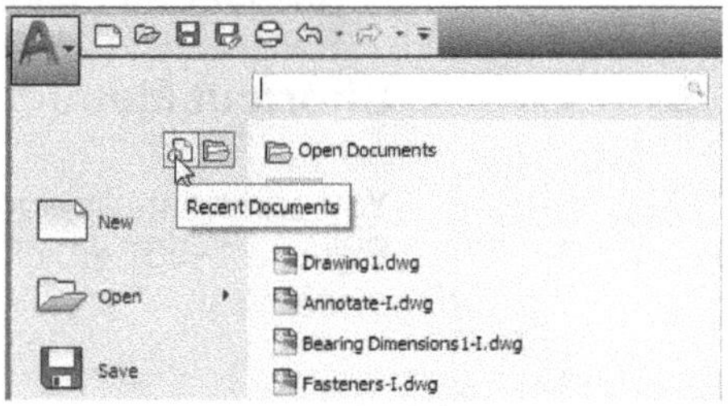

Figure 21–38

- When you hover the cursor over a drawing name, a thumbnail of the drawing displays. Hover the cursor a while longer to display more information about the file.

- Click (Recent Documents) to display a list of recently used drawing files or click (Open Documents) to display a list of open drawing files.
- You can customize the way the drawings are listed and displayed, as shown in Figure 21–39.

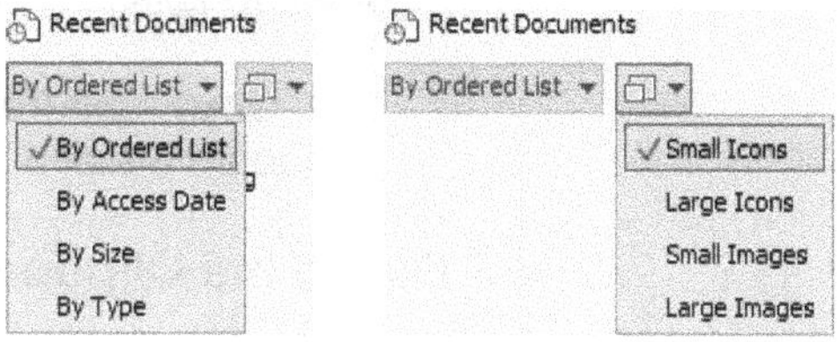

Figure 21–39

- Expand (Close) in the Application Menu to close either the current drawing or all open drawings, as shown in Figure 21–40.

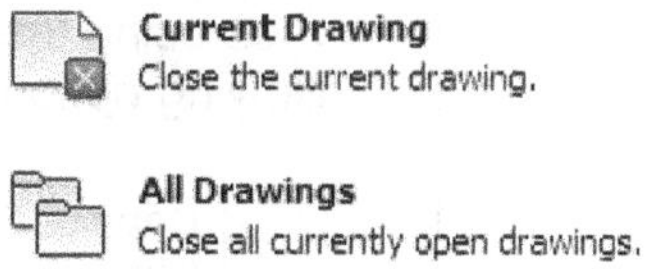

Figure 21–40

21.5 Copying and Pasting Between Drawings

*The AutoCAD **Copy** command does not work between drawings.*

You can place information on the clipboard by copying or cutting it from a document. You can then paste the information from the clipboard into the same document or into a different one, even in a different application. To copy, move and paste information between drawings you must use the Windows **Copy** command.

- **Cut**, **Copy**, and **Paste** are available in the *Home* tab> Clipboard panel and in the shortcut menu.

Cut to the Clipboard

As with other Windows applications, (Cut Clip) removes the selected objects from their file and places them on the clipboard.

Copy to the Clipboard

When using the Windows **Copy** command, you have the following options:

	Copy Clip	Copies the selected objects to the clipboard, using the lower left corner of the bounding box of all of the objects as the base point. <Ctrl>+<C> starts the command.
	Copy with Base Point	In the shortcut menu, expand **Clipboard** and select **Copy with Base Point**. It enables you to select the base point after the objects have been selected. This option provides more control over the location of the objects when they are placed. The base point is only significant when the objects are pasted into the AutoCAD software.
NA	**Copy Link**	Type **copylink** at the Command Line. It copies the contents of the current view to the clipboard.

Paste from the Clipboard

When using the Windows **Paste** command, you have the following options:

	Paste	Prompts you to select a location for the base point at which it then places the objects. <Ctrl>+<V> starts the command.

	Paste as Block	The copied objects are placed as a block. The AutoCAD software gives the block an arbitrary name. This option is only available if the objects on the clipboard are AutoCAD objects.
	Paste to Original Coordinates	Places the objects at the same coordinates as in the drawing from which they were taken. This option is only available if the objects on the clipboard are AutoCAD objects.
	Paste as Hyperlink	Creates a hyperlink of an object, text or file already copied to clipboard, and then associates it with another object.
	Paste Special	Enables you to control the format of an already copied data while pasting it into the active drawing.

Drag-and-Drop Copying

When two drawing windows are open, you can also *drag-and-drop* objects to copy them from one drawing into another.

How To: Copy using Drag-and-Drop

1. Without a command running, select the objects that you want to copy.
2. Hold the mouse button with the cursor on the objects (do not select a grip).
3. Drag the objects into the other drawing window and release the mouse button.

Match Properties Across Drawings

(Match Properties) works across drawings. You can select an object in one drawing and apply its properties to objects in another drawing.

Match Properties works for general object properties, such as color, linetype, and lineweight, and for the formatting of some specific object types, including text, dimensions, hatching, and tables.

Practice 21d Working in Multiple Drawings

Practice Objectives

- Switch between drawings and display them side by side.
- Copy and paste objects between drawings.

Estimated time for completion: 5 minutes

In this practice, you will switch between multiple drawings using *File* tabs and Open Documents. You will display drawings side by side using the Tile Vertical command. You will then copy and paste objects between the drawings, as shown in Figure 21–41.

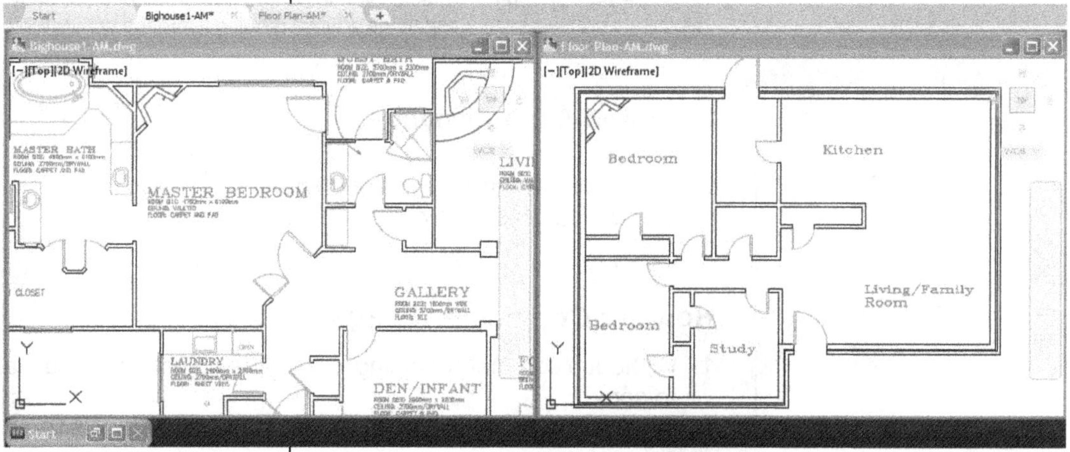

Figure 21–41

Use <Ctrl> to select both files in the Select File dialog box and click ***Open****.*

1. Open **Bighouse1-AM.dwg** and **Floor Plan-AM.dwg** from your practice files folder. Close any other open drawings.
2. If not already active, in the *Files* tab bar, select the **Bighouse1-AM.dwg** tab. Then, hover the cursor over the **Floor Plan-AM.dwg** tab to display its preview images. Select the **Model** preview to switch to **Floor Plan-AM.dwg** with its *Model* tab active.
3. Thaw the layer **Text**.

4. In the Application Menu, click (Open Documents) and display the thumbnails of the two floor plans by hovering the cursor over them, as shown in Figure 21–42. Select **Bighouse1-AM.dwg** to make that drawing current.

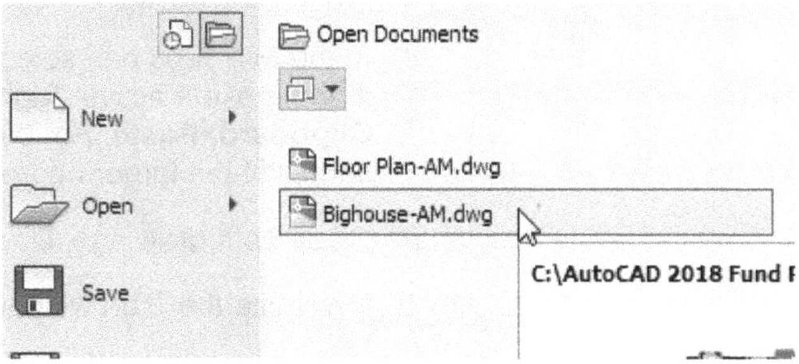

Figure 21–42

Depending on the selection of the filenames in the Select File dialog box, your drawing tabs might be reversed.

5. In the *View* tab>Interface panel, click (Tile Vertically) to display the drawings side-by-side. Minimize the *Start* tab display and click (Tile Vertically) again so that only the two drawings fill the drawing window.

6. In **Bighouse1-AM.dwg**, in the *Model* tab, zoom in on the Master Bedroom (upper left corner of floorplan) and start the **Match Properties** command (*Home* tab>Properties panel). Select the text **MASTER BEDROOM** as the source object. Click inside **Floor Plan-AM.dwg** once to activate it and then select each of the text labels in **Floor Plan-AM.dwg** as the destination object, as shown in Figure 21–43. Press <Enter> to exit the command. The text properties are matched in both drawings.

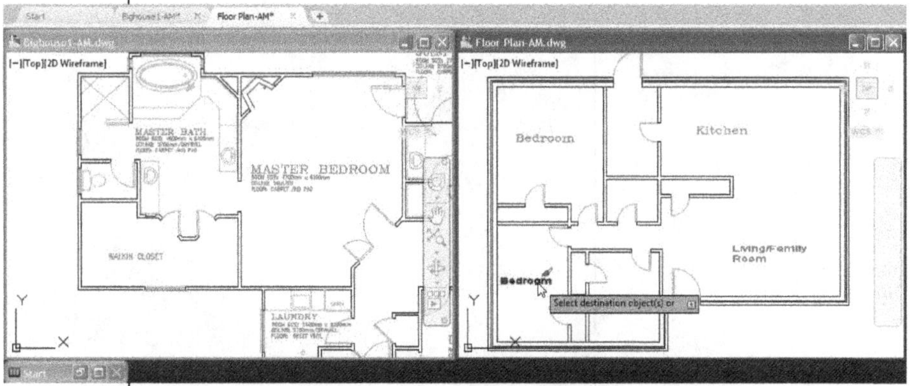

Figure 21–43

7. Make **Bighouse1-AM.dwg** the active window. Right-click and select **Clipboard>Copy with Base Point**. For the basepoint, select the corner of the walls behind the fireplace (in the master bedroom). Select the fireplace (they might be separate objects) and the short diagonal walls that frame it and press <Enter>.

8. In the *File Tabs* bar, select the *Floor Plan-AM* tab to switch to it and make it active. Right-click and select **Clipboard>Paste**. For the insertion point, select the top left corner of the larger bedroom to paste the fireplace there.

9. Close both drawings. Do not save changes.

10. Maximize the Start window.

21.6 Using Grips Effectively

Grips are a very powerful tool and using them helps you to quickly and easily modify drawings. You can increase the effectiveness of using grips by changing the base point, copying with grips, using the reference option, stretching multiple objects (as shown in Figure 21–44), and modifying grip settings.

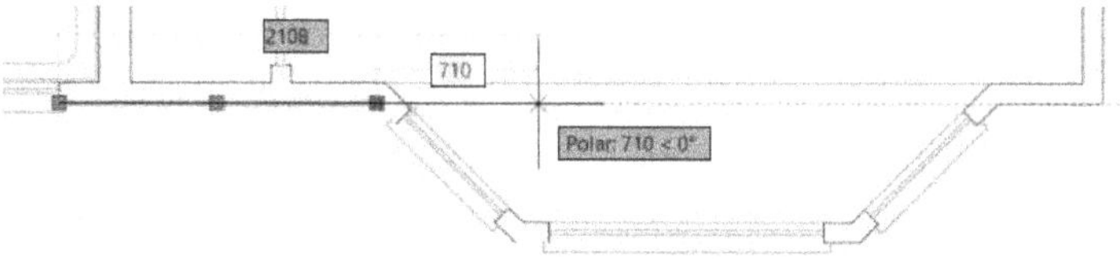

Figure 21–44

- If (Dynamic Input) is on, dynamic dimensions (and if it is a multifunctional grip, a dynamic list of options) display when you hover the cursor over a grip. Select one of the optional commands, such as **Stretch**, **Lengthen**, or **Add Vertex**.
- When you select a grip you can edit the dimensions to stretch the object. Use <Tab> to highlight the dimension that you want to change.
- Depending on which grip is selected, the Stretch mode either stretches or moves the object. Centers of circles and midpoints of lines move the objects. Standard blocks move because they cannot be stretched. Dynamic blocks have special grips.
- Pressing <Enter> while a grip is hot, sequentially toggles through **Move**, **Rotate**, **Scale**, **Mirror**, and then back to **Stretch**.
- To clear grips from objects, press <Esc> or right-click and select **Exit**.

Changing the Base Point

The hot grip becomes the default base point for moving, rotating, etc. To use a different base point, right-click and select **Base Point** as shown in Figure 21–45 (or type **B** in the Command Line). Select the new base point and continue with the command.

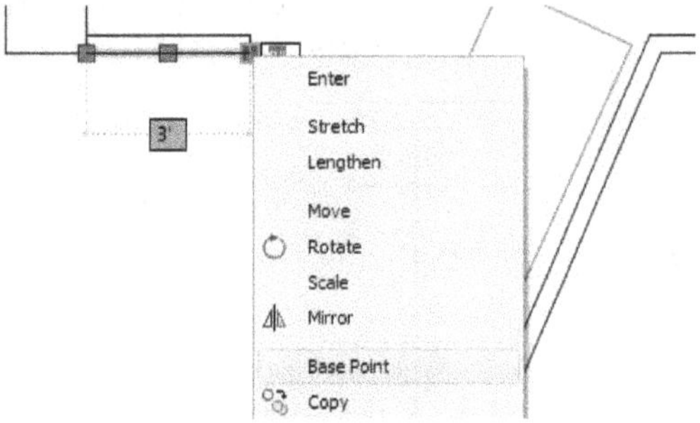

Figure 21–45

Copying with Grips

Use the **Copy** option with any of the grip editing modes to create multiple copies while you move, rotate, etc.

How To: Copy with Grips

Holding <Ctrl> while selecting the point for stretching, moving, rotating, etc., also starts the multiple copy mode.

1. Select the objects and make one grip hot.
2. Right-click and select the editing mode (**Stretch**, **Move**, **Rotate**, etc.).
3. Select the **Copy** option in the shortcut menu or Command Line.
4. Select (or type) the second point, rotation angle, mirror line, or scale factor.

- If you hold <Ctrl> while selecting the location for additional copies, the new objects snap to the same spacing as the first copy, as shown in Figure 21–46.

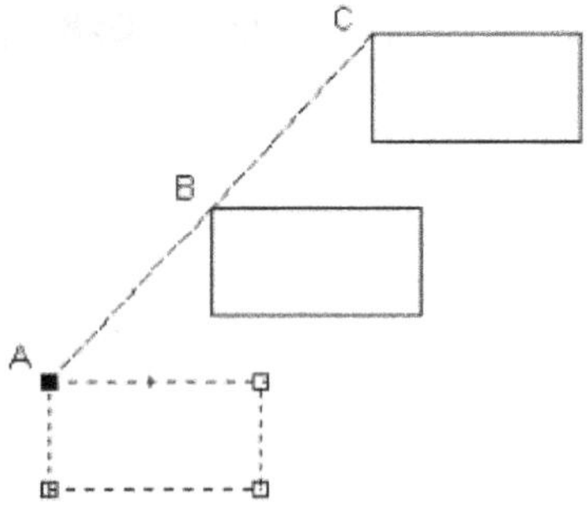

Figure 21–46

Rotate and Scale with the Reference Option

The **Reference** option enables you to select reference points in your drawing to describe the rotation angle or scale factor.

How To: Rotate and Scale with Grips and Reference

1. Select the objects that you want to rotate or scale.
2. Select the grip to be the base point for rotating or scaling.
3. Right-click and select **Rotate** or **Scale**.
4. Right-click and select **Reference**.
   - **For Rotate:** Specify the reference angle by typing the angle or selecting two points. Specify the new angle by typing the angle or selecting a second point. The first point of the new angle is the base point.
   - **For Scale:** Specify the reference length by typing the length or selecting two points. Specify the new length by typing the length or selecting a second point. The first point of the new length is the base point.

For example, you might want to straighten a rectangle that is rotated at an unknown angle, as shown in Figure 21–47. Select the rectangle and then select the grip at point 1 as the base point for rotation. Right-click and select **Rotate** and **Reference**. For the *Reference angle*, select the end points at **1** and **2** (this is the current angle of the object). For the *New angle*, type **0**.

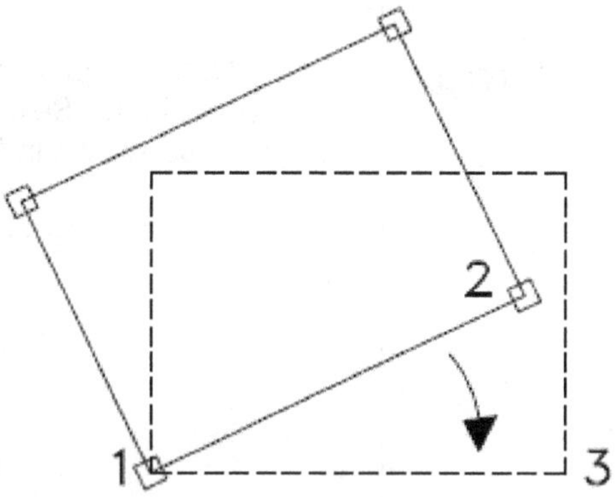

Figure 21–47

- The **Reference** option is also available with the regular **Rotate** and **Scale** commands.

Stretching Multiple Objects

In the Stretch mode, only hot grips or objects that contain hot grips are stretched. You can make multiple grips hot by holding <Shift> when selecting each grip, as shown in Figure 21–48.

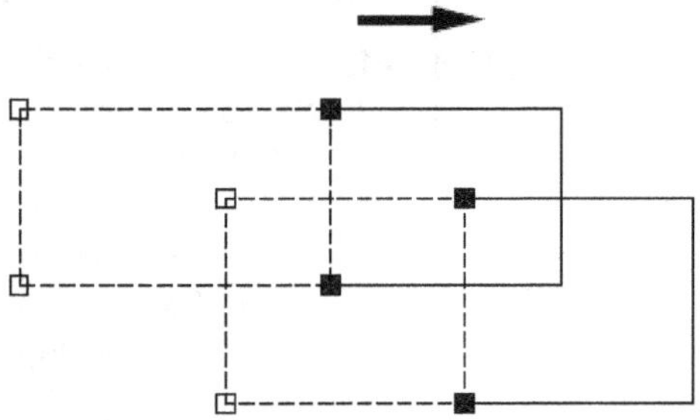

Figure 21–48

How To: Stretch with Grips

1. Select the objects that you want to stretch.
2. Hold <Shift> and select all of the grips that you want to move using **Stretch**.
3. Release <Shift>.
4. Select the grip that you want to use as a base point.
5. Select the point that you want to use as the second point of displacement.

Grip Settings

In the Options dialog box (expand the Application Menu and click **Options**), in the *Selection* tab, there are several settings related to grips, as shown in Figure 21–49.

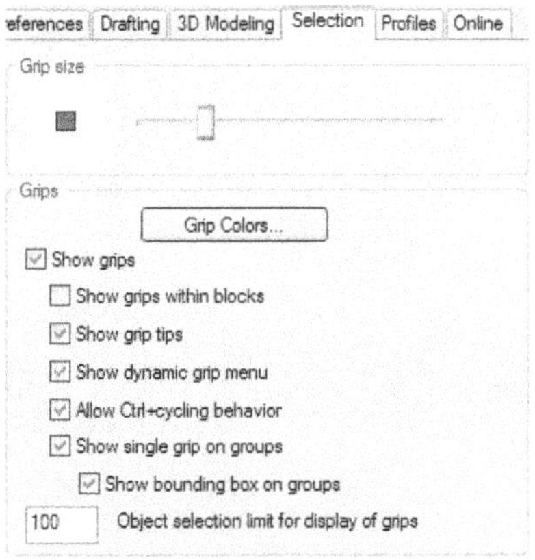

Figure 21–49

- *Grip size* enables you to control the size of the grip as it displays in the drawing window.

- You can also change the grip colors by clicking **Grip Colors...** and adjusting the values in the Grip Colors dialog box, as shown in Figure 21–50.

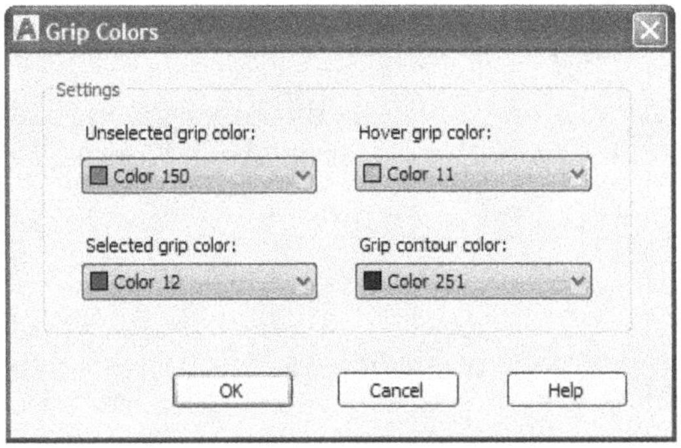

Figure 21–50

In addition to grip size and color, you can set the following:

Show grips	Turns grips on or off globally.
Show grips in blocks	Controls whether grips only display on a block's insertion point (off) or on all nested objects in the block (on). Normally it is easier to work with this option off. This only applies to standard blocks. Dynamic blocks still display grips.
Show grip tips	Grip tips are not available in the basic AutoCAD software, but can display for objects from software such as the AutoCAD® Architecture software.
Show dynamic grip menu	Controls whether a menu displays next to a dynamic grip.
Allow Ctrl+cycling behavior	Controls whether you can use <Ctrl> to cycle through the grip's options.
Show single grip on groups	Displays a single grip for an object group.
Show bounding box on groups	Displays a bounding box around the extents of grouped objects.
Object selection limit for display of grips	If you select more objects than the number set here, grips do not display on them.

Practice 21e Using Grips Effectively

Estimated time for completion: 10 minutes

Practice Objective

- Modify a drawing using grips.

In this practice, you will use grips to edit the schematic drawing, as shown in Figure 21–51.

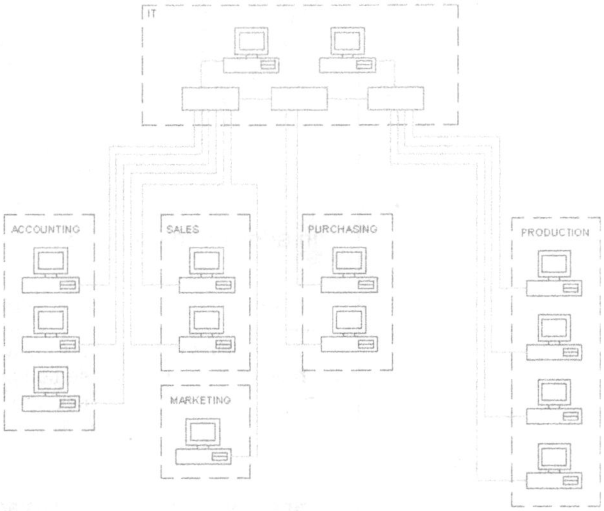

Figure 21–51

1. Open **Computer-M.dwg** from your practice files folder.
2. Use grips to add three, evenly spaced computers to **PRODUCTION**. Use <Ctrl> when selecting the locations for the copies, to place them at even intervals.
3. Use grips to stretch the red rectangle to include the new computers. Use <Shift> to select more than one hot grip.
4. Select the three, yellow polylines connecting the **ACCOUNTING** computers to the hubs. Use grips to **Mirror** and **Copy** the three polylines over to the **PRODUCTION** computers, using a base point at the midpoint of the middle hub. (After selecting one grip, use the shortcut menu to select **Mirror**, and then select **Base Point** before drawing the mirror line.)
5. Use grips to manipulate the new lines so they match up with the new computers.
6. Save and close the drawing.

21.7 Additional Layer Tools

The additional layer commands in the *Home* tab>Layers panel, can help you to work quickly with layers. They include commands that enable you to select layers rather than their names, and to change their layer state or current status.

Changing Object Layer States

The commands to freeze, toggle off, lock, and unlock layers are the most basic of the additional layer commands. They can be accessed in the *Home* tab>Layers panel, as shown in Figure 21–52.

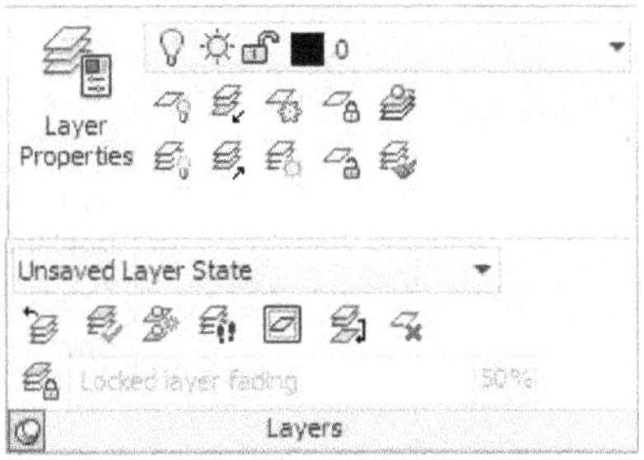

Figure 21–52

How To: Freeze or Turn Layers Off

1. Start (Layer Freeze) or (Layer Off).
2. Select an object on the layer that you want to change. It changes automatically.
3. You can continue selecting objects on other layers as required.
4. Press <Enter> to finish the command.

Two other commands are helpful with layer states:

- (Turn All Layers On)
- (Thaw All Layers)

Settings

In the Home tab>extended Layers panel, use (VP Freeze in All Viewports except Current) to freeze a selected layer in all other viewports except the active one.

Layer Freeze and **Layer Off** have settings for how blocks, Xrefs, and Viewports respond to the commands. These settings remain in effect until you change them.

Block selection	Sets the nesting level of a block or Xref: **Block (default):** Freezes or turns off the layer on which the block was inserted. If it is part of an Xref, it freezes the layer of the object. **Entity:** Only freezes or turns off the layer in the block or Xref that you actually select. **None:** Freezes or turns off the layer on which the block or Xref was inserted.
Viewports	Sets the way the command responds when you are working in a Paper Space viewport. **VPFreeze (default):** Only freezes or turns off the layer in the current viewport. **Freeze/Off:** Freezes or turns off the layer across the entire drawing.

How To: Lock or Unlock Layers

1. Click (Layer Lock) or (Layer Unlock).
2. Select an object on the layer that you want to change. It changes automatically.

- A small padlock icon displays when you hover the cursor over a locked layer, as shown in Figure 21–53.

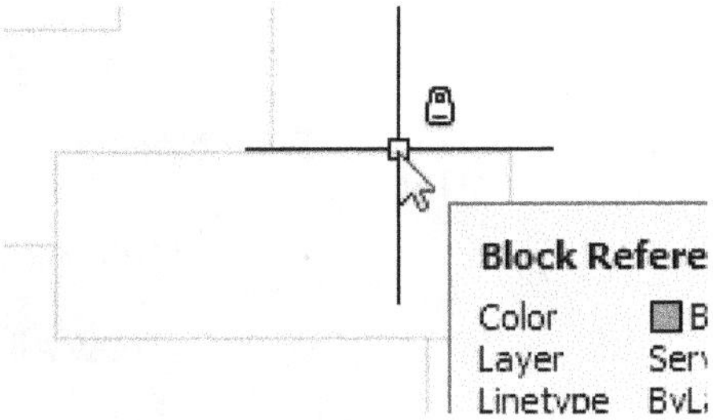

Figure 21–53

- Locked layers fade but are still displayed in the drawing. Use the **Locked layer fading** slider in the extended Layers panel to control how much the layers fade, as shown in Figure 21–54.

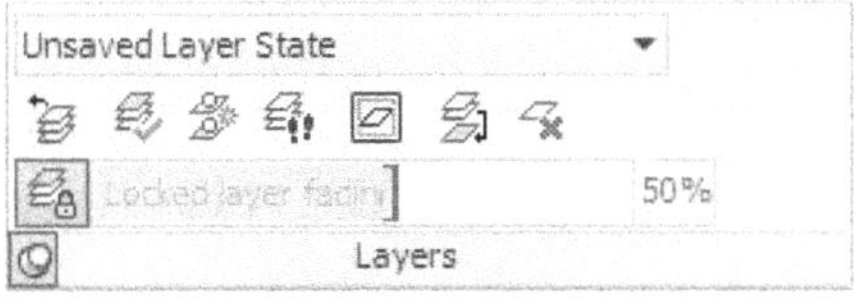

Figure 21–54

Isolating Layers

(Layer Isolate) is similar to changing the layer state, but it locks and fades (or turns off) all of the objects in a drawing EXCEPT those that are on the layers that you selected to isolate, as shown in Figure 21–55. When you have finished working with the isolated layers, you can return them to their original layer state.

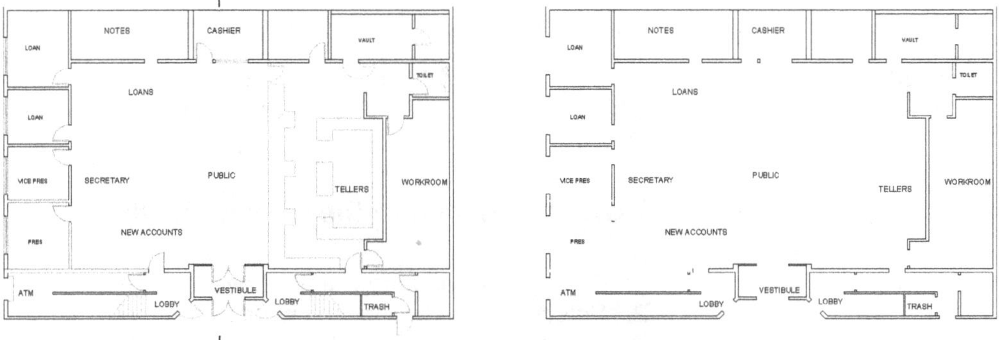

Figure 21–55

How To: Isolate Layers

1. Click (Layer Isolate).
2. Select objects on the layer(s) in which you want to work.
3. Press <Enter>. All of the other layers are locked and faded.

- If you only select one layer to isolate and it is not the current layer, it becomes current.
- The layers that are not selected to be isolated are either locked and faded or toggled off. To change this, start the **Layer Isolate** command, select **Settings**, and select the required option, as shown in Figure 21–56.

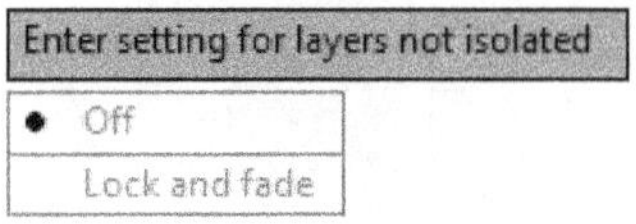

Figure 21–56

- When you select **Off** you are prompted to set the way it works in Paper Space viewports. The **Vpfreeze** option freezes the unisolated layers in the active viewport, and the **Off** option turns the unisolated layers off in all of the viewports.

How To: Unisolate Layers

1. Click (Layer Unisolate).
2. All of the isolated layers are restored.

- (Layer Previous) also restores layers that have been isolated and changes the current layer back to the original if **Layer Isolate** was last used to change it.

Changing an Object's Layer

There are other ways of changing the layers of objects in a drawing including: (Change to Current Layer) and (Copy Objects to New Layer). These commands change an object's layer by selecting other objects.

How To: Change to the Current Layer

1. Click (Change to Current Layer).
2. Select the objects that you want to place on the current layer.
3. Press <Enter> to finish the command and move the objects to the current layer.

How To: Copy an Object to a New Layer

This command creates new copies of selected objects and places them on a new layer. You can then move the copies to a new location while you are still in the command or leave them on top of existing objects.

1. Click (Copy Objects to New Layer).
2. Select the objects that you want to copy and press <Enter> to complete the selection set.
3. Select an object on the destination layer or use the **Name** option to open the Copy to Layer dialog box, in which you can select a layer name, as shown in Figure 21–57.

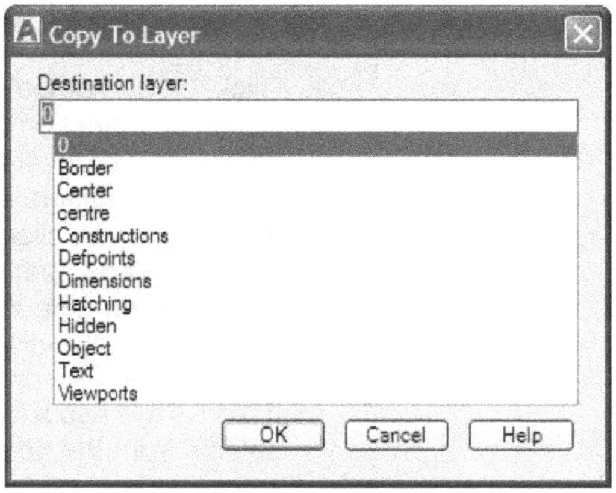

Figure 21–57

4. Select a base point from which to copy. If you want the new copies to be on top of the originals, you can press <Enter> to exit without moving the objects.
5. Select a second point to place the new objects on the selected layer.

- The new layer to which objects are going to be copied must exist for this command to be used.

Modifying Layers

In the *Home* tab>extended Layers panel use (Layer Merge) to move all of the objects on selected layers to a target layer and then delete the selected layers. (Layer Delete) removes a layer and any objects associated with that layer.

- The default response to the final prompt of *Do you wish to continue*? for each of these commands is **No**. You must specify **Yes** to complete the process.

How To: Merge Layers

1. Click (Layer Merge).
2. Select an object on the layer that you want to merge. You can select several layers before pressing <Enter> to continue.
3. Select an object on the target layer.
4. A warning box opens, listing the layers that you are going to merge into the target layer. If you type **Y** for **Yes**, the objects are moved to the target layer and the other layers are deleted from the drawing.

How To: Delete Layers

1. Click (Layer Delete).
2. Select an object on the layer that you want to delete. You can select several layers before pressing <Enter> to continue. If you select multiple layers, the objects disappear from the drawing as you click them.
3. A warning box opens, listing the layers that you are going to delete. If you type **Y** for **Yes**, the objects and layers are deleted from the drawing.

- If blocks are associated with the layer, they are redefined with objects from the deleted layer.

Layer Walk

Use this command to find out which layers the objects display on and then use other commands to move them to the correct layer.

(Layer Walk) provides an interface in which you can quickly display objects on specified layers and then modify them in a dialog box, as shown in Figure 21–58.

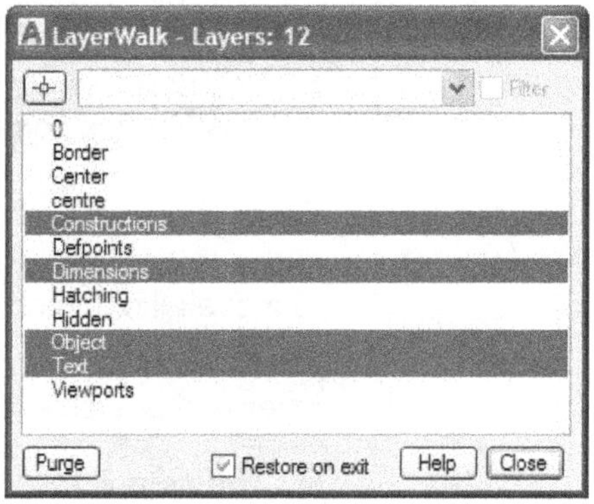

Figure 21–58

- You can either select from the list of layer names in the LayerWalk dialog box or use (Select Objects) to select objects in the drawing window.
- Use <Ctrl> and <Shift> or drag to select multiple layers.
- Double-click on the name if you always want a layer to be displayed. An asterisk displays next to the name. You can also right-click and select **Hold Selection**. You can release the hold layers individually or as a group by right-clicking and selecting **Release Selection** and **Release All**.
- If a layer does not contain any objects, you can click **Purge** to remove it from the drawing.

- When you have finished working in the dialog box, you can display the layer setup in your drawing if you clear the **Restore on exit** option. If it is selected, the modifications you made in the dialog box are not displayed in the drawing window.

Filtering Layers

You can use filters to select layers more quickly. Type information including a wildcard character (such as *) and press <Enter> to only display the layer names that match the filter, as shown in Figure 21–59.

*All of the layers display if you clear the **Filter** option.*

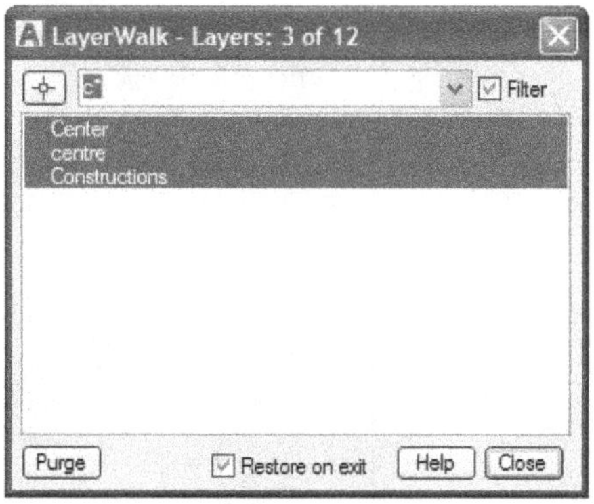

Figure 21–59

- To save a filter, right-click in the Layer list and select **Save Current Filter**. The filter is added to the drop-down list.
- In the LayerWalk dialog box, right-click and select **Save Layer State** to save the current selection of layers to be used later in the Layer State Manager.
- In the LayerWalk dialog box, right-click and select **Inspect...** to display the number of layers in the drawing, number of layers selected, and number of objects on the selected layers, as shown in Figure 21–60.

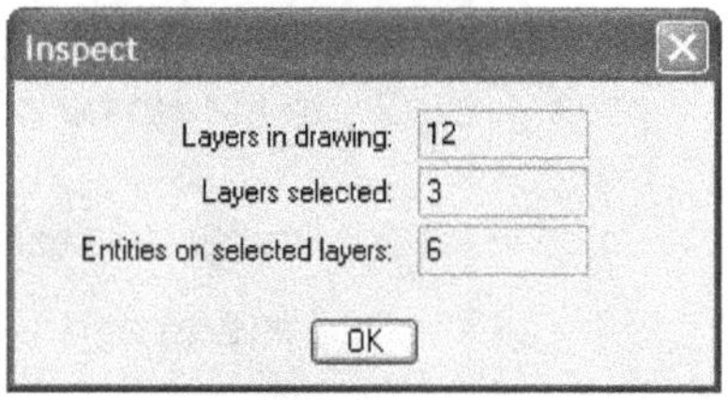

Figure 21–60

Practice 21f Layer Tools

Estimated time for completion: 10 minutes

Practice Objective

- Modify the layers using the additional layer commands.

In this practice, you will freeze and toggle off layers, as shown in Figure 21–61, and then restore the layer states. You will isolate and unisolate layers. You will use the **Layer Walk** and **Layer Merge** commands to determine whether any layers are incorrect in the drawing and then fix them as required.

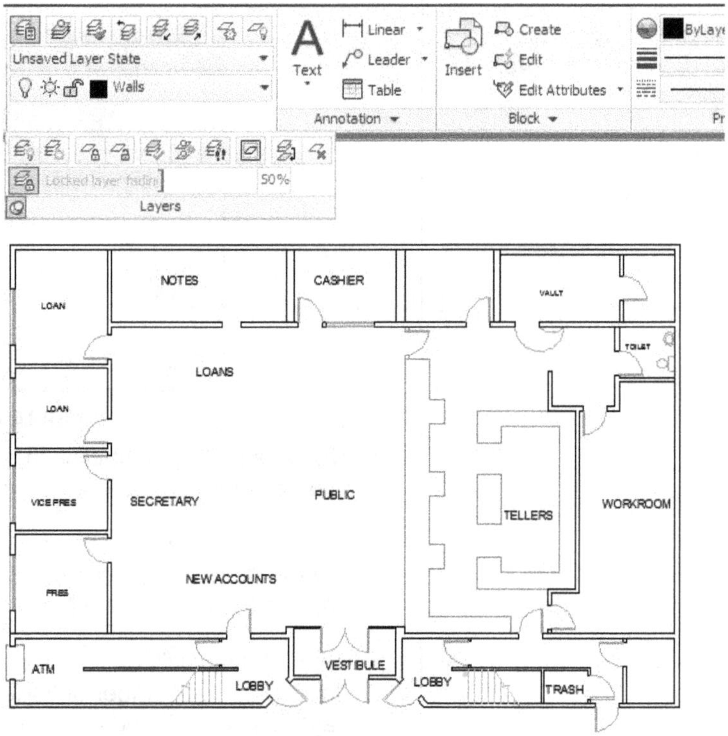

Figure 21–61

1. Open **Bank-AM.dwg** from your practice files folder.
2. In the *Home* tab, expand and pin the Layers panel.
3. Practice freezing and toggling off layers using (Layer Freeze) and (Layer Off).

4. Restore the layer states using (Turn all Layers On) and (Thaw All Layers).

5. You can also try isolating layers using (Layer Isolate) and (Layer Unisolate).

6. Set the current layer to **Electrical**.

7. Click (Layer Freeze). At the *Select an object* prompt, press <Down Arrow> and select **Settings>Block selection>Block** from the down arrow menus. Select a door to freeze and note what happens.

8. Click (Thaw All Layers).

9. Click (Layer Freeze) again. At the *Select an object* prompt, press <Down Arrow> and select **Settings>Block selection>Entity** from the down arrow menus. Select a door to freeze and note what happens (All of the doors disappear).

10. Click (Thaw All Layers).

11. Click (Layer Walk). Select **Doors**, **Furniture**, **STAIRS** to display the objects on each layer. Select the layer **Walls** first and then select the layer **WALL**. Note that the walls in the drawing are on two different layers. Close the Layer Walk dialog box.

12. Set layer **0** to be active. Click (Layer Merge) and select an object on the layer **WALL**. Press <Enter>. Select an object on the layer **Walls** and check the Layer Control in the Layers panel to verify that the one of the wall layers is deleted.

13. Save and close the drawing.

Chapter Review Questions

1. What do Workspaces control?
   a. The available tabs in the ribbon and the display of Tool Palettes.
   b. The settings in the Options dialog box.
   c. The default template location.
   d. The drawings that are open in the AutoCAD software.
2. You can reuse text that you have typed in the Command Line by pressing <Up Arrow> or <Down Arrow> to scroll to the text.
   a. True
   b. False
3. How can you paste AutoCAD objects into a drawing at the same location as in the drawing from which they were copied?
   a. Select **Edit>Paste Special** in the Application Menu.
   b. Right-click and select **Paste to Original Coordinates**.
   c. Right-click and select **Paste as Block**.
   d. Select **Edit>Paste Special** in the Menu Browser.
4. If you have multiple drawings open, how can you switch between them? (Select all that apply.)
   a. Use **Open** to open the drawing again.
   b. Press <Shift>+<Tab>.
   c. Use **Application Menu>Open Documents**.
   d. Use *View* tab>Interface panel, expanded Switch Windows drop-down list.
5. What is a function of the **Layer Walk** command?
   a. Toggle the visibility of layers on and off by selecting them in the LayerWalk dialog box.
   b. Change the properties of a layer.
   c. Change the layer on which an object is located.
   d. Create new layers in the LayerWalk dialog box.

6. When selecting an object and then a grip, which of the following commands is started by default?
    a. **Stretch**
    b. **Copy**
    c. **Scale**
    d. **Move**

Command Summary

Button	Command	Location
	**Clean Screen**	• **Status Bar** • **Command Prompt:** <Ctrl>+<0> (zero), cleanscreenON or cleanscreenOFF
	**Command Aliases**	• **Ribbon:** *Express Tools* tab>Tools panel
	**Workspace Switching**	• **Status Bar** • **Command Prompt:** wscurrent
Clipboard		
	**Copy**	• **Ribbon:** *Home* tab>Clipboard panel • **Shortcut Menu:** Copy • **Command Prompt:** copyclip or <Ctrl>+<O>
	**Copy with Base Point**	• **Shortcut Menu:** Copy with Basepoint • **Command Prompt:** <Ctrl>+<Shift>+<C> or copybase
	**Cut**	• **Ribbon:** *Home* tab>Clipboard panel • **Shortcut Menu:** Cut • **Command Prompt:** <Ctrl>+<X> or cutclip
	**Paste**	• **Ribbon:** *Home* tab>Clipboard panel • **Shortcut Menu:** Paste • **Command Prompt:** <Ctrl>+<V> or pasteclip
	**Paste as Block**	• **Ribbon:** *Home* tab>Clipboard panel • **Shortcut Menu:** Paste as Block • **Command Prompt:** pasteblock
	**Paste to Original Coordinates**	• **Ribbon:** *Home* tab>Clipboard panel • **Shortcut Menu:** Paste to Original Coordinates • **Command Prompt:** pasteorig
Layer		
	**Change to Current Layer**	• **Ribbon:** *Home* tab>expanded Layers panel • **Command Prompt:** laycur
	**Copy Objects to New Layer**	• **Ribbon:** *Home* tab>expanded Layers panel • **Command Prompt:** copytolayer
	**Layer Delete**	• **Ribbon:** *Home* tab>expanded Layers panel • **Command Prompt:** laydel
	**Layer Freeze**	• **Ribbon:** *Home* tab>Layers panel • **Command Prompt:** layfrz

	Layer Isolate/Layer Unisolate	• **Ribbon:** *Home* tab>Layers panel • **Command Prompt:** layiso or layuniso
	VP Freeze in All Viewports except Current	• **Ribbon:** *Home* tab>expanded Layers panel • **Command Prompt:** layvpi
	Layer Lock/Layer Unlock	• **Ribbon:** *Home* tab>Layers panel • **Command Prompt:** laylck or layulk
	Layer Merge	• **Ribbon:** *Home* tab>expanded Layers panel • **Command Prompt:** laymrg
	Layer Previous	• **Ribbon:** *Home* tab>expanded Layers panel • **Command Prompt:** layerp
	Layer Off	• **Ribbon:** *Home* tab>Layers panel • **Command Prompt:** layoff
	Layer Walk	• **Ribbon:** *Home* tab>expanded Layers panel • **Command Prompt:** laywalk
	Thaw All Layers	• **Ribbon:** *Home* tab>Layers panel • **Command Prompt:** laythw
	Turn all Layers On	• **Ribbon:** *Home* tab>Layers panel • **Command Prompt:** layon
Window		
	Cascade	• **Ribbon:** *View* tab>Interface panel
	Switch Windows	• **Ribbon:** *View* tab>Interface panel
	Tile Horizontally	• **Ribbon:** *View* tab>Interface panel
	Tile Vertically	• **Ribbon:** *View* tab>Interface panel

Chapter 22

Accurate Positioning

In this chapter you learn how to use absolute, relative, and relative polar coordinates to specify a point, to use tracking to specify a point based on existing points, to use construction lines, and to place reference points.

Learning Objectives in this Chapter

- Locate positions in a drawing and new points based on existing object snap points.
- Create guidelines that are infinite in one or both directions.
- Add individual points and multiple individual points.
- Create a pattern of multiple individual points.

22.1 Coordinate Entry

The AutoCAD® software has several ways of locating positions in a drawing by typing coordinates, or by coordinate entry, as shown in Figure 22–1:

- Absolute Cartesian Coordinates (X,Y)
- Relative Cartesian Coordinates (@X,Y)
- Relative Polar Coordinates (@Distance<Angle)

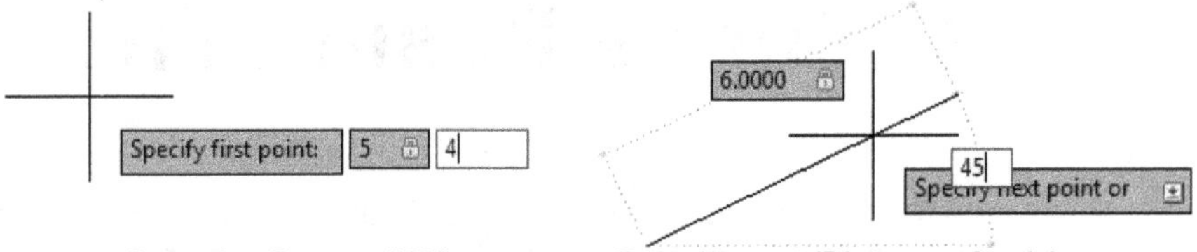

Cartesian Format (X,Y) *Polar Format (Distance<Angle)*

Figure 22–1

Absolute Cartesian Coordinates (X,Y)

Absolute Cartesian coordinates (X,Y) specify a point's absolute location based on the origin (0,0). You can use absolute coordinates to specify the first point of a line or the center point of a circle. For example, typing **8,2** locates a point eight units in the X-direction and two units in the Y-direction from the origin, as shown in Figure 22–2.

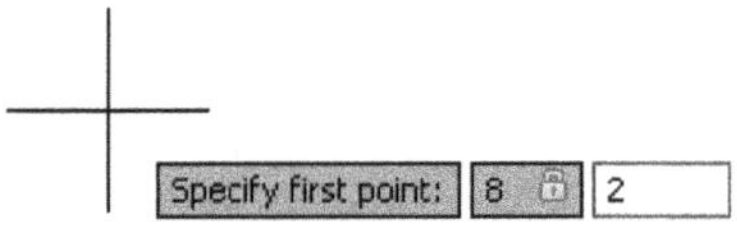

Figure 22–2

- Absolute Cartesian Coordinates are useful when you are given the coordinates to use, such as in some mapping applications or drawings for numeric control machinery.

Relative Cartesian Coordinates (@X,Y)

Relative Cartesian coordinates specify a point's distance away from the last point entered using X- and Y-values.

- Relative Cartesian coordinates are useful when you are given an X- and Y-distance rather than a distance and angle.
- When using (Dynamic Input), the coordinates you type for the *next point* or *second point* in a command are automatically relative by default.

- If (Dynamic Input) is toggled off, you have to force coordinates to be relative by putting **@** in front of them (@X,Y). **@** is a shorthand way of identifying the last point entered.
- When you type coordinates in the X,Y format, it overrides the default distance and angle format.

How To: Draw Using Relative Coordinates

In the example shown in Figure 22–3 the angled line is drawn using the specified dimensions and relative coordinates. The drawing requires X- and Y-values, rather than distance and angle values.

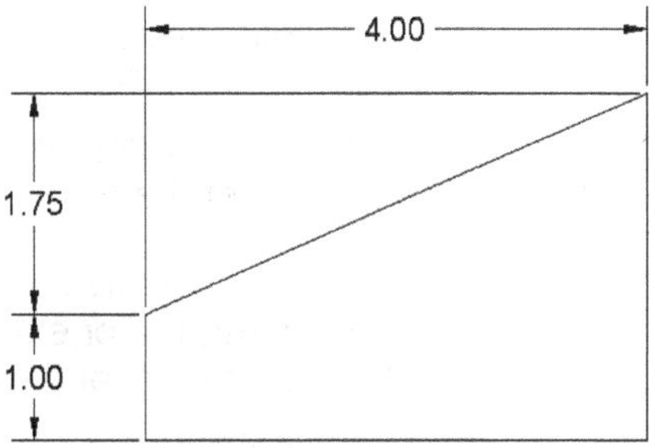

Figure 22–3

When (Dynamic Input) is toggled on, the coordinates you type for the next point or second point in a command are automatically relative by default. Therefore, @ is not required.

1. Verify that (Dynamic Input) is toggled on.
2. Start the **Line** command.
3. Draw the short vertical segment **1 unit** straight up.
4. At the *Specify next point:* prompt, type **4,1.75** and press <Enter>. This places the endpoint of the segment **4 units** to the right (X-value) and **1.75 units** up (Y-value) from the last point.
5. At the *Specify next point:* prompt, type **0,-2.75** and press <Enter>. This places the endpoint of the segment **0 units** to the right (X-value) and **2.75 units** down (Y-value) from the last point.
6. Type **C** to close the object and complete the drawing.

- The X- or Y-values can be either positive or negative. For example, @6,0 is a point 6 units straight to the right of the last point, but @-6,0 is a point 6 units to the left (back along the X-axis).

Relative Polar Coordinates (@Distance< Angle)

When you are selecting the *next point* for a line, dynamic dimensions display the distance from the last point and angle, as shown in Figure 22–4. Specifying the distance and angle is another form of coordinates, known as polar coordinates.

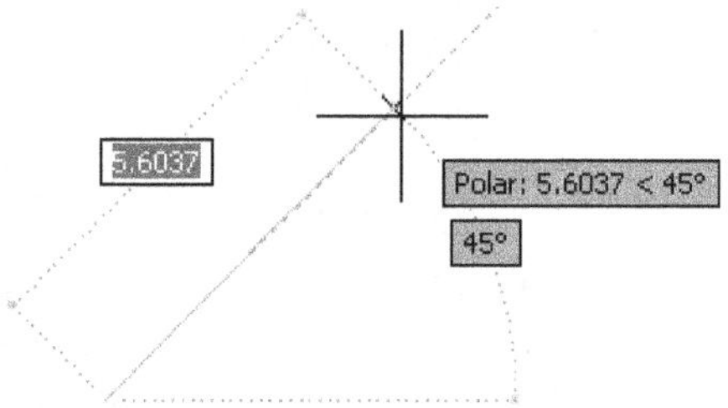

Figure 22–4

- Relative polar coordinates identify a point at a specific distance and angle from the last point selected.
- When drawing with (Dynamic Input) toggled on, you can enter the distance, press <Tab>, and enter the angle.
- You can also type polar coordinates in the form of **distance <angle**. For example, **@10<45** identifies a point ten units away, up, and to the right at a 45-degree angle from the last point entered (with (Dynamic Input) toggled off).
- You can use the AutoCAD angle scheme (shown in Figure 22–5) to help type the polar coordinates as **distance<angle** without needing to move the cursor to display the angle on the screen.

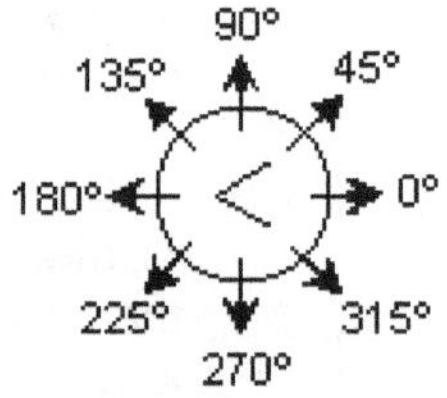

Figure 22–5

Notes on Coordinate Entry

- You can use coordinate entry with or without using (Dynamic Input). If (Dynamic Input) is toggled off, you must use **@** to make points relative to the last point.
- You can use **@** alone to indicate the last point.
- You can force coordinates to be absolute, rather than relative, by typing **#** in front of the X,Y value. For example, #1,1 always goes to the absolute point 1,1.

Right-click on (Dynamic Input) and select ***Dynamic Input Settings****.*

- The Dynamic Input settings can be changed so that the default for the second or next point is absolute instead of relative. In the Drafting Settings dialog box, in the *Dynamic Input* tab>*Pointer Input* area, click **Settings...** and modify the settings in the Pointer Input Settings dialog box.
- Relative coordinates can be useful in commands (such as **Move** and **Copy**), and in drawing commands. For example, you can use relative coordinates to copy an object at precise X- and Y- distances from the original. To copy the circle on the lower left (as shown in Figure 22–6), use the coordinates **5,3** as the second point.

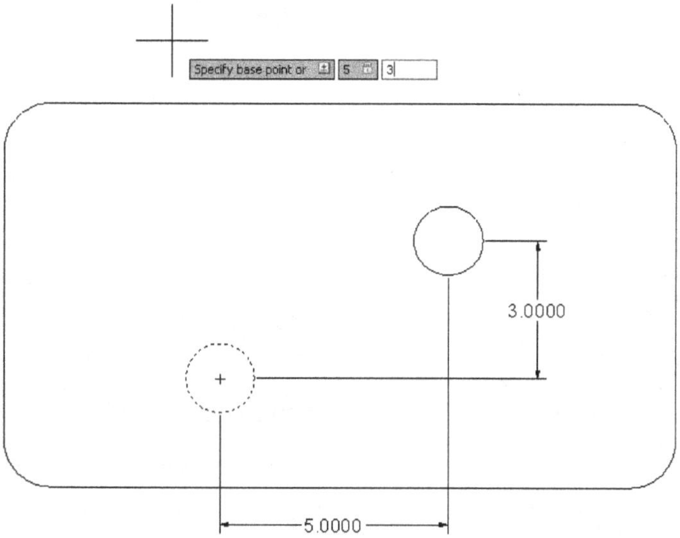

Figure 22–6

Hint: The User Coordinate System

The *User Coordinate System* (UCS) refers to the system of X-, Y-, and Z-coordinates, which define the AutoCAD Cartesian workspace. In the lower left corner of the window, a horizontal line labeled **X** and a vertical line labeled **Y** display. This is called the *UCS icon*, as shown in Figure 22–7.

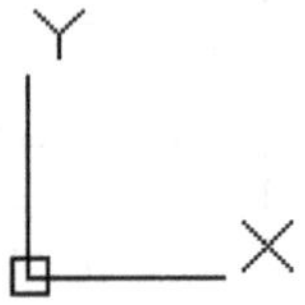

Figure 22–7

If the Coordinates panel is not displayed, right-click in any panel of the View tab and select ***Show Panels> Coordinates****.*

To hide the UCS icon, click (Hide UCS Icon) in the *View* tab>Coordinates panel, as shown in Figure 22–8. You might need to toggle on the Coordinates panel, as it is off by default. To have the UCS icon remain in the lower left corner of the screen (rather than moving with the 0,0 point), click (Show UCS Icon). By default, (Show UCS Icon at Origin) is selected.

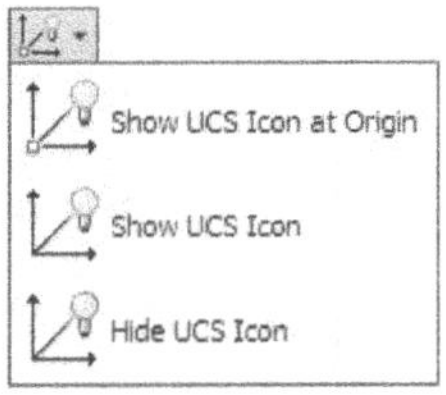

Figure 22–8

Typically, you work with a fixed coordinate system called the *World Coordinate System* or WCS. The UCS can also be changed to adjust the orientation of the drawing plane, which is primarily used in for 3D models.

- To return to the standard World Coordinate System at any time, click (World) in the *View* tab>Coordinates panel.

Practice 22a Drawing Using Coordinate Entry

Estimated time for completion: 5 minutes

Practice Objective

- Draw an object using typed coordinates.

In this practice, you will draw using typed coordinates, as shown in Figure 22–9.

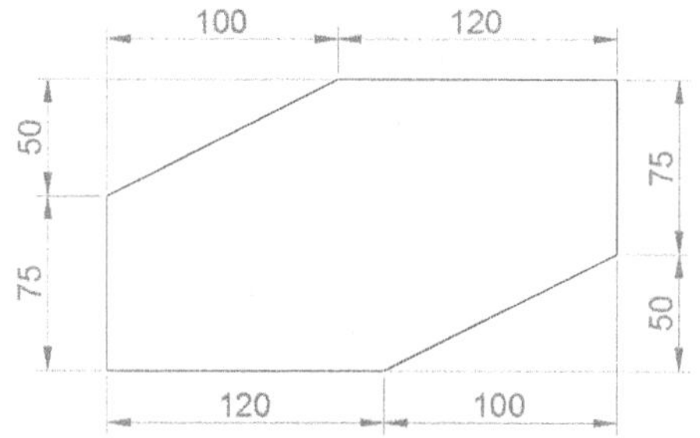

Figure 22–9

1. Start a new drawing based on **Mech-Millimeters.dwt**, which is located in your practice files folder. Save it as **New Plate.dwg**.
2. Toggle on  (Dynamic Input) if it is not already on.
3. Start the **Line** command.
4. For the first point, type the absolute coordinates **120,120** and press <Enter>.
5. For the next point, type **120<0** and press <Enter>. This draws the first segment **120** units straight to the right (angle 0) from the last point.
6. For the next point, type **100,50** and press <Enter>. This places the endpoint **100** units to the right (X-value) and 2 units up (Y-value) from the last point.
7. For the next point, type **75<90** and press <Enter>.
8. For the next point, type **120<180** and press <Enter>.
9. For the next point, type **–100,–50** and press <Enter> to draw the angled segment down and to the left.
10. Type **C** and press <Enter> to close the figure.
11. Save and close the drawing.

22.2 Locating Points with Tracking

Object Snap Tracking Review

You can track from two points to find the intersection point of their tracking lines.

You can use the technique of Object Snap Tracking to locate a new point based on existing object snap points. For example, you can find the precise center of an object in your drawing by tracking from the midpoints of two sides, as shown in Figure 22–10.

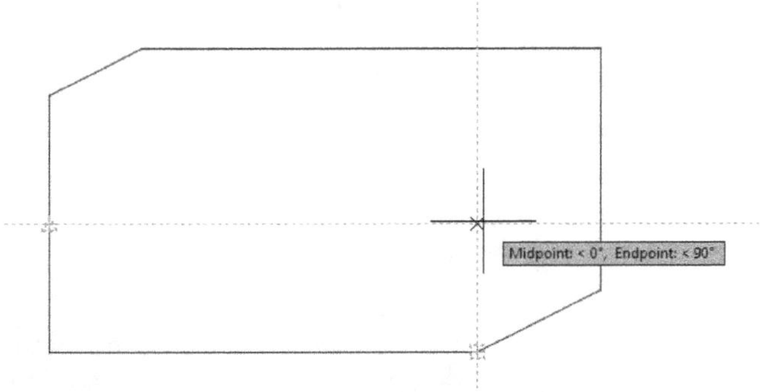

Figure 22–10

- (Object Snap) and (Object Snap Tracking) must both be toggled on to use Object Snap Tracking.
- Hover the cursor over the object snap point and then move it away vertically or horizontally to display the tracking line.
- You can select one point and type a distance to move in one direction along a tracking line from that point.

Temporary Track Point

(Temporary Track Point) can create additional tracking points, which can be useful when you are using Object Snap Tracking and need to have more than two tracking points. It enables you to find a location based on two distances from another point. For example, if you need to position a circle with its center five units to the left and three units up from an endpoint, you need to use Temporary Track Point to add the additional point.

- (Object Snap) and (Object Snap Tracking) must both be toggled on to use Temporary Track Point.

- You can start a Temporary Track Point by right-clicking and selecting **Snap Overrides>Temporary track point** in the shortcut menu or by typing **TT** in the Command Line, after invoking a draw command.

How To: Use a Temporary Track Point

1. In the Status Bar, toggle on (Object Snap) and (Object Snap Tracking).
2. Start a command, such as **Line** or **Circle**.
3. When prompted for a point, start (Temporary Track Point) by typing **tt**.
4. Hover the cursor over an existing point, which is then marked with a small plus mark.
5. Move the cursor to lock the required tracking angle from the temporary point, and then type a distance to move in relation to the temporary point, as shown in Figure 22–11.

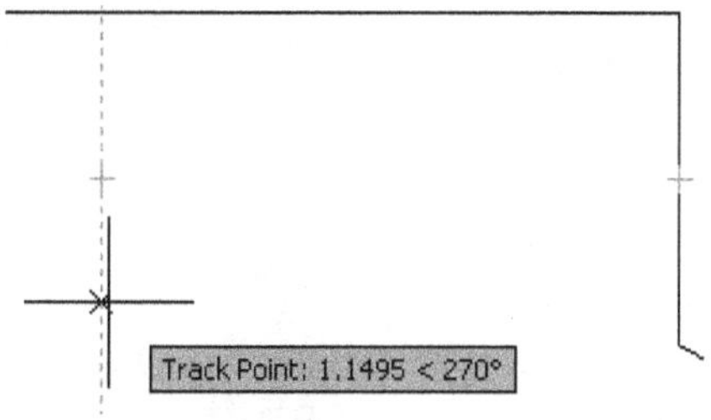

Figure 22–11

- Tracking lines display when you have locked a tracking angle from the temporary point.

- **IMPORTANT:** Do not move the cursor directly over the cross that marks the temporary point. Doing so clears the point.

Practice 22b Locating Points with Tracking (Mechanical)

Estimated time for completion: 5 minutes

Practice Objective

- Place holes at certain locations.

In this practice, you will use Object Snap Tracking and Temporary Track Point to place holes on a machine part, as shown in Figure 22–12.

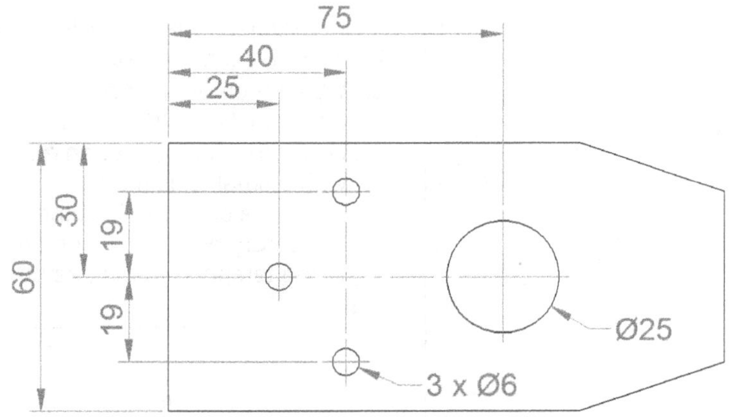

Figure 22–12

1. Open **Track-M.dwg** from your practice files folder.
2. Set the Object Snap Settings to **Midpoint**, and verify that  (Object Snap) and  (Object Snap Tracking) are toggled on.
3. To draw a circle using the **Circle** command, hover the cursor over the midpoint of the left line as a tracking point, and then pull the cursor to the right. Type **75,** press <Enter>, and set the *diameter* (using the <Down arrow>) to **25**.
4. Repeat this process to place the **6 diameter** circle, **25 unit** from the midpoint on the left, as shown in Figure 22–12.
5. Start the **Circle** command again and start the **Temporary Track Point** override, by right-clicking anywhere and selecting **Snap Overrides>Temporary track point**.

6. Hover the cursor over the midpoint of the left line, and pull the cursor to the right. Type **40** (as shown on the left in Figure 22–13) and press <Enter>. A small plus mark displays at the temporary track point. Move the cursor directly below the plus mark. A tracking line displays. Type **19** (as shown on the right in Figure 22–13) and press <Enter> to select another point 0.75 units down from the temporary point.

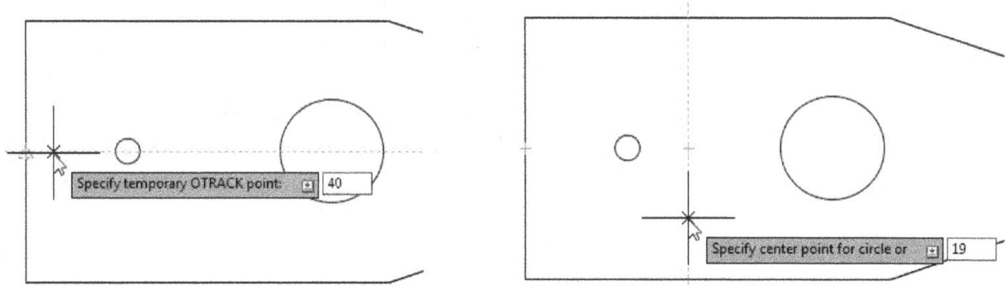

Figure 22–13

7. Place a **6 diameter** circle at this temporary track point location.

8. Repeat this process to place the last circle (**6 diameter**), but move the cursor directly above the cross as shown in Figure 22–12.

9. Save and close the drawing.

Practice 22c Locating Points with Tracking (Architectural)

Practice Objectives

- Draw the walls of a building.
- Position additional wall lines using tracking methods.

Estimated time for completion: 10 minutes

In this practice, you will create walls for a simple building outline using the Polyline command and then use Object Snap Tracking and Temporary Track Point methods to help position interior partitions, as shown in Figure 22–14.

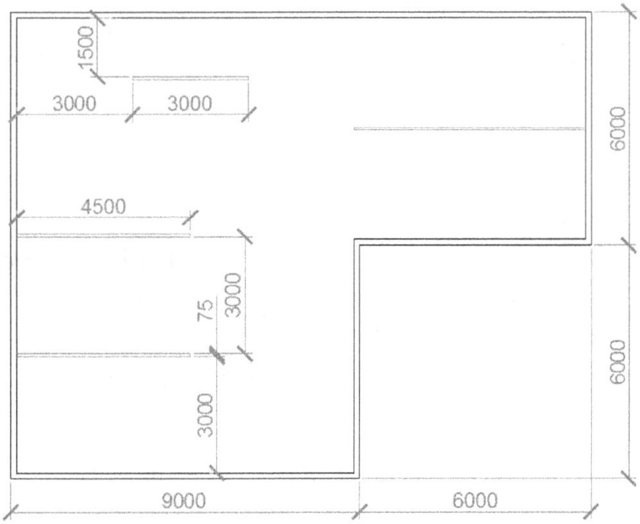

Figure 22–14

1. Start a new drawing based on **AEC-Millimeters.dwt,** which is found in your practice files folder.

2. Make the layer **Walls** current and draw the outside of the building as shown in Figure 22–14, using the **Polyline** command (verify that the **Width** option is set to **0**). Start from the lower left corner and draw counter-clockwise.

   -  (Object Snap Tracking) can help to position the point for the top left corner.

Note: Ignore the undimensioned partition wall.

3. Offset the exterior walls **150mm** to the inside.
4. Make the layer **Partitions** current and draw the interior partitions as shown in Figure 22–14. Use  (Object Snap Tracking) and **Temporary Track Point** to help position the lines precisely. Make all of the interior partitions **75mm** wide.
5. Save the drawing as **Open Office.dwg** and close the drawing.

22.3 Construction Lines

Use temporary construction lines as guidelines for creating the more permanent parts of your design, as shown in Figure 22–15. Regular lines can serve as construction lines, but do not always provide the required length. Construction Lines and Rays are infinite lines that can be used to help construct your drawing.

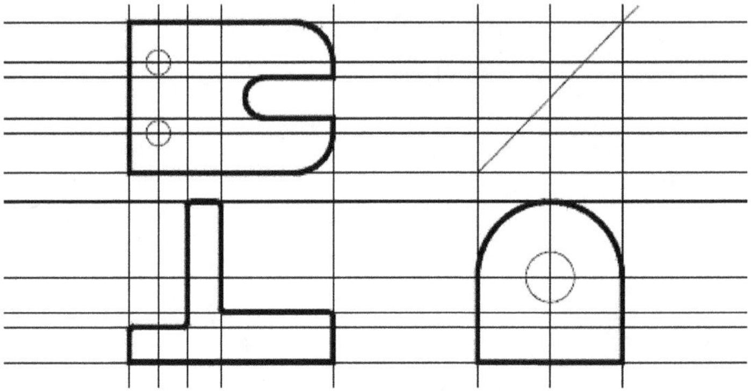

Figure 22–15

Construction Lines

The **Construction Line** command creates a line that is infinite in both directions.

The command options provide several methods of specifying the location and angle of the line.

How To: Draw a Construction Line

1. In the *Home* tab>expanded Draw panel, click (Construction Line).
2. Select two points on the screen for the line to go through or select an option in the menu. If you select two points, you can create additional construction lines by continuing to select points at different angles around the first point.
3. Select the **Hor**, **Ver**, or **Ang** options before selecting the first point if you want to make a series of horizontal, vertical, or angled construction lines.
4. If you want to create construction lines offset by a specific distance, select the **Offset** option.
5. The **Bisect** option creates a construction line that bisects a selected angle. It is determined by three points: angle vertex point, angle start point, and angle endpoint.

- Construction lines are not affected by zooming.
- Construction lines should be placed on a separate layer that can be toggled off or made non-plotable.

Rays

A ray extends infinitely in one direction from a specified point and you can input more than one ray from the same point.

Ray *does not have the same options as* ***Construction Line****.*

How To: Draw a Ray

1. In the *Home* tab>expanded Draw panel, click  (Ray).
2. Select the start point for the ray. This becomes the end point of the ray.
3. Select a through point for the ray.
4. Continue to select other through points to create additional rays at different angles, but with the same end point.
5. Press <Enter> to end the command.

- Use object snaps to place construction lines and rays precisely on existing objects.

Practice 22d Construction Lines

Estimated time for completion: 10 minutes

Practice Objective

- Create guidelines that are used to add geometry.

In this practice, you will draw circles and then add more circles to the plate using construction lines for precise placement, as shown in Figure 22–16.

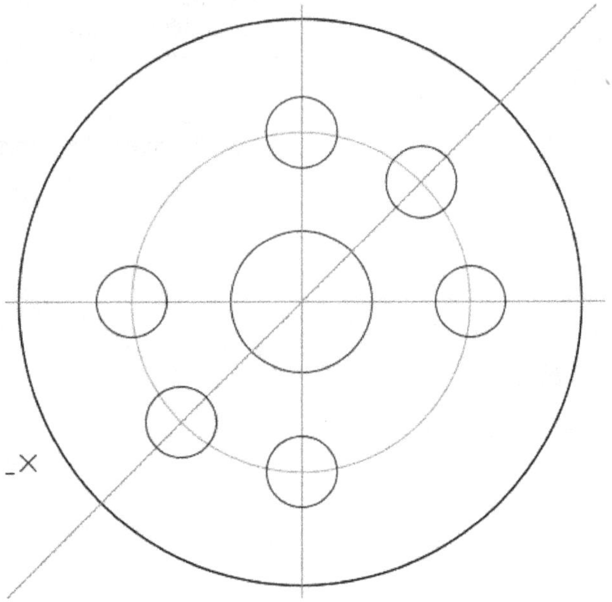

Figure 22–16

1. Create a new drawing based on **Mech-Millimeters.dwt**, which is located in your practice files folder. Save it as **Round Plate.dwg**.
2. Draw two circles (**R=50** and **R=200**) around the *center point* **250,120**. Use the **Zoom Extents** command to display the entire drawing.
3. Set the current layer to **Construction**.
4. Draw a third circle (**R=120**) around the same center point.
5. Toggle on the **Center** object snap.

6. In the *Home* tab>expanded Draw panel, click (Construction Line). Place the following three construction lines through the center point of the circles:
   - Horizontal
   - Vertical
   - Angular at 45 degrees

   Select the **Hor**, **Ver**, or **Ang** options in the <Down Arrow> menu before selecting the first point, as shown in Figure 22–17.

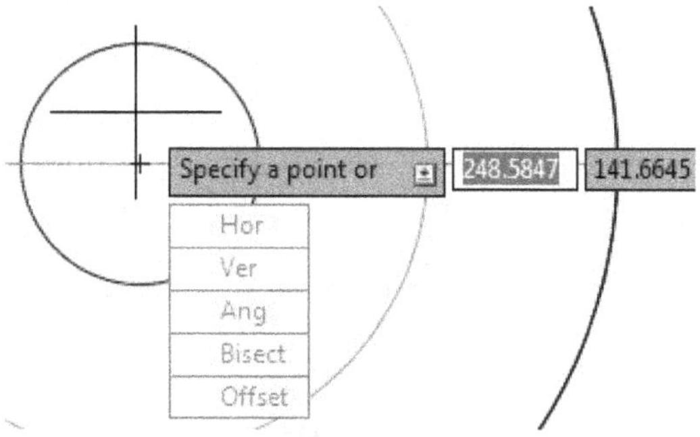

Figure 22–17

7. Set the current layer to **Object**.
8. Draw six circles with **R=25** at the intersection (**Intersection** object snap) of the construction lines and the middle circle.
9. Toggle off the layer **Construction**.
10. Save and close the drawing.

22.4 Placing Reference Points

The **Point** command places permanent reference markers into a drawing. For example, a point could be used to mark the center point of an arc for future reference, or to mark the precise location of survey points on a map, as shown in Figure 22–18. The visibility of this reference marker can be toggled on and off as required.

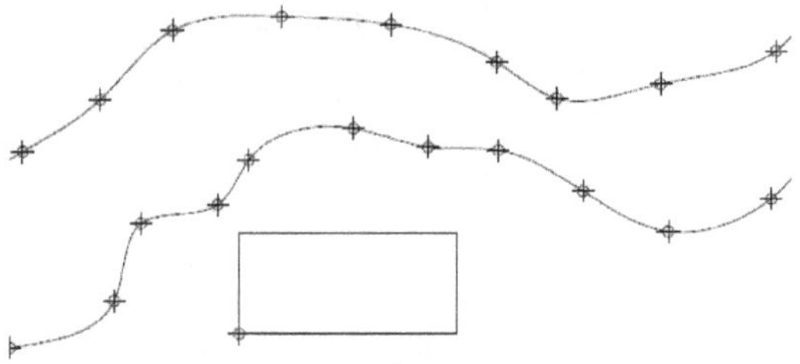

Figure 22–18

- You can add multiple individual points using (Multiple Points). Two other commands, (Divide) and (Measure), create groups of points in a pattern. You can access these point commands in the expanded *Home* tab>Draw panel, as shown in Figure 22–19.

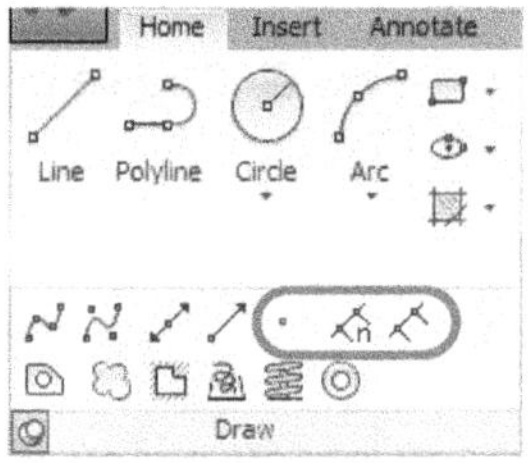

Figure 22–19

- Once placed in a drawing, points can be moved or erased like other objects.
- Use the **Node** object snap to snap to a point.

Setting the Point Style

To change the appearance of points in your drawing, click (Point Style...) in the *Home* tab>expanded Utilities panel. The Point Style dialog box opens (as shown in Figure 22–20), enabling you to select from the available point styles.

Changing the point style changes the display of all of the points in the drawing. The drawing must be regenerated before the change displays.

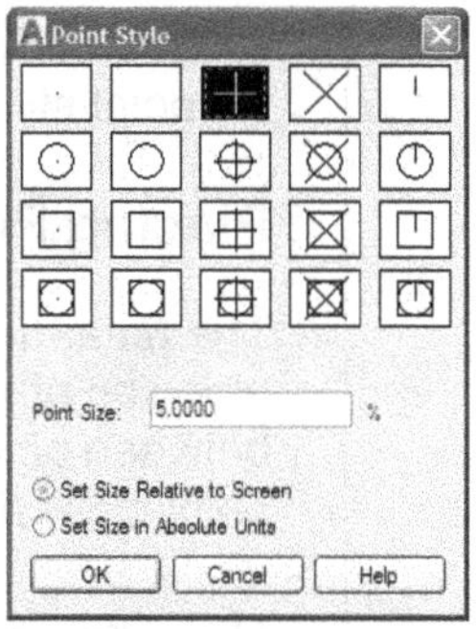

Figure 22–20

Creating Groups of Points

Creating groups of points can be very useful. For example, you might need to space electrical outlets evenly around a large room in a floor plan (as shown in Figure 22–21), or to place markers every 300 meters along a runway on a map.

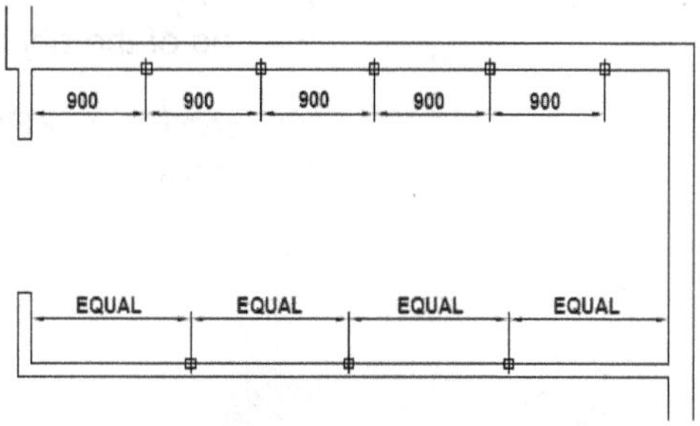

Figure 22–21

Placing Evenly Spaced Points on an Object

The **Divide** command places points to divide an object into a specified number of equal segments. You can specify the number of segments. This is not the number of points: a line divided into three segments has two points placed along it as shown in Figure 22–22.

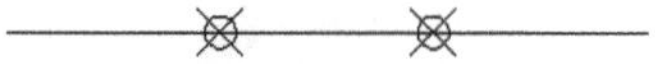

Figure 22–22

How To: Divide an Object

1. In the *Home* tab>expanded Draw panel, click (Divide).
2. Select the object that you want to divide.
3. Enter the number of segments. The points are evenly spaced, dividing the object into equal length segments between the points.

- You can use the **Block** option to insert a block instead of a point style.

Placing Points at Specified Intervals on an Object

The **Measure** command places points at a specified distance along an object. You specify the *length of segments* (the distance between points). The software begins to measure from the end point closest to the location used to select the object.

How To: Measure an Object

1. In the *Home* tab>expanded Draw panel, click (Measure).
2. Select the object that you want to measure.
3. Specify the length of the segment. The points are spaced at the specified distance along the object.

- If the object cannot be divided evenly, the remainder is left at the end of the object, opposite to where it was selected.

- You can use the **Block** option to insert a block instead of a point style.

Practice 22e Placing Points

Practice Objective

- Place points to mark the locations on objects.

Estimated time for completion: 5 minutes

In this practice, you will place points to mark the locations of the centers of holes in a plate. You will use **Point**, **Divide**, and **Measure** commands to position the points, as shown in Figure 22–23.

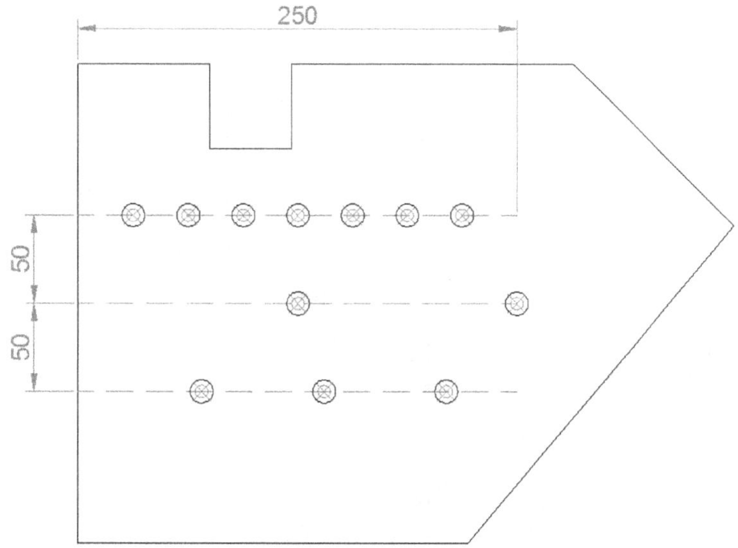

Figure 22–23

1. Open **Points-M.dwg** from your practice files folder.
2. Change the current layer to **Constructions**.
3. Draw a line from the midpoint of the left side (vertical line) of the plate, **250 units** straight to the right side.
4. Offset the line **50 units** on either side.
5. In the *Home* tab>expanded Utilities panel, click  (Point Style) to open the Point Style dialog box. Select the cross and circle or other visible point style and click **OK**.
6. In the *Home* tab>expanded Draw panel, click  (Multiple Points). Place points at the midpoint and right endpoint of the middle construction line. Press <Esc> to end the command.

7. In the *Home* tab>expanded Draw panel, click (Divide) and select the top construction line. Type **8** as the number of segments. Seven points should be displayed, evenly dividing the line.

8. In the *Home* tab>expanded Draw panel, click (Measure) and select the bottom construction line near the left endpoint. Type **70** as the length of segments and press <Enter>. Three points should display, spaced at that distance apart.

9. Add **Node** as additional Object snap.

10. Set the current layer to **Object**.

11. Start the **Circle** command and place a **13** radius circle on one of the nodes (points).

12. Use the **Copy** command to copy the circle to the other points.

13. Toggle off the layer **Constructions**.

14. Save and close the drawing.

Chapter Review Questions

1. With Dynamic Input toggled off, after you pick the first corner for a rectangle, what are the typed coordinates that can be used to make it 20 units long and 8 units high?
   a. 20,8
   b. @8,20
   c. 8,20
   d. @20,8
2. What does @ represent in the AutoCAD software?
   a. Indicates that Object Snap is going to be used.
   b. Indicates that a temporary tracking point is going to be used.
   c. Indicates a point relative to the last point.
   d. Used in place of 0.
3. What does the Temporary Tracking Point enable you to do that Object Snap Tracking alone does not?
   a. Find a location based on two distances from another point.
   b. Draw circles, lines, and rectangles.
   c. Find a location based on the midpoints of two objects.
   d. Precisely pick a point without using an object snap.
4. The difference between construction lines and regular lines is that construction lines extend infinitely.
   a. True
   b. False
5. Which command would enable you to position points every 5 units along a line?
   a. **Temporary Tracking Point**
   b. **Divide**
   c. **Point**
   d. **Measure**

6. Relative coordinates are relative to the _______.
    a. Origin (0,0).
    b. Last point picked.
    c. Nearest object snap.
    d. Current screen display.

Command Summary

Button	Command	Location
	**Construction Line**	• **Ribbon:** *Home* tab>expanded Draw panel • **Command Prompt:** xline or xl
	**Divide**	• **Ribbon:** *Home* tab>expanded Draw panel • **Command Prompt:** divide or div
	**Hide UCS Icon**	• **Ribbon:** *View* tab>Coordinates panel
	**Measure**	• **Ribbon:** *Home* tab>expanded Draw panel • **Command Prompt:** measure or me
	**Point (Multiple Points)**	• **Ribbon:** *Home* tab>expanded Draw panel • **Command Prompt:** point or po
	**Point Styles**	• **Ribbon:** *Home* tab>expanded Utilities panel • **Command Prompt:** ddptype
	**Ray**	• **Ribbon:** *Home* tab>expanded Draw panel • **Command Prompt:** ray
	**Show UCS Icon**	• **Ribbon:** *View* tab>Coordinates panel
	**Show UCS Icon at Origin**	• **Ribbon:** *View* tab>Coordinates panel
	**Temporary Track Point**	• **Shortcut Menu:** Snap Overrides> Temporary Track Point • **Command Prompt:** tt
	**World**	• **Ribbon:** *View* tab>Coordinates panel

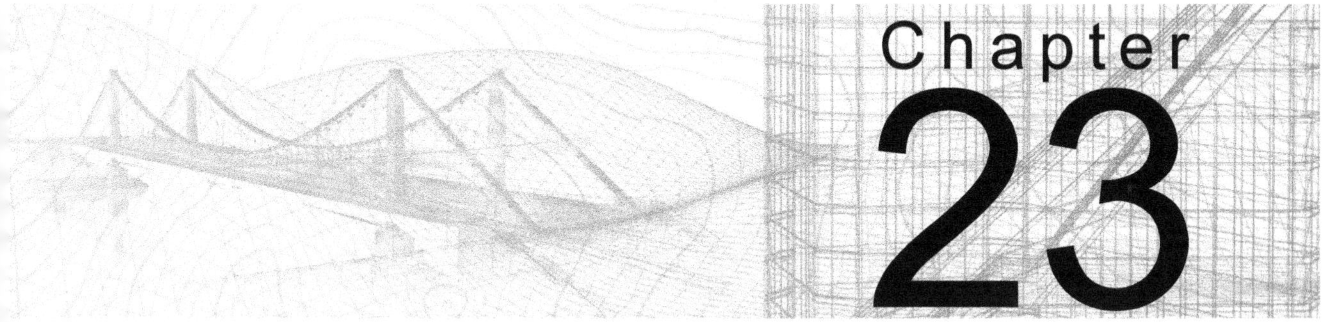

Chapter 23

Projects: Productivity Tools

This chapter contains practice projects that can be used to gain additional hands-on experience with the topics and commands covered so far in this student guide. These practices are intended to be self-guided and do not include step by step information.

Learning Objectives in this Chapter

- *Schematic:* Modify a piping diagram using editing techniques such as trim and stretch.
- *Mechanical:* Create several parts and objects using various Drafting Settings.
- *Architectural:* Create several plans using various tracking and placement commands.

23.1 Schematic Project: Purifier Unit

Estimated time for completion: 15 minutes

In this project you will use editing techniques to modify the piping diagram shown in Figure 23–1.

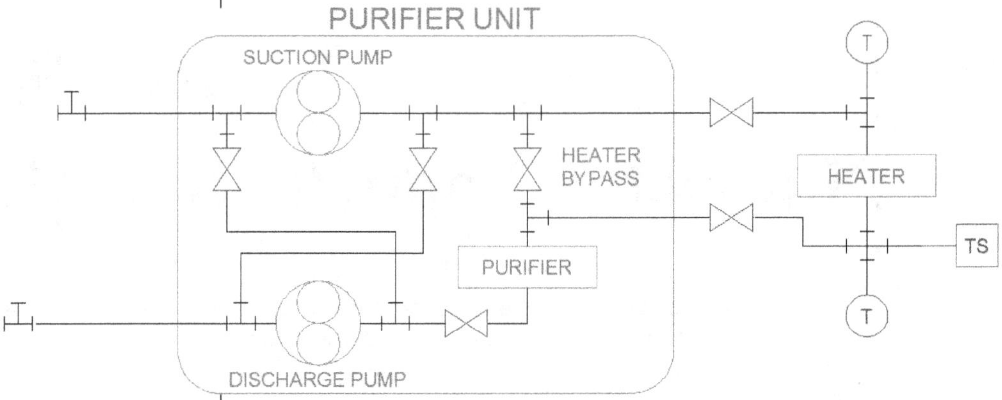

Figure 23–1

1. Open **Piping-M.dwg** from your practice files folder.
2. Use the **Stretch** command to stretch the Heater elements farther to the right, as shown in Figure 23–2.

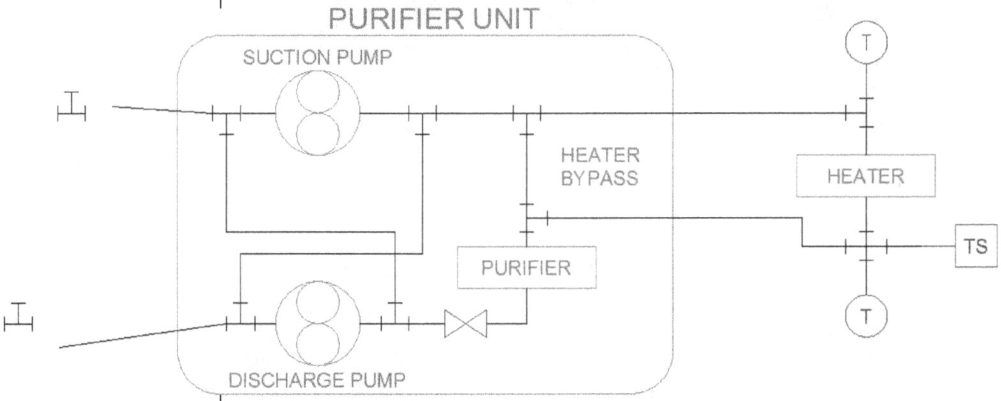

Figure 23–2

3. Use grips to copy and rotate the gate valve (the blue hourglass shape) to the locations shown in Figure 23–3. Use the **Nearest** object snap to place the valves precisely on the lines.

4. Use **Trim** to remove the section of the line inside the valves, as shown in Figure 23–3.

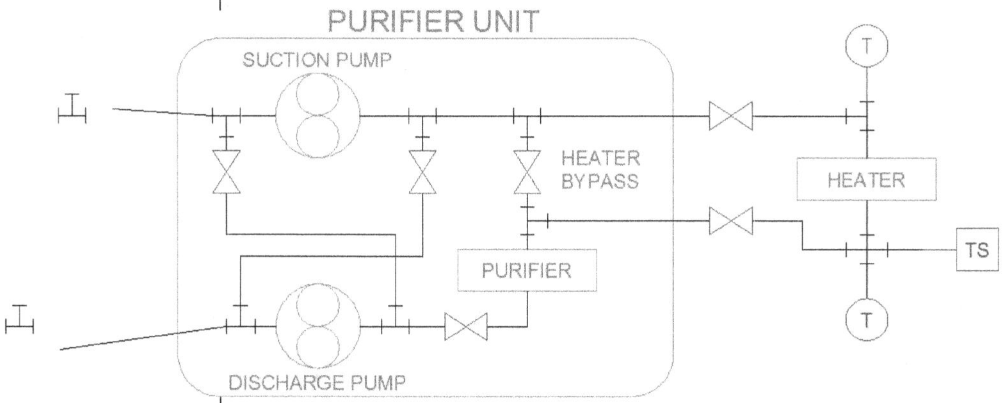

Figure 23–3

5. Use grips to stretch the endpoint of the lines on the left side to connect with the **T** fittings, as shown in Figure 23–4.

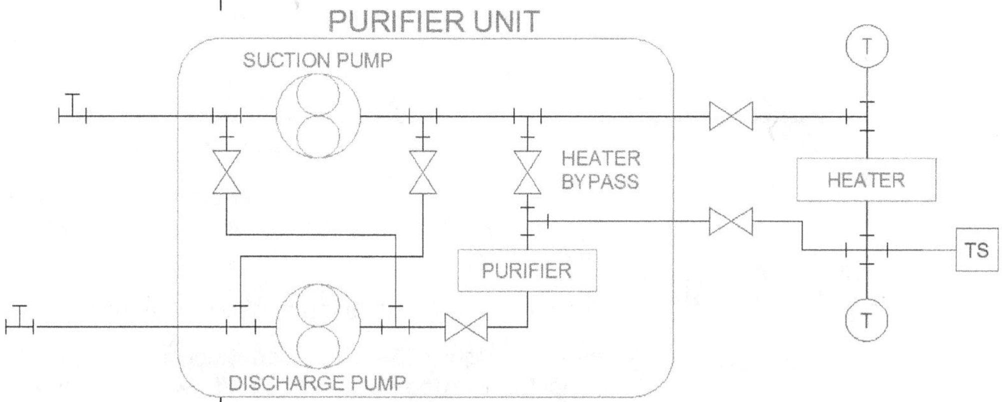

Figure 23–4

23.2 Mechanical Project: 2 Views

Estimated time for completion: 20 minutes

In this project you will create the front and top views of a part, as shown in Figure 23–5.

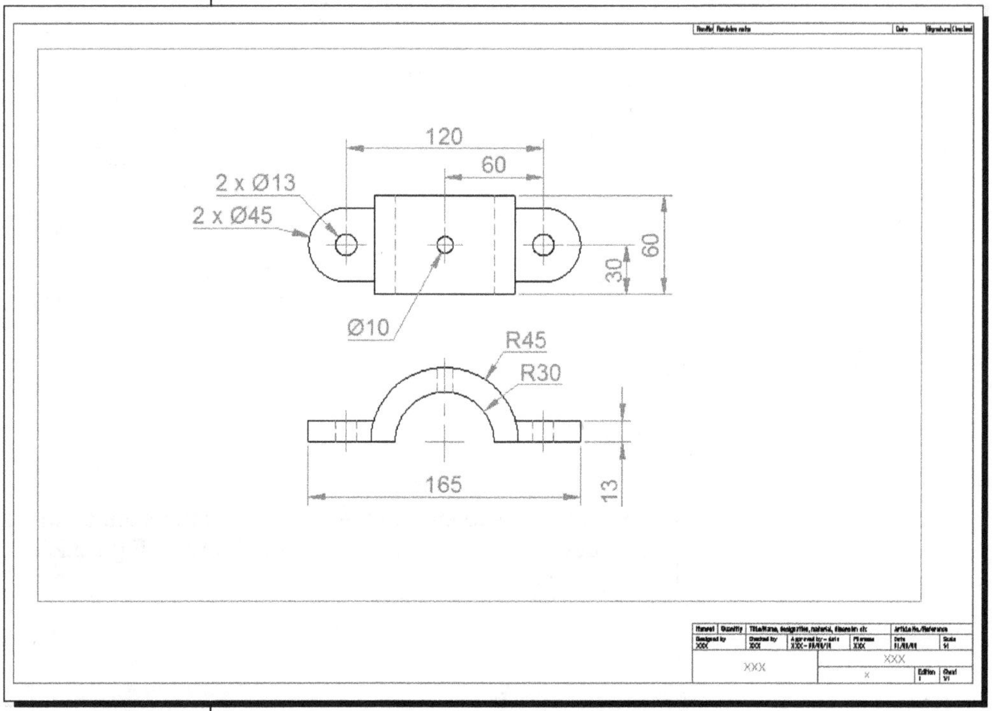

Figure 23–5

1. Start a new drawing based on **Mech-Millimeters.dwt**, which is located in your practice files folder and save it as **2Views.dwg**.
2. Use the tools you have learned to create the two views, as shown in Figure 23–5. Use construction lines or (Object Snap Tracking) to help align and draw the views. Place the hidden lines on the layer **Hidden**.
3. If time permits, switch to the **ISO A2** Layout tab and display the views in a viewport scaled at **1:1**. Add annotative dimensions in the viewport as required.

23.3 Architectural/Civil Project: Formal Garden

Estimated time for completion: 40 minutes

In this project you will create a formal garden plan. Use a construction line to establish the center line, and then use tracking and other methods to help place the various components as shown in Figure 23–6.

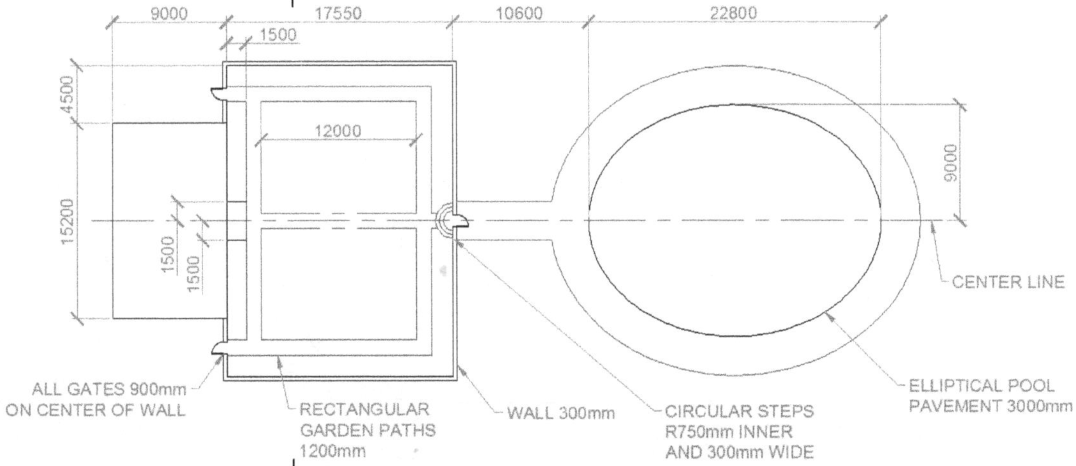

Figure 23–6

1. Start a new drawing named **Formal Garden.dwg** based on **Civil-Millimeters.dwt,** which is located in your practice files folder.
2. Draw the **9000 x 15200 building** with the **1500 x 3000 porch** shown in black (midpoint of right vertical wall of building) in Figure 23–6.
3. Use the **Construction Line** command to establish the center line.
4. Draw the rectangular garden wall and paths with gates, as shown in Figure 23–6. Use tracking or other construction lines to help you. Place the objects on the layer **Pavement Edge New**.
5. Add the semi-circular stairs.
6. (Optional) If time permits, add the elliptical pool.

23.4 Mechanical Project: Cover Plate

Estimated time for completion: 30 minutes

In this project you will draw one view of a mechanical part, as shown in Figure 23–7.

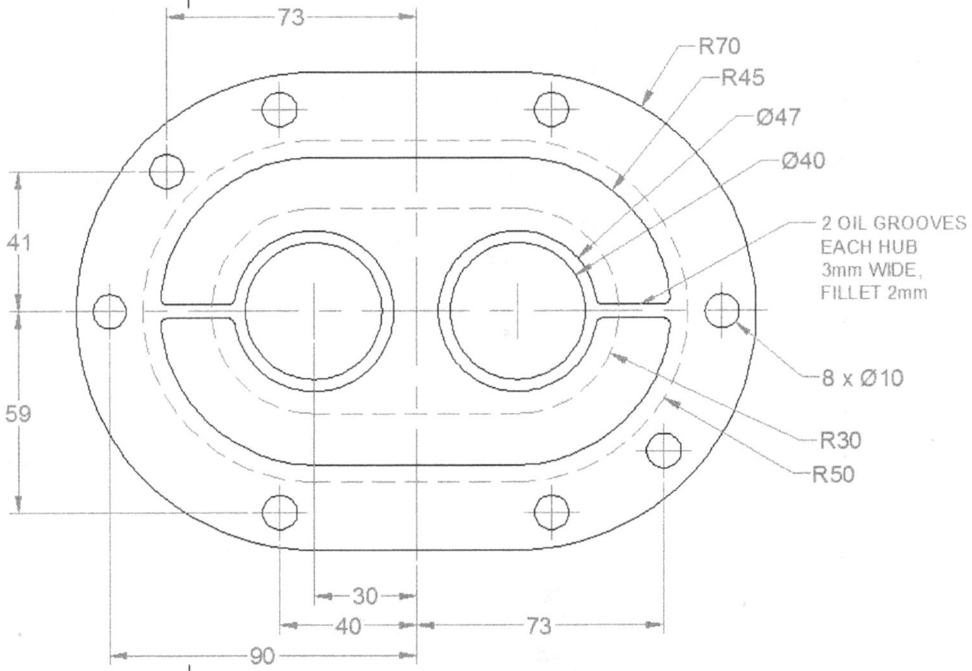

Figure 23–7

1. Start a new drawing based on **Mech-Millimeters.dwt**, which is located in your practice files folder.
2. Draw the objects shown in Figure 23–7 using tools such as Dynamic Input, Direct Distance Entry, Polar Array, and Object Snap Tracking. Draw only the objects, not the dimensions. Note that all of the dimensions are mirror images unless otherwise indicated.
3. Save the drawing as **Cover Plate.dwg**.

23.5 Architectural Project: Addition

Estimated time for completion: 15 minutes

In this project you will draw an addition to an existing house plan, as shown in Figure 23–8.

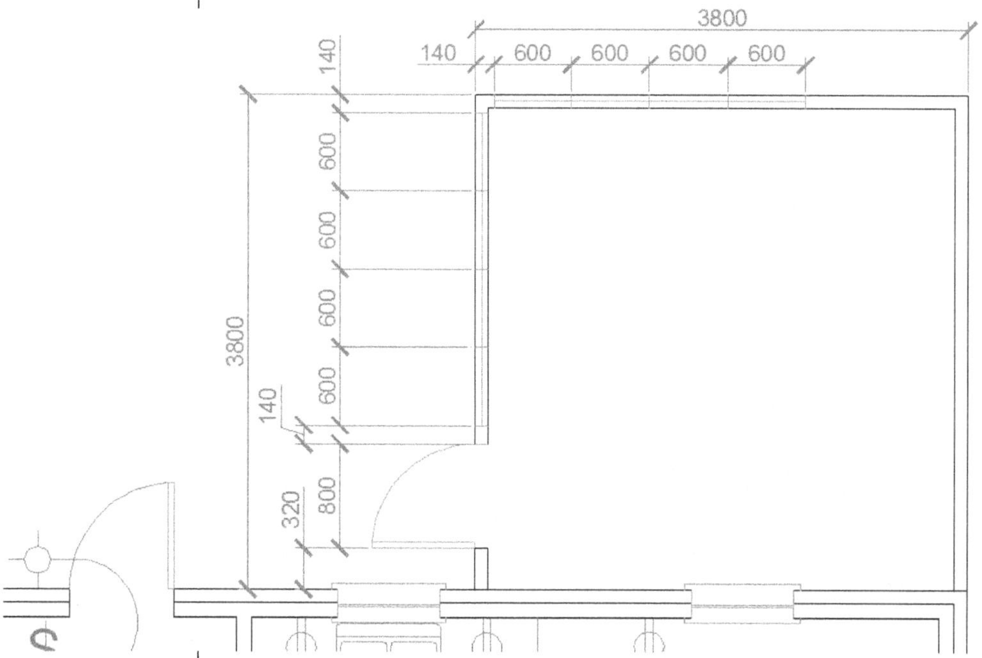

Figure 23–8

1. Open **Addition-AM.dwg** from your practice files folder.
2. Draw the addition along the top right horizontal wall of the building, as shown in Figure 23–8. The walls are **100mm** thick. Remember to use the appropriate layers. Use Dynamic Input, Direct Distance Entry, Object Snaps, Object Snap Tracking, and other drafting tools to help create the drawing.
   - Use the dynamic **Door** and **Window** blocks from the *Architectural* tab in the Tool Palettes.
   - Use grips to adjust the depth of the window and door blocks to match the depth of the wall.
3. Save and close the drawing.

23.6 Mechanical Project: Block

Estimated time for completion: 10 minutes

In this project you will use the Drafting Settings tools to help draw a mechanical object, as shown in Figure 23–9.

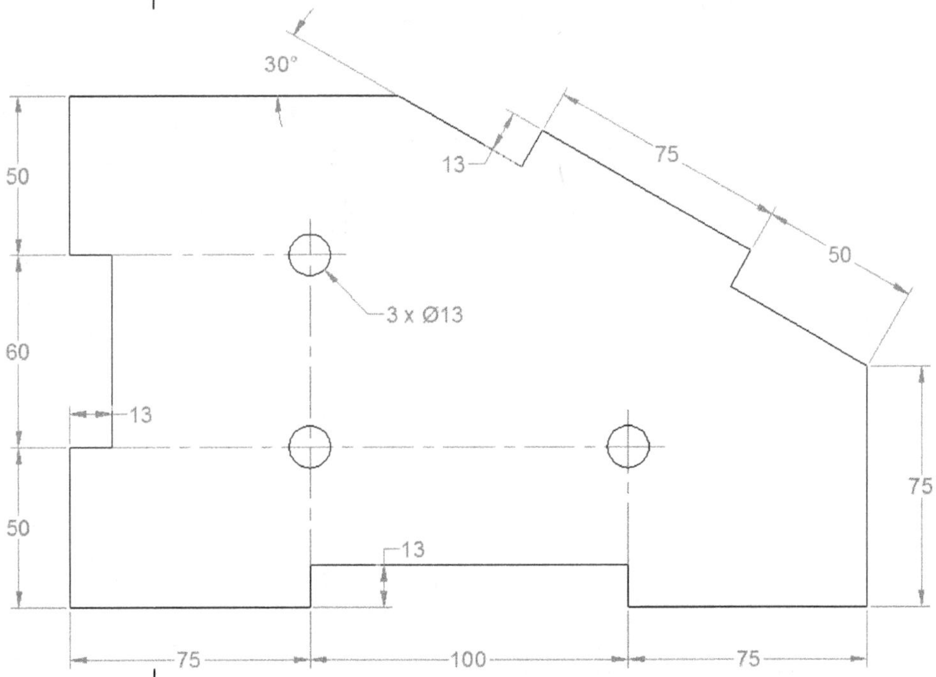

Figure 23–9

1. Start a new drawing based on **Mech-Millimeters.dwt**, which is located in your practice files folder. Save it as **Block.dwg**.
2. Draw the objects shown in Figure 23–9. Draw only the objects, not the dimensions.

Construction Hints:

- With Dynamic Input, use Polar Tracking to draw the outline. Set the *Polar Angle* to **30 degrees** to draw the angled segments. Depending on how you construct the lines, Object Snap Tracking can help you to draw the top undimensioned segment.
- Use Object Snap Tracking to place the three circles in relation to the outline.

3. Save and close the drawing.

23.7 Mechanical Project: Plate

Estimated time for completion: 15 minutes

In this project you will use the Drafting Settings tools to help draw the object shown in Figure 23–10.

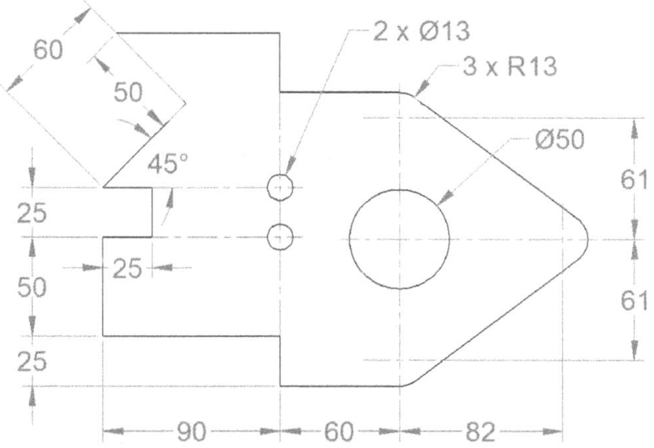

Figure 23–10

1. Start a new drawing based on **Mech-Millimeters.dwt**, which is located in your practice files folder. Save it as **Angled Plate.dwg**.

2. Draw the objects shown in Figure 23–10. Draw only the objects, not the dimensions.

Construction Hints:

- Start with the circle with a *diameter* of **50**.
- Use Object Snap Tracking to place the three **R13** fillets (drawn as full circles) in relation to the larger circle. Draw the two angled segments on the right **Tangent** to the **R13** fillets (circles). (You will trim the circles later, to make them into fillets.)
- Start at the bottom quadrant of the bottom circle and begin drawing the outline clockwise. Use Polar Tracking. Set the *Polar Angle* to **45 degrees** to draw the angled segments at the upper left side. Use Object Snap Tracking to draw the remaining segments of the outline.
- Use Object Snap Tracking to position the two circles with a *diameter* of **13**.
- Trim the three circles with a *radius* of **13** to finish.

Chapter 24

Parametric Drawing

In this chapter you learn how to add geometric and dimensional constraints to objects, modify parameters, and create user parameters.

Learning Objectives in this Chapter

- Control how geometry reacts using the Geometric constraints.
- Specify distances, radii, or angles that must be fulfilled by the geometry.
- Specify, modify, and delete and object's geometric constraints, and customize the constraint settings.
- Add dimensional constraints and convert the existing dimensions into constraints.
- Modify and add formulas to dimensional constraints.

24.1 Working with Constraints

In the AutoCAD LT® software, you cannot create constraints. However, you can view, edit, and delete them.

Constraints and parametric tools provide ways of testing design options while maintaining specific relationships in a drawing. They are used extensively in software, such as the Autodesk® Inventor® software and the Autodesk® Revit® Architecture software. The AutoCAD® software uses them to enhance 2D sketching. There are two types of constraints: Geometric and Dimensional, as shown in Figure 24–1.

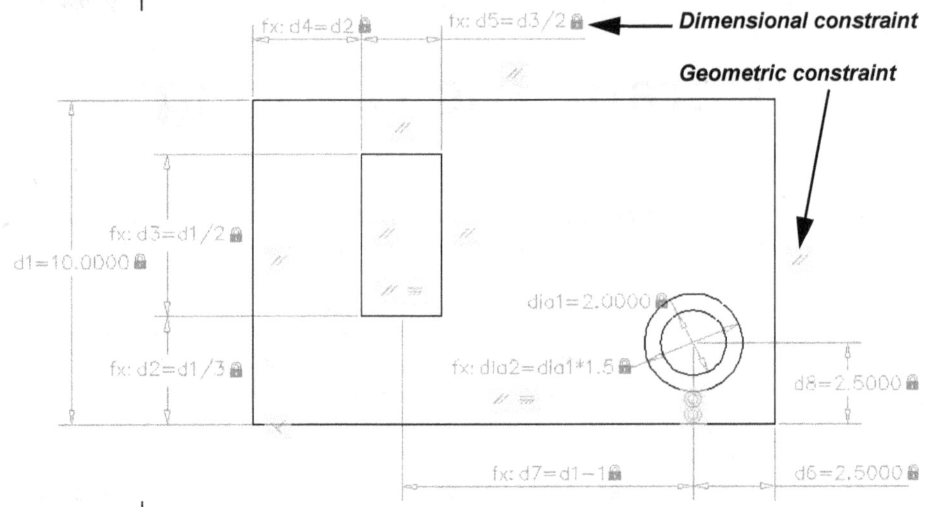

Figure 24–1

In the AutoCAD LT software, you need to show all geometric or dimensional constraints before this icon displays. By default, when you open a drawing containing constraints in the AutoCAD LT software, they are hidden.

- Geometric constraints control how geometry reacts. For example, you can specify that a line remain horizontal or that two circles are concentric.
- Dimensional constraints specify distances, radii, or angles that must be fulfilled by the geometry. Dimensional constraints can include formulas referencing other constraints or using basic mathematical functions.
- When you hover the cursor over an object that has constraints,  displays, as shown in Figure 24–2.

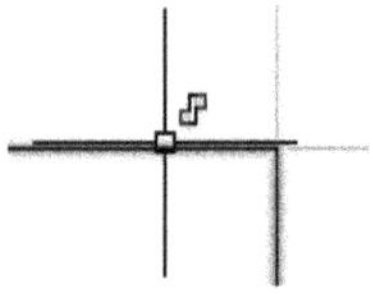

Figure 24–2

24.2 Geometric Constraints

Once objects have been sketched, you can automatically and manually add constraints to the geometry by selecting them in the *Parametric* tab>Geometric panel, as shown in Figure 24–3. Click the required constraint icon and select the objects that you want to constrain.

*In the AutoCAD LT software, in the Geometric panel, you only have access to the **Show/Hide**, **Show All**, and **Hide All** commands.*

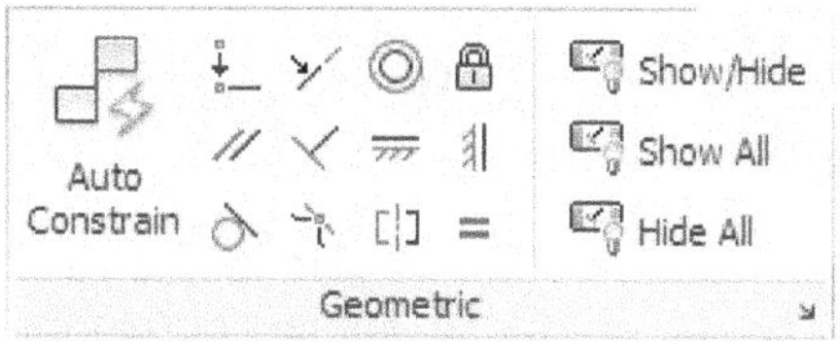

Figure 24–3

Auto Constraining Objects

If you are working with rectangles and some lines or polylines, you can use the **Auto Constrain** command first to set up the parallel, perpendicular, horizontal, or vertical relationships. This command is best used with rectangles, or applying other constraints could force the rectangle away from the correct shape.

How To: Auto Constrain Objects

1. Draw the objects in the design.
2. In the *Parametric* tab>Geometric panel, click (Auto Constrain).
3. Select the objects that you want to constrain.The constraints are applied as shown on the rectangle in Figure 24–4.

One perpendicular, one horizontal, and four parallel constraints help a rectangle to keep its shape.

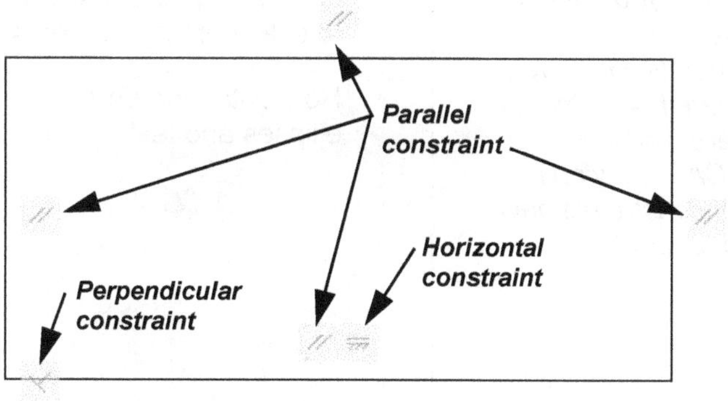

Figure 24–4

- Commands that duplicate objects, such as **Copy**, **Mirror**, and **Array**, also duplicate any related constraints.

Specifying Geometric Constraints

Before you start adding constraints, draw the objects, including any fillets or chamfers. The exact sizes and angles of the objects are not important.

- Linear objects include lines and polyline segments. For the purpose of constraints, a polyline segment can be selected separately from the rest of the polyline.
- Radial objects include circles, arcs, and ellipses.

Horizontal and Vertical

(Horizontal) and (Vertical) constraints force linear objects to remain horizontal or vertical. Select the linear object that you want to be horizontal or vertical, as shown in Figure 24–5.

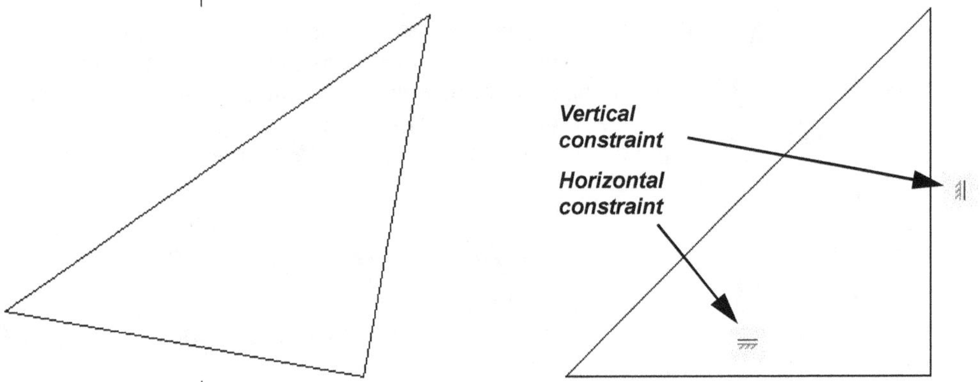

Figure 24–5

In the AutoCAD LT software, you cannot create these constraints. However, you can modify them if you are working in an AutoCAD drawing in which constraints have been created.

- You can also use these tools to align two points horizontally or vertically, such as center points for circles. When prompted to select an object, press <Enter> to select two points.
- Horizontal and Vertical constraints can also be used with ellipses and text.

Parallel and Perpendicular

(Parallel) constrains two linear objects, forcing them to take on the angle of the first object. (Perpendicular) constrains the second linear element to rotate 90 degrees from the angle of the first linear object. Select a linear object and then a second linear object. The objects take on the angle or right angle of the first object, depending on the selected constraint. Examples of these constraints are shown in Figure 24–6.

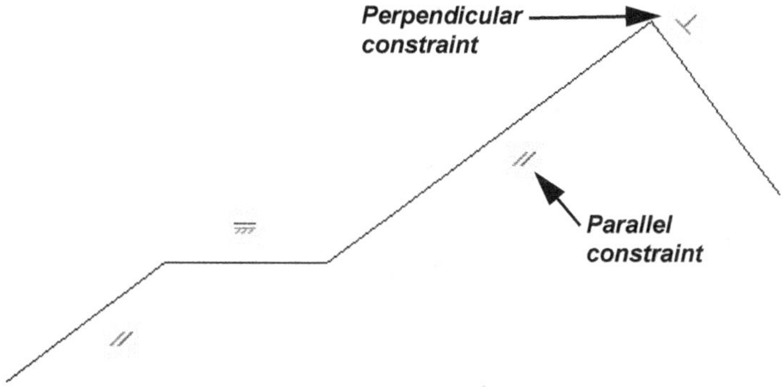

Figure 24–6

- Parallel and Perpendicular constraints can also be used with ellipses and text.

Tangent

(Tangent) constrains an object to the tangent of a radial object. At least one object needs to be a circle, arc, or ellipse, but the objects do not have to touch. Select one object and then select a second object. The elements are then forced to be tangent, as shown in Figure 24–7.

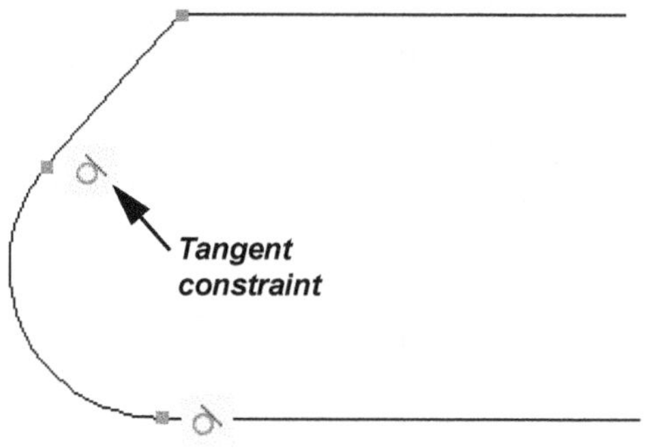

Figure 24–7

Smooth

(Smooth) ensures that the selected objects continue the same curvature values between a spline and other linear objects. Select the spline at the endpoint at which you want the curve to continue. Select the second linear element, which can be a line, polyline, or another spline. In Figure 24–8, the endpoint of the spline and the endpoint of the line (indicated by their grips) are selected.

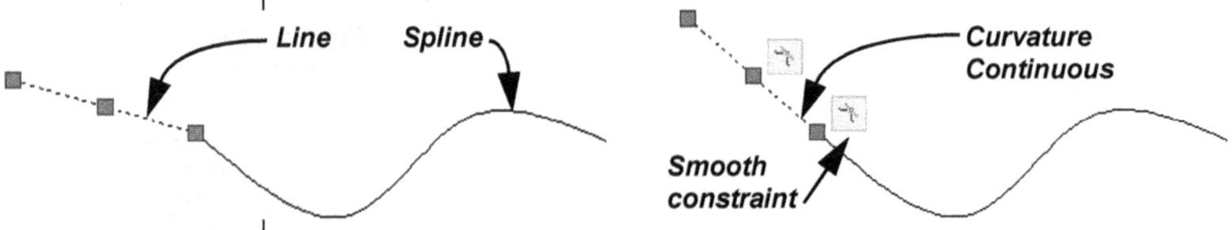

Figure 24–8

Coincident

(Coincident) constrains two points to remain together or a point to remain touching another point on an object. Select a point on one object and then a point on a second object. The point on the second object is moved coincident to the point on the first object. In the example shown in Figure 24–9, the center of the circle has been constrained to the midpoint of the line.

A constraint bar does not display with coincident constraints, but a small blue square displays.

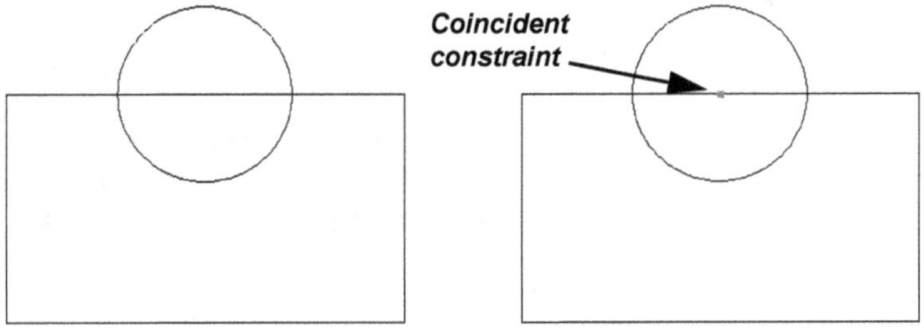

Figure 24–9

- Coincident constraints can also move along an object, such as the end of the arc constrained to the line.

Concentric

 (Concentric) constrains two radial objects, such as arcs, circles, or ellipses, to maintain the same center point. Select the first center point of a radial object, and then the second center point of another radial object. The two objects take on the center point of the first object, as shown on the right in Figure 24–10.

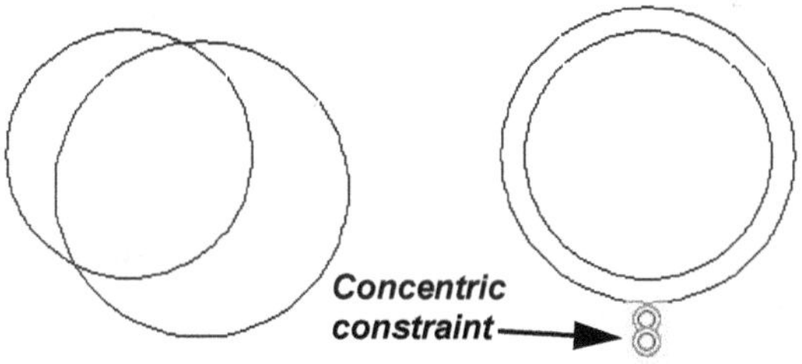

Figure 24–10

Colinear

 (Colinear) constrains two lines to lie along the same infinite line. They do not need to be touching. Select the first line and then select the second line. The second line moves to line up with the first line, as shown in Figure 24–11.

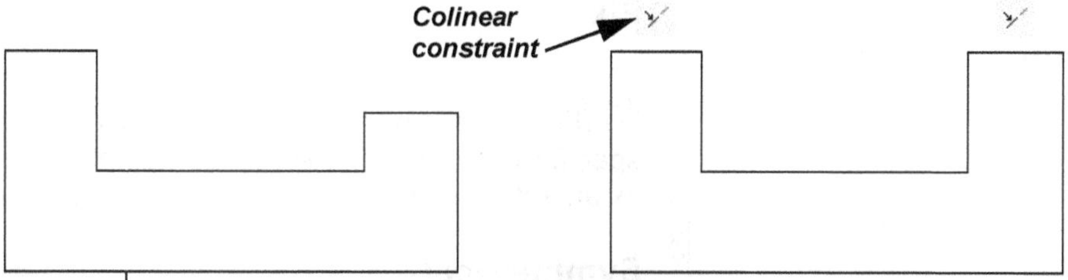

Figure 24–11

- Colinear constraints can also be used to make ellipses and text colinear with other objects, such as lines or ellipses.

Equal

= (Equal) constrains two linear elements to maintain the same length or two radial elements to maintain the same radius.

How To: Apply an Equal Constraint

1. Select the first object and then the second object.
2. The second object takes on the measurements of the first object. In Figure 24–12, the object on the right was not constrained and only the selected segment of the polyline changed in distance.

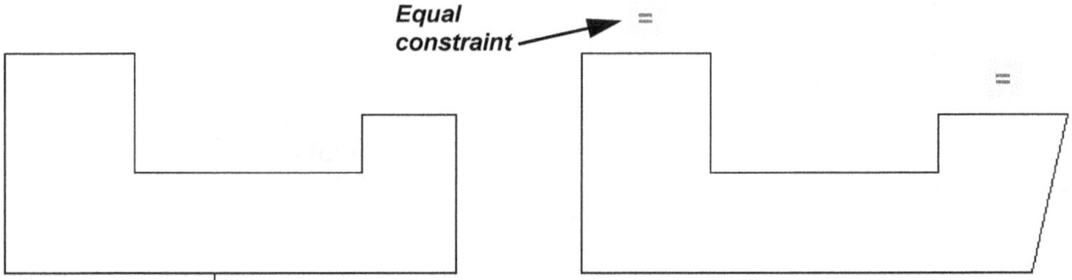

Figure 24–12

- When using Auto Constrain and the Equal constraint, it is applied to lines or polylines of the same length and circles of the same diameter.

Fix

(Fix) constrains a point on an object to remain fixed to a specific location on the World Coordinate System. You can also fix an entire object, rather than just a single point.

Symmetrical

(Symmetrical) constrains two points on objects or forces objects to be symmetrical about a symmetry line.

- Add other constraints first before applying the symmetrical constraint.

How To: Add a Symmetrical Constraint

1. Select the first object or press <Enter> to select a point on an object.
2. Select the second object or point.
3. Select the symmetry line. The objects move into symmetry about the symmetry line, as shown in Figure 24–13.

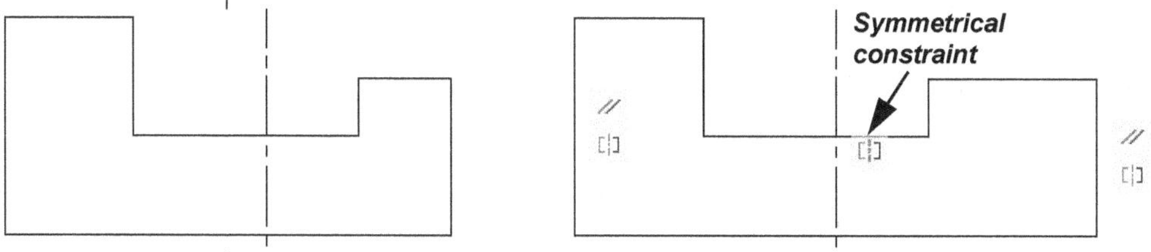

Figure 24–13

Constraint Bars

Constraint bars are icons that display when geometric constraints are applied to objects. If more than one constraint is applied to an object, the icons touch, forming a bar. When you hover the cursor over a constraint in the constraint bar, the related objects highlight in the drawing.

Toggling off the display of a constraint bar or an icon does not delete or remove the constraint. It only hides the icon.

- To toggle off individual constraint bars, click the close (X) icon, which displays when you hover the cursor over the bar, as shown in Figure 24–14.

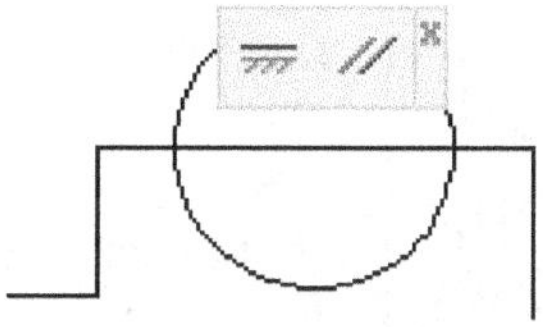

Figure 24–14

In the AutoCAD LT software, in the Geometric panel, click (Show All) to display all of the constraints in the drawing.

- To display the constraints of selected objects, click (Show/Hide Geometric Constraints) in the Geometric panel.
- To display all of the constraints in a drawing, click (Show All Geometric Constraints).
- To hide all of the constraints in a drawing, click (Hide All Geometric Constraints).

Modifying Geometrical Constraints

Objects that are constrained can still be modified using grips. When you select the grip, you can still stretch, move, rotate, and scale the objects as long as the constraints are satisfied, as shown on the left in Figure 24–15. Press <Shift> to cycle between maintaining and relaxing constraints. Relaxing constraints (as shown on the right in Figure 24–15), removes those constraints.

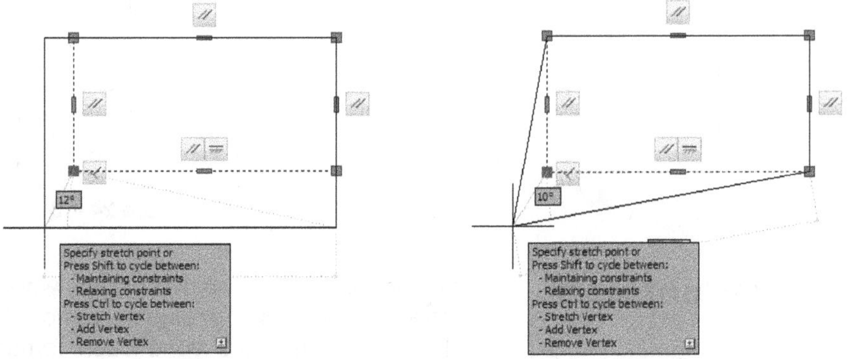

Constraints applied ***Constraints released***

Figure 24–15

- If you modify the location of the grip when the constraints are released, any unfulfilled constraints are automatically deleted.
- You can relax (remove) a constraint by pressing <Shift> while modifying an object.

Deleting Constraints

To delete a constraint, select the constraint in the constraint bar, right-click and select **Delete**, as shown in Figure 24–16.

You can also select the constraint and press <Delete>.

In the AutoCAD LT software, you can use these methods to delete constraints as required.

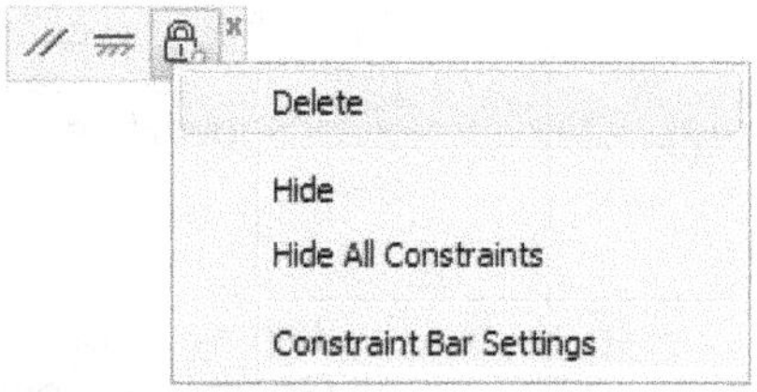

Figure 24–16

- In the *Parametric* tab>Manage panel, you can click  (Delete Constraints) and then select the object from which you want to delete all of the constraints.

Constraint Settings

Click in the Geometric panel to open the Constraint Settings dialog box in the *Geometric* tab, as shown in Figure 24–17. It contains three tabs: *Geometric*, *Dimensional*, and *AutoConstrain*. The options in these tabs enable you to control how the constraints are displayed and used in the drawing.

In the AutoCAD LT software, you can control the constraint bar display settings and transparency. However, the ***Infer geometric constraints****,* ***Show constraint bars after applying constraints to selected objects****, and* ***Show constraint bars when objects are selected*** *options are not available.*

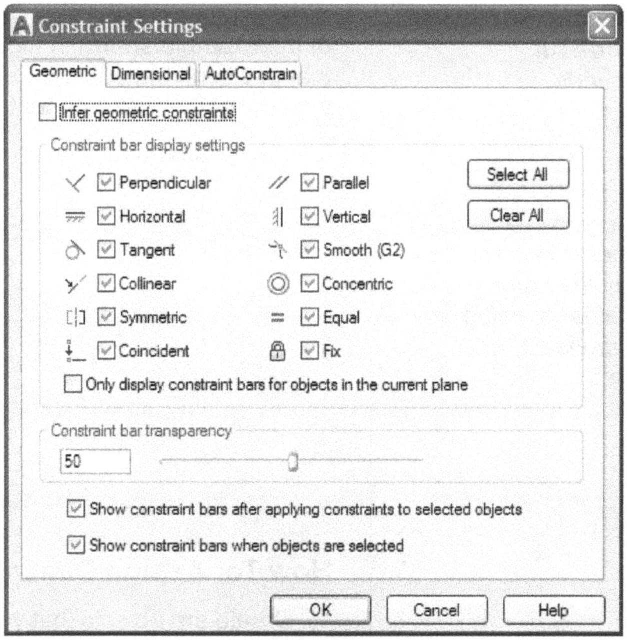

Figure 24–17

- The *Geometric* tab enables you to control the constraints that display in the constraint bar and the transparency of the bar.
- The **Show constraint bars after applying constraints to selected objects** controls whether or not constraint bars display when you have applied constraints to objects.
- The **Show constraint bars when objects are selected** controls whether or not the constraint bars display when objects are selected.
- The **Infer geometric constraints** option uses existing constraints to determine whether additional constraints are required as more objects are added to the drawing. The constraints are then automatically added as required.
- The *AutoConstrain* tab sets the priority in which constraints are applied when **Auto Constrain** is used. You can also control the Tolerance.

Use ***Infer Constraints*** *in the Customization list in the Status Bar to toggle the* ***Infer geometric constraints*** *option on or off.*

24.3 Dimensional Constraints

*In the AutoCAD LT software, in the Dimensional panel, you only have access to the **Show/Hide**, **Show All**, and **Hide All** commands.*

The AutoCAD software automatically assigns names (e.g., d1 or d2) to dimensions. You can display the name, name and value, or value of the dimension, as required.

The dimensional constraints that are created to define a feature's shape are considered parameters. They drive the object's size, distance, and angle and can be changed at any time, causing the features to update automatically.

In the example shown in Figure 24–18, the dimensional value that positions the cut feature has been changed. Therefore, the position of the feature updates to reflect the design change.

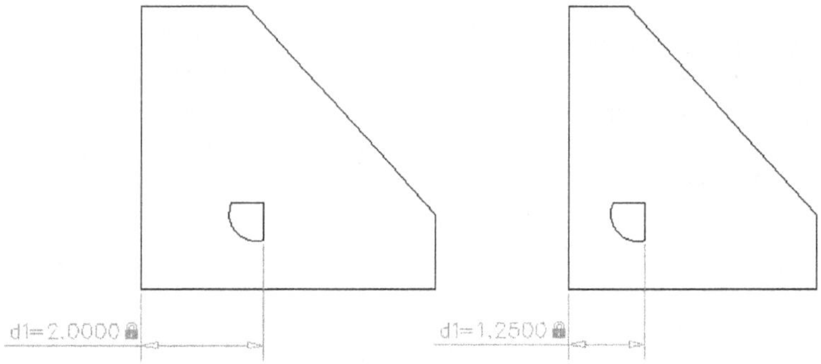

Figure 24–18

How To: Assign Dimensional Constraints

The dimensional constraints work in the same way as the standard dimension commands.

1. Create the objects that you want to constrain and apply geometrical constraints to them.
2. In the *Parametric* tab>Dimensional panel (shown in Figure 24–19), select the type of dimension that you want to place.

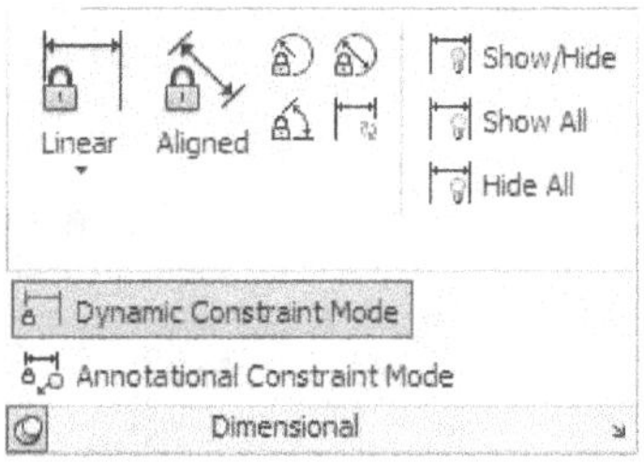

Figure 24–19

3. Specify the points that you want to dimension and then pick the dimension line location.
4. When the dimension highlights, type a number value, expression, or formula for the dimension.

Types of Dimensional Constraints

All available dimensional constraints are described as follows:

	Linear: Constrains the horizontal or vertical distance between two points. The direction depends on the placement of points and dimension line.
	Horizontal: Constrains the X distance between two points or objects (in the Linear fly-out).
	Vertical: Constrains the Y distance between two points or objects (in the Linear fly-out).
	Aligned: Constrains the distance between two points on an object or on two different objects.
	Radius: Constrains the radius of a circle or arc.
	Diameter: Constrains the diameter of a circle or arc.
	Angular: Constrains the angle between two lines or polyline segments, or between three points (vertex, first, and second angle constraint points).

In the AutoCAD LT software, in the Dimensional panel, click (Show All) to display all of the constraints in the drawing.

- For some Dimensional Constraints, you can select entire objects.
- Click (Show/Hide Dynamic Constraints) to toggle the visibility of the selected dimensional constraints on and off.

  You can also click (Show All Dynamic Constraints) or (Hide All Dynamic Constraints) to toggle all of the constraints on or off.
- Dimensional constraints are dynamic. They display at the same size when you zoom, but they do not plot.

- You can change dynamic constraints to annotation constraints in the Properties palette, as shown in Figure 24–20. Annotation constraints use the active annotation scale and dimension style.

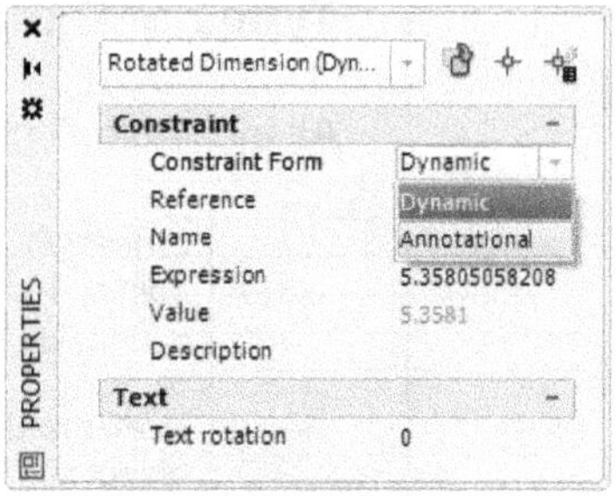

Figure 24–20

- By default, the *Name* and *Expression* display in both the dynamic and annotation constraints. This can be changed in the Constraint Settings dialog box, as shown in Figure 24–21.

  Open the dialog box by clicking the icon in the *Parametric* tab> Dimensional panel.

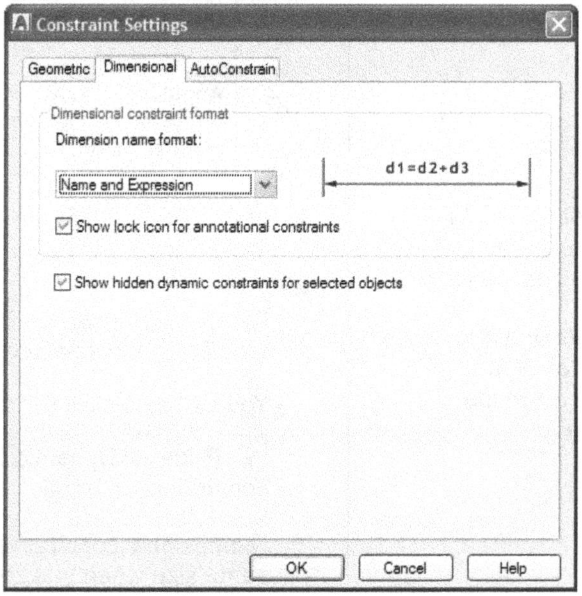

Figure 24–21

- You can turn existing dimensions into Dimensional Constraints.

How To: Convert Dimensions into Constraints

1. Draw the dimension(s) using standard dimension commands.
2. In the *Parametric* tab>Dimensional panel, click (Convert).
3. Select the dimension and press <Enter>. The dimension becomes a parameter, as shown in Figure 24–22. The parameter value can then be modified.

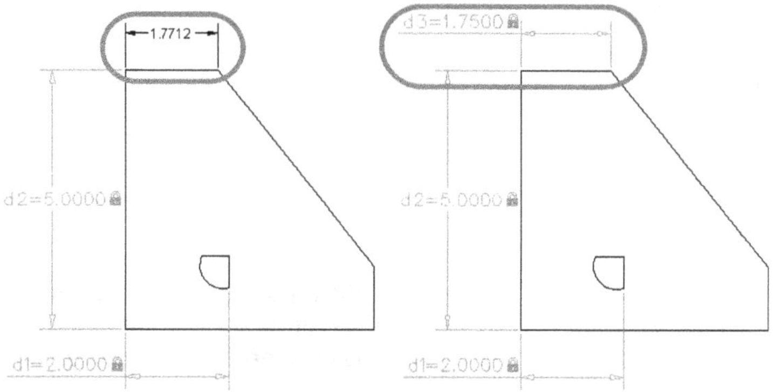

Figure 24–22

Hint: Best Practices for Dimensional Constraints

When creating dimensions, use the following guidelines:

- Consider the dimensions that are going to be displayed in drawings and note the resulting feature relationships.
- Consider changes that might be made to the model in the future and how easily the dimensions facilitate those changes.
- Periodically modify dimensions to test *what if* scenarios. This is called *flexing the model* and helps eliminate future problems by verifying that the model behaves correctly.

Modifying Dimensional Constraints

In the AutoCAD LT software, you can double-click on the text and modify the parametric dimension value.

To modify a dimensional constraint, you can double-click on the text and type the new information in the text field, as shown in Figure 24–23.

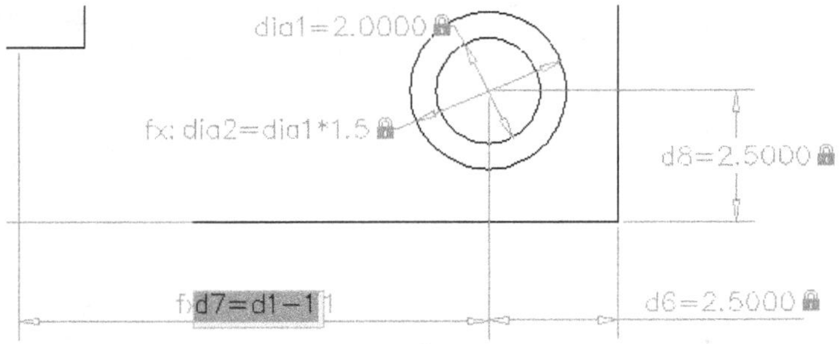

Figure 24–23

- When dimensional constraints reference one another, **fx:** is added to the beginning of the dimension to indicate that a reference already exists.

In the AutoCAD LT software, you can use the Parameters Manager to modify constraints.

You can also modify the constraints in the Parameters Manager palette, as shown in Figure 24–24. Click *fx* (Parameters Manager) in the *Parametric* tab>Manage panel.

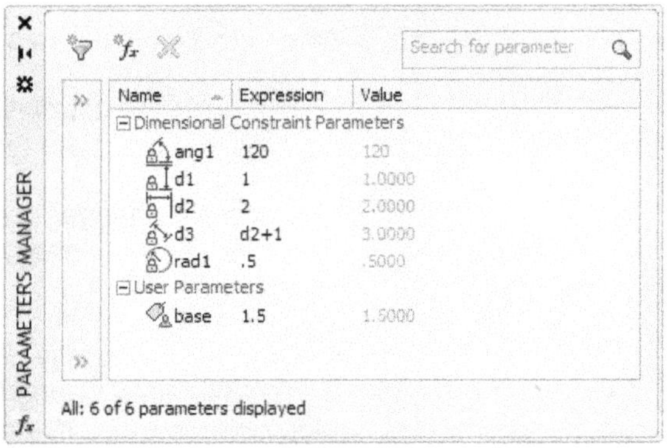

Figure 24–24

- In the Parameters Manager, modify the *Expression*. The *Value* updates automatically.
- To remove a dimensional constraint, select it in the Parameters Manager and click ✖ or press <Delete>.

- By default, all of the parameters in a drawing display. Click (Filter) and select **All Used in Expressions** to only display the parameters used in expressions, as shown in Figure 24–25.

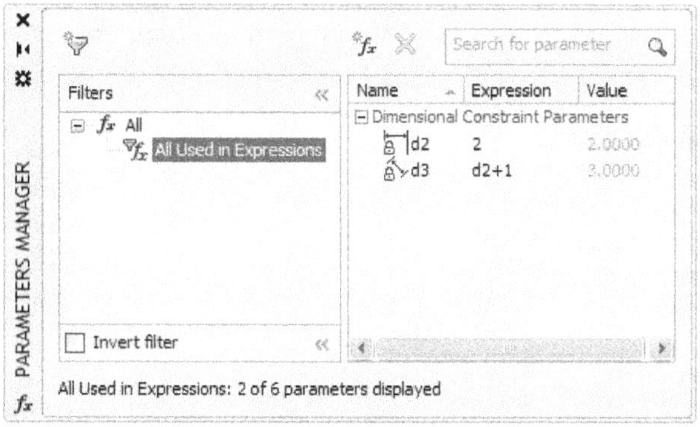

Figure 24–25

In the AutoCAD LT software, you can use the Parameters Manager to filter constraints.

- You can search for parameters by typing a value in the *Search for parameter* field in the Parameters Manager.

Formulas in Constraints

Formulas can be added to dimensional constraints when they are inserted or in the Parameters Manager.

- Formulas are user-defined mathematical relations that are used to capture and control design intent.
- An equation is created by writing a relation using dimensions or parameters from the model. For example, equations can be used to keep a hole centered on a block, as shown with the dimensions for **d3** and **d4** in Figure 24–26.

In the AutoCAD LT software, you can add formulas to existing dimensional constraints.

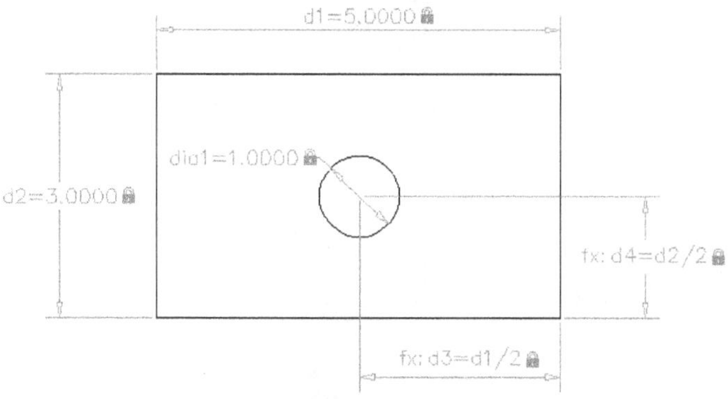

Figure 24–26

Creating User Parameters

User parameters can be added to strengthen the formulas. For example, you might have a bolt size that impacts several other parameters in the drawing, as shown in Figure 24–27. By creating a user parameter, you can easily flex the object by changing the user variable and noting how the other objects react. Changing the user value modifies the object.

In the AutoCAD LT software, (Create User Parameter) is not available. You can only modify existing constraints.

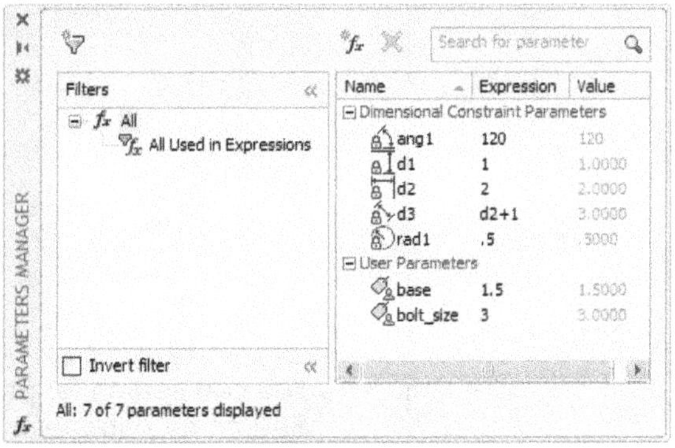

Figure 24–27

How To: Create a User Parameter

1. In the Parameters Manager, click (Create User Parameter). A new parameter displays in the *User Parameters* area.
2. Type a name and an expression.
3. Use the parameter in the expression of other parameters.

User parameter names cannot contain spaces, begin with a number, or be over 256 characters.

Practice 24a Working with Constraints

Practice Objectives

- Add Geometric constraints to the drawing.
- Add dimensional constraints to the drawing.

Estimated time for completion: 30 minutes

In this practice, you will add Geometric constraints to a drawing using the Auto Constrain command. You will then add Dimensional constraints to drive an existing model's shape and size, as shown in Figure 24–28.

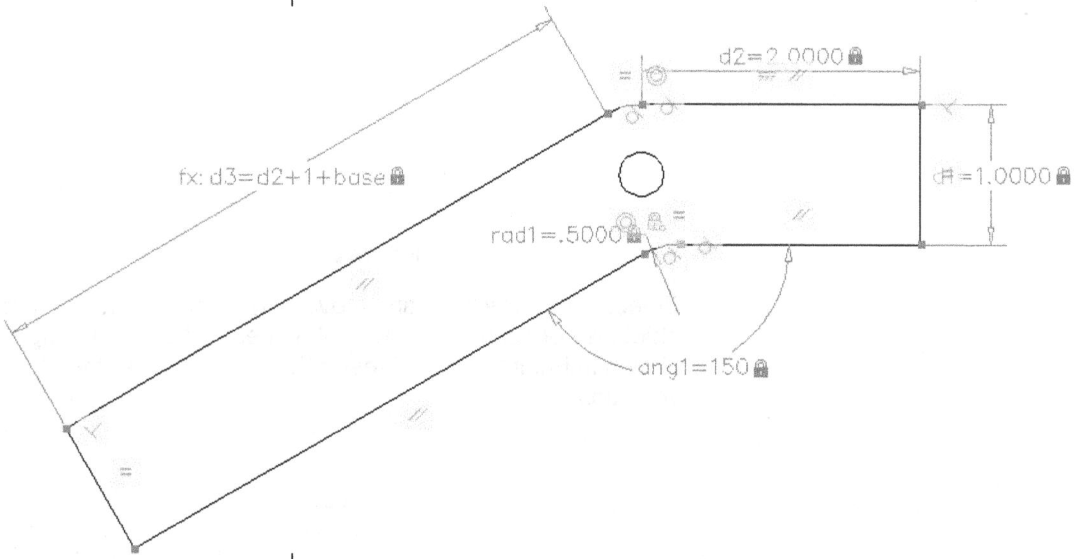

Figure 24–28

Task 1 - Add automatic geometric constraints.

1. In the AutoCAD software, open **Entry-Clamp-M.dwg** from your practice files folder.
   - *In the AutoCAD LT software, you cannot create Geometric or Dimensional constraints. Skip to Task 3.*
2. In the *Parametric* tab>Geometric panel, click (Auto Constrain).

*If the constraints were not applied correctly, open the Constraint Settings dialog box and check the settings in the **AutoConstrain** tab.*

3. Select all of the objects in the drawing (use crossing or window selection) and press <Enter>. Many constraints are applied, as shown in Figure 24–29.

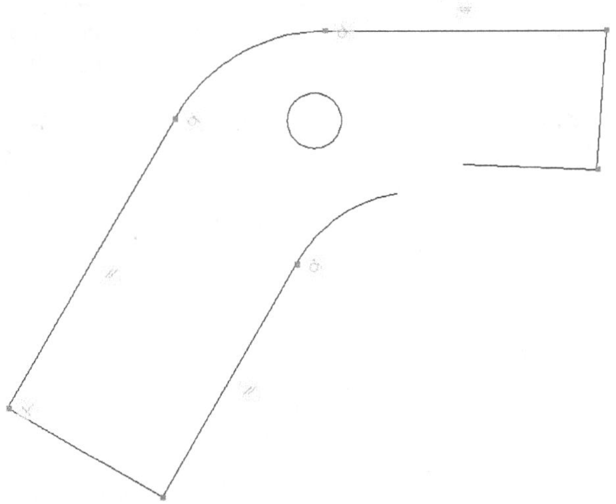

Figure 24–29

4. Select one of the lines and move it by its grip. Note that the object is not constrained enough to keep it from distorting, as shown in Figure 24–30. Press <Esc> twice to exit the selection.

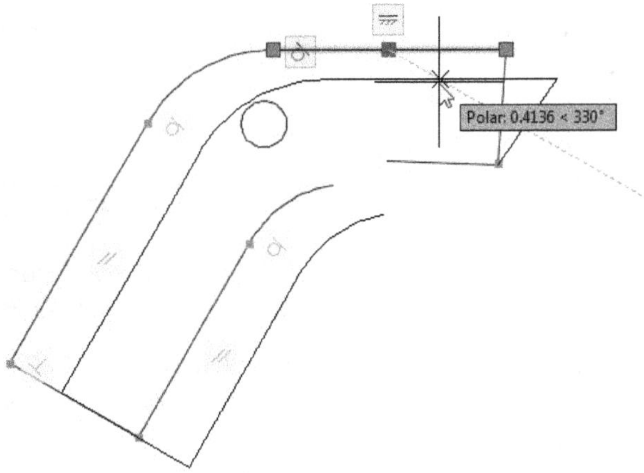

Figure 24–30

5. In the Geometric panel, click (Coincident).

6. Select the right end point of the bottom arc and then the left end point of the closest line, as shown in Figure 24–31. The arc and the line is joined.

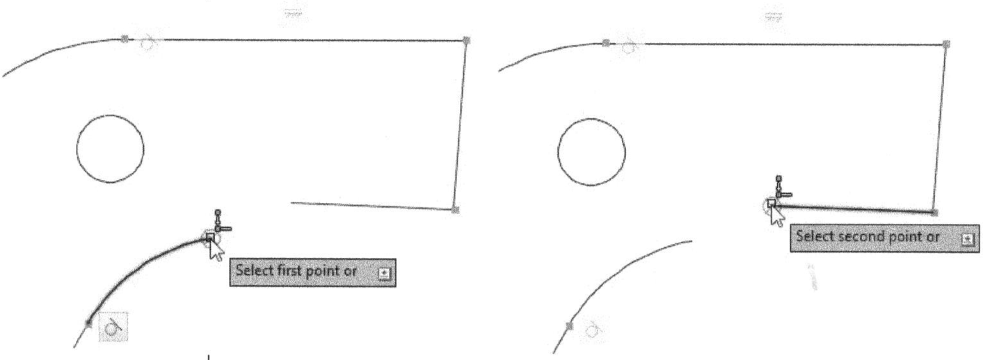

Figure 24–31

7. Add a Tangent constraint to the arc and coincident line. In the Geometric panel, click (Tangent) and select the arc and its corresponding line (the line to which you joined it).
8. To make the same line parallel to the line above, click (Parallel) and select the top line and the bottom line.
9. Click (Perpendicular) to make the right line touching the two horizontal parallel lines perpendicular. Select the top line and then the right line. The object should now be similar to the one shown in Figure 24–32.

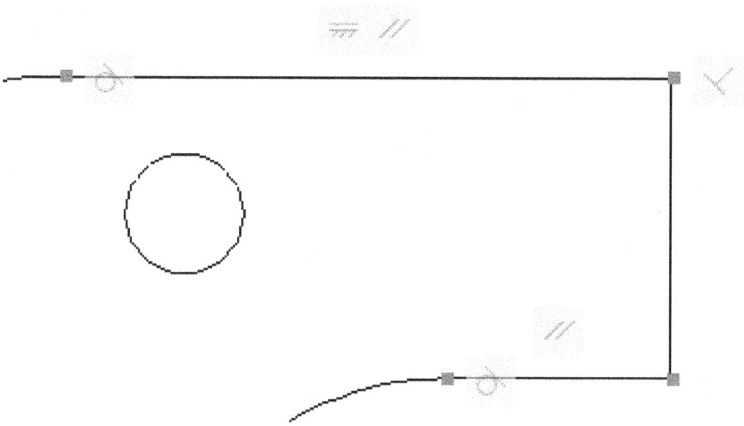

Figure 24–32

10. In the Geometric panel, click (Equal). Select the vertical line on the right and then the angled line on the bottom left, as shown in Figure 24–33.

11. Modify one of the lines using grips. The vertical lines automatically adjusts to stay equal in length.

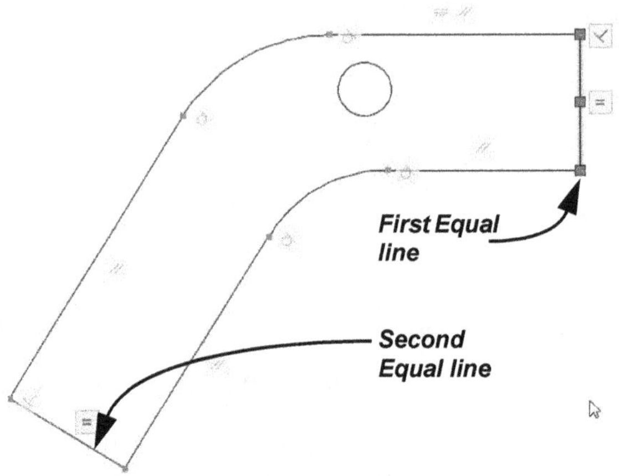

Figure 24–33

12. Make the two arcs (Equal). Select the bottom arc and then the top arc.

13. Use (Concentric) to have the circle and top arc share the same center point. Select the top arc and then the circle.

14. The circle might be outside the figure. Move the bottom left parallel line to resize the object slightly such that the circle is inside the lines, as shown in Figure 24–34. Press <Esc>.

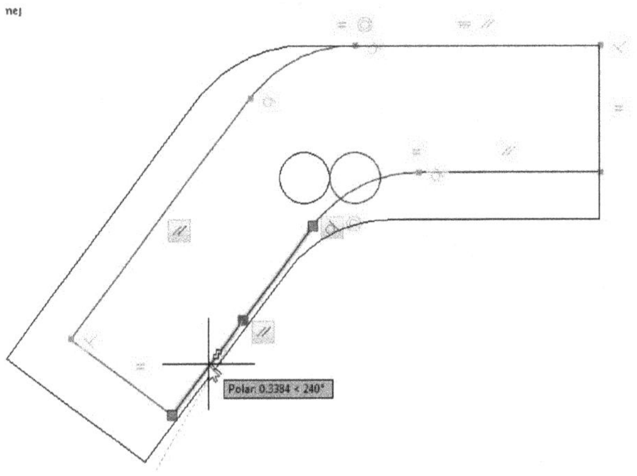

Figure 24–34

15. In the Geometric panel, click (Fix). Select the circle to make this a fixed point.
16. Flex the object by moving one of the lines. Note that it is still not fully constrained and needs to be finished with Dimensional constraints. Undo the flex action.
17. Click (Hide All) to hide the Geometric constraints.

Task 2 - Add dimensional constraints.

If the Annotation Scale dialog box opens, click ***OK****.*

1. In the *Parametric* tab>Dimensional panel, click (Linear).
2. Press <Enter> to change to the **Object** option.
3. Select the vertical line on the right and then click to the right of it to place the dimensional constraint value field.
4. Type **1** in the *Dimensional constraint* field and press <Enter>, as shown in Figure 24–35.

Both the vertical line on the right and the angled line on the bottom left automatically adjust their lengths because they are equal.

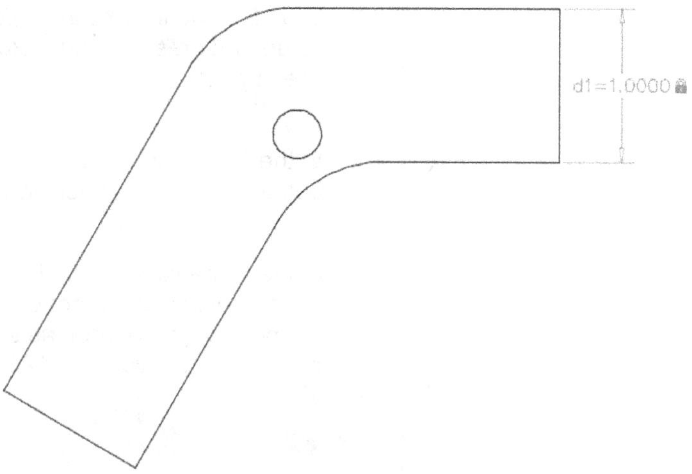

Figure 24–35

5. Use (Linear) with the **Object** option to select the top horizontal line. Set the value of the dimension text to **1**.

6. Use (Aligned) with the **Object** option to select the top left angled line. Set the value of the dimension text to **d2+1**, as shown in Figure 24–36.

If the name of the top horizontal line Dimensional constraint is something other than ***d2****, type its current name in the formula expression of the Dimensional constraint value field for the angled line in the top left.*

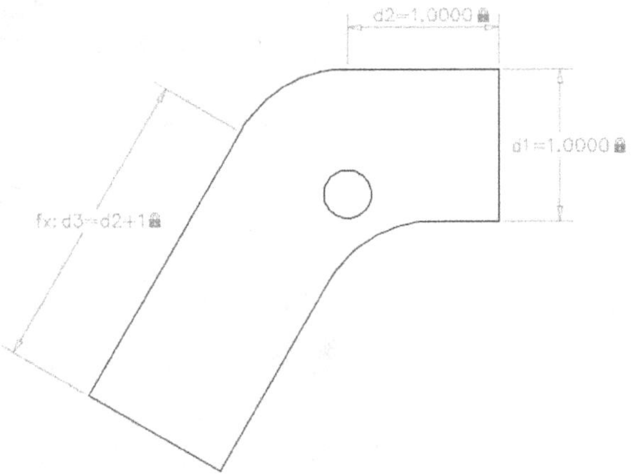

Figure 24–36

7. Double-click on the linear Dimensional constraint **d2**.

8. Type **2** in the linear *Dimensional constraint* field to change its value and press <Enter>. Both the d2 line and the d3 aligned lines update.

9. In the Dimensional panel, click (Radius) and set the bottom arc to the dimension text value of **0.5**.

10. In the Dimensional panel, click (Angular). Select the horizontal line at the bottom right and then the angular line at the bottom (left of arc), as shown in Figure 24–37. Set the dimension text value to **120**.

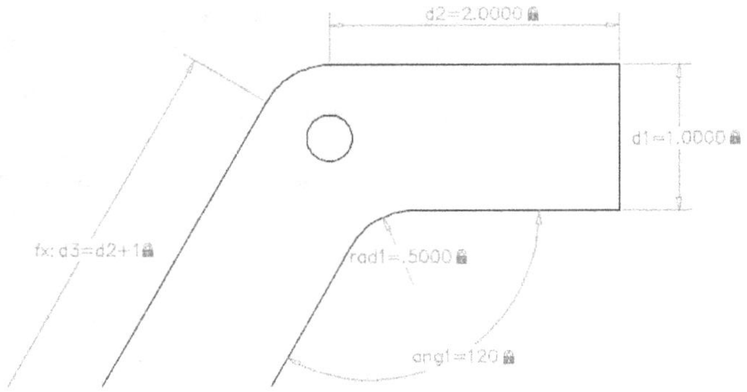

Figure 24–37

Task 3 - Modify values in the Parameters Manager.

1. In the *Parametric* tab>Manage panel, click (Parameters Manager), if it is not already open.

2. In the Parameters Manager, under the *Expression* column for *ang1*, change the value to **100** and press <Enter>. The model updates accordingly. Change the same parameter to **150** and press <Enter> to update the model.

3. At the top of the Parameters Manager, click (Create User Parameter) to create a new user parameter.

   - *In the AutoCAD LT software, you cannot create new user parameters. Skip to Step 6.*

4. Change the name of the new user-defined parameter to **base**, and change its *Expression* to **1.5**.

5. In the Parameters Manager, change the *Expression* for **d3** to **d2+1+base**, as shown in Figure 24–38, and press <Enter>. Note how the model updates.

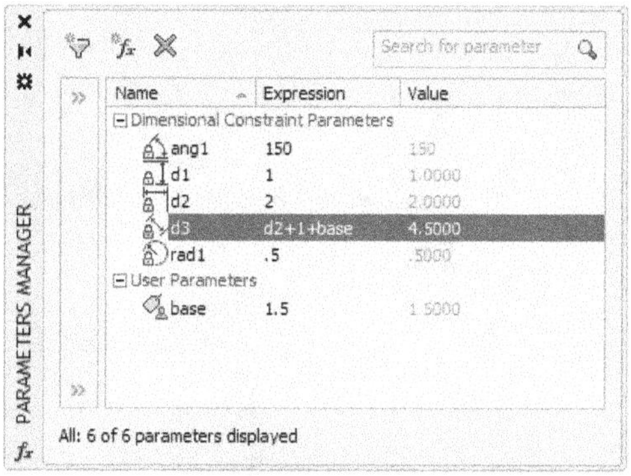

Figure 24–38

6. Flex the model several times using different values in the Parameters Manager.

7. Minimize or toggle off the Parameters Manager.

Task 4 - Modify constraint settings.

1. In the Geometric panel, click (Show All) to display the geometric constraints.

2. In the Dimensional panel, click to open the Constraint Settings dialog box.

3. Select the *Geometric* tab. In the *Constraint bar display settings* area, clear the **Tangent** option, as shown in Figure 24–39.

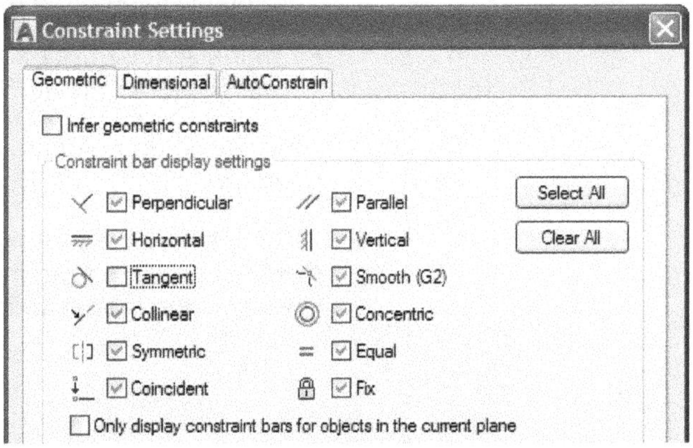

Figure 24–39

4. Select the *Dimensional* tab and change the *Dimension name format* to **Value**, as shown in Figure 24–40.

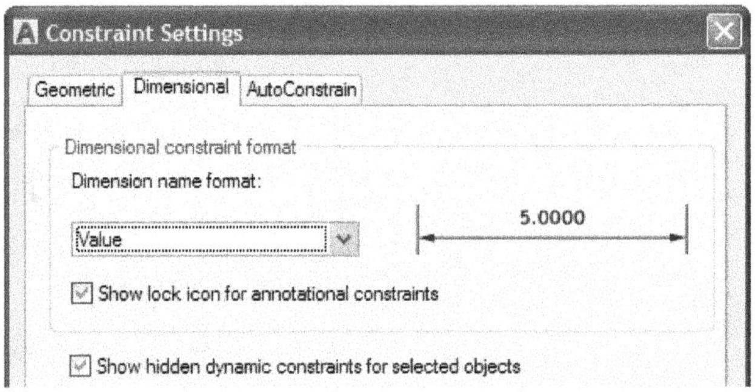

Figure 24–40

5. Click **OK**.

6. The dimensional constraints now only display the value and the tangent constraint glyphs are no longer displayed, as shown in Figure 24–41.

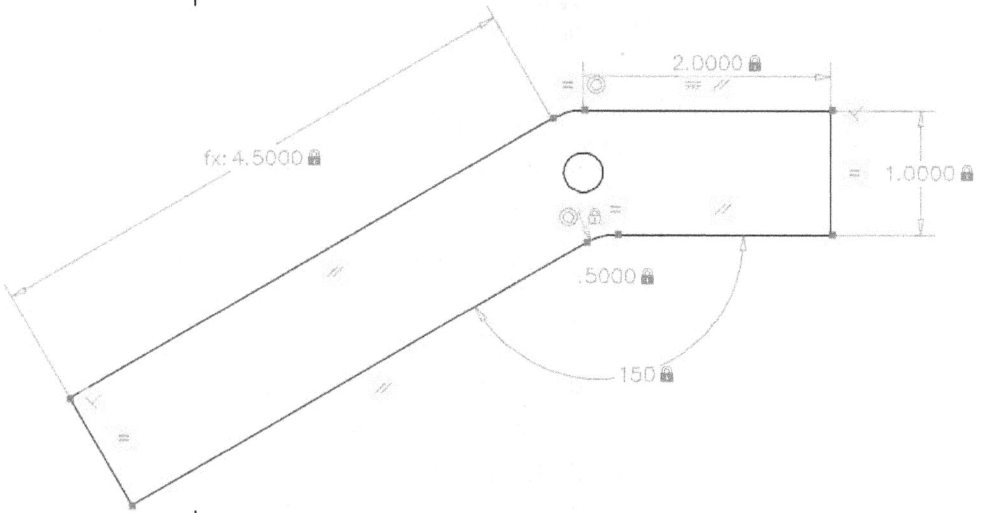

Figure 24–41

7. Save the drawing.

Chapter Review Questions

1. Which Geometric constraint forces two linear objects to take on the angle of the first object?
   a. Symmetrical
   b. Parallel
   c. Vertical
   d. Perpendicular
2. Which of the following can be displayed for Dimensional constraints?
   a. Symmetrical
   b. Tangent
   c. Name and Value
   d. Equal
3. You can convert existing dimensions into Dimensional Constraints.
   a. True
   b. False
4. How can you add Formulas in Dimensional Constraints?
   a. You cannot add Formulas in Dimensional Constraints.
   b. When the Dimensional Constraints are inserted.
   c. Use the Tool Palettes.
   d. Use the Layer Properties Manager.
5. The **Auto Constrain** command is best used with the ______object type.
   a. Ellipse
   b. Circle
   c. Rectangle
   d. Arc

6. If you create user parameters, how do they affect the constrained object?
    a. They delete all of the formulas.
    b. They control Geometric constraints.
    c. Changing the user value modifies the object.
    d. They remove Dimensional constraints.

Command Summary

Button	Command	Location
Constraint Management		
	Delete Constraints	• **Ribbon:** *Parametric* tab>Manage panel
	Parameters Manager	• **Ribbon:** *Parametric* tab>Manage panel
Dimensional Constraints		
	Aligned	• **Ribbon:** *Parametric* tab>Dimensional panel
	Angle	• **Ribbon:** *Parametric* tab>Dimensional panel
	Convert	• **Ribbon:** *Parametric* tab>Dimensional panel
	Diameter	• **Ribbon:** *Parametric* tab>Dimensional panel
	Hide All Dynamic Constraints	• **Ribbon:** *Parametric* tab>Dimensional panel
	Horizontal	• **Ribbon:** *Parametric* tab>Dimensional panel
	Linear	• **Ribbon:** *Parametric* tab>Dimensional panel
	Radius	• **Ribbon:** *Parametric* tab>Dimensional panel
	Show All Dynamic Constraints	• **Ribbon:** *Parametric* tab>Dimensional panel
	Show/Hide Dynamic Constraints	• **Ribbon:** *Parametric* tab>Dimensional panel
	Vertical	• **Ribbon:** *Parametric* tab>Dimensional panel
Geometric Constraints		
	Auto-Constrain	• **Ribbon:** *Parametric* tab>Geometric panel
	Coincident	• **Ribbon:** *Parametric* tab>Geometric panel
	Colinear	• **Ribbon:** *Parametric* tab>Geometric panel
	Concentric	• **Ribbon:** *Parametric* tab>Geometric panel
	Equal	• **Ribbon:** *Parametric* tab>Geometric panel

	**Fix**	• **Ribbon:** *Parametric* tab>Geometric panel
	**Hide All Geometric Constraints**	• **Ribbon:** *Parametric* tab>Geometric panel
	**Horizontal**	• **Ribbon:** *Parametric* tab>Geometric panel
	**Parallel**	• **Ribbon:** *Parametric* tab>Geometric panel
	**Perpendicular**	• **Ribbon:** *Parametric* tab>Geometric panel
	**Show All Geometric Constraints**	• **Ribbon:** *Parametric* tab>Geometric panel
	**Show/Hide Geometric Constraints**	• **Ribbon:** *Parametric* tab>Geometric panel
	**Smooth**	• **Ribbon:** *Parametric* tab>Geometric panel
	**Symmetrical**	• **Ribbon:** *Parametric* tab>Geometric panel
	**Tangent**	• **Ribbon:** *Parametric* tab>Geometric panel
	**Vertical**	• **Ribbon:** *Parametric* tab>Geometric panel

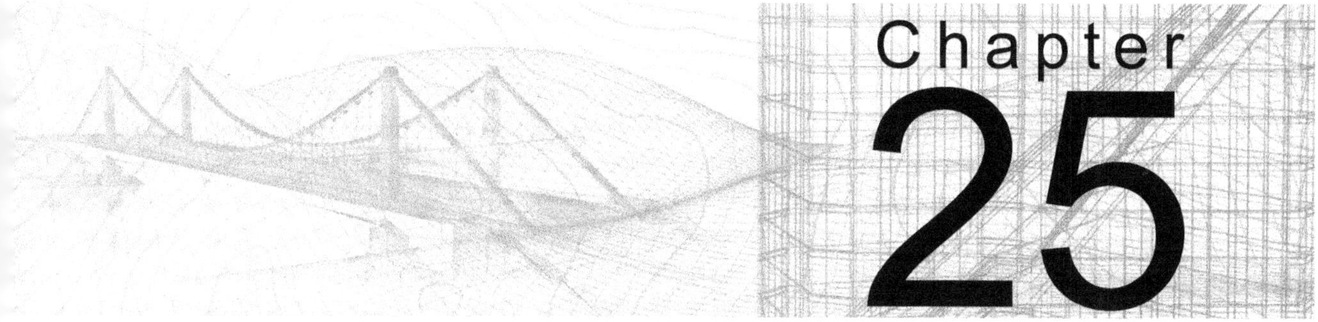

Working with Blocks

In this chapter you learn how to create local blocks, edit blocks, and remove unused elements by purging. You also learn how to add blocks to tool palettes and to modify tool properties in palettes.

Learning Objectives in this Chapter

- Create different types of blocks that can be used in the same drawing or inserted into other drawings.
- Modify block objects and customize block settings to remove elements from a drawing.
- Create a palette and add blocks to it.
- Modify the properties of a tool.

25.1 Creating Blocks

The objects that are reused frequently can be saved as a blocks. The blocks you need to use might already exist in your drawings, or you can buy block libraries for almost any type of drawing. You can also easily create your own blocks. A block can be locally defined in a drawing or saved as a file for use in other drawings.

Creating Single Named Objects

The **Create Block** command converts a group of selected objects into a single named object or *local block definition* that only belongs to the current drawing.

How To: Create a Block

1. Draw the objects that you want to include in a block.
2. In the *Insert* tab>Block Definition panel or *Home* tab>Block panel, click (Create Block).
3. In the Block Definition dialog box (as shown in Figure 25–1), specify the *Name*, *Base point*, *Objects*, *Behavior*, *Settings*, and *Description*.

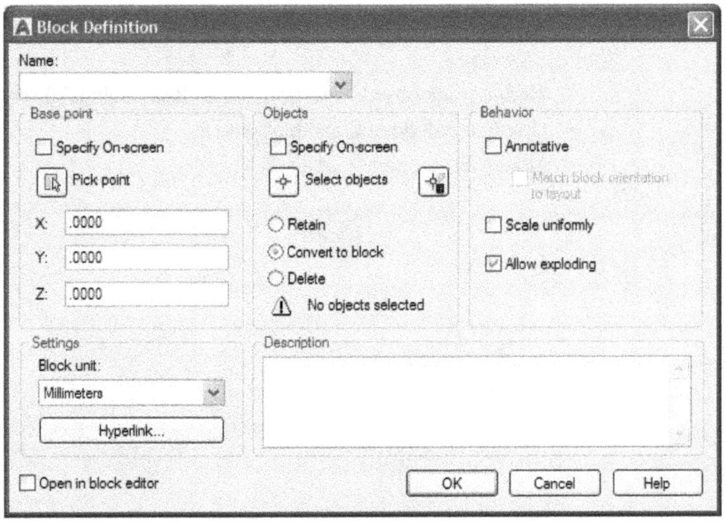

Figure 25–1

4. Click **OK**.

Block Settings

When you create a block, you need to specify various parameters in the Block Definition dialog box, as shown in Figure 25–2.

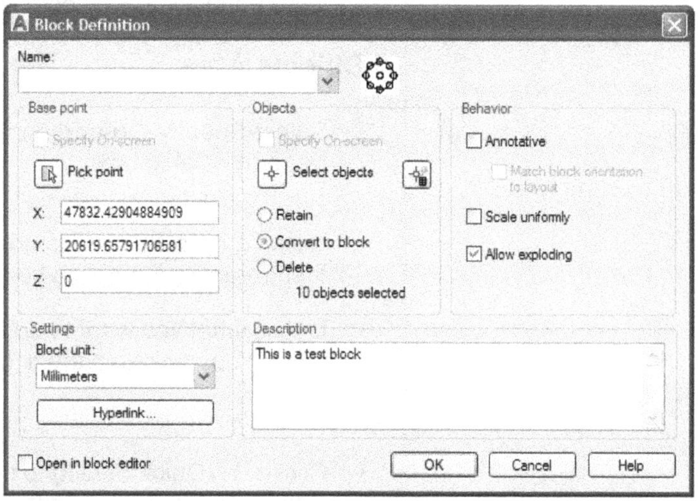

Figure 25–2

Base Point Area

The *Base point* is a critical setting, which controls the handle of the block when it is inserted. In the example shown in Figure 25–3, the block for a door has its base point at the hinge corner, where it attaches to the end of the wall and the block for the manhole cover has its base point at the center of the cover.

A good base point makes a block much easier to insert.

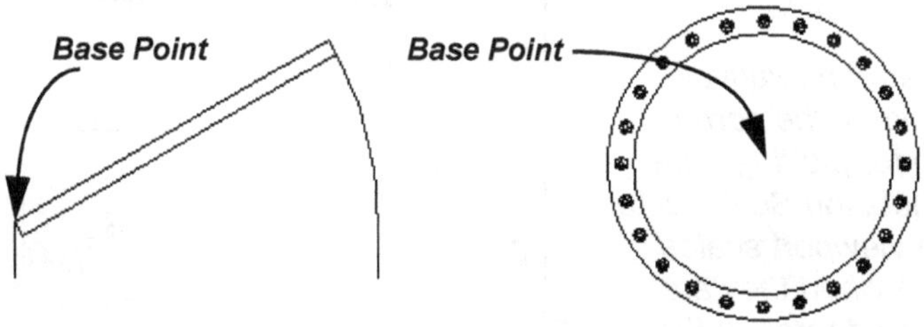

Figure 25–3

In the *Base point* area, you can specify the base point by doing one of the following:

- Select **Specify On-screen** to select the base point after you close the dialog box.

- Click (Pick point) to select a point on the screen and then return to the dialog box.
- Type an exact X,Y,Z coordinate.

Objects Area

- Select **Specify On-screen** to select the objects after you close the dialog box.
- Click (Select objects) to select objects on the screen and then return to the dialog box.
- Define what you want to do with the objects after you select them. You can retain them, convert them to a block, or delete them.
- Click (Quick Select) to start the **Quick Select** command, which can be used to filter out objects in your selection as required.

Behavior Area

- Blocks can be annotative, which means they scale appropriately to the sheet of paper when they are plotted. This is used when you are creating annotation blocks, which often include text (such as a section callout bubble or room tags), as shown in Figure 25–4. Use **Annotative** to make the new block annotative.

Create annotative blocks at the correct size for plotting. The Annotation Scale factor of a viewport scales them when they are inserted through the viewport.

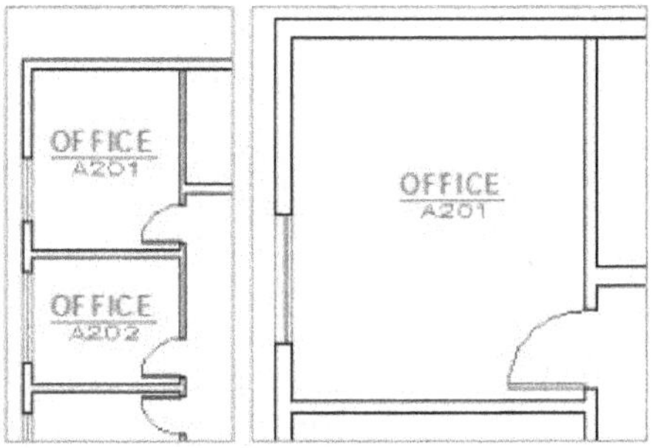

Figure 25–4

- When you insert an annotative block, an annotative icon displays in the preview in the Insert dialog box, as shown in Figure 25–5.

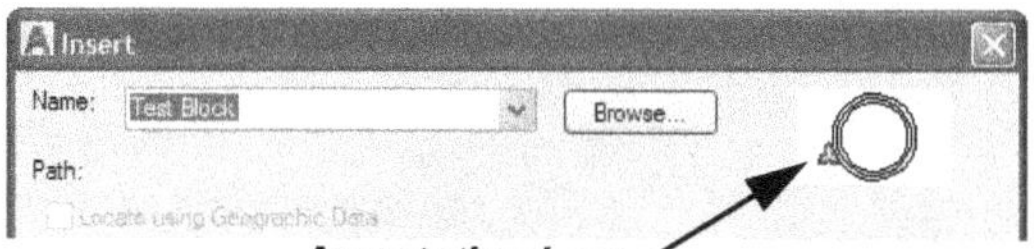

Figure 25–5

- You can also use **Scale uniformly** to force the X- and Y-scaling of the block to be the same when the block is inserted into the drawing.
- Use **Allow exploding** to explode the block into its components when it is inserted into the drawing.

Settings Area

- Select a type of measurement in the Block unit drop-down list. This controls the scaling of the block when it is inserted into another drawing that uses a different type of unit. For example, if the unit in the block and the units in the drawing are different, the block is automatically scaled when it is inserted.
- Click **Hyperlink...** to add a link to another file or to a web address.
- Select **Open in block editor** to add dynamic features to the block.
- In the *Description* area, you can type a description of the block or any notes as required.

Creating Drawing Files from Objects (WBlock)

Blocks created with the **Create (Block)** command are stored in the drawing file in which they were created and are only available through that drawing. If you want to select objects and save them as a separate drawing file that can be used in other drawings, use the **Write Block (Wblock)** command.

- The **Write Block** command saves a copy of a block definition on your computer as a drawing file. Each use of **Write Block** creates a separate drawing file (.DWG).

- As with any .DWG file, the drawing files created with the **Write Block** command can be inserted into other drawings. Drawings to be used as blocks are often stored in a *block library*, which is a shared network folder containing drawings that are available to everyone in an office.

- You can use **Write Block** to break a large drawing into smaller components.

- To insert a file made with **Write Block** into another drawing, use **Browse...** in the Insert dialog box and select a file to insert.

- Once you have inserted the file, it creates a local block definition in the drawing. The local block definition is not linked to the DWG file that was made with **Write Block**.

How To: Create a Wblock

1. In the *Insert* tab>Block Definition panel, expand Create Block and click  (Write Block). The Write Block dialog box opens, as shown in Figure 25–6.

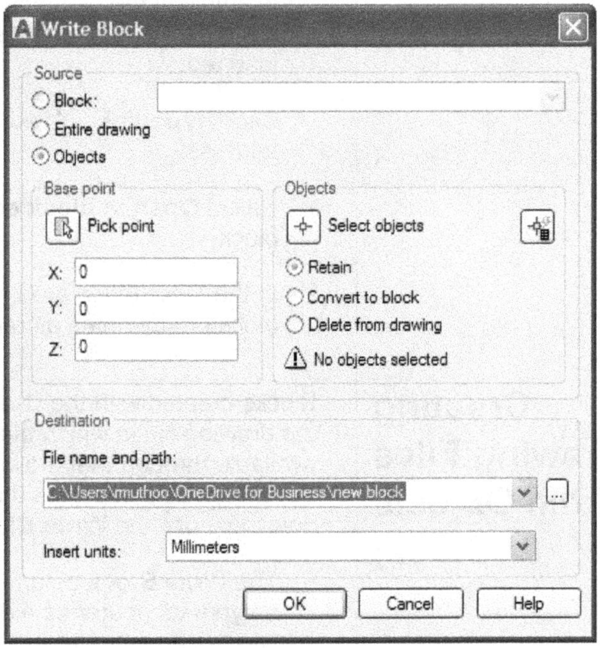

Figure 25–6

2. Select an option in the *Source* area:
   - **Block:** Select a block name from the drop-down list to create a Wblock from an existing block in the drawing.
   - **Entire Drawing:** Selects all of the objects in the drawing including any named objects (such as layers and dimension styles that are associated with the objects), and the current layer. Any unused named objects (such as empty layers) are not included. This is a quick way to clean up a file before it is stored.
   - **Objects:** Select the objects using the options in the *Base point* and *Objects* areas.
3. In the *Destination* area, specify the destination filename and path.
4. Also, specify the *Insert units* if they are to be different than the default units.
5. Click **OK**.

25.2 Editing Blocks

You might have a library of standard details, but need to change one of them for your current project. You can change a local block definition in a drawing using the **Block Editor**, as shown in Figure 25–7.

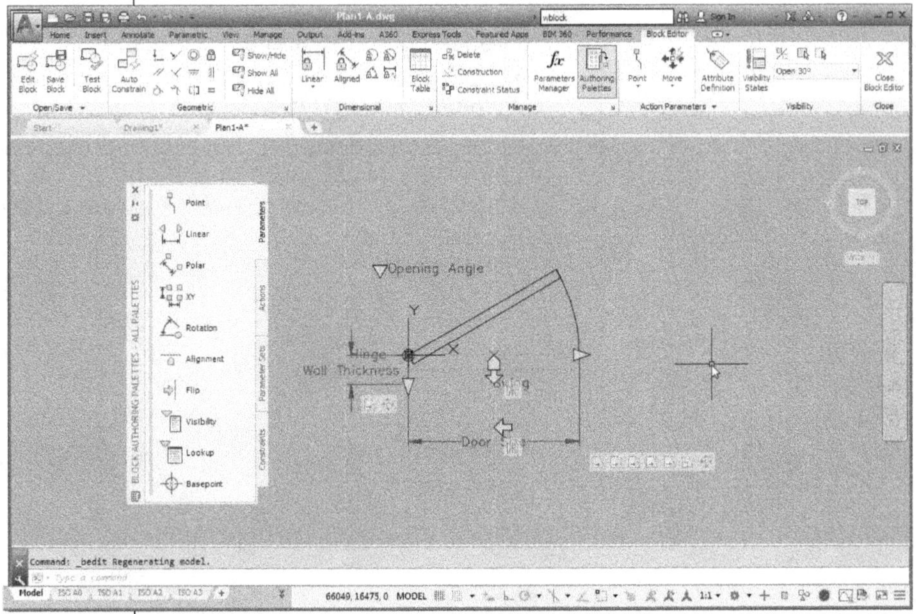

Figure 25–7

- When you open the Block Editor, the *Block Editor* contextual tab opens containing the tools that are required to create complex dynamic blocks, including constraints and special parameters. You can use the tools on any of the other tabs as well to create or modify block objects.
- Changing the block definition modifies all of the instances of the block in the drawing.
- The fastest way to start the Block Editor is to double-click on the block that you want to edit.

How To: Edit a Block in the Block Editor

1. Double-click on the block that you want to edit. Alternatively, in the *Insert* tab>Block Definition panel, click (Block Editor).
2. In the Edit Block Definition dialog box (as shown in Figure 25–8), select the block that you want to edit and click **OK**.

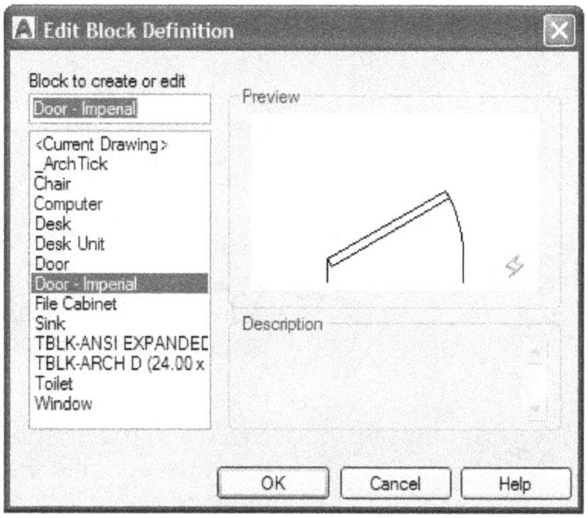

Figure 25–8

3. The *Block Editor* contextual tab opens, the drawing window background changes to gray, the Block Authoring Palette displays, and many of the constraint tools display with the selected block.
4. Modify the block.
5. When you are finished, click (Close Block Editor).

- The selected block displays in the Block Editor in its original position, even if you selected an instance that was rotated.

Remaking Blocks

- To modify a single instance of a block (rather than the block definition), you can **Explode** the block into its original raw components, provided that the **Allow Exploding** option was toggled on when the block was created. This command also converts polylines into lines and arcs.
- If the block objects were originally created on layer **0**, they revert to this layer when the block is exploded.
- If you have exploded a block and modified its components, you can use the **Create (Block)** command to make the components into a block again.
- If other instances of the block are in the drawing, select the insertion point that was used for the previous block.
- If you use the same name as the original block when you redefine it, all of the instances of that block in the drawing update to match the new block definition.
- If you make changes to a drawing file that you inserted as a block, you need to click **Browse...** in the **Insert** command to insert the updated drawing file. You are then prompted to redefine the existing local block definition.

Practice 25a Create and Edit Blocks

Practice Objectives

- Define a block.
- Create a new drawing file from a local block.
- Create a new file and then redefine the block.

Estimated time for completion: 20 minutes

In this practice, you will define a block for a couch, first drawing the objects and then using the **Create Block** command. You will then use **Write Block** to create a new drawing file from your local block. You will also use **Write Block** to select part of a drawing and create a new file, and then use **Block Editor** to redefine a block.

Task 1 - Creating a local block.

In this task you will define a block for a couch, first drawing the objects and then using the **Create Block** command, as shown in Figure 25–9.

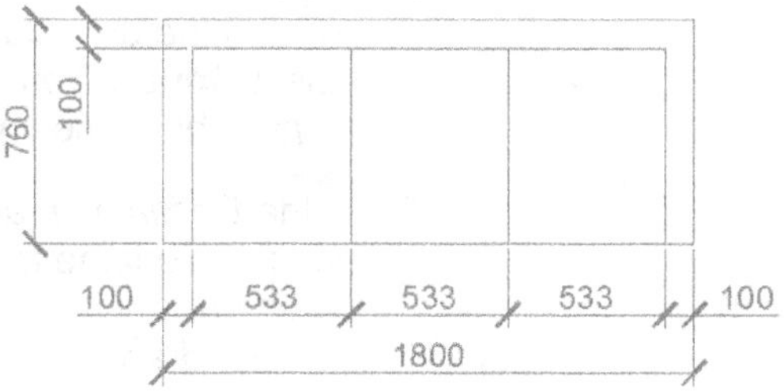

Figure 25–9

1. Open **California House-AM.dwg** from your practice files folder.

For quick access, you can display the Layer Control in the Quick Access Toolbar.

2. Set the current layer to **Furniture**. (Hint: You will draw the block on this layer so that it retains the properties of the layer **Furniture** no matter what layer you insert it on.)
3. Zoom in on one of the rooms and draw a couch, as shown in Figure 25–9.
4. In the *Insert* tab>Block Definition panel, click (Create Block). In the Block Definition dialog box, name the block **Couch**.
5. In the *Base point* area, click (Pick point) and select the midpoint at the back of the couch as the base point.

6. In the *Objects* area, click (Select objects), select the couch objects, and press <Enter>. Select the **Delete** option.
7. Verify that the *Block unit* is set to **Millimeters**.
8. Verify that **Open in block editor** is NOT selected.
9. Click **OK**. The couch is deleted from the active drawing.
10. Set the current layer to **0**.
11. Use the **Insert (Block)** command to insert a couch in several rooms (note that it is still the color of the layer **Furniture**).
12. Save the drawing with a few couches inserted.

Task 2 - Creating a drawing file from a block.

1. In the *Insert* tab>Block Definition panel, expand Create Block and click (Write Block).
2. In the Write Block dialog box, for the *Source*, select **Block**, expand the drop-down list of local blocks in the drawing, and select **Couch**. You do not need to select the *Base point* or *Objects* because you are using an existing block definition.
3. In the *Destination* area, set the path to your practice folder and the filename to **Couch,** as shown in Figure 25–10. The *Insert units* should be set to **Millimeters**. Click **OK** to create the new drawing file.

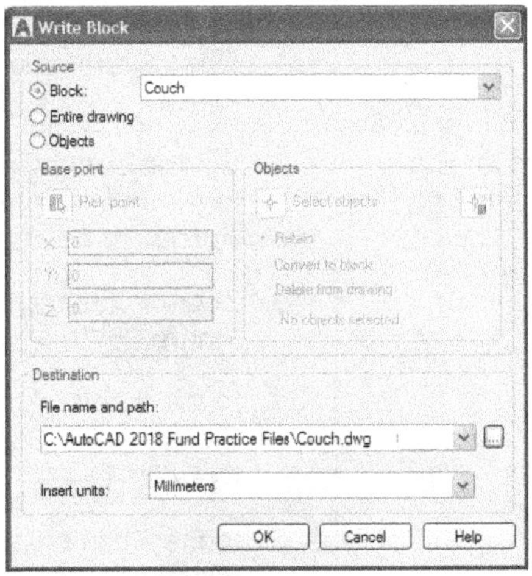

Figure 25–10

4. In the practice files folder, open the new drawing **Couch.dwg**.

5. Use the **Zoom Extents** command to display the couch. Save and close the drawing.

6. Open **Plan1-AM.dwg** from your practice files folder.

7. Start the **Insert Block** command and note the list of blocks. The **Couch** block is not in the graphics list. Click **More Options...** to open the Insert dialog box. Click **Browse...** and select the **Couch.dwg** file in your practice folder. Insert a couch into one of the rooms. It becomes a local block in the drawing **Plan1-AM.dwg**.

8. Save and close all of the drawings.

Task 3 - Create a new drawing from part of a drawing.

In this task you will toggle off most of the layers in a drawing and use **Write Block** to copy the remaining objects to a new file, as shown in Figure 25–11.

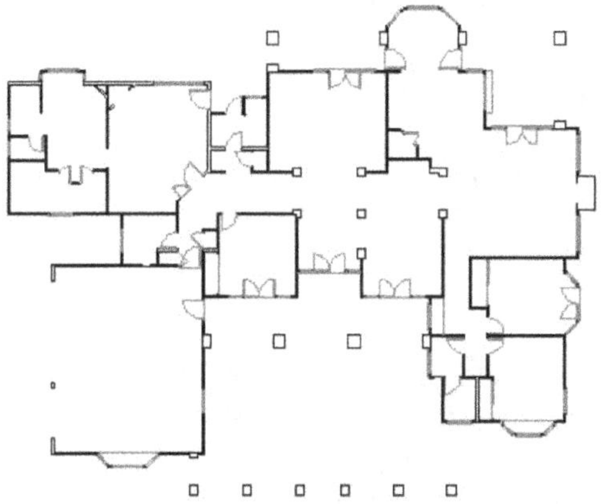

Figure 25–11

1. Open **California House-AM.dwg** from your practice files folder.

2. Use the **Zoom Extents** command to display the entire plan.

3. Freeze all of the layers except **0**, **Doors**, **Walls**, and **Windows** (many layers are already frozen).

4. Start the **Write Block** command. In the Write Block dialog box, in the *Source* area, select **Objects**.

5. In the *Objects* area, click (Select objects) and select all of the visible objects. Right-click to return to the dialog box.
6. Leave the *Base point* at **0,0,0**. Set the path to your practice folder and name the file **Floorplan-AM.dwg**.
7. Click **OK** to close the dialog box.
8. Close **California House-AM.dwg**. Do not save changes.
9. Open **Floorplan-AM.dwg**. Only the objects that you selected display along with the layers related to those objects.
10. Close the drawing. Do not save changes.

Task 4 - Edit a block.

In this task you will use the Block Editor to redefine a block with a new design, as shown in Figure 25–12.

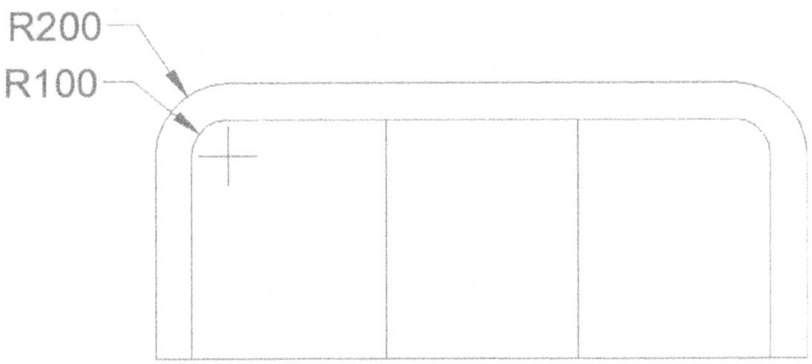

Figure 25–12

1. Open **California House-A.dwg** from your practice files folder.
2. Toggle on the layer **Furniture** if the Couch is not displayed. Double-click on one of the **Couch** blocks.
3. In the Edit Block Definition dialog box, **Couch** is highlighted with its preview displayed. Click **OK** to continue.
4. The Block Editor opens with the block filling the drawing area. Also the background changed to gray and the Block Authoring Palette displays. Close or hide the Block Authoring Palette.
5. Fillet the back corners of the couch, as shown in Figure 25–12. Zoom in as required.

6. In the *Block Editor* contextual tab, click (Close Block Editor) and save the changes.
7. All of the instances of the **Couch** block in this drawing are automatically updated to the new style. Insert another **Couch** and note that it has also changed.
8. Save and close the drawing.

25.3 Removing Unused Elements

A drawing might contain elements that were defined once but are no longer used. Common examples of this include:

- Blocks that are defined but not inserted anywhere.
- Layers that do not contain any objects.
- Named components that are no longer used.

These unused (or unreferenced) definitions use disk space and can significantly increase the size of your drawing. Use the **Purge** command to remove these items.

How To: Purge All Unreferenced Items

1. In the Application Menu, select **Drawing Utilities>Purge**. The Purge dialog box opens, as shown in Figure 25–13.

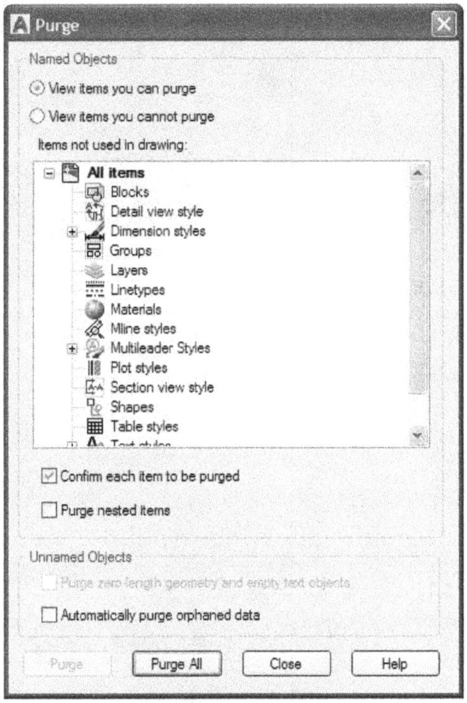

Figure 25–13

2. Click **Purge All** and click **Close** to end the command.

How To: Purge Specific Types of Items or Individual Items

1. In the Application Menu, select Drawing Utilities> **Purge**.
2. In the Purge dialog box, in the *Items not used in drawing area*, select the category of the item that you want to purge (such as *Blocks*, *Layers*, etc.). You can also expand the list for any category (by clicking **+**) and select individual items to purge.
3. Click **Purge**.
4. Click **Close** when you are finished.

- If the **Confirm each item to be purged** option is selected, you are prompted to verify each item before it is purged.
- To completely purge all of the unreferenced elements in the drawing, select the **Purge nested items** option. For example, this enables you to purge any unreferenced layers that are part of (or *nested in*) an unreferenced block definition.
- If the **View items you cannot purge** option is selected, a list of these items displays. Select an individual item for an explanation of why it cannot be purged.

Practice 25b Purging

Practice Objective

- Remove unused block definitions and empty layers.

Estimated time for completion: 5 minutes

In this practice, you will remove unused block definitions and empty layers from a drawing using the **Purge** command.

1. Open **Purge-AM.dwg** from your practice files folder.
2. Open the Layer Control and review the list of layers.

There are around 25 layers in the list.

3. Expand the **Insert Block** command and note that several blocks are defined in this drawing, but are not used. Cancel the command without inserting any blocks.
4. In the Application Menu, expand Drawing Utilities and select **Purge**.
5. In the Purge dialog box, expand the list of blocks to display the blocks that can be purged, as shown in Figure 25–14.
6. Expand the list of layers to display the layers that can be purged.
7. Click **Purge All**. In the Purge - Confirm Purge dialog box, select **Purge all items**.
8. Most of the unused items are purged, but some still remain. These items were nested in blocks, as shown in Figure 25–14.
9. Click **Purge All** again and select **Purge all items**. All of the unused items are purged, as shown in Figure 25–14.

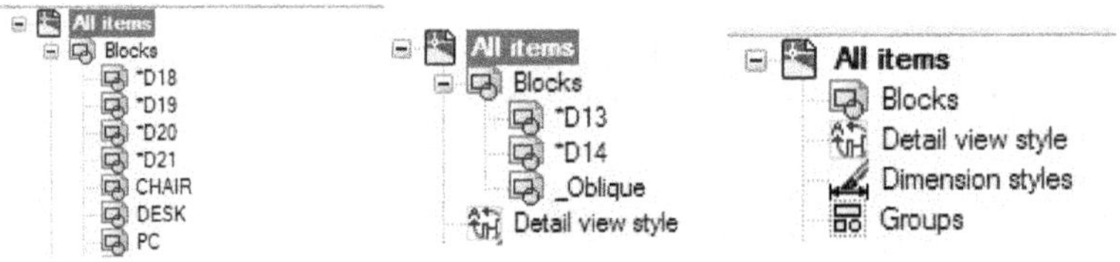

Figure 25–14

10. Close the Purge dialog box.
11. Open the Layer Control again. The unreferenced layers have been removed.
12. Start the **Insert Block** command. The unused blocks have been removed.
13. Save and close the drawing.

25.4 Adding Blocks to Tool Palettes

Tool palettes are the easiest way of inserting blocks into your drawing. You can create custom palettes in the Tool Palettes to organize your blocks into logical categories.

Once the palette has been created, drag and drop blocks into it to create tools for those blocks. Then use the palette tools to insert the blocks into the drawings in which you want to use them, whether or not the block has been defined in the drawing.

How To: Create a New Tool Palette

1. Right-click in the Tool Palettes title bar or tab and select **New Palette**.
2. In the *Edit* field, type a name for the palette (as shown in Figure 25–15), and press <Enter>. The new palette does not contain any tools.

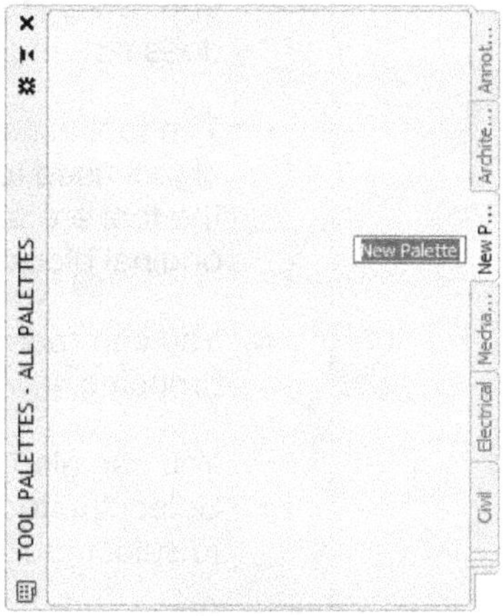

Figure 25–15

- Although you can add tools to the default palettes supplied with the AutoCAD software, creating custom palettes enables you to better organize the tools as you want.

- You can also right-click on the tab and select **Delete Palette** or **Rename Palette** to delete or rename existing palettes.

How To: Add Blocks to a Palette

The file containing the blocks must be saved before you can add a block to a palette.

1. Select a block in the drawing area.
2. Drag and drop it onto the palette, as shown in Figure 25–16.

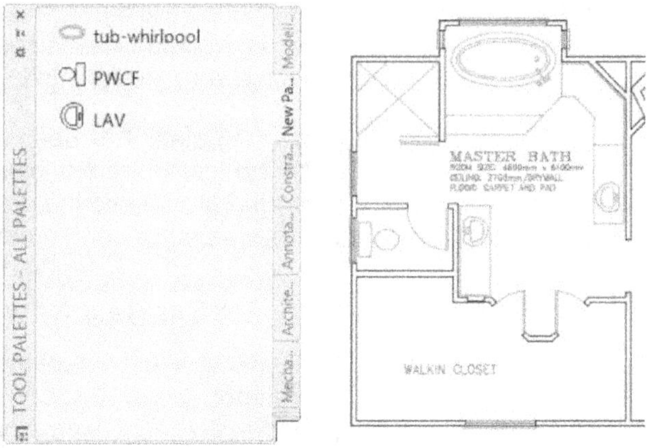

Figure 25–16

- Drag the block onto the palette by its *edge*, not by its blue grip. Dragging the grip moves the block in the drawing but does not enable you to drop it into the palette.
- The tool uses the layer, color, and other properties of the object used to create it. Therefore, blocks that you insert with the tool are automatically placed on the same layer as the original block, no matter which layer is current.
- You can rearrange the tools in the palette by dragging and dropping.
- You can also delete individual tools from the Tool Palettes. Select the tools that you want to delete (use <Shift> or <Ctrl> to select multiple icons), right-click, and select **Delete**.
- You must add blocks to the palette one at a time using this method.

Preparing Blocks for a Tool Palette

- The drawing from which you add the block to a palette becomes the source file for the block tool in the palette. If you move or delete this source drawing file, the palette tool no longer works.
- Create and store your blocks in a library drawing, or several such drawings for different categories of blocks. For example, you can define your furniture blocks in a drawing called *Furniture Library* and then add the blocks to a palette from that drawing.
- Keep your block library drawings in a location from which they cannot be moved or deleted. Make it a network location if everyone needs to access these blocks.

Hint: Creating a Tool Palette from DesignCenter

DesignCenter offers a quick way of creating a tool palette using the entire set of blocks in a drawing. Right-click on the drawing name in DesignCenter and select **Create Tool Palette**, as shown in Figure 25–17. A palette is created with the same name as the drawing, containing tool icons for all of the blocks defined in that drawing.

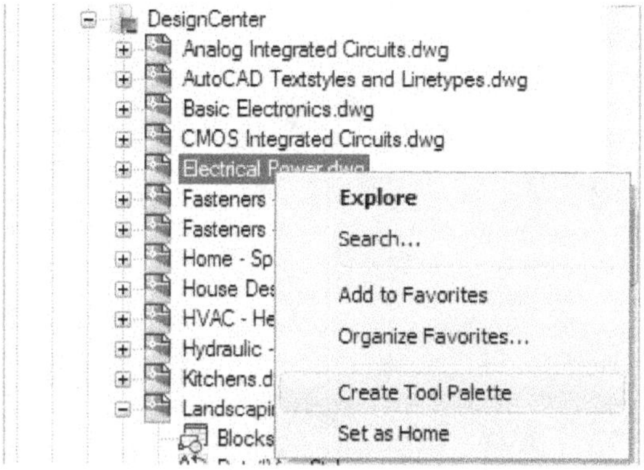

Figure 25–17

25.5 Modifying Tool Properties in Tool Palettes

Each tool in a palette can be modified to insert the object using specific properties, such as layer, scale, or rotation. For example, you might need to place a block at two different angles.

- You can create two tools in the palette for inserting the block, each preset to be inserted at the required angle.
- Once a tool has been added to a palette, you can drag and drop it to different places in the palette or to other tabs as required.

Modifying Tool Properties

To modify a tool's properties, right-click on a tool in the palette and select **Properties...** The Tool Properties for a block tool are shown in Figure 25–18. Other types of tools (e.g., for hatching or commands) have different properties.

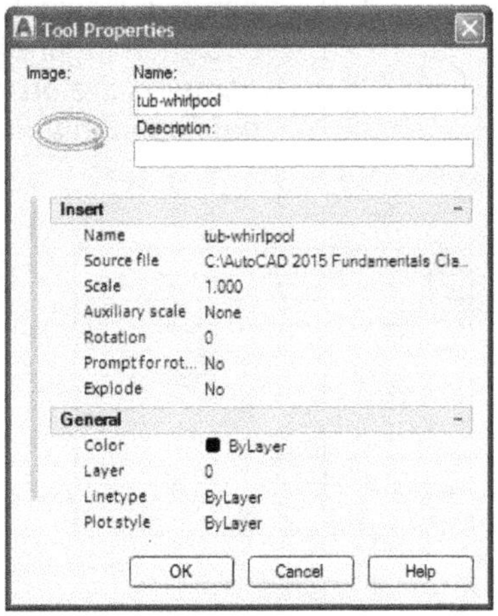

Figure 25–18

Command Options

Image	The preview image that displays for the tool.
Name	The name that displays with the tool in Tool Palettes. By default, this is set to the name of the block.
Description	An optional description for the tool, taken from the block description.

Insert Options

Name	The name of the block in the source file.
Source file	The drawing file used to create this tool in the palette and where the block definition is stored.
Scale	Insertion scale for the block. You can preset a value here. **Auxiliary scale** enables you to scale based on the current dimension scale factor or plot scale factor.
Rotation	Sets the rotation angle for the block when inserted.
Prompt for Rotation	If set to **Yes**, you are prompted for the rotation angle in the Command Line when you insert using the click and pick point method. This has no effect when you insert using the drag-and-drop method.
Explode	If set to **Yes**, the block is inserted as its component pieces, not as a single block object.

General Options

Layer	Sets the layer on which the block is inserted.
Other Options	The other General options (**Color**, **Linetype**, etc.) are normally set to **ByLayer** so that their properties are controlled by the layer.

- If the layer specified in the Tool Properties does not exist in the current drawing, it is automatically created when you insert the block.
- If the specified layer is toggled off or frozen, the block is still placed on that layer. However, it does not display until you toggle on or thaw the layer.

Redefining Blocks in Tool Palettes

If the block definition in the source file changes, it does not automatically update in the palette. Open the Tool Properties dialog box and select the source file again.

- You can update a block definition in the current drawing to match a block in the tool palettes by right-clicking and selecting **Redefine**, as shown in Figure 25–19.

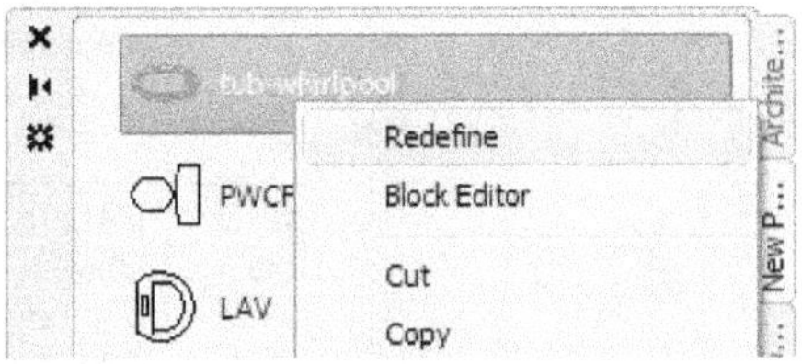

Figure 25–19

- If you open a block in the Tool Palettes in the **Block Editor**, any changes are saved to the block in the palette and automatically update in the active drawing.
- You can specify an image for a tool palette icon. Right-click on the tool and select **Specify image...**, as shown in Figure 25–20. In the Select Image File dialog box, you can select the file you want to use. BMP, JPG, PNG, GIF, and TIF files are all supported image types.

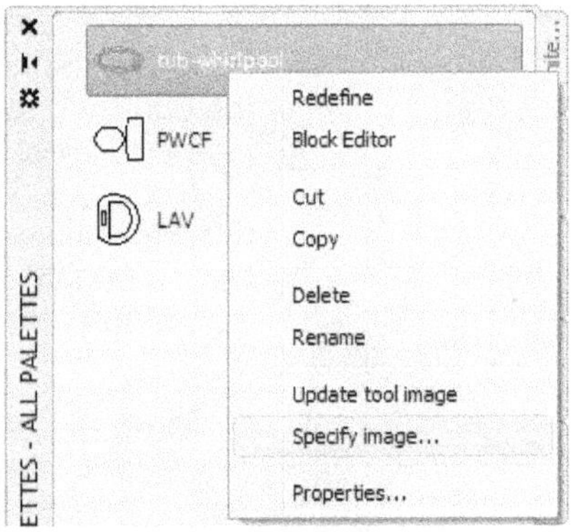

Figure 25–20

Practice 25c Modifying Tool Properties

Estimated time for completion: 10 minutes

Practice Objectives

- Create a custom tool palette and add blocks to the palette.
- Copy and modify a block tool.

In this practice, you will create a custom tool palette with blocks and use the palette to insert the blocks. You will then add blocks to the custom tool palette using the drag and drop method. You will also modify the properties of the blocks in the tool palette.

Task 1 - Add blocks to a custom tool palette.

In this task you will create a custom tool palette with blocks and use the palette to insert the blocks, as shown in Figure 25–21.

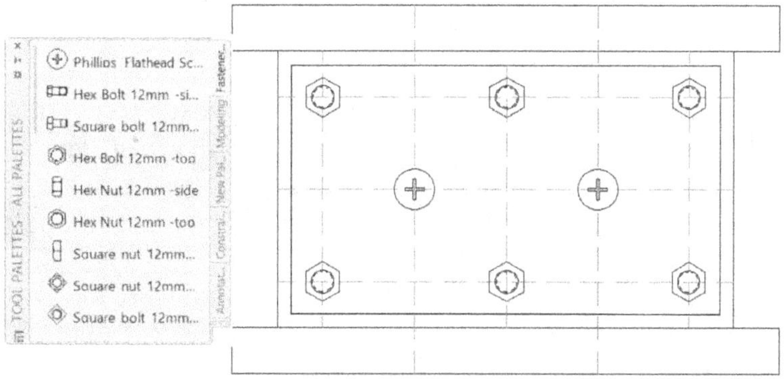

Figure 25–21

1. Open **Fasteners-M.dwg** from your practice files folder. The objects are all defined as blocks in this drawing.
2. In the *View* tab>Palettes panel, click (Tool Palettes) to open Tool Palettes if it is not already open.
3. Right-click in the palette title bar or the tab bar and select **New Palette**. In the *New Palette* edit field, type **Fasteners** and press <Enter>. A new blank palette is created with the *Fasteners* tab active.

Do not select the object by its grip. Select any other highlighted part instead.

4. In the Drawing window, select the round Phillips screw and drag and drop it onto the palette. An icon and description for the block is added automatically, as shown in Figure 25–22.

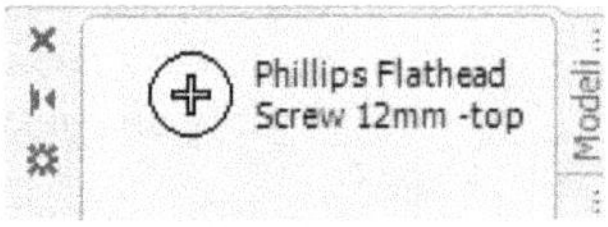

Figure 25–22

5. Repeat Step 4 to add the other bolt and nut blocks to the palette. You must add them one at a time.

6. Close **Fasteners-M.dwg**. Do not save changes.

7. Open **Assembly-M.dwg** from your practice files folder.

8. Set *OSNAP* to **Endpoint** and **Intersection**.

9. Drag and drop the block **Phillips Flathead Screw 12mm -top** to the intersections of the construction lines as shown in Figure 25–21.

10. Drag and drop the **Hex Bolt 12mm -top** blocks into the drawing, as shown in Figure 25–21.

Task 2 - Modify the tool properties.

In this task you will copy a block tool in the new tool palette and modify the tool properties, as shown in Figure 25–23.

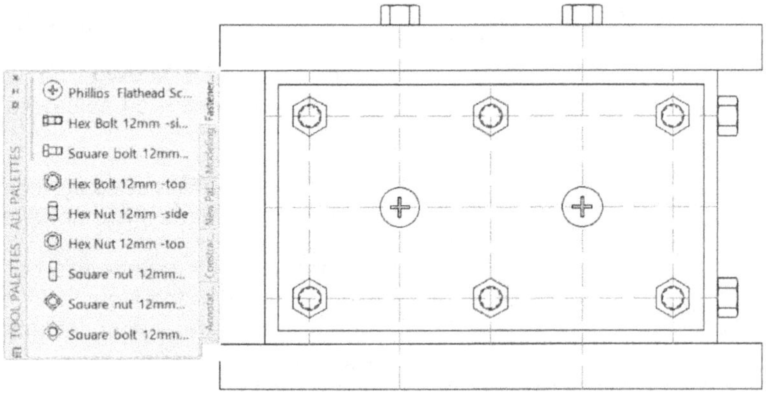

Figure 25–23

1. To make a copy of the **Hex Nut 12mm -side** tool, hold <Ctrl> and drag and drop the tool directly below the original one in the palette. The copy of the tool has the same name.

2. Right-click on the new tool icon and select **Properties,** as shown in Figure 25–24.

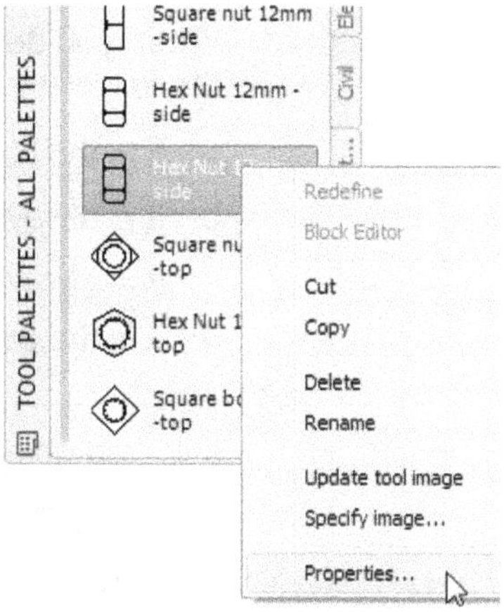

Figure 25–24

3. In the Tool Properties dialog box, change the *Name* next to the image to **Hex Nut – Horizontal**. (Do not change the name under the Insert properties. Doing so breaks the link to the block definition.)

4. In the Insert properties, change the *Rotation* to **90**. As you press <Enter> to accept the values, note that the image in the dialog box displays horizontally.

5. In the General properties, verify that the *Layer* is set to **Object**, so that the block is always inserted on this layer. Click **OK**.

6. Insert the **Hex nut- Horizontal** and the **Hex Nut 12mm -side** along the top and side respectively, as shown in Figure 25–23.

7. Save and close the drawing.

Chapter Review Questions

1. When you define a block, you specify a base point. Which of the following are true about the base point?
    a. It is the handle that you use when inserting the block.
    b. It is always at 0,0.
    c. It is always at the center of the block.
    d. It is the point used to select the block objects.
2. Which command creates a separate drawing file from selected objects, that can be used in other drawings?
    a. **Make Block**
    b. **Wblock**
    c. **Purge**
    d. **Annotative Block**
3. If you change the definition of a block, what happens to any instances of that block that were already inserted in the drawing?
    a. They are automatically renamed.
    b. They are erased.
    c. They change to match the new definition.
    d. Nothing.
4. After adding blocks from a drawing to a Tool Palette, it does not matter if you move or delete the source drawing file.
    a. True
    b. False
5. Which of the following can you set in the Tool Properties for inserting a block?
    a. Offset
    b. Rotation
    c. Freeze
    d. Flip

6. If a layer that is specified in the Tool Properties of a block does not exist in the current drawing, what happens when you insert that block into that drawing?

    a. The block is inserted on layer 0.

    b. The block cannot be inserted into that drawing.

    c. You are prompted for a new name for the layer.

    d. The layer is automatically created in the drawing.

Command Summary

Button	Command	Location
	**Block Editor**	• **Ribbon:** *Home* tab>Block Definition panel or *Insert* tab>Block panel • **Command Prompt:** bedit or BE
	**Create Block**	• **Ribbon:** *Home* tab>Block panel or *Insert* tab>Block Definition panel • **Command Prompt:** block or B
	**Purge**	• **Application Menu:** Drawing Utilities>Purge • **Command Prompt:** purge or PU
	**Tool Palettes**	• **Ribbon:** *View* tab>Palettes panel • **Command Prompt:** toolpalettes, toolpalettesclose, or <Ctrl>+<3>
	**Write Block**	• **Ribbon:** *Insert* tab>Block Definition panel, Create Block drop-down list • **Command Prompt:** wblock

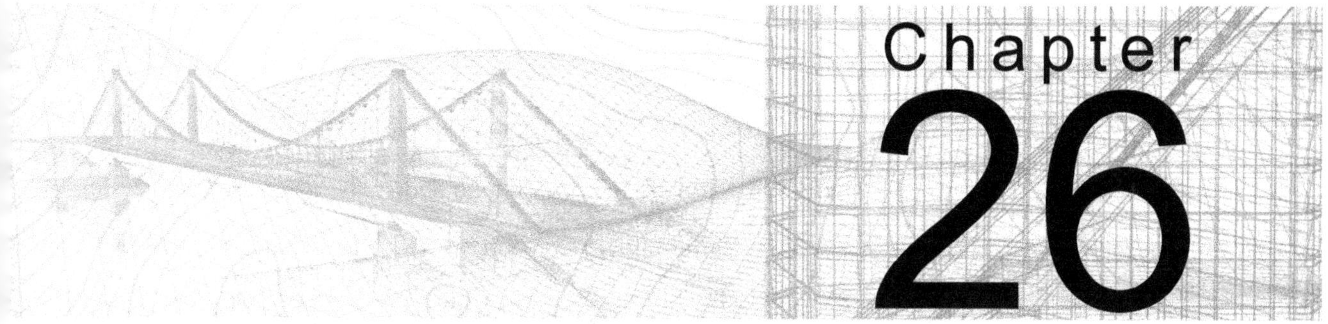

Projects: Creating and Organizing Blocks

This chapter contains practice projects that can be used to gain additional hands-on experience with the topics and commands covered so far in this student guide. These practices are intended to be self-guided and do not include step by step information.

Learning Objectives in this Chapter

- *Mechanical:* Create a control panel that contains objects and blocks.
- *Architectural:* Create a floor plan that contains office furniture using features such as blocks.
- *Civil:* Create a utility layout that contains objects and blocks.

26.1 Mechanical Project: Control Panel

Estimated time for completion: 45 minutes

In this project you will draw objects to represent components in a control panel, make blocks of those objects, and insert the blocks to complete the drawing, as shown in Figure 26–2.

1. Open **Panel-M.dwg** from your practice files folder.
2. Create the blocks shown in Figure 26–1. All objects should be drawn on layer **0**. Do not include the text or dimensions.

- Tip: To draw the hexagons, use the **Polygon** command. Select the **Circumscribed** option with a radius of **2.2**.

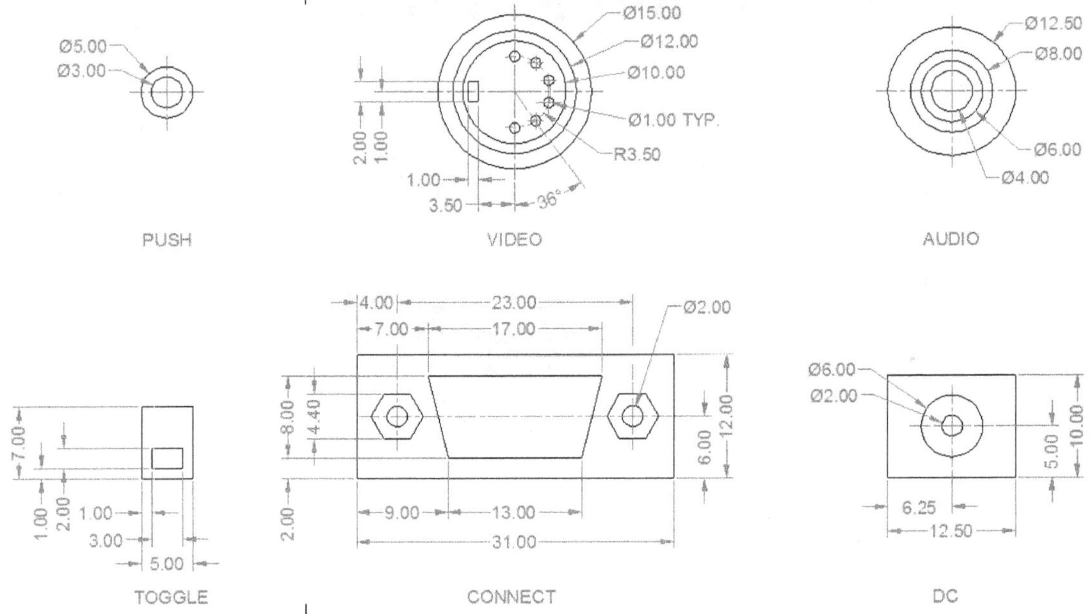

Figure 26–1

3. Insert the blocks on the layer **Component** as shown in Figure 26–2.

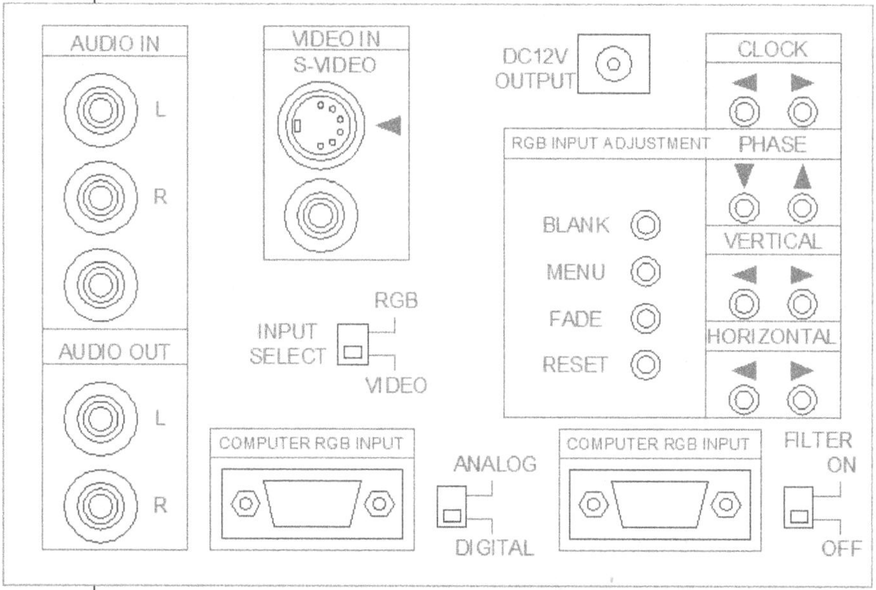

Figure 26–2

4. (Optional) Create a tool palette with the blocks from this project, so that you can use it to insert them into the current drawing or other drawings.

26.2 Architectural Project: Furniture Layout

Estimated time for completion: 45 minutes

In this project you will create blocks for office furniture and insert them into a floor plan as shown in Figure 26–3.

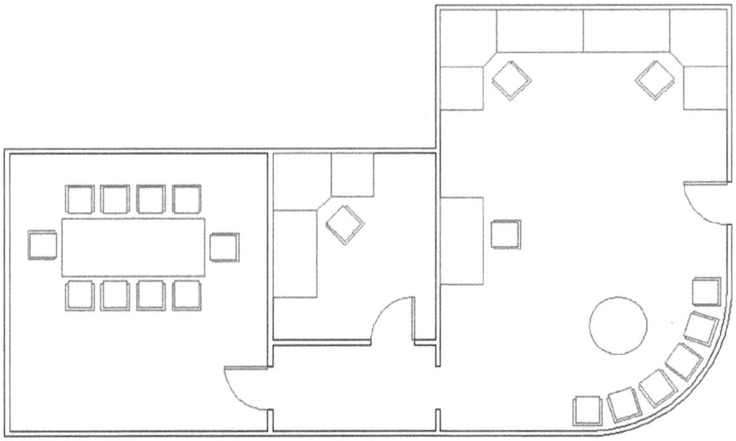

Figure 26–3

1. Open **Office3-AM.dwg** from your practice files folder.
2. Create the blocks shown in Figure 26–4. All of the objects should be drawn on the layer **Furniture**, except the door (layer **Doors**).

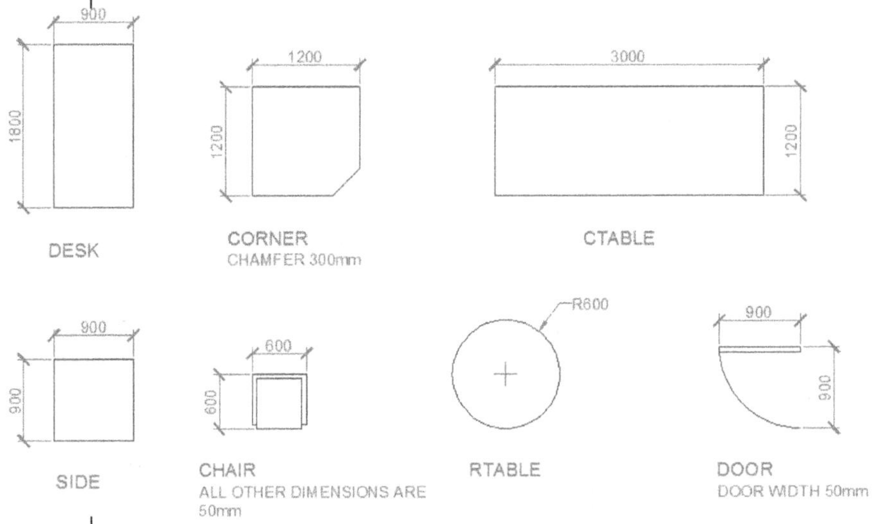

Figure 26–4

3. Insert the blocks as shown in Figure 26–3. (**Tip:** Use the **Array** and **Mirror** commands to help place some of the furniture).

4. (Optional) Create a tool palette with the blocks from this project, so that you can use it to insert these blocks into the current drawing or other drawings.

26.3 Civil Project: Utility Layout

Estimated time for completion: 60 minutes

In this project you will create blocks for a utility layout and insert them into an existing plan, as shown in Figure 26–5.

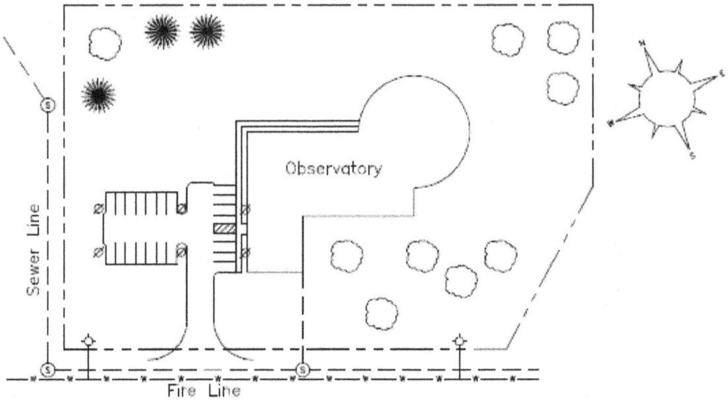

Figure 26–5

1. Open **Observatory Site-CM.dwg** from your practice files folder.

2. Pan to an empty part of the drawing and create the blocks shown in Figure 26–6. All of the objects should be drawn on layer **0**.

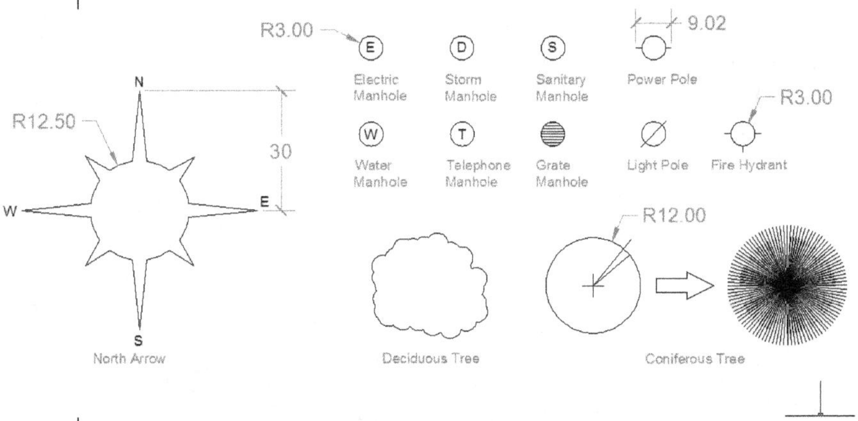

Figure 26–6

3. Insert the blocks in the drawing as shown in Figure 26–5. Insert the blocks on the appropriate layers.

4. (Optional) Create a tool palette with the blocks from this project, so that you can use it to insert the blocks into the current drawing or other drawings.

Chapter 27

Creating Templates

In this chapter you learn how to create template drawings, control drawing units and limits, create new layers, set up standard layouts, and save template drawings.

Learning Objectives in this Chapter

- Set standards for creating templates.
- Set the type of drawing units and their precision used in a drawing.
- Create new layers, customize their options, and organize them.
- Create custom page setups and associate them to specific Layout tabs.
- Apply a new page setup or an imported page setup to a Layout tab.
- Set up layouts to be used in a template.
- Save a drawing as a template file.

27.1 Why Use Templates?

Creating templates is an important step in customizing the AutoCAD® software to your specific work and drawing projects. A template is a drawing that contains the settings that you want to include as the foundation for new drawings. When correctly defined, these settings also establish a set of standards for each project.

Features that should be set in a template include the following (as shown in Figure 27–1):

- Units (coordinates) and limits.
- Layers.
- Annotation styles for Text, Dimensions, and Multileaders.
- Layouts with page setup, border, and title block.

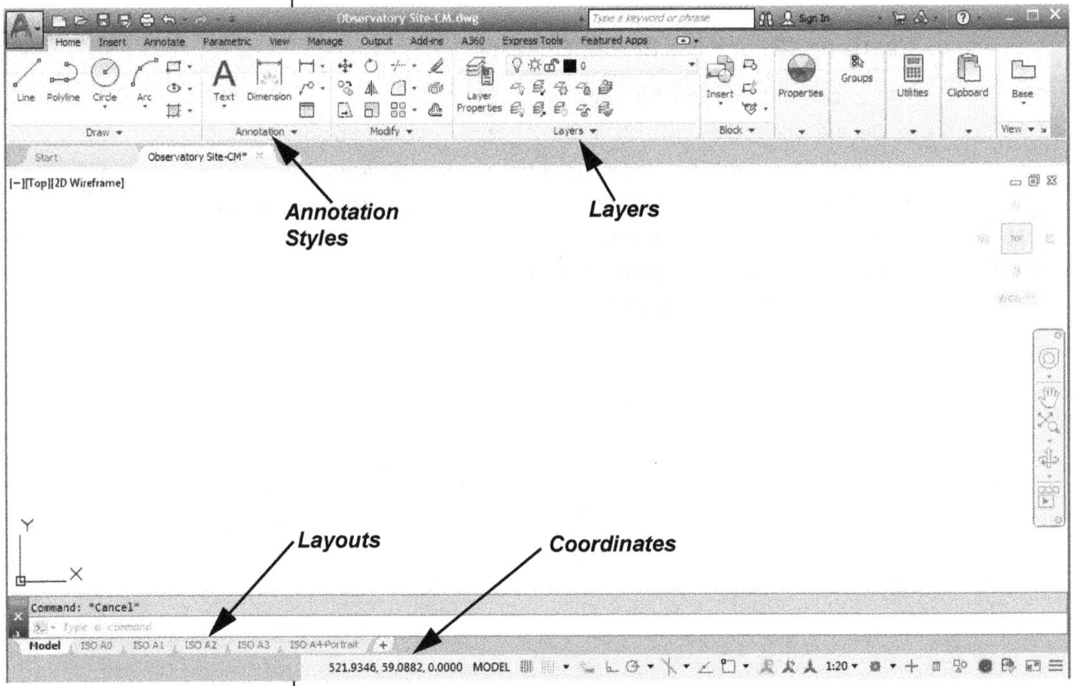

Figure 27–1

- Several predefined templates are supplied with the AutoCAD software, some with title blocks and borders at standard sizes. You need to add layers, text styles, and dimension styles if you use these templates.
- Other settings that can be saved in a template are system variables (such as **Global Linetype Scale**), and the Snap and Grid drafting settings. The Object Snap, Polar Tracking, and Object Snap Tracking drafting settings are stored in the AutoCAD system files and cannot be saved in a template.

Drawing Standards

In addition to templates, you should consider the other standards that you might need to add. Creating standards for using with the software enables you to work efficiently and faster without having to search for them when required.

Standards are important in the following key areas:

- **Naming Standards:** Establish a consistent scheme for drawing filenames, folders, and servers.
- **Layer Standards:** Your office or organization should have a standard layer scheme that everyone follows.
    - Your standard layer scheme should be included in your template drawings so that it is available in new drawings. You should rarely need to create a new layer.
    - A logical approach to layer names can simplify layer management. For example, if you name all of the layers related to plumbing with the prefix **P-**, they are grouped together in the Layer Control and are easy to manipulate as a group.
- **Block Standards:** Establish a consistent naming scheme for blocks. Store drawings (that are to be inserted into other drawings) as blocks in a shared network folder that is accessible to everyone who needs them. Alternatively, place sets of related blocks into block library drawings to be accessed using Tool Palettes or DesignCenter.
- You can also include standard blocks in your template file. (Tool Palettes are not related to templates. When you create custom Tool Palettes, they are available for any drawing).

- **Annotation Styles:** Use text, dimensions, and multileader styles to ensure consistency and minimize the formatting required each time you add text, a table, or dimensions to the drawing.

*In the AutoCAD LT® software, the **Sheet Set Template File Location** and **Default Template for Sheet Creation and Page Setup Overrides** options are not available.*

Hint: Default Template for QNEW

In the Quick Access Toolbar, click (New) to launch the **QNew** command. **QNew** can be set to use a default template file, so that you are not prompted to select the template when creating a new drawing. You can specify the template along with its path in the **Default Template File Name for QNEW** option in the *Files* tab in the Options dialog box, as shown in Figure 27–2.

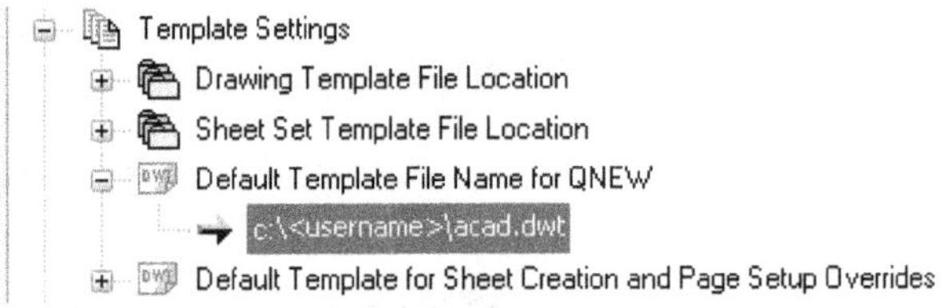

Figure 27–2

- If a default for **QNew** has not been specified, the command opens the Select Template dialog box, similar to the regular **New** command.
- The **QNew** template also controls which template is used for the new drawing that automatically opens at startup.

27.2 Controlling Units Display

The first setting you should establish in your template is the type of drawing units to be used. By setting the units in a template, you ensure that any new drawing based on that template automatically starts with the correct units. The **Units** command enables you to specify the type of drawing units used and the precision that the AutoCAD software displays for those units, as shown in Figure 27–3.

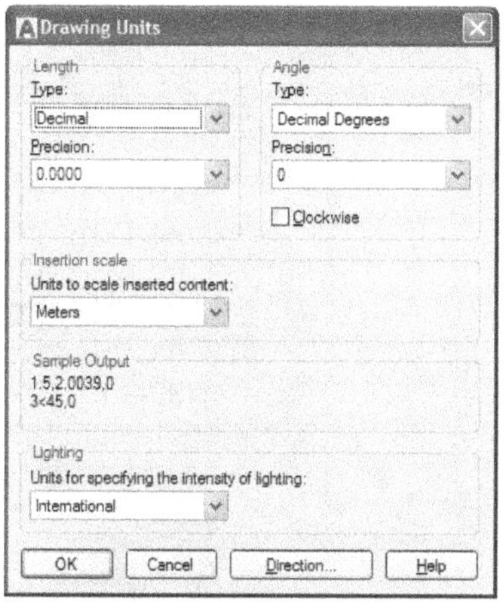

Figure 27–3

How To: Set the Drawing Units

1. Open the template drawing that you are creating.
2. In the Application Menu, select **Drawing Utilities>Units**.
3. In the *Length* area, select an option in the Type and Precision drop-down lists.
4. In the *Angle* area, select an option in the Type and Precision drop-down lists and set the angle rotation to be **Clockwise** from **0** as required.
5. In the *Insertion scale* area, select an option in the Units to scale inserted content drop-down list.
6. In the *Lighting* area, select an option in the Units for specifying the intensity of lighting drop-down list (this is only required if you are working in 3D).
7. Click **OK**.

In the AutoCAD LT software, the Lighting area is not available.

- The Length Type options include **Architectural**, **Decimal**, **Engineering**, **Fractional**, and **Scientific**.

- The Angle Type options include **Decimal Degrees**, **Deg/Min/Sec**, **Grads**, **Radians**, and **Surveyor's Units**. By default, angles are measured in a counter-clockwise direction. If you need them to go in the other direction, select the **Clockwise** option.
- Note the *Sample Output* area as you modify the settings, as shown in Figure 27–4.

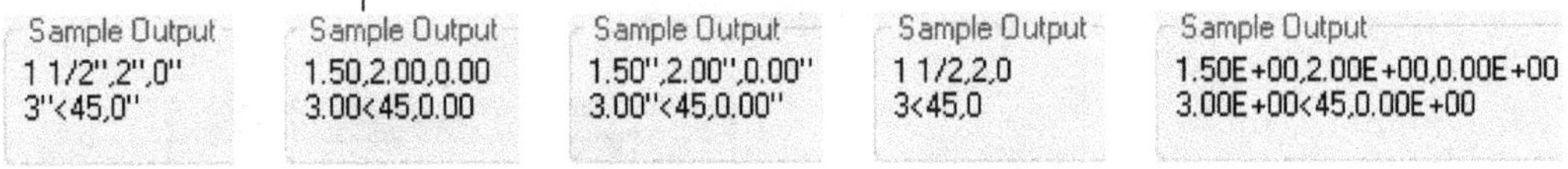

Architectural ***Decimal*** ***Engineering*** ***Fractional*** ***Scientific***

Figure 27–4

- Decimal units can stand for many unit types: inches, feet, meters, millimeters, miles, etc.
- The **Insertion scale** controls how blocks created in different units, are scaled when inserted into the drawing. For example, if the block units are inches and the drawing units are millimeters, the AutoCAD software scales the block based on the conversion factor for inches to millimeters (25.4).
- For Architectural or Engineering units, the *Insertion scale* units should be set to **Inches, millimeters, or meters**.
- Changing the precision here only controls the degree of precision that displays and does not affect the size of objects that are drawn. The AutoCAD software still works with its full degree of accuracy, regardless of the precision setting.
- Click **Direction...** to open the Direction Control dialog box in which you can set the base angles for **East**, **North**, **South**, **West**, and **Other**. This is usually used in civil engineering drawings.

Hint: Editing the Scale List

The Scale List (used for the Viewport Scale, Annotation Scale, and Plot Scale), is stored in each drawing file and can vary from drawing to drawing. Therefore, if you want to use a standard scale list in each drawing, you should set it in the template drawing as you want it to be displayed.

To edit the scale list, click **Custom...** in the Annotation scale list (as shown in Figure 27–5), or click (Scale List) in the *Annotate* tab>Annotation Scaling panel to open the Edit Drawing Scales dialog box.

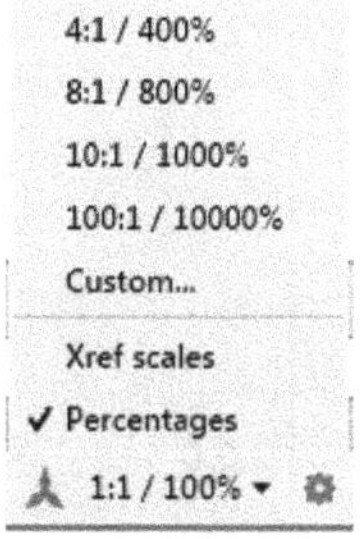

Figure 27–5

You can **Add**, **Edit**, and **Delete** scales, as shown in Figure 27–6. You can also move them up and down in the list so that the most commonly used scales are at the beginning. Click **Reset** to return to the default scale list.

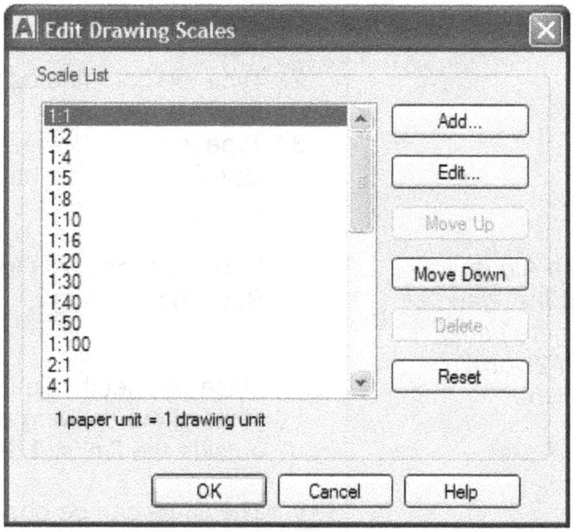

Figure 27–6

Drawing Limits

When you begin drawing, it helps to start with an area of an appropriate size displayed on the screen. For example, a site plan in Engineering units needs to have a larger area displayed than a small mechanical part in the same units.

The *limits* of a drawing define the rectangular area (extents of the area) in which you are going to draw. You can set the limits by selecting a lower left and upper right corner. For example, you might set the upper right limits of a site plan to **300m,150m** while a mechanical part is set to **300mm,180mm**, as shown in Figure 27–7.

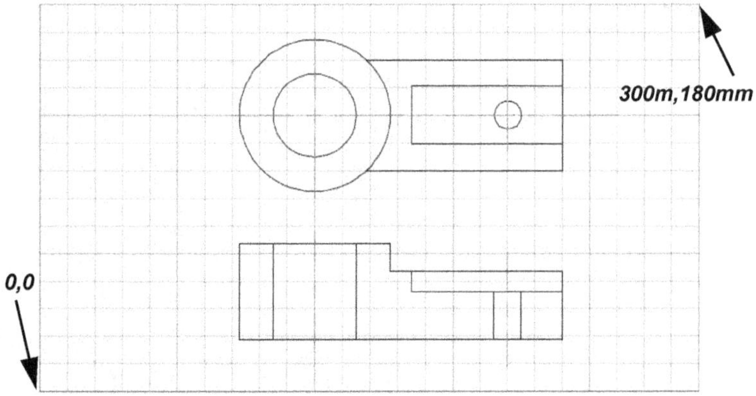

Figure 27–7

How To: Set the Drawing Limits

1. Start the **Limits** command by typing **limits** in the Command Line.
2. Type the coordinates for the lower left corner, which is normally set to **0,0**.
3. Type the coordinates for the upper right corner. They should define an area slightly larger than the objects you are planning to draw.

(Zoom All) is located in the View tab>Navigate panel, expanded ***Zoom Extents*** *flyout.*

4. Use (Zoom All) to fit the drawing in the drawing area.
5. Save the drawing.

- Once you set the limits, use (Zoom All). It zooms to fit the limits of the drawing in the drawing area (if there are objects outside the limits, it displays them as well).
- The limits can be changed at any time without harming your drawing.

27.3 Creating New Layers

A layering scheme is the most important organizing tool in any drawing. A standard layer scheme should be included in your template drawings. Use the Layer Properties Manager to create new layers and change the properties or status of existing layers, as shown in Figure 27–8.

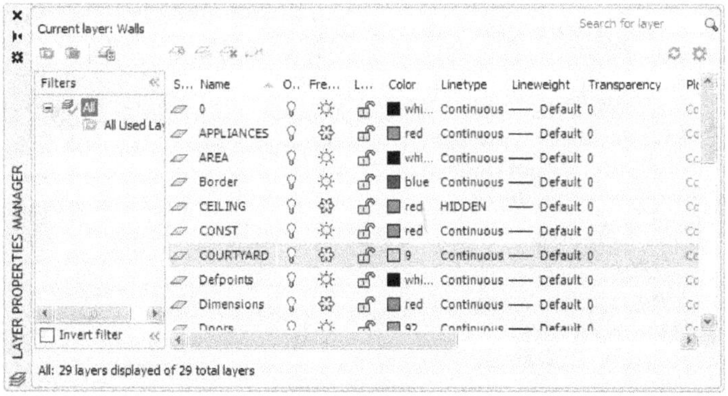

Figure 27–8

Layer Properties Manager

The Layer Properties Manager is a palette and can stay open while you are working in the drawing. It can also be docked and hidden to create space in the drawing area. When layers are modified in the Layer Properties Manager, the changes are automatically applied to the drawing and listed in the Layer Control list in the *Home* tab>Layers panel.

- When you create layers, you set their color, linetype, lineweight, and plot or no-plot status, and the plot style (if applicable).
- Layers defined in a template establish a consistent layer standard for all drawings based on that template.
- The icon in the *Status* column indicates whether the layer contains objects ( ), does not contain objects ( ), or is the current layer ( ).

How To: Create a New Layer

1. in the *Home* tab>Layers panel, or in the View tab> Palettes panel, click (Layer Properties).
2. Click (New Layer). A new layer is added to the list with the default name, **Layer1**.
3. Type a name for the new layer. Layer names can have up to 255 characters and can include letters, numbers, spaces, and most other special characters (the following symbols are not permitted: < > / \ ? * | , = `.).
4. To set the **Color**, select the color swatch for that layer, select a color in the Select Color dialog box (as shown in Figure 27–9), and click **OK**.

To create several new layers quickly, click (New Layer) once and then type the layer names separated by a comma.

The Select Color dialog box has three tabs: Index Color, True Color, and Color Books. The Index Color list (256 colors) is adequate for most needs.

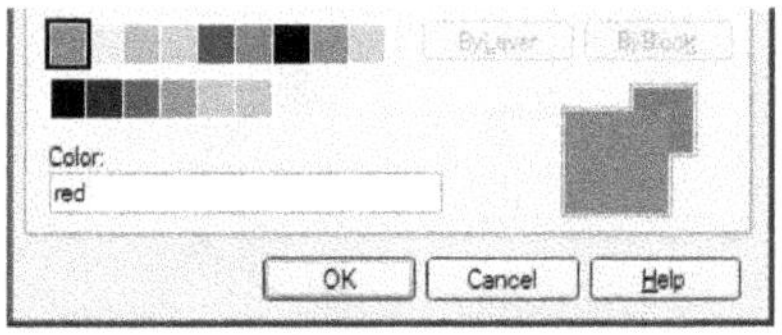

Figure 27–9

5. To set the **Linetype**, select the linetype name for that layer, select a different linetype in the Select Linetype dialog box (as shown in Figure 27–10), and click **OK**.

Linetypes are set by default to display in a Paper Space viewport according to the current viewport scale.

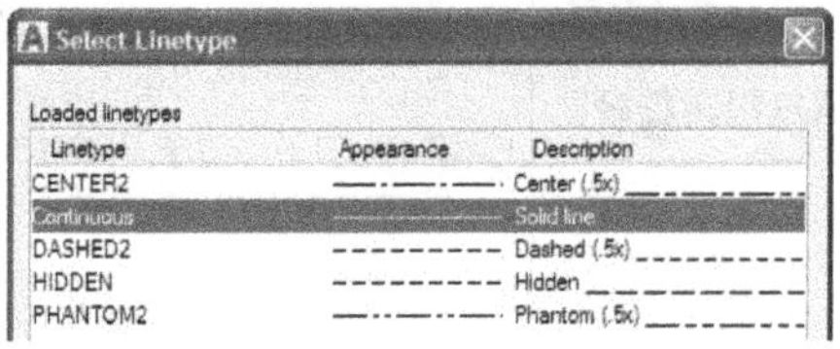

Figure 27–10

6. To set the **Lineweight**, select the lineweight setting for that layer, select a width in the Lineweight dialog box (as shown in Figure 27–11), and click **OK**.

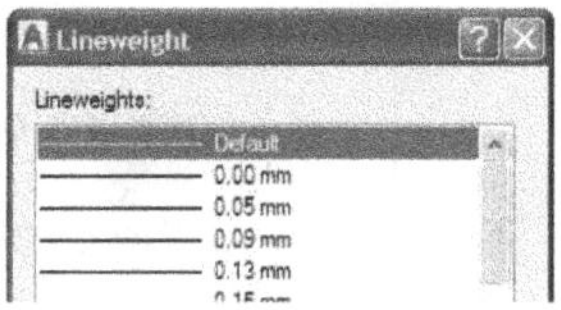

Figure 27–11

7. To make the layer non-plotting, click (Plot) or (No Plot), as shown in Figure 27–12. No Plot layers are useful for construction lines, notes, viewports, and other information that is required for drawing construction, but not for the plotted output.
8. If you want to freeze a layer by default in a new viewport, click (New VP Freeze), as shown in Figure 27–12. For example, you might want to create a layer that is only displayed in one viewport.

Figure 27–12

9. To add a description, click in the *Description* column and type the description.

- The changes are automatically applied to the drawing.
- If a layer is selected in the Layer Properties Manager when you click (New Layer), the new layer copies the properties of the selected layer.

Sorting Layers by Properties

- You can sort layers in the list according to their properties by selecting any of the column headings at the top of the list. For example, selecting the *Name* column sorts the list alphabetically by name, and selecting the *Freeze* column separates the frozen from the thawed layers. Clicking on a heading again reverses the sort order.
- You can rearrange the display order of columns in the Layer Properties Manager by dragging the column header to a new location, as shown in Figure 27–13. The new location is saved by the AutoCAD software.

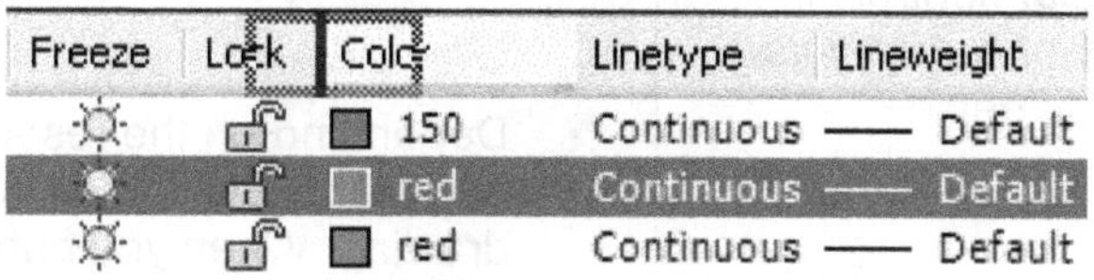

Figure 27–13

- You can resize the width of the columns in the Layer Properties Manager by dragging the border between the column headings. You can also right-click on a column header and select **Maximize column** to maximize one column, or select **Maximize all columns** to resize all of the columns to the width of their largest cell.

- You can remove any columns that you do not want displayed. Right-click on any column header and select a column name to clear the checkmark and remove it from the display. **Name** is grayed out and cannot be removed, as shown in Figure 27–14.

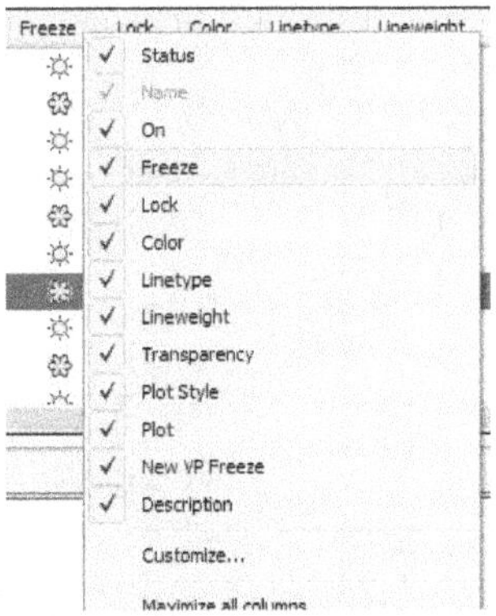

Figure 27–14

- Additional column names display if you are in a layout.

Lineweights

Lineweight refers to how heavy or wide the lines are in an object, as shown in Figure 27–15. Heavier lineweights are used to emphasize parts of the drawing. This becomes important when the drawing is plotted.

 *(Show/Hide Lineweight) in the Status Bar controls the visibility of lineweights on the screen.*

Figure 27–15

- Depending on the resolution of your monitor, you might not be able to distinguish between similar lineweights in your drawing. When you print the drawing, the lineweights are easier to differentiate.

- Plotted lineweight in the AutoCAD software is often controlled by color.

Linetypes

Linetype refers to whether the objects are drawn with dashed, dotted, continuous, or other line styles, as shown in Figure 27–16. Usually, specific types of lines are used for specific types of objects. For example, hidden lines are usually dashed, while most objects are drawn with continuous linetypes.

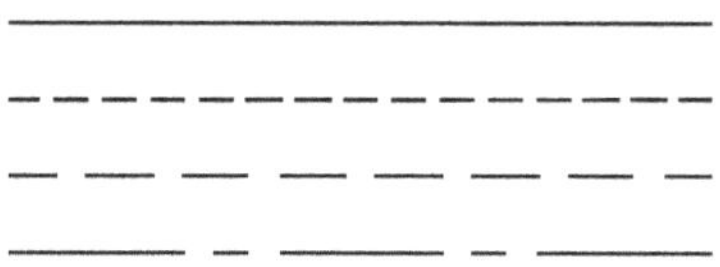

Figure 27–16

How To: Load a Linetype

The AutoCAD software comes with a wide selection of standard linetypes. If the required style does not display in the Select Linetype dialog box, you can load other linetypes into the drawing.

1. In the Layer Properties Manager, select the linetype name for the layer that you want to modify. The Select Linetype dialog box opens.
2. Click **Load...**.
3. In the Load or Reload Linetypes dialog box, select the Linetype(s) that you want to use. To select more than one, hold <Shift> or <Ctrl> while selecting.
4. Click **OK**. The linetypes are now available for use.

- The standard linetype definitions are stored in the file **Acad.lin**.

Hint: Linetype Scale

The Linetype Scale controls the length of segments and gaps for all of the linetypes in the drawing. A larger value for the linetype scale places longer segments and gaps. Depending on the size of your drawing, you might need to adjust the linetype scale so that linetypes display and plot at an appropriate size.

- By default, the linetype scale is set to display in Paper Space viewports so the linetypes are scaled correctly for each viewport.
- You can type **ltscale** in the Command Line to launch the command.

Other Layer Options

The left panel in the Layer Properties Manager displays the layer filter tree. Layer filters are an advanced layer management tool that are used to control the layer list and to group layers.

- One layer filter, **All Used Layers**, is predefined. Selecting this filter only lists layers that contain objects. To return to the full list, select **All** in the Layer Filter tree.
- If you do not use layer filters, you can hide that portion of the Layer Properties Manager by clicking « (Collapses Layer filter tree), as shown in Figure 27–17.

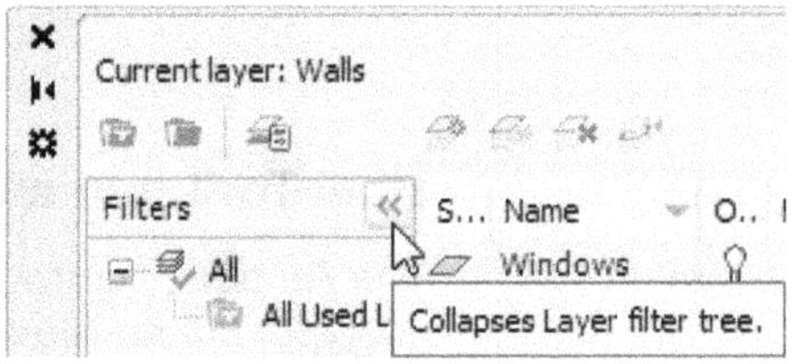

Figure 27–17

How To: Delete a Layer

1. Select a layer name in the list.
2. Click (Delete Layer). The layer is removed.

- You cannot delete layers that contain objects or certain special layers, such as layer **0**.

How To: Rename a Layer

1. In the list, click once on the layer name to select it and then click it again. An edit box displays around the highlighted name (you can also right-click on a Layer name and select **Rename Layer**).
2. Type a new name.

- You cannot rename layer **0** and should not rename the default layer **defpoints**.

How To: Merge Layers

You can select multiple layers in the Layer Properties Manager and merge their objects into one layer. All of the objects on the selected layers are moved to the merged layer and the selected layers are removed from the drawing.

1. In Layer Properties Manager, use <Shift> or <Ctrl> to select one or more layers to merge.
2. Right-click and select **Merge selected layer(s) to...**
3. In the Merge to Layer dialog box, select the layer to which you want to merge the other layers.
4. Click **OK**.
5. In the warning box, click **Yes**.
6. The AutoCAD Text window opens displaying the progress of the merge procedure. The selected layers are merged to the target layer. The selected layers are then deleted.

27.4 Adding Standard Layouts to Templates

You can simplify your day-to-day work by creating layouts in your template files that match the printers and paper sizes that you normally use, as shown in Figure 27–18. These layouts are then ready to use in new drawings based on the templates.

*To create a new Layout tab from an existing layout, right-click on the one that you want to use and select **Move or Copy**. In the dialog box, select **Create a copy** and select a layout before which the copy is going to be placed.*

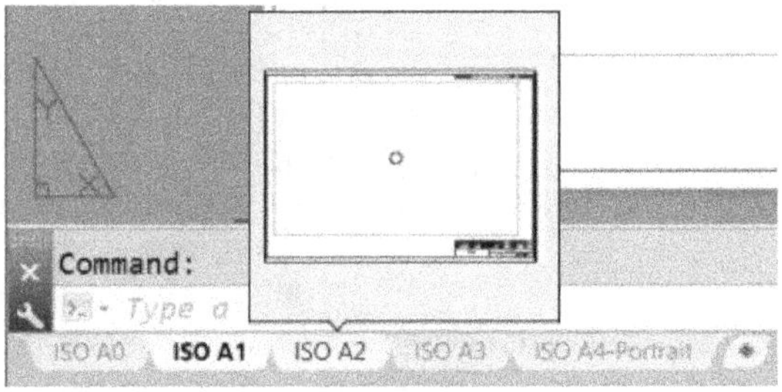

Figure 27–18

Working in the Page Setup Manager

In the Page Setup Manager, you can assign an existing page setup to the current Layout tab, create new page setups, modify existing page setups, and import page setups from another file.

When you set up template files for your office, you need to be able to specify the layouts that use your office printers and title blocks. To do so, create page setups in the Page Setup Manager (as shown in Figure 27–19), and then associate standard page setups with the Layout tabs.

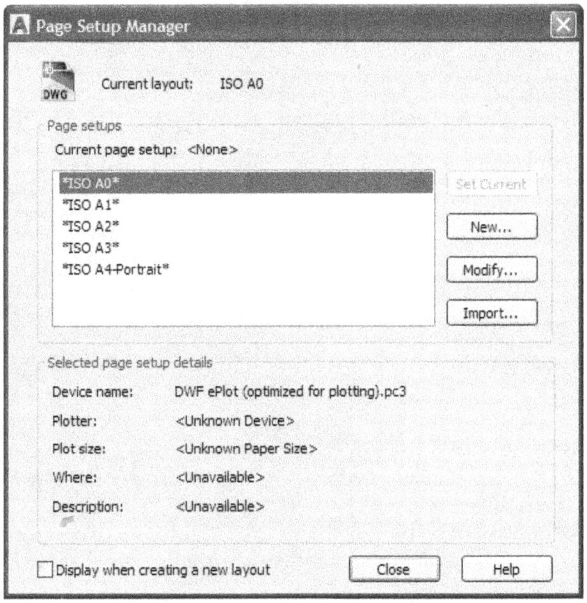

Figure 27–19

How To: Create a Page Setup

1. In the *Output* tab>Plot panel, click (Page Setup Manager). Alternatively, in the Application Menu, select **Print>Page Setup**.
2. In the Page Setup Manager dialog box, click **New**.
3. In the New Page Setup dialog box shown in Figure 27–20, type a name for the setup. Select an existing setup in the *Start with* area if the new setup is similar to an existing one.

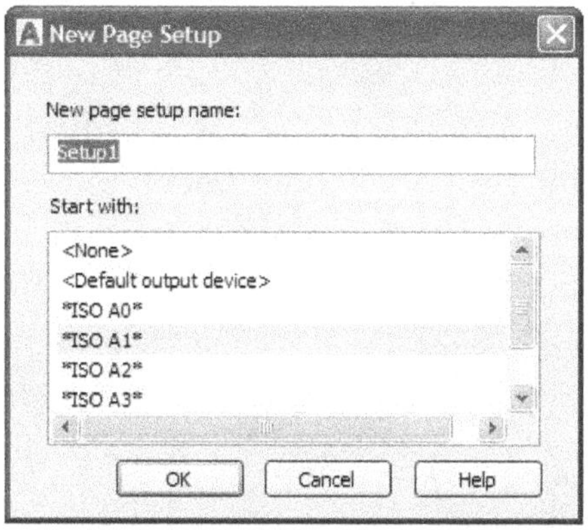

Figure 27–20

4. Click **OK**.

5. In the Page Setup dialog box (shown in Figure 27–21), select the printer or plotter that you want to use. This determines the paper sizes from which you can select.

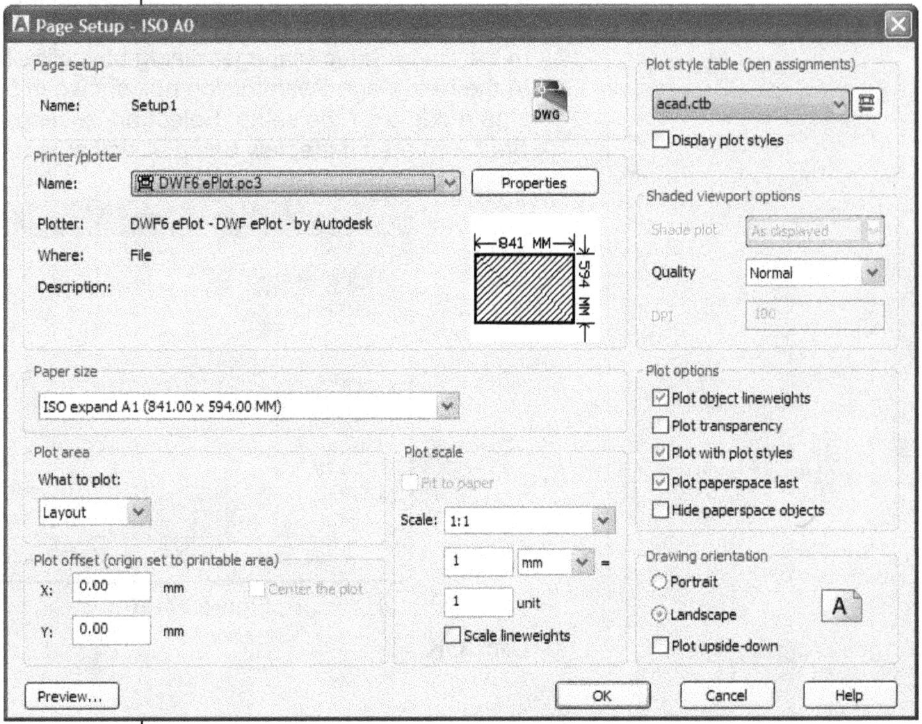

Figure 27–21

6. Specify the *Paper size*, *Plot area*, *Plot offset*, *Plot scale*, *Plot style table*, *Shaded viewport options*, *Plot options*, and *Drawing orientation*.
7. Click **Preview...** to display a preview of how the setup is going to print on the sheet.
8. Right-click in the preview and select **Exit**.
9. When the page setup is finished, click **OK** to return to the Page Setup Manager. The new page setup can now be applied to a layout.

Page Setup Options

Printer/ plotter

Enables you to select from the list of available printing devices. Check with your CAD manager if the printer/plotter you want to use is not in the list. The AutoCAD software includes several predefined plotter configurations, such as DWF6 e-plot.

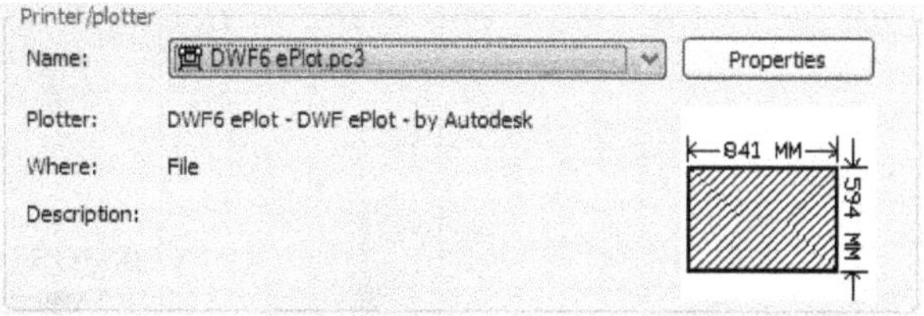

Paper size

Enables you to set the size of the layout. The available sizes depend on the selected plotter.

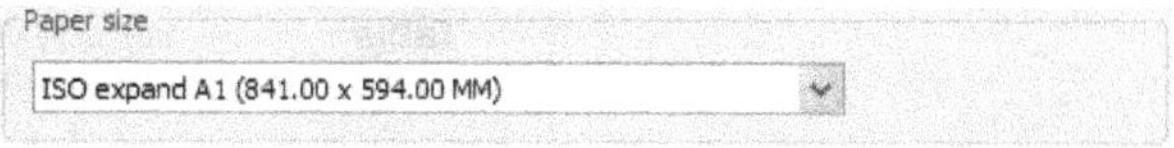

Plot area

Sets the printable area. Normally, you use the **Layout** option to plot the entire layout to the extents of the printable area. You can also print the Extents of the drawing, the Display in the drawing area, a Window that you select, or a View that has been defined in the drawing.

Plot offset

Controls where the drawing starts to plot on the paper. Depending on your plotter, you might need to set this so that the drawing fits correctly on the paper. The **Center the plot** option is not available when the *Plot area* is set to **Layout**.

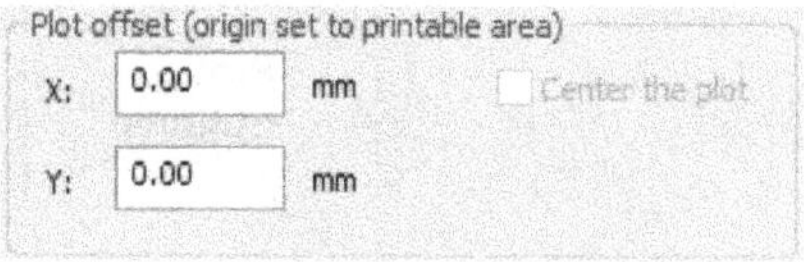

Plot scale	Sets the scale when you are printing from a layout. The default scale is 1:1. However, you can set a different scale if you are creating a check plot on a smaller piece of paper. 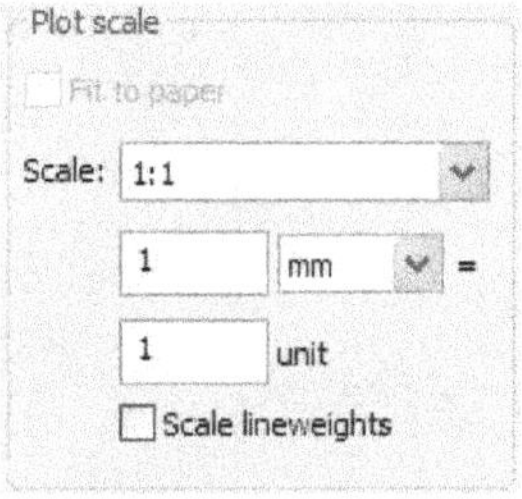 **IMPORTANT**: The *Plot scale* for a layout is almost always 1:1 because the layout is created at the actual size required to fit on the piece of paper. The scaling of the model is done using the Viewport Scale.
Plot style table	Coordinates the layer color to pen weight, or sets up other special effects for plotted output. Consult your CAD manager about which one you should use. 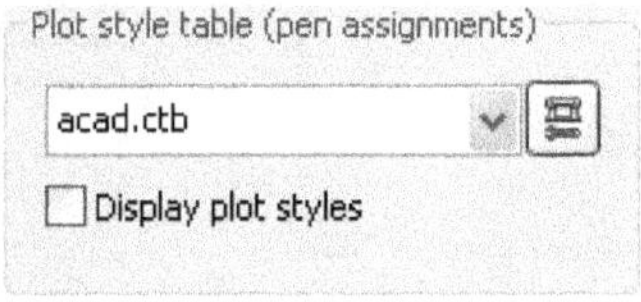
Shaded viewport options	For 3D models, this enables you to set viewports to be hidden or rendered and to control the image quality. 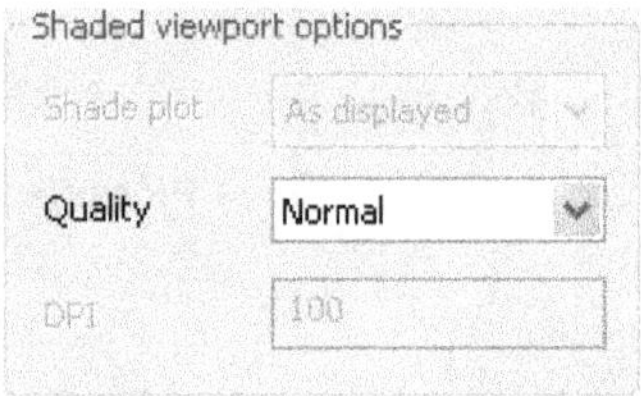
Plot options	Enables you to plot using lineweights or plot styles and to specify how to treat Paper Space objects. 

Drawing orientation	Sets the paper orientation to **Portrait** (the short edge of the paper is at the top of the page) or **Landscape** (the long edge of the paper is at the top of the page). 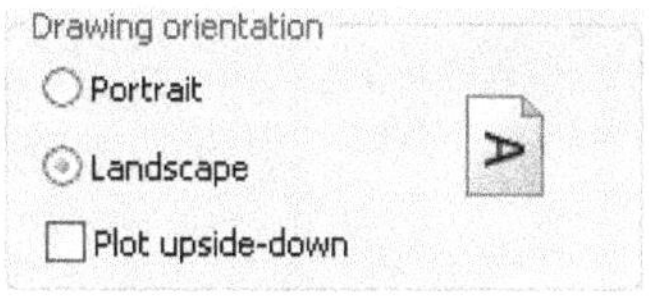

Layout Size: Printable Area

The AutoCAD software displays the *printable* area of the layout as a dashed boundary, as shown in Figure 27–22. Because printers or plotters cannot print to the edges of the sheet, the printable area is smaller than the actual paper size. The size of the margins varies from one printer model to another, and even from one sheet size to another. Ensure that the objects you place on the layout fit in the printable area.

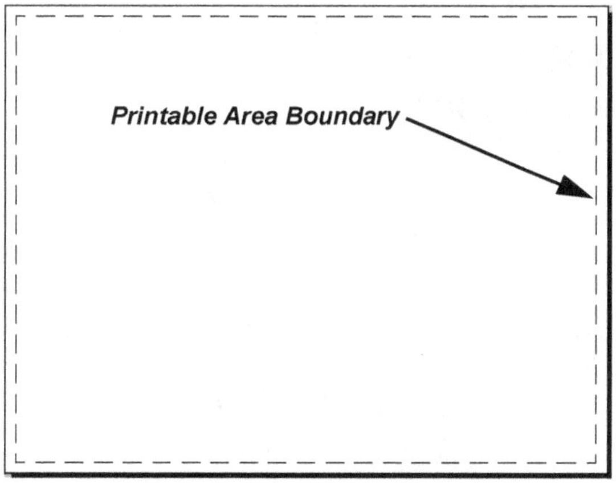

Figure 27–22

How To: Apply a Page Setup to a Layout

1. Right-click on the layout that you want to set and select **Page Setup Manager...**
2. In the Page Setup Manager, select a page setup with the required plotter and paper size.
3. Click **Set Current** to apply it to the layout.
4. Click **Close** to close the Page Setup Manager.

How To: Import a Page Setup from Another File

If names are not displayed in the list, the drawing might have layouts but they have not been saved as page setups.

1. Open the Page Setup Manager.
2. Click **Import...**.
3. In the Select Page Setup From File dialog box, select the file that contains the page setup you want to use and click **Open**.
4. In the Import Page Setups dialog box, select the setup that you want to import, as shown in Figure 27–23.

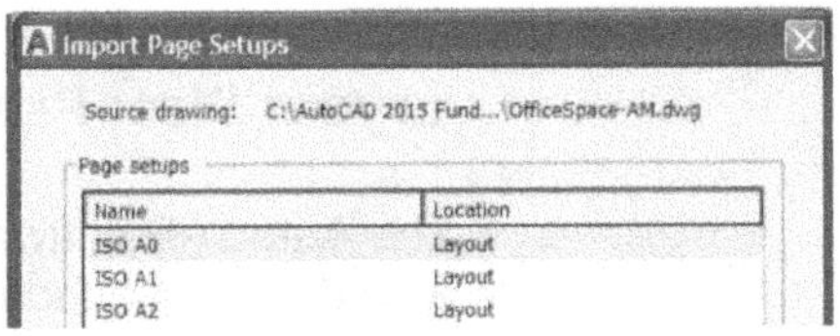

Figure 27–23

5. Click **OK** to complete the process. The imported page setup can now be used in your current drawing.

Setting Up Layouts to Use in a Template

To prepare layouts to be used in a template, specify generic names for the *Layout* tabs, add title blocks, and set up at least one viewport on each Layout.

- Rename new layouts using a generic name. For example, it might be one that reflects the printer and paper size, such as **Printer-ANSI C**. When it is used in a project, you can change the label to match the sheet number and/or sheet name.
- Your company title block should be designed to fit on the paper size specified in the page setup.
- Verify that the viewport is on the layer **Viewport**.
- Repeat the steps for each plotter and paper size required.

27.5 Saving Templates

All of the established settings can be saved in a template file. By saving the settings in a template, you automatically make them available in every new drawing based on that template.

How To: Create a Template

*If you select **Save As>Drawing Template**, the dialog box opens in the AutoCAD Template folder with **AutoCAD Drawing Template (*.dwt)** already selected as Files of type.*

1. Start a new drawing or open an existing drawing.
2. Establish all of the drawing settings as required (e.g., units or layers).
3. In the Application Menu, select **Save As** to save the drawing as a template.
4. In the Save Drawing As dialog box, expand the Files of type drop-down list and select **AutoCAD Drawing Template (*.dwt)**.
5. Assign the correct folder, give the file a name, and click **Save**.
6. In the Template Options dialog box, in the *Description* area, type a brief description of the template, as shown in Figure 27–24.

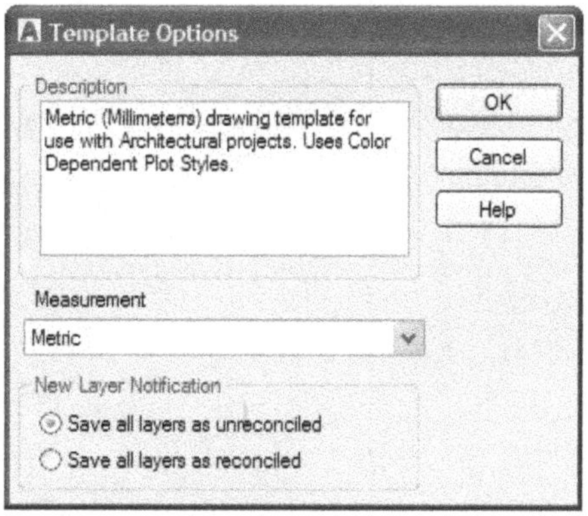

Figure 27–24

For more information on reconciled layers, see Reconcile New Layers in the AutoCAD Help system.

7. Select the system of measurement (Metric).
8. Select whether to save all of the layers as unreconciled or reconciled.
9. Click **OK**.

- Templates have the file extension .DWT to distinguish them from normal .DWG files.
- Templates should be saved in a separate folder to which everyone has access.
- You can modify an existing template as you would a normal drawing. To open a template, start the **Open** command and select **Drawing Template (*.dwt)** in the expanded Files of type drop-down list, as shown in Figure 27–25.

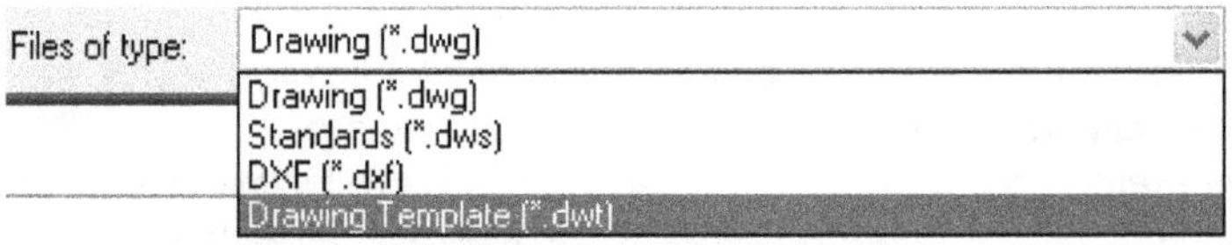

Figure 27–25

Practice 27a Saving a Template

Practice Objectives

- Set the units and limits in a drawing.
- Create a set of layers in a drawing.
- Create a page setup and apply it to a Layout tab.
- Add a title block to a Layout tab.
- Save the drawing as a template.

Estimated time for completion: 30 minutes

In this practice, you will create a drawing that you will turn into a template. You will set the units and test them by measuring distances using grips and use the Layer Properties Manager to create and modify new layers. You will also create a Page Setup and apply it to a standard layout, and then save the drawing as a template.

Task 1 - Control and test the units display.

In this task you will create a drawing that you will turn into a template. You will set the units and test them by measuring distances using grips, as shown in Figure 27–26.

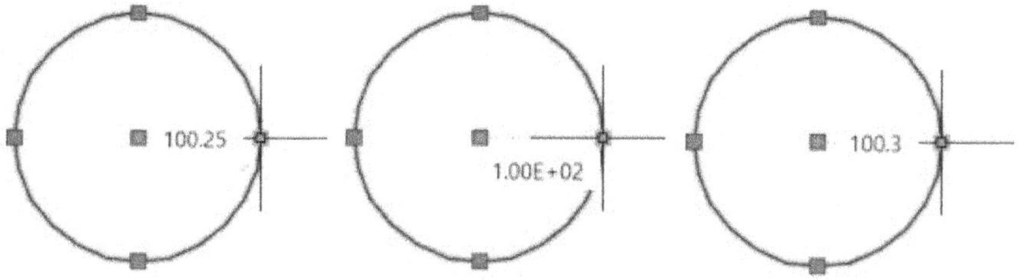

Figure 27–26

In the AutoCAD LT software, select ***acadlt.dwt****.*

1. Start the **New** command and select **acad.dwt** from the AutoCAD 2018 Template folder (default folder). Save the new drawing as **AEC-Facilities.dwg** in you practice files folder.
2. In the Application Menu, select **Drawing Utilities>Units**. In the Drawing Units dialog box, in the *Length* area, set the *Type* to **Decimal** and the *Precision* to **0.00**.
3. Verify that the *Insertion scale* is set to **Millimeters**. Click **OK**.
4. Draw a **100.25mm** radius circle (type **100.25** for the radius).
5. Use **Zoom Extents** to display the circle.

6. Select the circle and hover the cursor over one of the outer grips. The radius should be listed as **100.25**.

7. Start the **Units** command again to open the Drawing Units dialog box. Change the *Length Type* to **Scientific** and the *Length Precision* to **0.00E+01**, and click **OK**.

8. Select the circle again and hover the cursor on one of the grips. The radius is reported as **1.00E+02**.

9. Start the **Units** command to open the Drawing Units dialog box. Change the *Type* to **Decimal** and *Length Precision* to **0.0**.

10. Select the circle and hover the cursor over one of the outer grips. The radius is reported as **100.3**.

11. Start the **Units** command to open the Drawing Units dialog box. Set the *Length Type* to **Decimal** with a *Precision* of **0**.

12. In the Command Line, type **limits**. Set the lower left corner to **0,0** and the upper right corner to **30400,22800**.

13. Use (Zoom All) to fit the drawing on the screen. The circle displays very small near the bottom of the drawing window.

14. (Optional) Set the *Scale List* to only display **Metric** scales.

15. Save the drawing.

Task 2 - Create new layers.

In this task you will use the Layer Properties Manager to create new layers and change their properties, as shown in Figure 27–27.

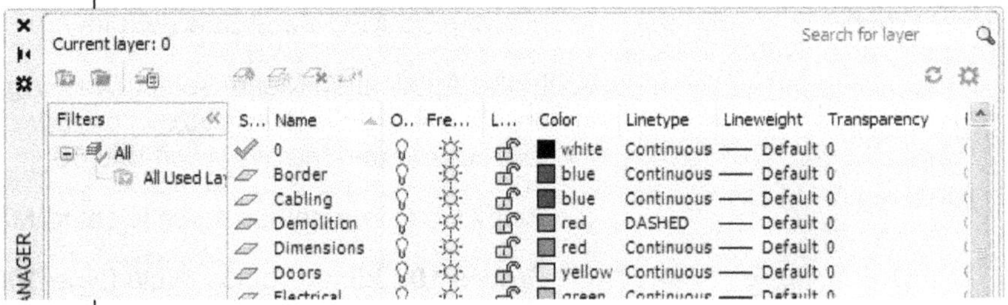

Figure 27–27

1. Open the Layer Properties Manager and using (New Layer), create the layers specified in the following table, as shown for few layers in Figure 27–28.

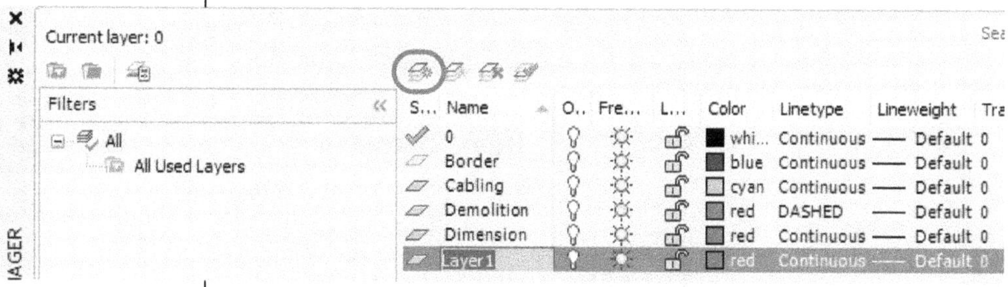

Figure 27–28

*The DASHED linetype is not listed in the Select Linetype dialog box. Select **Load...** and then **DASHED** in the list.*

Layer Name	Color	Linetype	Other
Border	blue	Continuous	
Cabling	cyan	Continuous	
Demolition	red	DASHED	
Dimensions	red	Continuous	
Doors	yellow	Continuous	
Electrical	green	Continuous	
Equipment	green	Continuous	
Furniture	green	Continuous	
HVAC	blue	Continuous	
Notes	cyan	Continuous	
Plumbing	magenta	Continuous	
Titles	blue	Continuous	
Viewports	gray (8)	Continuous	No plot
Walls	white	Continuous	
Windows	yellow	Continuous	

If you have a white background then the white color will display as black in the Select Color dialog box.

- You are using a color-to-lineweight scheme, in which red is the lightest color and white the heaviest. Gray is used to indicate a no plot layer.
- The layers are automatically added to the Layer Control.

2. Close the Layer Properties Manager and verify that all of the layers display in the Layer Control.

Task 3 - Create a page setup.

In this task, you will create a page setup and apply it to a standard layout for the template file, as shown in Figure 27–29.

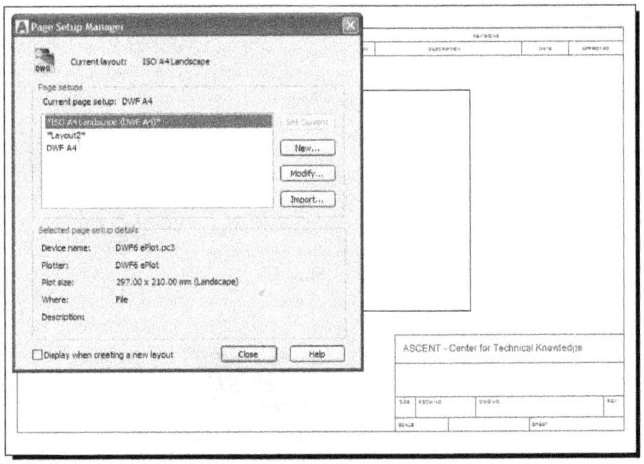

Figure 27–29

1. Switch to **Layout1**. In the Status Bar, right-click on the *Layout* tab and select **Page Setup Manager...**.
2. In the Page Setup Manager, click **New**, enter the name as follows (**DWF A4**) and click **OK**. In the Page Setup dialog box set the remaining information from the table below and click **OK**.

Name:	DWF A4
Printer/plotter:	DWF6 ePlot.pc3
Paper size:	ISO expand A4 (297.00 x 210.00 MM)
Drawing Orientation:	Landscape

3. In the Page Setup Manager, click **Set Current** to apply the setup to **Layout1**. Close the Page Setup Manager.
4. Rename *Layout1* as **ISO A4**.

Task 4 - Add a title block and border.

1. Make the layer **Border** current.
2. Using the **Insert** command, insert **Tblk-A4-M.dwg** from the practice folder. Use **0,0,0** for the insertion point.
3. Select the viewport and change it to the layer **Viewports**.
4. Resize the viewport as required to fit title block inside the border.
5. Center the circle in the viewport.
6. In the Status Bar, set the *Viewport Scale* to **1:100**. The circle is very small at this scale.
7. Save the drawing.

Task 5 - Save a template.

In this task you will save a drawing file as a template, as shown in Figure 27–30.

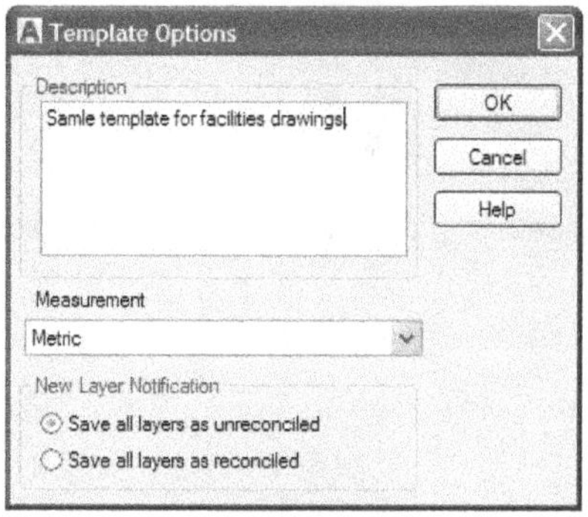

Figure 27–30

1. Switch to the **Model** layout.
2. Erase everything in the drawing, zoom all, and set the current layer to **Walls**.
3. In the Application Menu, select **Save As>Drawing Template**. In the Save Drawing As dialog box, navigate to your practice files folder. Verify that the *Files of type* is set to **AutoCAD Drawing Template (*.dwt)**. For the name, verify that **AEC-Facilities.dwt** is already displayed. Click **Save** to continue.
4. In the Template Options dialog box, enter the description **Sample template for facilities drawings** and verify that **Metric** is selected as the *Measurement*. Click **OK** to finish.
5. Close the template file.
6. Start a new drawing based on **AEC-Facilities.dwt**, which you saved in the practice files folder.
7. Verify that the settings you built into the template (units, layers, and layouts) work in the new drawing.
8. Close the file without saving changes.

Chapter Review Questions

1. Which objects should be set in the template file?
   a. Layers
   b. Polygons
   c. Constraints
   d. Polylines
2. Which of the following is controlled by the Drawing Limits?
   a. The drawing precision.
   b. The extents of the area where you intend to draw.
   c. The scale of the drawing.
   d. The maximum number of objects added in the drawing.
3. Changing the Units Precision in a drawing changes the size of objects that you have drawn.
   a. True
   b. False
4. When creating a template file, you want to add custom layouts. Which of the following commands enables you to define the printer, paper size, and plot scale for a layout?
   a. **Page Setup**
   b. **Plotter Setup**
   c. **Layout Setup**
5. Which command enables you to create a template file?
   a. **Template**
   b. **New**
   c. **Save As**
   d. **Open**

Command Summary

Button	Command	Location
	**Layer Properties Manager**	• **Ribbon:** *Home* tab>Layers panel or *View* tab>Palettes panel • **Command Prompt:** layer or LA
N/A	**Limits**	• **Command Prompt:** limits
	**New**	• **Quick Access Toolbar** • **Command Prompt:** qnew
	**Page Setup Manager**	• **Ribbon:** *Output* tab>Plot panel • **Application Menu:** Print>Page Setup • **Shortcut Menu:** (*right-click on Model tab or Layout tab*) Page Setup Manager • **Command Prompt:** pagesetup
	**Save As**	• **Application Menu:** Save As • **Command Prompt:** saveas
	**Scale List**	• **Ribbon:** *Annotate* tab>Annotation Scaling panel • **Command Prompt:** scalelistedit
	**Units**	• **Application Menu:** Drawing Utilities>Units • **Command Prompt:** units or UN
	**Zoom All**	• **Ribbon:** *View* tab>Navigate 2D panel • **Navigation Bar:** Zoom All • **Command Prompt:** zoom+a or ZA

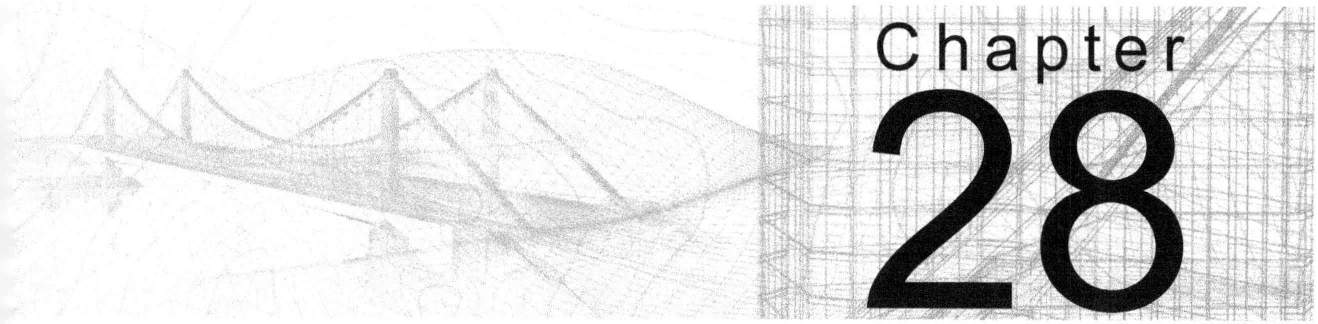

Advanced Layouts

In this chapter you learn how to work with named views, create multiple viewports, create additional viewports, add layer overrides in viewports, and modify annotative scales.

Learning Objectives in this Chapter

- Create viewport configurations and named views of specific areas in a drawing.
- Modify a viewport by removing portions so that it displays more clearly in the layout.
- Override layer properties in a viewport and freeze one or multiple layers in a drawing.
- Control the display of objects in viewports.
- Modify annotative object scales.

28.1 Creating and Using Named Views

If you are working on a large complex drawing, you might want to break it into views that you can readily access in both Model Space and in the Paper Space viewports.

The **View Manager** command (shown in Figure 28–1), stores areas of the drawing under specific names. For example, you can use named views to define a view of each quadrant in a map, or an area in a large mechanical assembly or architectural plan. These named views can easily be restored in the drawing area.

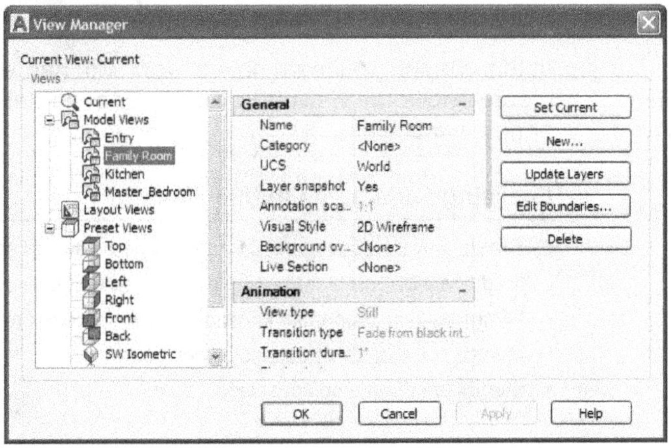

Figure 28–1

- In a large or complex drawing, named views provide a faster method of display control than the **Zoom** command.

*The Views panel is not displayed by default. You need to right-click anywhere in the View tab and select **Show Panels>Views** to display the panel.*

- Once named views have been created, you can access them in the list in the *View* tab>Views panel as shown in Figure 28–2.

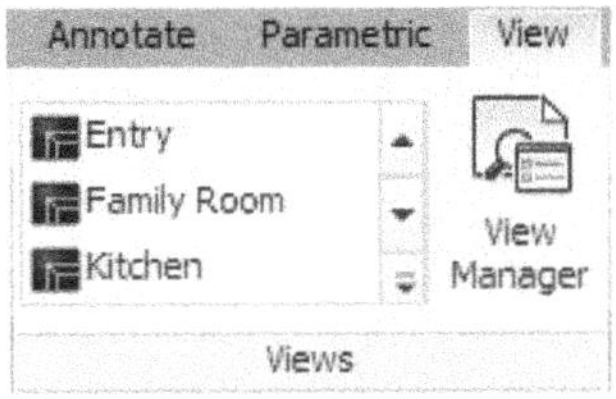

Figure 28–2

How To: Create a Named View

In the AutoCAD LT® software, the ***Shot Properties*** *and* ***ShowMotion*** *commands are not available. The* ***View Manager*** *command opens the New View dialog box.*

In the AutoCAD LT software, the New View dialog box contains the View Name field, and the Boundary and Settings areas. In the Settings area, only the ***Save layer snapshot with view*** *option and UCS drop-down list are available.*

1. In the *View* tab>Views panel, click (View Manager).
2. In the View Manager dialog box, click **New...**.
3. In the New View / Shot Properties dialog box, type a name in the *View name:* field, as shown in Figure 28–3.
4. The *View type* should be set to **Still**, as this option is typical for 2D views. The other *View type* options relate to 3D features.

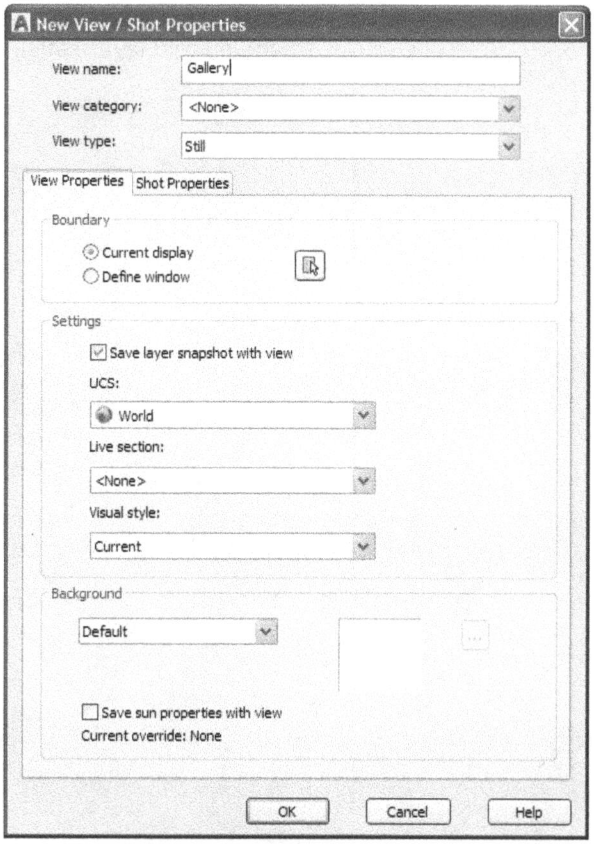

Figure 28–3

5. In the *Boundary* area, select the **Current display** option to save the current screen view, or select the **Define window** option to define a different view by clicking (Define view window).
6. In the *Settings* area, select whether to save the layer snapshot with the view.
7. Click **OK** to create the view.

- The view can be defined to store the current layer settings (On/Off, Freeze/Thaw, etc.), so that these layers are automatically displayed when the view is restored.
- After a view has been defined, you can modify its boundaries by selecting it in the list and clicking **Edit Boundaries....** The current view area is then highlighted. Select two points on screen to define a new area and press <Enter>.
- Views that store layer settings are marked **Yes** in the *Layer snapshot* under General in the View Manager dialog box. You can select a view in the list and click **Update Layers** to save the current layer settings with the view.

28.2 Advanced Viewport Options

To be more efficient in the creation of layouts, you can use previously created Named Views of your model as the basis for Viewports in a layout. You can also modify the shape of existing viewports, as shown in Figure 28–4.

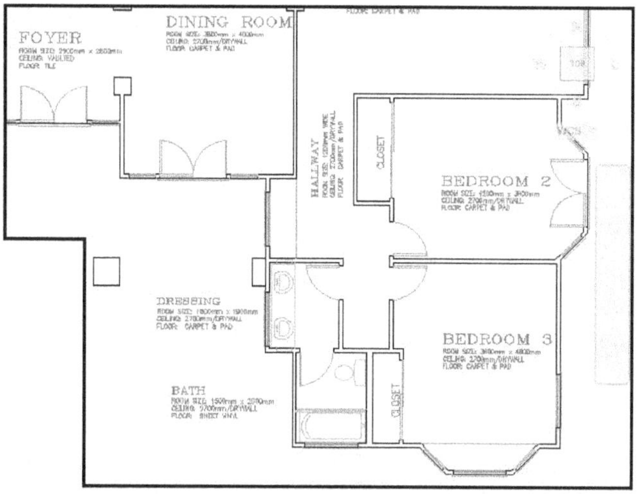

Figure 28–4

Creating Viewports from Named Views

You are required to be in one of the layouts to display the Layout tab in the Ribbon.

The Viewports dialog box enables you to select Named Views to use as the basis for new viewports in a layout. You can create single or multiple Named View Viewports at the same time.

How To: Use Named Views as Viewports

1. Verify that you are in an active layout.
2. Set the layer to which you want to add the viewports to be current.
3. In the *Layout* tab>Layout Viewports panel, click  (Named).
4. In the Viewports dialog box, select the *New Viewports* tab.
5. In the *Standard viewports* area, select the standard viewport configuration that you want to use. If required, set the **Viewport Spacing**.

6. In the *Preview* area, select one of the Views as shown in Figure 28–5. The Preview View is highlighted.

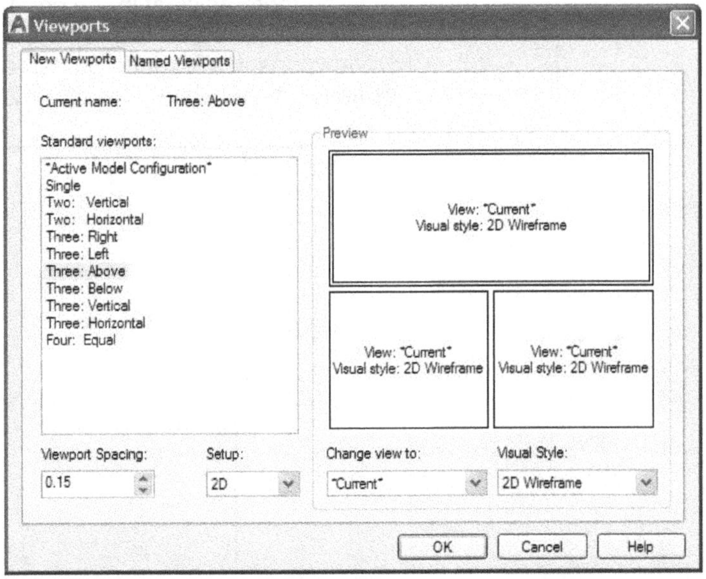

Figure 28–5

*By default, **2D** puts the current view in all of the viewports. **3D** puts standard 3D views (Top, Front, and SE Isometric) in the new viewports.*

7. In the Change view to drop-down list, select a Named View (if any have been saved), as shown in Figure 28–6, to display in that Viewport location.

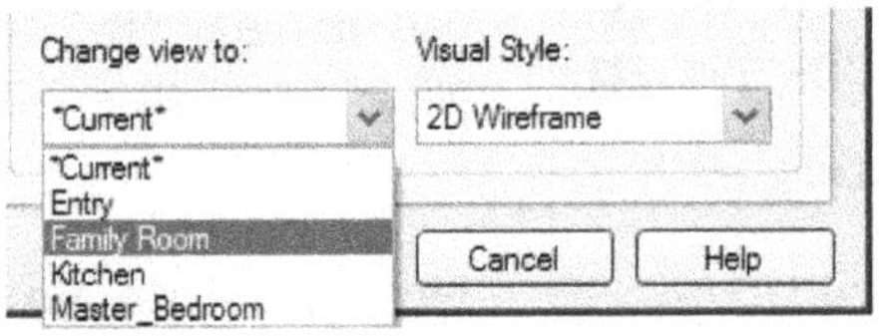

Figure 28–6

8. The view name displays in the *Preview* area, as shown in Figure 28–7.

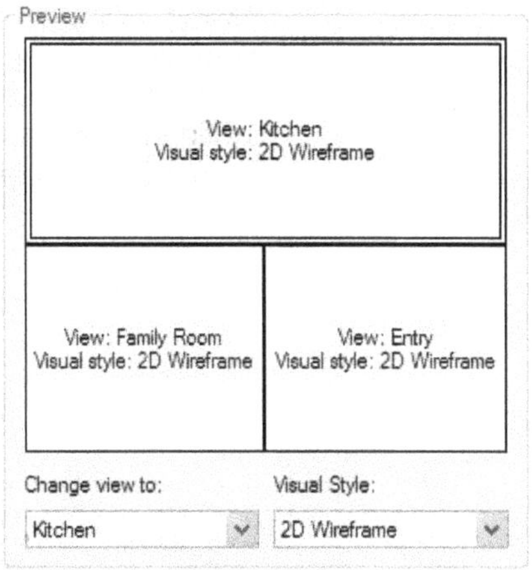

Figure 28–7

In the AutoCAD LT software, the Visual Styles drop-down list is not available.

9. The Visual Style can be preselected if you are working in 3D.
10. Click **OK** to continue.
11. If you are working in a layout, you are prompted to select two corners or to use fit to place all of the viewports on the sheet.

- The *Named Viewports* tab enables you to restore the saved configurations of Model Space viewports. However, the configuration of viewports in a layout cannot be saved.
- The Viewports dialog box works in both Model Space (for *tiled* viewports) and Paper Space or Layout mode (for *floating* viewports).

Hint: Model Space Viewports

Model Space can also be divided into viewports, but only for viewing. For example, if you have a very complex drawing you might need to display multiple close-up views at the same time as shown in Figure 28–8. The viewport that is currently active is highlighted with a blue border. You can drag the edges of the viewports to resize them.

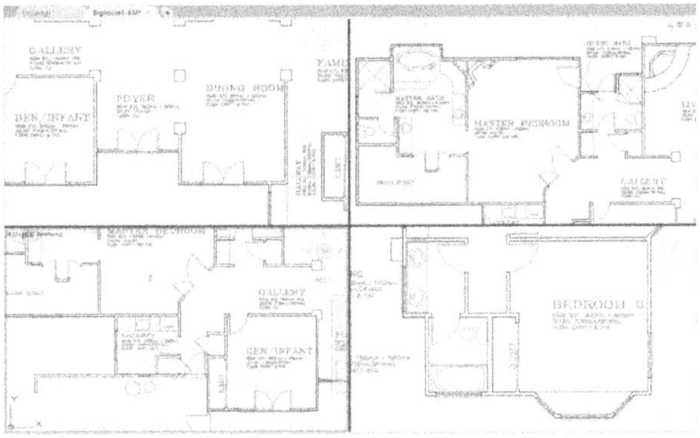

Figure 28–8

In Model Space, you can use **Named** in the *View* tab>Model Viewports panel to create a new viewport configuration.

However, it is easier to expand (Viewport Configuration) in the *View* tab>Model Viewports panel and select the required arrangement, as shown in Figure 28–9.

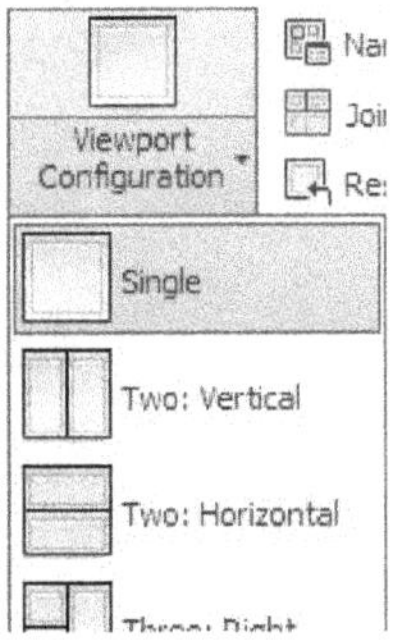

Figure 28–9

Clipping Viewports

You can remove any portions of a viewport that are not required, or make its shape fit better in the available layout space. This is most effective if you have already created the viewport with the correct scale and view of the drawing.

How To: Clip a Viewport

1. In the *Layout* tab>Layout Viewports panel, click (Clip).
2. Select the viewport that you want to clip.
3. Select a clipping object (which has already been created) or press <Enter> to draw a polygonal object, as shown in Figure 28–10.

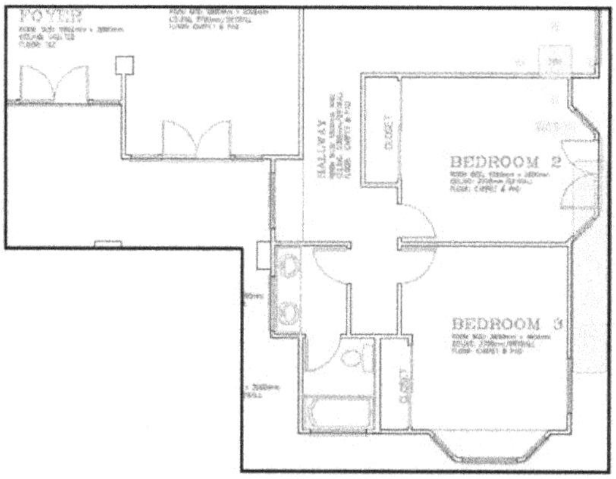

Figure 28–10

- Use the **Delete** option to remove the clipping boundary and restore the original viewport.
- If the clipping boundary extends outside the current viewport boundary, the viewport is extended in that direction.
- You can reclip a viewport without needing to delete the old clip boundary first.
- You can also change the shape of a polygonal viewport (without clipping) by using grips to stretch the vertices to new locations.

28.3 Layer Overrides in Viewports

When you are working in viewports, you might want to modify the layers that display in the various viewports, as shown in Figure 28–11. You can modify layers per viewport and change their color, linetype, lineweight, and plot style using the Layer Properties Manager. To create the viewport specific changes, you need to be working in a *Layout* tab.

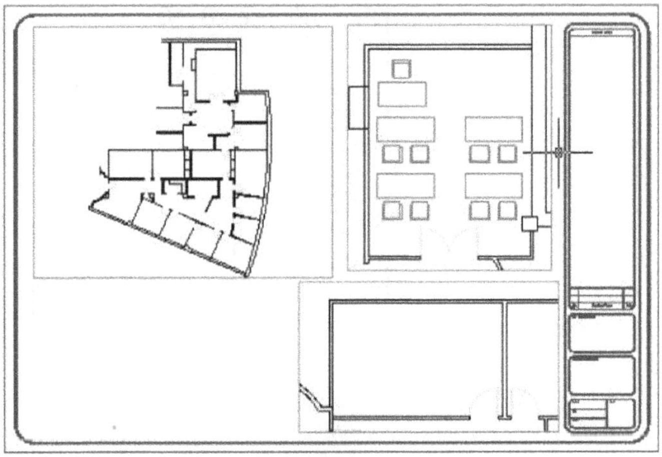

Figure 28–11

Overriding Layer Properties in Viewports

You can use the Layer Properties Manager to change layer properties (such as color, linetype, and lineweight) in a single viewport without the change being made in other viewports. The changes only affect the current viewport and not the model or other viewports, as shown in Figure 28–12.

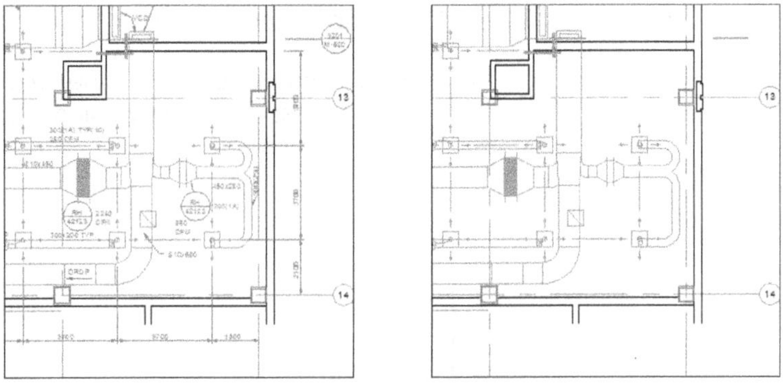

Figure 28–12

- Viewport specific settings include: **New VP Freeze**, **VP Freeze**, **VP Color**, **VP Linetype**, **VP Lineweight**, **VP Transparency**, and **VP Plot Style**. As the name specifies, the **VP Freeze** can be used to freeze/thaw a layer in only one viewport. Similarly, **VP Color** enables you to change the color of a layer in a single (current) viewport. The **New VP Freeze** tool can be used to freeze/thaw a layer in any subsequent viewport that you might create and does not affect the current viewport.

- To create these changes, you must be in a Layout tab and working through a viewport.

How To: Modify Layer Properties in a Viewport

You might need to extend the Layer Properties Manager to display all the columns.

1. In a *Layout* tab, double-click in a viewport to enter Model Space.
2. Open Layer Properties Manager and modify the viewport properties as required. They are highlighted as they are modified, making it easy to see the changes, as shown in Figure 28–13.

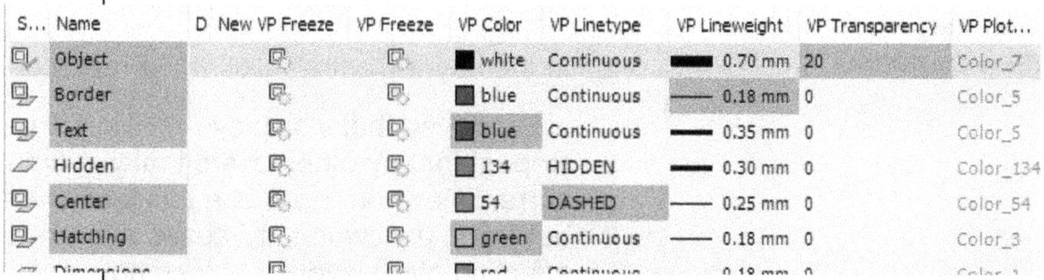

Figure 28–13

3. These changes are immediately and automatically reflected in the viewport.

- The layers also highlight in the Layer Control in the Layers panel as shown in Figure 28–14.

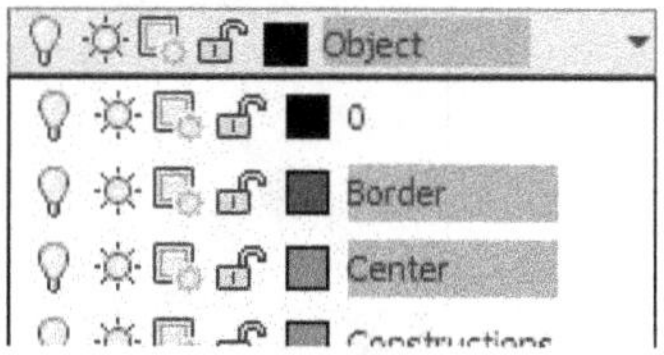

Figure 28–14

- The Viewport Overrides layer filter is automatically created when you use viewport overrides, as shown in Figure 28–15.

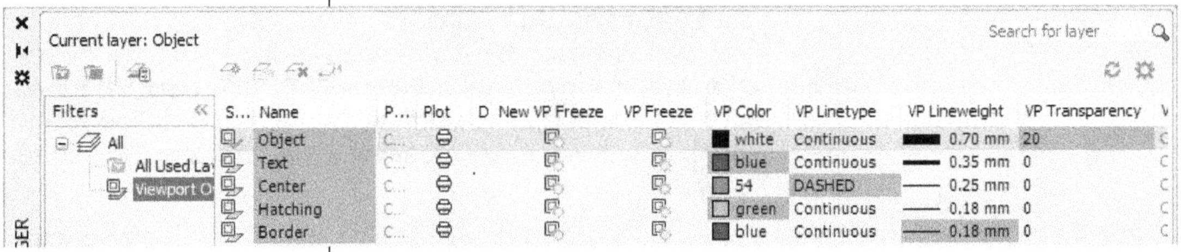

Figure 28–15

Freezing Layers in Viewports

If you freeze a layer or toggle it off using the standard tools, it becomes hidden in all of the viewports.

The **VP Freeze** tool is also available in the Layer Control for easily freezing a layer in a viewport. In the Layer Control, use (Freeze or Thaw in current viewport) to freeze/thaw a layer in only one viewport.

How To: Freeze a Layer in a Viewport

1. Make the viewport active in which you want to freeze the layer.
2. In the Layer Control, click (Freeze or thaw in current viewport) so that it displays for the required layer.
3. Repeat for any other layers that you want to freeze in the current viewport.If you use this tool when you are in a layout but not in a viewport, it freezes a layer in the layout without affecting other layouts. It does not affect the layer display in any viewports when used this way.

Practice 28a Viewports and Named Views

Practice Objectives

- Create and use named views.
- Modify an existing viewport and remove a viewport clip.
- Apply viewport overrides.

Estimated time for completion: 25 minutes

In this practice, you will create and use named views using the Viewport Manager and the **Viewports** command. You will set up multiple viewports based on Named Views. You will remove a viewport clip using the **Clip** command. You will also freeze layers in individual viewports and apply layer overrides to the color settings for layers in a viewport.

Task 1 - Create and use named views.

In this task you will create and restore views in a drawing.

1. Open **Office-M.dwg** from your practice files folder.
2. Zoom in on the stairway in the upper right corner, as shown in Figure 28–16.

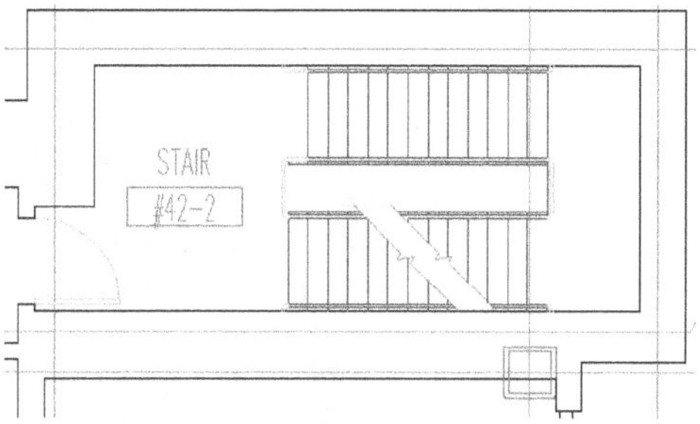

Figure 28–16

In the View tab, if the Views panel is not displayed by default, right-click anywhere in the View tab and select ***Show Panels>Views****.*

In the AutoCAD LT software, the ***Named Views*** *command opens the New View dialog box.*

3. In the *View* tab>Views panel, click (View Manager). The View Manager dialog box opens.
4. Click **New...** to open the New View / Shot Properties dialog box.
5. In the *View name* field, type **Stairs** and verify that the **Save layer snapshot with view** option is selected.
6. Accept the other default settings and click **OK**. Click **OK** to close the View Manager dialog box.

7. Zoom to display the entire drawing, and toggle off the layer **HVAC**.

8. Open the View Manager dialog box again and click **New...**. Type **Elevators** for the view name.

9. Verify that the **Save layer snapshot with view** option is selected.

10. In the *Boundary* area, click (Define view window). The drawing area displays.

11. Use **Zoom** and **Pan** to display the two elevators in your drawing window. Select two corner points to define the view, as shown in Figure 28–17, and press <Enter> to return to the dialog box.

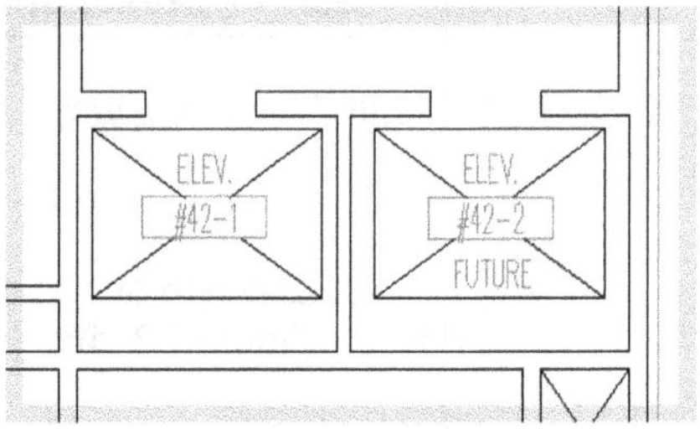

Figure 28–17

12. Click **OK** to complete the view creation. Click **OK** again to close the View Manager dialog box.

13. In the *View* tab>Views panel, use the View Control to select the view **Stairs,** as shown in Figure 28–18. The stairs area displays in the drawing window. Zoom out and note that the **HVAC** layer is toggled on (green HVAC components display).

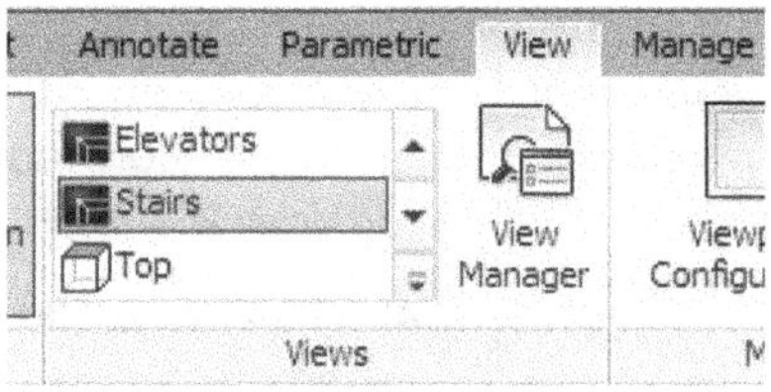

Figure 28–18

14. In the View Control, select the view **Elevators**. Zoom out and note that the layer **HVAC** is toggled off.

Task 2 - Create multiple viewports from Named Views.

In this task you will create multiple viewports based on Named Views using the Viewports dialog box as shown in Figure 28–19.

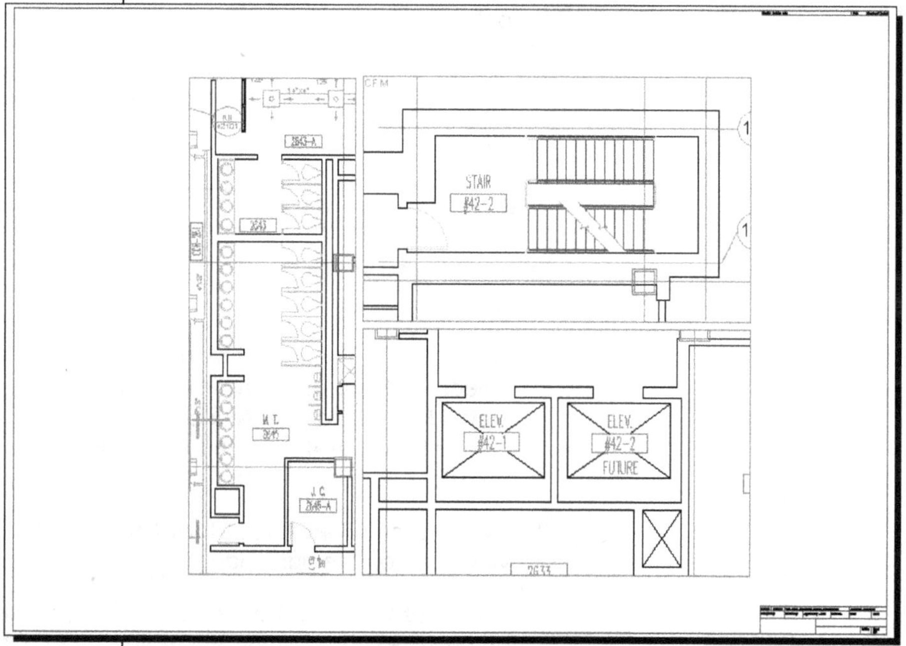

Figure 28–19

1. Switch to the **A-401 Detail Plans** layout and set the current layer to **Viewports**.
2. In the *Layout* tab>Layout Viewports panel, click (Named). In the Viewports dialog box, select the *New Viewports* tab. In the *Standard viewports* area, select **Three: Left**, and set the *Viewport Spacing* to **10** (distances in this drawing are in millimeters).
3. In the *Preview* area, click in the top right viewport. In the Change view to drop-down list, select **Stairs**. Click in the bottom right viewport and change the *View* to **Elevators**. Click **OK** to close the Viewports dialog box.
4. Select two corners to place the three viewports in the layout, as shown in Figure 28–19.

5. Activate the top right viewport, and in the Status Bar, scale it to **1:20**. It automatically scales the top right viewport to **1:20.**
6. Activate the viewport on the left scale it to **1:30** and pan inside it to display the restrooms located near the center left of the drawing. Use grips to make this viewport narrower to only display the restrooms, as shown in Figure 28–19.
7. Use grips to make the other 2 viewports wider. Move the three viewports as required to center them better in the layout.

Task 3 - Clip a viewport.

In this task you will clip an existing viewport using the **Polygonal** option.

1. Copy the existing layout by right-clicking on the tab and selecting **Move or Copy**. In the dialog box select **A-401 Detail Plans** and **Create a copy**. Click **OK**. The new layout is placed before **A-401 Detail Plans.** Rename the new layout as **A-201 1st Floor Plan**.
2. Switch to the **A-201 1st Floor Plan** layout. Delete the two viewports on the right side.
3. Use grips to resize the remaining viewport so that it fills most of the sheet. Display the entire floor plan at a *scale* of **1:50**. Pan to center the drawing in the viewport.
4. In the *Layout* tab>Layout Viewports panel, click (Clip).
5. Select the viewport, press <Enter> to select the **Polygonal** option. Starting from the lower left corner of the viewport, select points to define a clipping boundary that cuts out the bottom right portion of the view, as shown in Figure 28–20. Select the **Close** option to complete the polygon.
6. In Paper Space, draw a circle with a *radius* of **150** in the area cleared (right bottom corner area) by clipping the other viewport.
7. In the *Layout* tab>Layout Viewports panel, expand (Viewports, Rectangular) and click (Viewports, Object) and select the circle. Scale this *circular viewport* to **1:30** and pan in it to display one room of the plan, as shown in Figure 28–20.

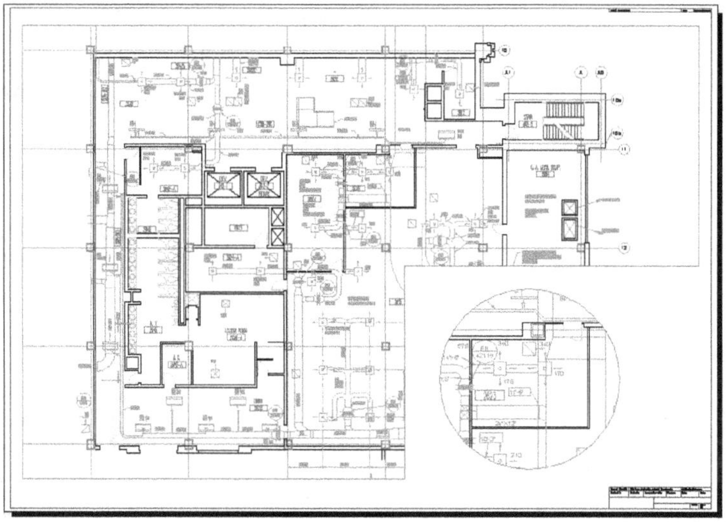

Figure 28–20

Task 4 - Remove viewport clip and apply viewport overrides.

In this task you will remove a viewport clip, freeze layers in individual viewports, and apply layer overrides to the color settings for layers in a viewport, as shown in Figure 28–21.

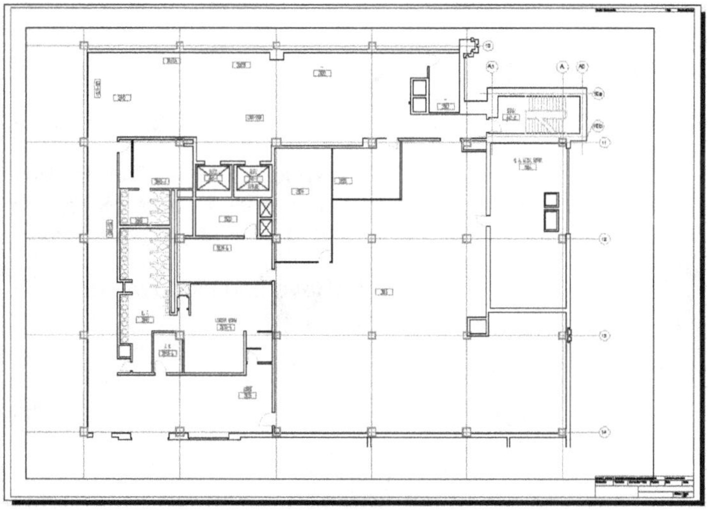

Figure 28–21

1. Copy the **A-201 1st Floor Plan** layout and rename it as **H-201 1st HVAC Floor Plan**.

2. Switch to the **H-201 1st HVAC Floor Plan** layout.

3. Delete the circular viewport.

4. Select the large clipped viewport. Start the **Clip Viewport** command. At the *Select clipping object* prompt, select the **Delete** option (as shown in Figure 28–22) to remove the clipping boundary. It becomes a rectangular area again.

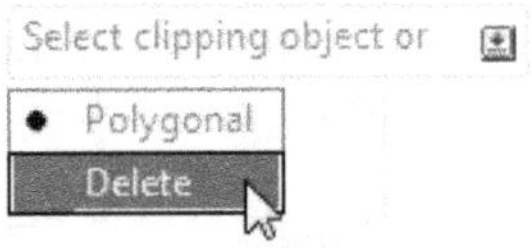

Figure 28–22

5. Activate the large viewport. Freeze the layer **HVAC** in this viewport, so that the HVAC components do not only display in this viewport.

6. Open the Layer Properties Manager and change the *VP Color* for the layer **Stair** to **Green**, as shown in Figure 28–23, so that the stairs are only green in this viewport.

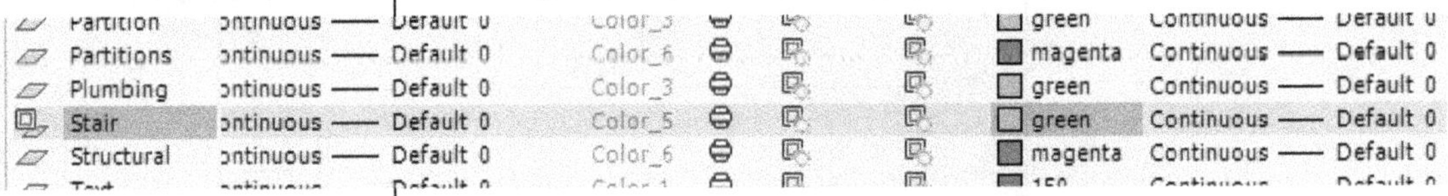

Figure 28–23

7. Switch to the **A-201 1st Floor Plan** layout. It should display differently from the **H-201 1st HVAC Floor Plan** layout. The **HVAC** layer should be visible and the stairs should be blue.

8. Save and close the drawing.

28.4 Additional Annotative Scale Features

The Annotation Scale is connected to the Viewport Scale. Therefore, annotative objects, such as dimensions and text, display in viewports that have the same scale. You can add Annotation Scales to objects, enabling them to display in viewports of different scales. This ensures that all of the relevant information always displays at the correct scale and in the required viewports. For example, for the drawing shown in Figure 28–24, you might want the room names to display in each view, and to display different dimensions for each view.

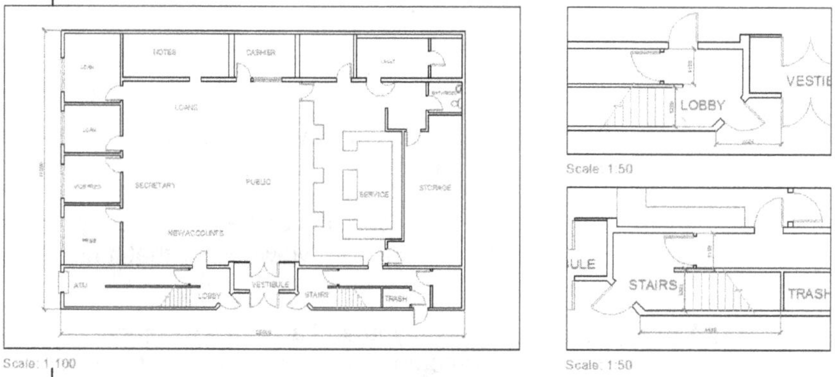

Figure 28–24

- When you change a Viewport Scale, the annotation objects displayed in the viewport change as well. The display of objects depends on what the annotation visibility is set to and whether or not the scale is automatically added to the object.

	Annotation Visibility: When toggled **Off**, only annotative objects with the current scale display. It is recommended that you use this option most of the time. It is what is plotted.
	Annotation Visibility: When toggled **On**, annotative objects for all of the scales display. Use when you need to add or remove an annotative object to the current scale.
	Add scales to annotative objects when the annotation scale changes Off: When toggled **Off**, annotation scales are not automatically added to objects in the viewport.
	Add scales to annotative objects when the annotation scale changes On: When **On**, annotation objects in the drawing update to match the new annotation scale.

- When you add a scale to an object, a scale representation is created. When you select an annotative object that has more than one scale, all of its scale representations display, as shown in Figure 28–25. There is no limit to the number of scales that can be added to an object, but too many scales can be confusing when you try to grip edit the object.

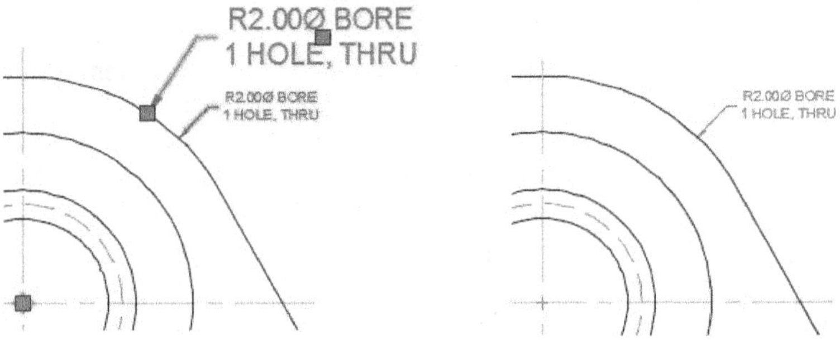

Figure 28–25

- If you modify the information contained in the annotation, it updates in all of the scale representations.
- You can grip edit each scale representation separately in its associated viewport so that it fits the location.

Modifying Annotative Object Scales

When you add annotative objects to a viewport, they automatically use the scale of the viewport. If you need to change the scale or move annotative objects out of a viewport, you can modify the scales associated with the objects or with the viewport, as shown in Figure 28–26.

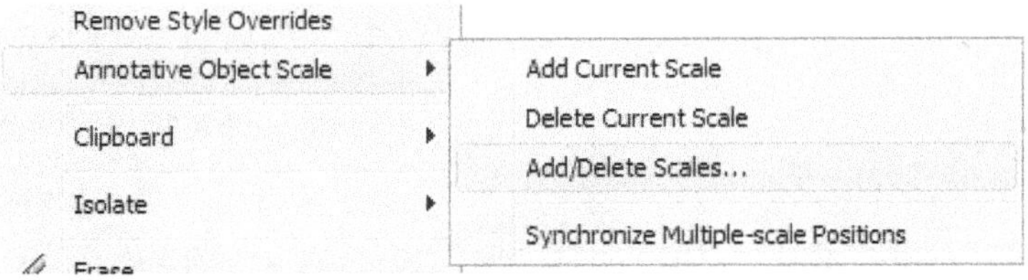

Figure 28–26

- These tools are available in the *Annotate* tab>Annotation Scaling panel or when you right-click on an annotative object.

- To display an annotative object in several viewports that use different scales, use **Add/Delete Scales** under **Annotative Object Scale** in the shortcut menu. This opens the Annotation Object Scale dialog box, where you can click **Add** and then add all the other annotative scales that are used in each viewport.

If you do not want an annotative object to display in the current viewport, but do want it to be visible in a viewport at a different scale, **Delete** the current scale.

If you want to include an annotative object in your viewport that is not displayed in the current viewport scale, toggle on **Annotation Visibility** in the Status Bar to display all of the scale representations of the objects. Then **Add** the current scale.

If you want to add or delete multiple scales, click this icon in the Annotation Scaling panel to open the Annotation Object Scale dialog box.

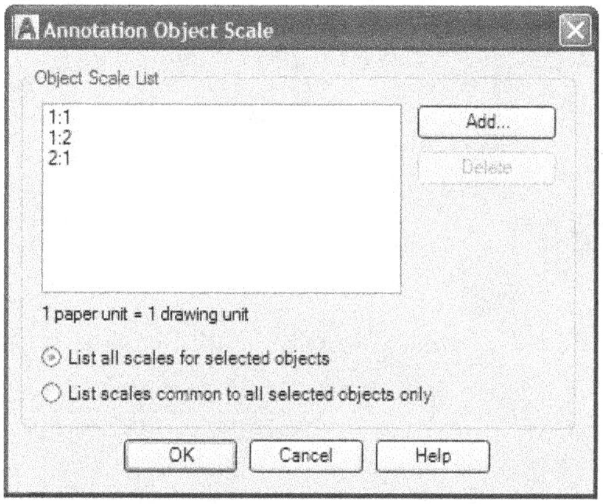

- You can change the locations of individual scale representations, but you might need to have them all return to one position. In the Annotation Scaling panel, click  (Sync Scale Positions) to move all of the related representations to the same location as the selected item.

Practice 28b Additional Annotative Scale Features

Practice Objectives

- Create annotative styles and annotative hatching.
- Control the visibility of annotation objects.

Estimated time for completion: 15 minutes

In this practice, you will specify annotative styles for text, dimensions, and multileaders. You will create annotative hatching using the Hatch command. You will then create viewports at different scales and add annotative objects to them, as shown in Figure 28–27.

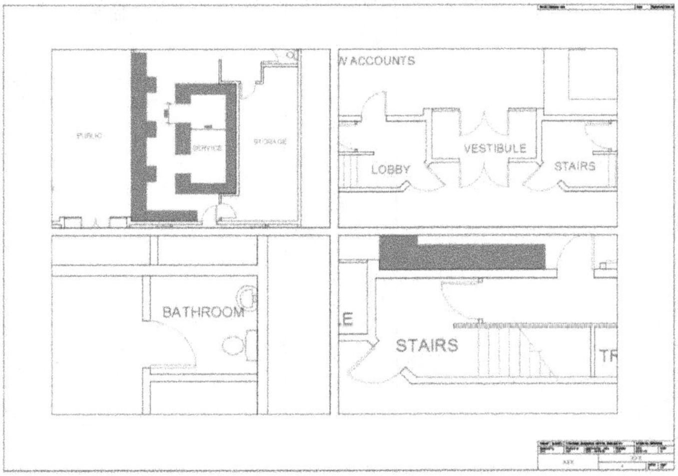

Figure 28–27

Task 1 - Define Annotative Text and Dimensions.

1. Open **Service-AM.dwg** from your practice files folder.
2. In the *Annotate* tab, set the *Dimension style* to **Architectural-MM** (an annotative style), as shown in Figure 28–28.
3. Set the *Text style* to **Hand** (an annotative style), as shown in Figure 28–28.

4. Set the *Multileader style* to **Annotative**, as shown in Figure 28–28.

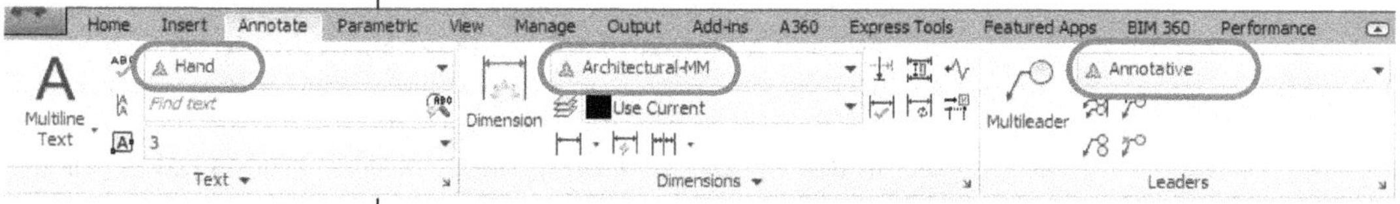

Figure 28–28

5. Switch to the **ISO A1** layout tab, which contains four viewports.
6. Select each viewport in Paper Space by clicking on the viewport border. Confirm the Viewport Scale in the Status Bar. They should be as follows: *Service*: **1:50**, *Vestibule*: **1:30**, *Bathroom*: **1:16**, and *Stairs*: **1:20**.
7. Click (Lock/Unlock Viewport) to lock the Viewport Scales for each viewport.
8. Set the layer **Dimensions** to be current. Double-click in the viewport that displays the Service area and add the dimensions and text shown in Figure 28–29. They only display in the current viewport.

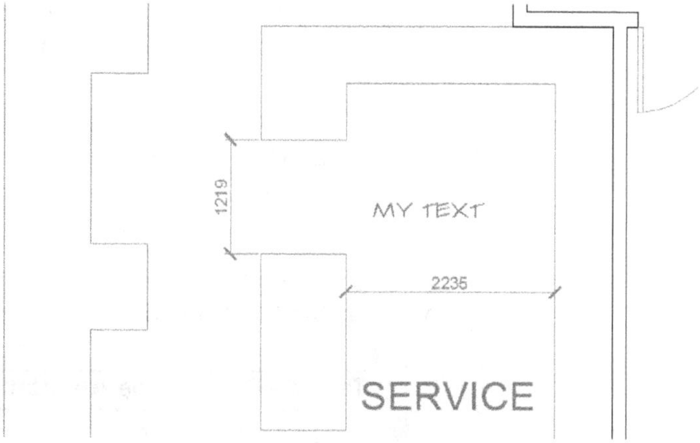

Figure 28–29

Task 2 - Define the annotative hatching.

1. Activate the viewport displaying the Service area, if it is not already active, and set the layer **Hatching** to be current.
2. Start the **Hatch** command.
3. In the *Hatch Creation* contextual tab>Options panel, click (Annotative).
4. Set the *Hatch Pattern* to **ANSI 31** and the *Hatch Pattern Scale* to **1**. Add hatching to the three counter areas inside the Service area viewport.
5. Close the Hatch Creation. The hatching only displays in the current viewport.

Task 3 - Add annotative scales.

1. Select the hatch object that you just created.
2. Right-click on the selected hatching and select **Annotative Object Scale>Add/Delete Scales**. The Annotation Object Scale dialog box opens. The current Annotation Scale displays.
3. Click **Add...** to add the other scales. The Add Scales to Object dialog box opens.
4. Select the *scales* **1:16** and **1:20**. Doing so enables the annotative hatch object to display in the Vestibule viewport and the Bathroom viewport.
5. Click **OK**. The scales display in the Annotation Object Scale dialog box.
6. Click **OK**. The annotation objects (hatches) now display in the Vestibule and Bathroom viewports.

Task 4 - Change the Annotation object display.

1. Switch to the Model tab and note how the annotative objects (text, dimensions, hatch) display.
2. In the Status Bar, click (Annotation Visibility On) to toggle it off. Note that the annotative objects no longer display.
3. Save and close the drawing.

Chapter Review Questions

1. What is the purpose of the View Manager?
   a. To create layouts using different areas of a drawing.
   b. To create a new block using selected objects.
   c. To create a new drawing file using selected objects.
   d. To store areas of a drawing under specified names.
2. It is possible to create a single or multiple Named View viewports at the same time.
   a. True
   b. False
3. What does the (Clip) command do?
   a. Fillets the corners of an existing viewport to make it circular.
   b. Removes the portions of a viewport that are not required.
   c. Joins multiple viewports to create a single one.
   d. Breaks a viewport to create multiple viewports.
4. How can you change the color of a layer in a single (current) viewport?
   a. In the Layer Properties Manager, change the *VP Color* property.
   b. In the Layer Properties Manager, change the *New VP Freeze* property.
   c. In the viewport, switch to Model space and change the color of the layer.
   d. Create a new layer and move the objects to the new layer.

5. If you want to display an annotative object in several viewports that use different scales, what should you do?
    a. Create separate layers for each viewport and put the objects on each layer.
    b. Create annotative styles (dimension, text, etc.) for each viewport.
    c. Use **Add/Delete Scales** to add the scales for each viewport.
    d. Lock each viewport.

Command Summary

Button	Command	Location
	**Clip**	• **Ribbon:** *Layout* tab>Layout Viewports panel • **Command Prompt:** vpclip
	**Named (Paper Space)**	• **Ribbon:** *Layout* tab>Layout Viewports panel • **Command Prompt:** viewports or vports
	**Named (Model Space)**	• **Ribbon:** *View* tab>Model Viewports panel • **Command Prompt:** viewports or vports
	**View Manager**	• **Ribbon:** *View* tab>Views panel • **Command Prompt:** view or V
	**Viewport Configuration Control**	• **Ribbon:** *View* tab>Model Viewports panel

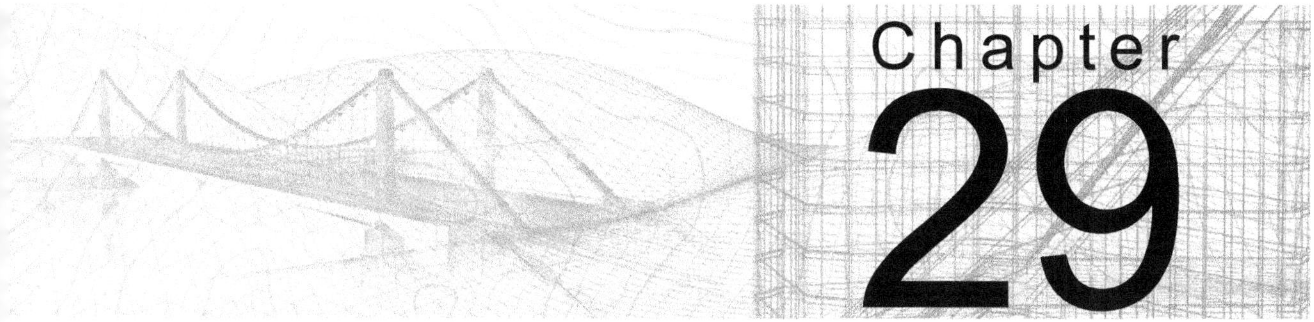

Annotation Styles

In this chapter, you learn how to create annotation styles including Text Styles, Dimension Styles, and Multileader Styles.

Learning Objectives in this Chapter

- Create and modify text, dimensions, and multileader styles.
- Create sub-styles of existing dimension styles.

29.1 Creating Text Styles

When you add text to your drawing, it uses the properties (e.g., height, font, etc.) of the current *text style,* as shown in Figure 29–1. Text styles should be created in the template file so that everyone on the same project uses the same styles. You can create a new style by assigning the height, width, and slant to a text font, or to a typeface design.

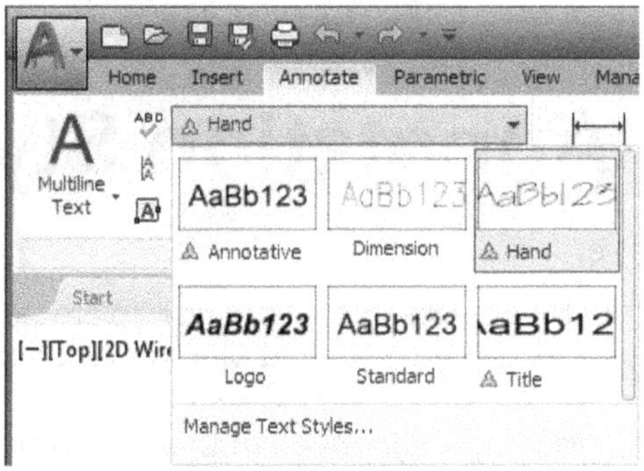

Figure 29–1

- There are two default styles: **Standard** and **Annotative**. You can create other styles as required.
- A variety of font files are available for creating different styles of text. There are two different types of fonts: Truetype fonts (used by most Microsoft Windows software) and AutoCAD® shape fonts. You can use the fonts that the AutoCAD software installs or the other Truetype fonts that were installed with Windows.

How To: Create a Text Style

You can also open the dialog box by clicking the panel arrow in the *Annotate tab>Text panel.*

1. In the *Annotate* tab>Text panel>Text Style list, select **Manage Text Styles...**.
2. In the Text Style dialog box (shown in Figure 29–2), click **New...**. The new style takes on the attributes of the current text style.

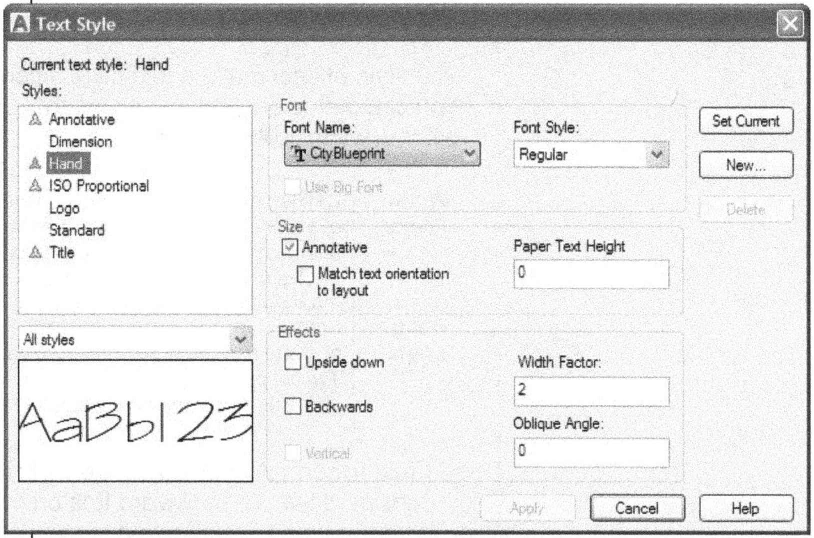

Figure 29–2

3. In the New Text Style dialog box, type a new name and click **OK**.
4. Expand the Font Name drop-down list, select a font (a preview of the font displays in the *Preview* area). For some fonts, you can also specify a Font Style (such as bold or italic).
5. Select the **Annotative** option if you want the text style to scale per viewport. You can also set a default height for the style, but this is typically left at **0** so that you can use one style for different sizes of text.
6. In the *Effects* area, set up the required properties.
7. Click **Apply** to continue working in the dialog box or **Close** to close the dialog box. The style that was created is now the current style.

- You can change the current style in the Text Style Control in the *Home* tab>expanded Annotation panel, the *Annotate* tab>Text panel, or the *Text Editor* contextual tab>Style panel when you have started the **Multiline Text** command.

- You can change the style of existing text by selecting the text object and then selecting a style in the *Home* tab>Annotation panel or *Annotate* tab>Text panel.

- If you modify an annotative style, you need to use **annoupdate** to update any existing objects to match the revised annotative style.

Style Effects

The style effects make a text style different from a standard font. You can define several text styles that use the same font but differ in width, oblique angle, etc.

Width Factor	Defines the character width relative to the height. A width factor of **1** is the default. Numbers greater than one increase the width and numbers less than one decrease the width. Typical width factors are in the range of 0.8 to 1.5.
Oblique Angle	Enables you to slant the lettering. Positive values incline the top of the text to the right and negative values slant it to the left. Typical obliquing angles range from +10 to -10. Angles of +30 and -30 are commonly used to label isometric drawings.

- Text is normally placed horizontally in a drawing. Vertical, upside-down, or backward text orientation can also be defined when creating text styles.

Notes on Text Styles

- The *Preview* displays an image of how your text style is going to be displayed when used in the drawing. All of the effects of a text style are previewed except the height.
- To rename a text style, double-click on the style name. In the Edit box, type the new name.
- To delete a text style, highlight it in the list and click **Delete**. It is only deleted if it is not in use.
- Some TrueType fonts can be filled or outlined. To have them filled in your drawing, you need to set the **textfill** system variable to **ON** (textfill = 1).
- **Match Properties** (in the *Home* tab>Properties panel) enables you to copy the style from one text object to another in your drawing. It is also available in the *Text Editor* contextual tab.

Practice 29a Creating and Using Text Styles

Estimated time for completion: 10 minutes

The color has been changed to black for printing clarity.

Practice Objective

- Create several new text styles.

In this practice, you will define several new text styles using the **Text Style** command, as shown in Figure 29–3.

Figure 29–3

1. Open **AEC-Facilities1-AM.dwg** from your practice files folder. It is an empty file.
2. Make the layer **Notes** active.
3. In the *Annotate* tab>Text panel, note that the active text style is **Standard.**
4. Switch to one of the layouts. Start the **Multiline Text** command. If the preview text (abc) is not visible with the cursor, zoom in until it displays. Place the text **The Standard Style** anywhere in the drawing.
5. In the Text Style list, select **Manage Text Styles...**. Modify the Standard Style and change the *Font Name* to **romans**. Click **Apply** and **Close**. Note how the text you just entered has updated.
6. Open the Text Style dialog box again and click **New**.
7. Create a new style named **Title**. Set the *Font Name* to **Arial**, the *Font Style* to **Bold** and the *Width Factor* to **1.5**. Click **Apply** to save the changes.
8. Create another new text style named **Hand2**. For the *Font Name*, select **CityBlueprint**. Set the *Width Factor* to **1.5**. Click **Apply** to save the changes.
9. Create another new text style named **Dimensions**. For the *Font Name*, select **romans**. Set the *Width Factor* to **0.8**. Click **Apply** to save the changes and click **Close**.
10. Make each style current and then add text to the drawing using a text string to test the styles.
11. Set the current style to **Hand**. Erase all of the text and save the drawing.

29.2 Creating Dimension Styles

The dimension style controls all aspects of how your dimensions display (type and size of arrows, type of units displayed, text specifications, text placement, etc.). You might need to have several styles in a drawing to display different information, as shown in Figure 29–4. For example, in mechanical drawings you might have one style with decimal units that displays two decimal places of precision, another that displays three decimal places, and a third that displays both English and Metric units at the same time.

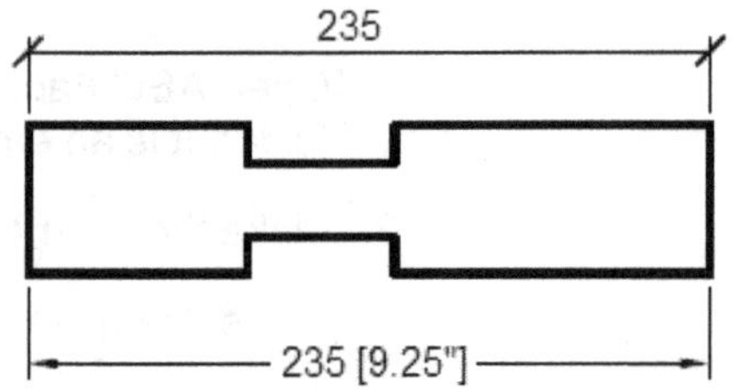

Figure 29–4

- You can set the current dimension style in the Dimension Style Control in the *Home* tab>Annotation panel or *Annotate* tab>Dimensions panel.
- There are two default styles: **Standard** and **Annotative**. You can create other styles as required.

You can also open the dialog box by clicking the panel arrow in the *Annotate tab> Dimensions panel.*

How To: Create a Dimension Style

1. In the *Annotate* tab>Dimensions panel>Dimension Style list, select **Manage Dimension Styles...**.
2. Click **New...** in the Dimension Style Manager, as shown in Figure 29–5.

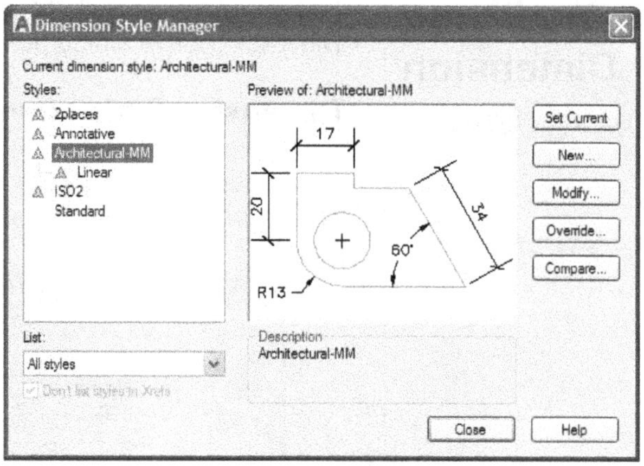

Figure 29–5

3. The Create New Dimension Style dialog box opens, as shown in Figure 29–6. In the Start With drop-down list, select a style to use as a template. In the *New Style Name* field, type a new style name and then select the **Annotative** option as required. Click **Continue**.

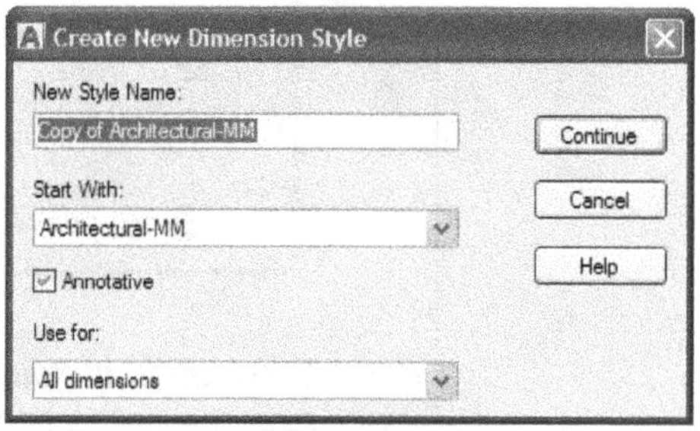

Figure 29–6

4. Modify the tabs as required and click **OK**.
5. If you want to make the new style current, double-click on its name in the *Styles* area or select it and click **Set Current**.
6. Click **Close**.

- All of the distances and sizes specified for the dimension style should be at their final plotted distance or size.

Modifying Dimension Styles

In the Dimension Sytle Manager, click **Modify** to open the Modify Dimension Style dialog box.

Dimension Style Lines Tab

The *Lines* tab controls the appearance of the dimension lines and extension lines, as shown in Figure 29–7.

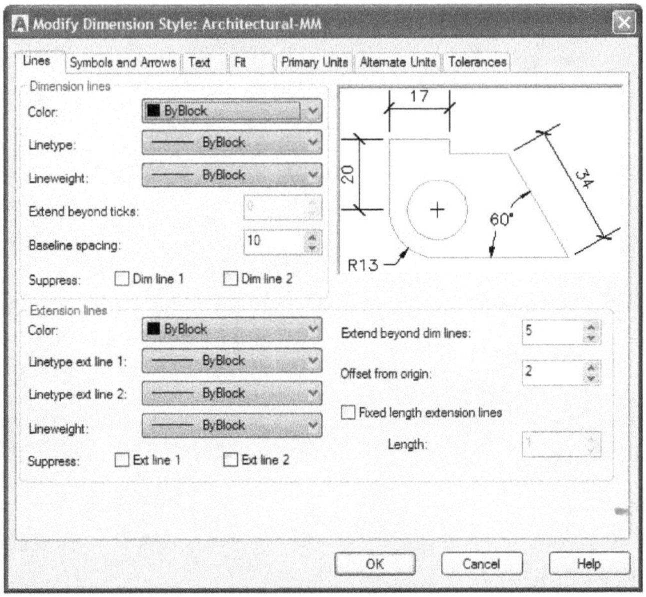

Figure 29–7

- *Color* and *Lineweight* are set to **ByBlock** by default. This is essentially the same as **ByLayer**. The dimension elements use the color and linetype of the current layer.
- *Extend beyond ticks* only applies if ticks are used rather than arrowheads.
- *Baseline spacing* is used for baseline dimensions that are applied with the **Baseline** or **Quick Dimension** commands.
- *Offset from origin* controls the size of the gap between the object and the start of the extension line.
- *Fixed length extension lines* controls how far the line reaches from the dimension line toward the dimensioned object.

Dimension Style Symbols and Arrows Tab

The *Symbols and Arrows* tab controls the size and style of the arrowheads on the dimension lines and leaders, and other symbols, such as Center marks (for circles and arcs) or the Arc length symbol, as shown in Figure 29–8.

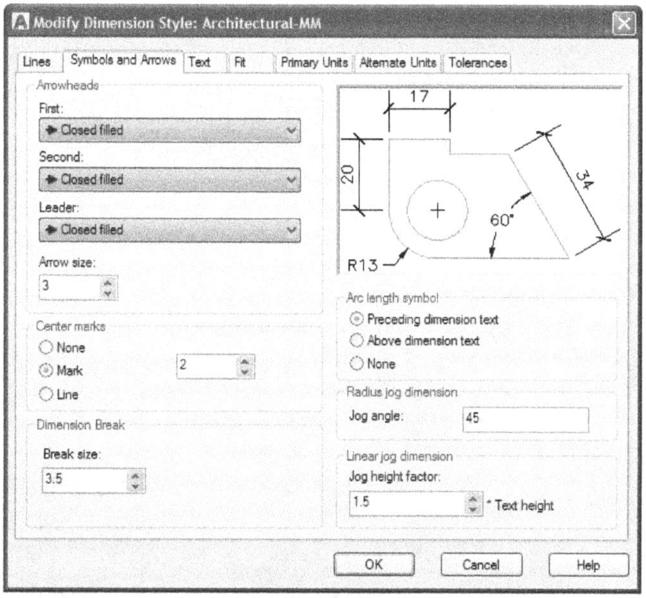

Figure 29–8

- The *Leader* (used for Radius, Diameter, and Angular dimensions) can have a different arrow style from the dimension lines.
- *Center Marks* are used with Radius and Diameter dimensions and the **Center Mark** command.

Dimension Style Text Tab

The *Text* tab controls the placement and appearance of the dimension text, as shown in Figure 29–9.

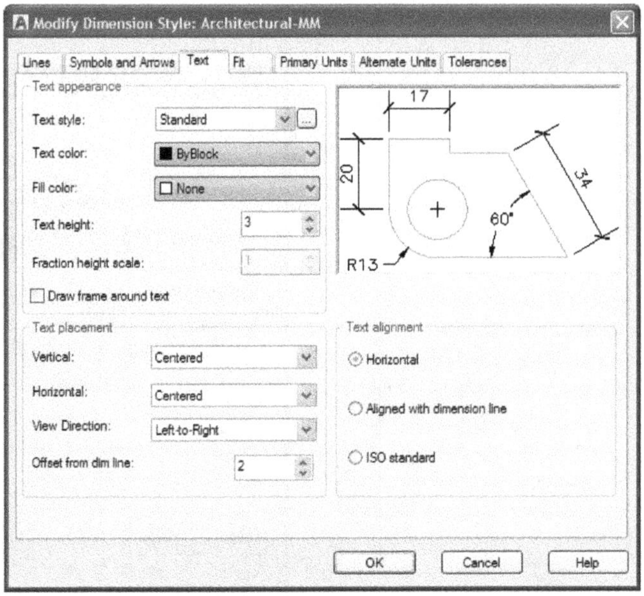

Figure 29–9

Do not set a height in text styles to be used for dimensioning. Use the dimension style to control the height.

- You can specify a text style in the Text style drop-down list. If you have not defined one, you can click  (Browse) to open the Text Style dialog box to create a new style. The text height should be set to the required plotted height.
- If you want the text to plot at a heavier weight than the rest of the dimensions (a standard drafting technique), set the text color to be a color that plots to a medium weight and leave the rest of the dimension elements with the *Text color* set to **ByBlock**. You can set the layer **Dimensions** to be a lightweight color.
- The *Fill* color can be set to **Background** or another color so that the text masks any objects behind it.
- *Offset from dim line* controls the size of the gap between the text and dimension lines. This applies when the text is centered on the line and above the line.
- *Text placement* can be set for **Vertical** and **Horizontal** dimensions.

- *View Direction* displays the dimension text **Left-to-Right** or **Right-to-Left**.

Dimension Style Fit Tab

The *Fit* tab controls the positions of arrows, text, leader lines, and the dimension line, as shown in Figure 29–10. It also controls the scale for dimension features.

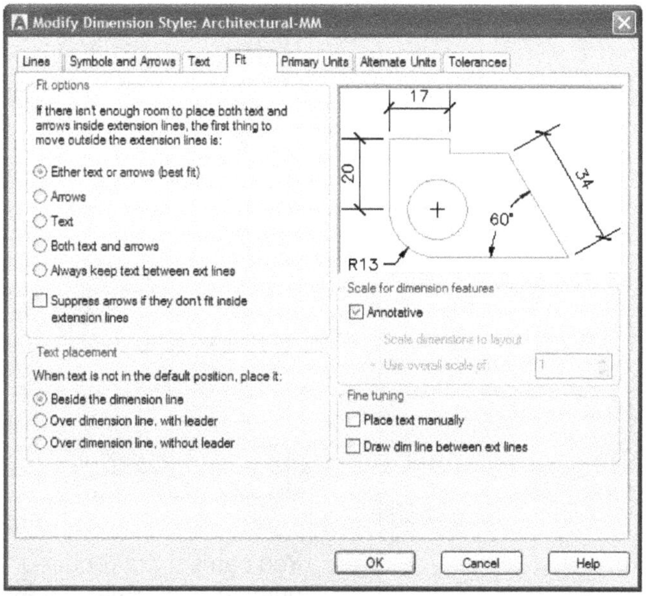

Figure 29–10

- When you set the *Scale for dimension features* to **Annotative**, the other options are grayed out. The dimensions are scaled according to the scale of the viewport through which they are inserted.

- If you are not using Annotative dimensions, you can use **Scale dimensions to layout** to display the objects in all viewports. You can also select **Use overall scale of** to dimension directly on the model when you are plotting from Model Space.

Dimension Style Primary Units Tab

The *Primary Units* tab controls the format of the primary units in the dimension text, as shown in Figure 29–11. This is independent of the type of units that are used in the drawing.

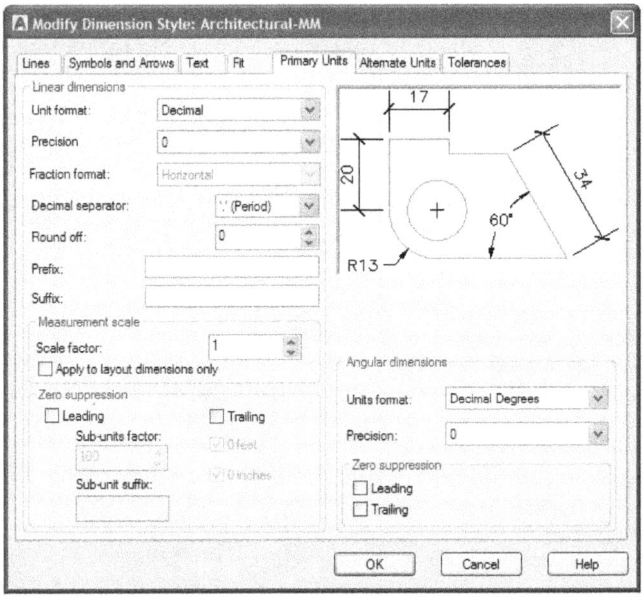

Figure 29–11

- You can set the required type of units for dimensioning, the number of decimal places, and other information to define the appearance of the text.
- A default *Prefix* and *Suffix* can be added in front or after all of the dimension values (for example, a suffix of mm for millimeters).
- The *Scale factor* multiplies the actual dimension value. For example, if the actual distance is 5 and the scale factor is 2, the value that displays in the dimension text is 10. If objects are drawn at full size, the scale should normally be set to 1.
- The *Sub-units factor* eliminates the leading zeros in dimension values by specifying that any measurement less than one primary unit be dimensioned in a smaller unit of measure. The *Sub-unit suffix* automatically appends a different dimension suffix to such dimensions.

Dimension Style Alternate Units Tab

The *Alternate Units* tab is very similar to the *Primary Units* tab.

- *Multiplier for alt units* is the conversion factor between the units in which your drawing was created and the units you want to use for alternative dimensions. For example, if the Primary Units are decimal inches and the Alternate Units are millimeters, *Multiplier for alt units* should be **25.4** (1 inch = 25.4mm).

Dimension Style Tolerances Tab

The *Tolerances* tab is usually used in mechanical design to indicate the degree of precision required in manufacturing.

- *Method* determines how the tolerance is calculated and displayed. The options are **None**, **Symmetrical** (equal bilateral), **Deviation** (unequal bilateral), **Limits**, and **Basic** (places a box around the dimension and is used with Geometric Dimensioning & Tolerancing).

Creating Dimension Sub-Styles

You might need to use a slightly different style for a specific type of dimension. For example, you might want linear dimensions to use tick marks instead of arrows and to always be forced above the dimension line. You can create a style that uses arrows, and then create a sub-style that is only used for linear dimensions, as shown in Figure 29–12. When using that style, all of the dimensions that you place have arrows, except for the linear dimensions.

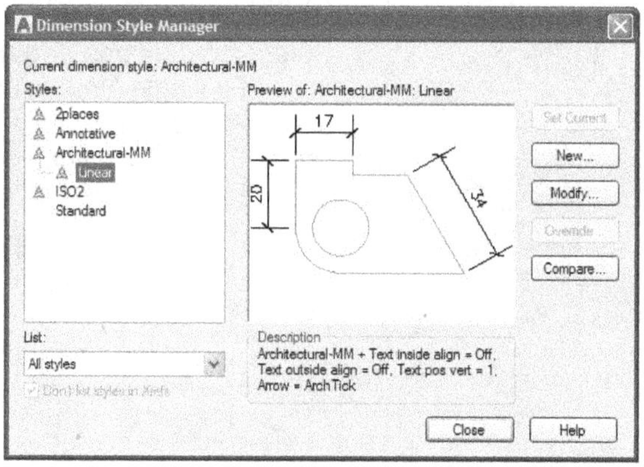

Figure 29–12

How To: Set Up a Dimension Sub-Style

1. Open the Dimension Style Manager.
2. Click **New...**.
3. In the Create New Dimension Style dialog box, in the Start With drop-down list select the style to use as a template.
4. In the Use for drop-down list, select a dimension type for the sub-style (linear, angular, etc.) that you are creating, as shown in Figure 29–13.

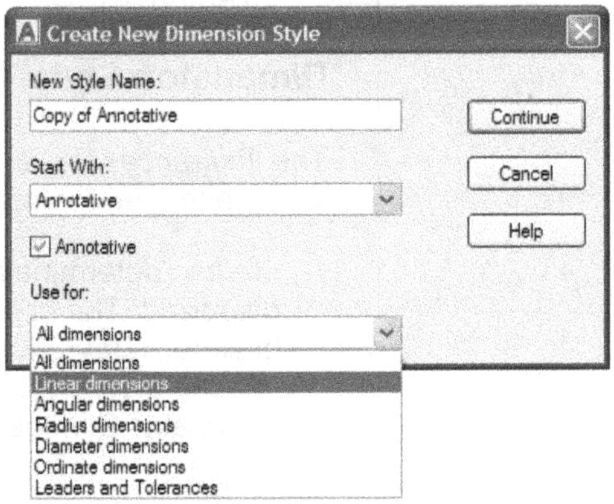

Figure 29–13

5. Click **Continue**.
6. In the New Dimension Style dialog box, define the sub-style as required with settings for lines, arrows, text, fit, etc.
7. When all of the settings have been adjusted, click **OK**. The new sub-style is listed in the Dimension Style Manager under the main style.

Hint: Modifying a Single Dimension

Select a dimension and use the Properties palette to modify the style of a single dimension without changing the style definition. In the Properties palette, all of the dimension style settings are listed. Each setting can be changed for the selected dimension.

Practice 29b Creating Dimension Styles (Architectural)

Estimated time for completion: 10 minutes

Practice Objectives

- Change the dimension style of various dimensions.
- Create a new dimension style and a related sub-style.

In this practice, you will test existing dimension styles and change them as required. You will also create a new dimension style with a related sub-style, as shown in Figure 29–14.

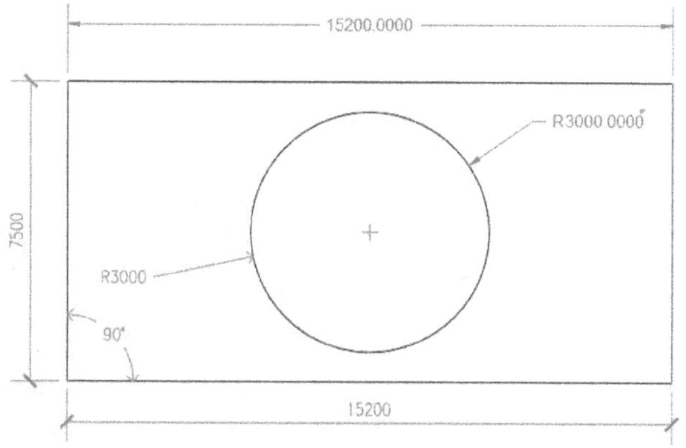

Figure 29–14

Task 1 - Test the existing dimension styles.

1. Open **AEC-Facilities2-AM.dwg** from your practice files folder.
2. If required, switch to the Model layout.
3. Change the current layer to **Walls** and draw a **15200 x 7500** rectangle with a **3000** radius circle at its center.
4. Switch to the **ISO A3** layout.
5. Double-click in the viewport to activate it. If required, pan in the viewport to display the rectangle and the circle. Return the *Viewport Scale* to **1:100** if it changed.

6. Set the current layer to **Dimensions**. Using the **Standard** dimension style, add a linear dimension for the top length line and a radius dimension to the circle. The dimension text and arrows are not displayed because this dimension style is not annotative.
7. Using the Properties panel for each of the dimensions, change the *Dim style* to **Annotative**. The dimension information is now available, but it is not designed to work with architectural dimensions.

Task 2 - Create a new dimension style.

1. In the Dimension Styles list, select **Manage Dimension Styles...** to open the Dimension Style Manager.and click **New...**.
2. In the Create New Dimension Style dialog box, set the *New Style Name* to **Decimal**. In the Start With drop-down list, select the **Standard** style to use as a template. Select **Annotative** and click **Continue**.
3. In the New Dimension Style dialog box, set the following options and click **OK**:

Symbols & Arrows tab	*Arrowheads* area	First, Second, and Leader: **Right angle**
Text tab	*Text appearance* area	Text style: **Dimensions**
Fit tab	*Scale for dimension features* area	Annotative
Primary Units tab	*Linear dimensions* area	Unit format: **Decimal**; Precision: **0**

4. Select **Decimal** and click **Set Current** in the Dimension Style Manager. Click **Close**.
5. Using the new style, add linear dimensions for the left and bottom edges of the rectangle. Add radial dimensions to the circle and angular dimensions to the left corner of the rectangle. Note the differences from the dimensions in the previous style.

Task 3 - Create a dimension sub-style.

1. In the Dimension Styles list, select **Manage Dimension Styles...**.
2. In Dimension Style Manager., select the new **Decimal** style and click **New...**.
3. Delete **Copy of Decimal** and leave the *New Style Name* blank.
4. In the Use for drop-down list, select **Linear dimensions** and click **Continue**.
5. Modify the options as follows:

Symbols & Arrows tab	*Arrowheads* area	First and Second: **Architectural tick**
Text tab	*Text alignment* area	Aligned with dimension line
Text tab	*Text placement* area	Vertical: Above

6. Click **OK** and **Close** to exit the Dimension Style Manager. Note that he linear dimensions update to display the new format, as shown in Figure 29–14.
7. Erase all of the dimensions.
8. Double-click outside the viewport to return to Paper Space.
9. Save the drawing.

Practice 29c Dimension Styles (Mechanical)

Estimated time for completion: 15 minutes

Practice Objective

- Create dimension styles and apply them to dimensions.

In this practice, you will create two dimension styles and then apply dimensions with those styles, as shown in Figure 29–15 and Figure 29–16.

1. Open **Dim-M.dwg** from your practice files folder.
2. Create the two dimension styles (Tolerance and Metric_Imperial) listed in the tables. *Start With* the **Standard** style, make each style **Annotative**, and use the default settings for options that are not specified.

	Tolerance	**Metric_Imperial**
Lines tab		
Baseline spacing	10	13
Symbols and Arrows tab		
Arrowheads	Right angle	Closed filled
Center marks	Mark	Line
Text tab		
Text style	Standard	Standard
Text color	ByBlock	Magenta
Text height	5	5
Vertical Placement	Centered	Above
Horizontal Placement	Centered	Centered
Text Alignment	Horizontal	Aligned with dimension line
Primary Units tab		
Unit format	Decimal	Decimal
Precision	0.00	0
Alternate Units tab		
Alternate Units	None	Architectural, precision 0'-0"
		Multiplier 25.4

Tolerances tab		
Method	Limits	None
Upper Value	0.5	
Lower Value	0.8	
Scaling for height	1	

For Metric_Imperial, include the following sub-styles:

	Angular	**Diameter**
Text tab		
Vertical text placement	Centered	Centered
Text alignment	Horizontal	Horizontal

3. Use the new dimension styles to dimension the objects shown in Figure 29–15 and Figure 29–16.
   - Set the layer **Dimensions** to be current.
   - A layout is prepared for each style. Use the **Add/Delete Scales** command to control which dimensions display in the appropriate viewport on each layout. The scale of the viewport in the **ISO A2 TOL** layout is 1:1 and the scale of the one in the **ISO A1 MET-IMP** layout is 2:1.

Tolerance

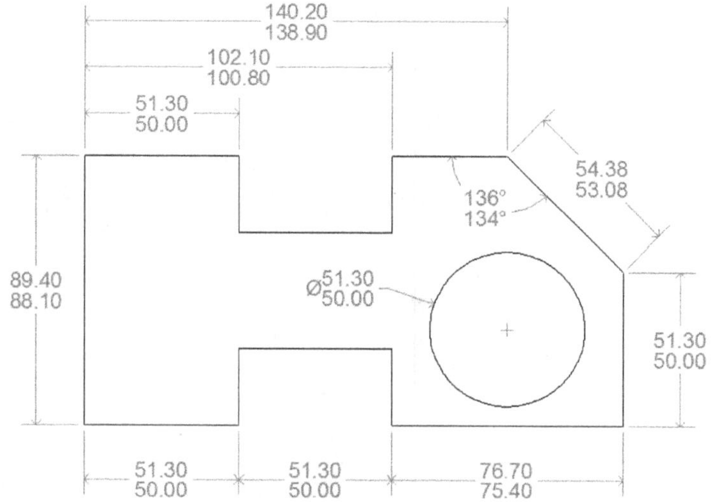

Figure 29–15

Metric_Imperial

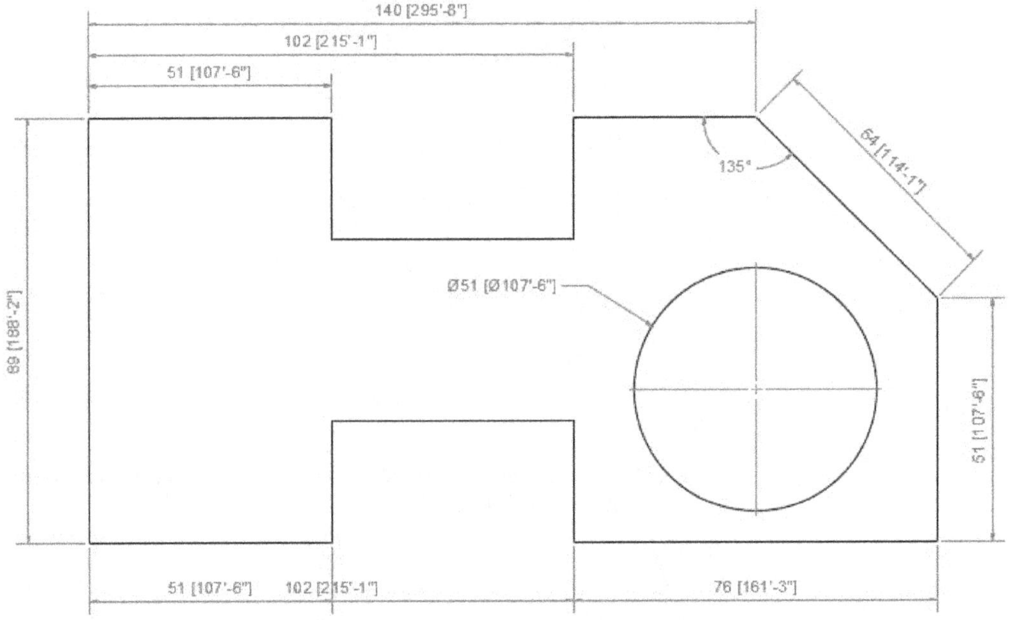

Figure 29–16

29.3 Creating Multileader Styles

Multileaders are used to point to objects in your drawing with text or symbols. Use the Multileader Style Manager to create styles that control the display options for different multileaders. The styles can be annotative or a specified scale, and have different arrowheads, text styles, colors, linetypes, etc., as shown in Figure 29–17. You can create styles for specific uses and then use the Multileader Style Manager to update them as required. This ensures accuracy throughout the drawing and makes it easy to modify multileaders.

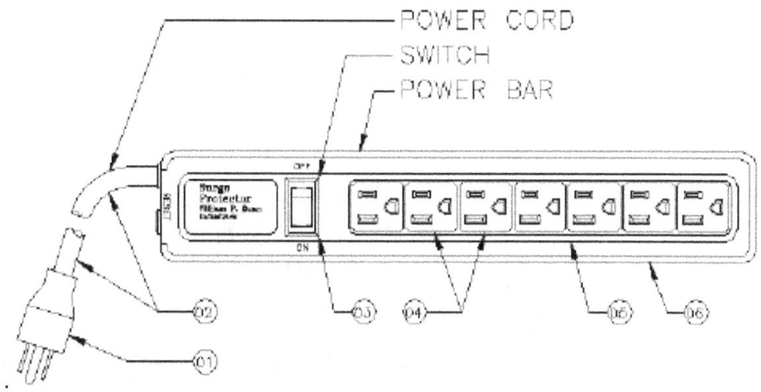

Figure 29–17

How To: Create a Multileader Style

You can also open the dialog box by clicking the panel arrow in the *Annotate tab>Leaders panel.*

1. In the *Annotate* tab>Leaders panel>Leader Style list, select **Manage Multileader Styles....** The Multileader Style Manager opens, as shown in Figure 29–18.

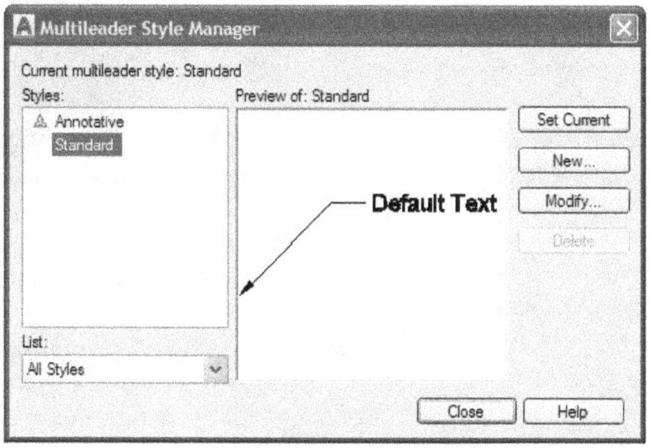

Figure 29–18

2. Click **New...**
3. In the Create New Multileader Style dialog box, type a *New style name*, expand the Start with drop-down list and select a style, and select or clear the **Annotative** option, as shown in Figure 29–19.

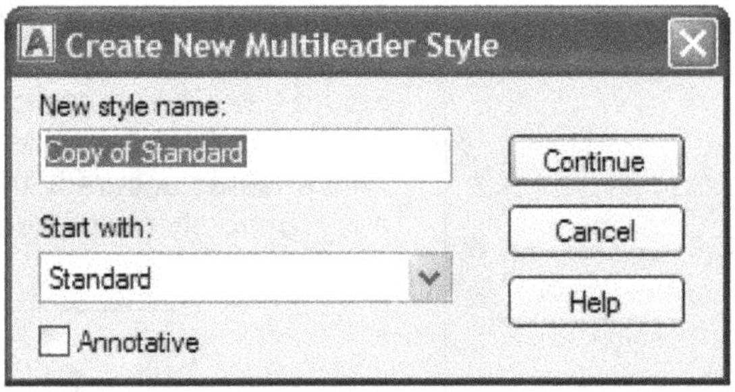

Figure 29–19

4. Click **Continue**. The Modify Multileader Style dialog box opens.
5. In the *Leader Format* tab, specify the leader's *Type* (**Straight**, **Spline**, or **None**), its formatting, the style and size of the Arrowhead, and the distance for the Leader break, as shown in Figure 29–20.

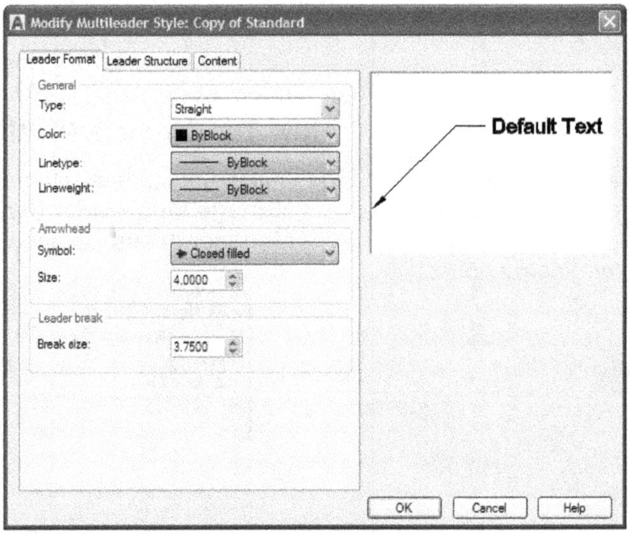

Figure 29–20

6. In the *Leader Structure* tab, specify how you want the leader to work, as shown in Figure 29–21. For example, the default leader style has the *Maximum leader points* set to **2** and *Landing Settings* toggled on. Select **Annotative** if you are using the annotative scaling tools.

*If you are creating a spline leader style, you might need to clear the **Constraints** and **Landing Settings** options.*

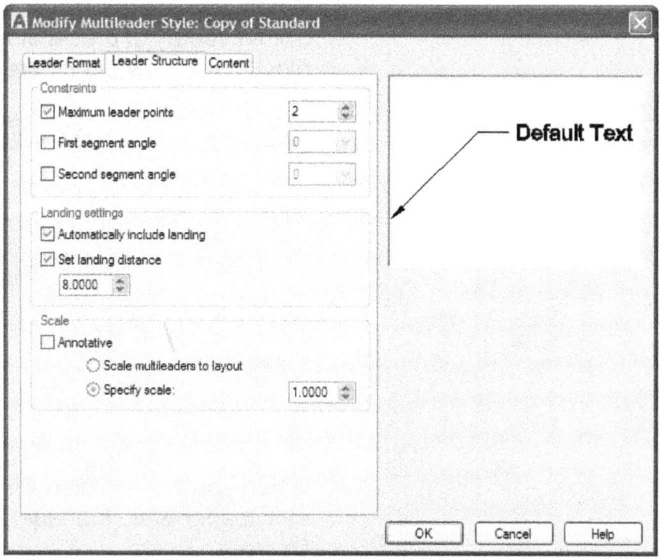

Figure 29–21

7. In the *Content* tab, you can specify whether you want the multileader content to be **Mtext**, **Block**, or **None**. Once you set the *Multileader type*, the rest of the options vary according to the selection. The **Mtext** option is shown in Figure 29–22.

*When you have selected text, you can set the attachment to be **Horizontal** or **Vertical**.*

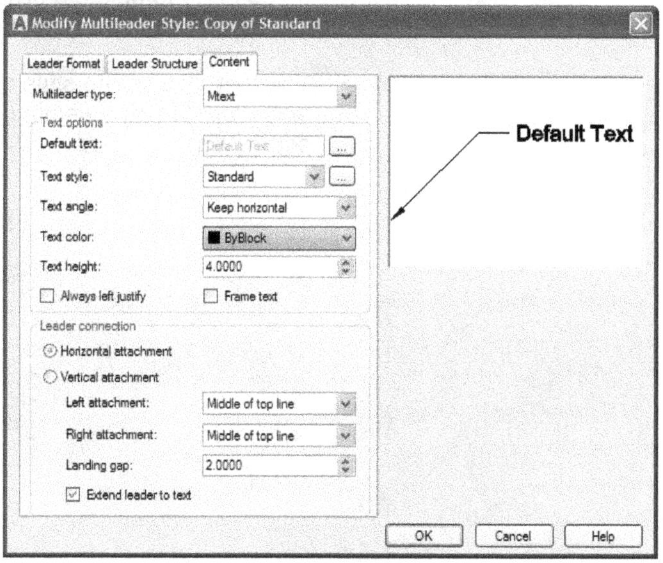

Figure 29–22

8. When you use the **Block** *Multileader type*, you can select from a variety of preset blocks with attributes or use your own blocks, as shown in Figure 29–23.

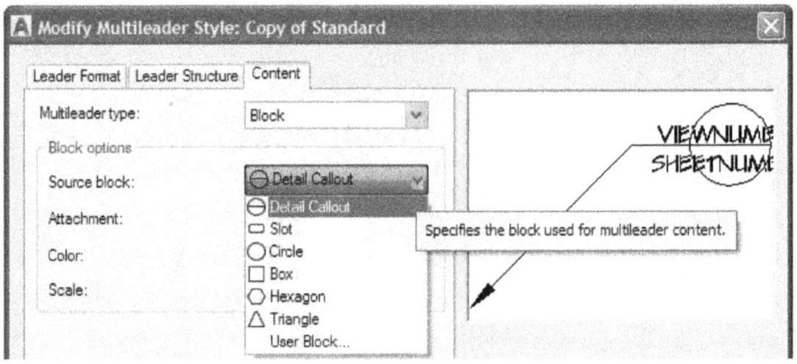

Figure 29–23

9. When you are satisfied with the style, click **OK**. In the Multileader Style Manager, select the new style and click **Set Current**.
10. Click **Close**.

- If you need to make a change to a style, open the Multileader Style Manager, select the style that you want to change, and click **Modify**.
- If you need to delete a style, open the Multileader Style Manager, select a style, and click **Delete**.
- You can also create style overrides for the Leader, Content, and Workflow by selecting **Options** in the **Multileader** command.

Practice 29d Creating Multileader Styles

Practice Objective

- Create a multileader style.

Estimated time for completion: 10 minutes

In this practice, you will create a multileader style using a spline and a block, as shown in Figure 29–24.

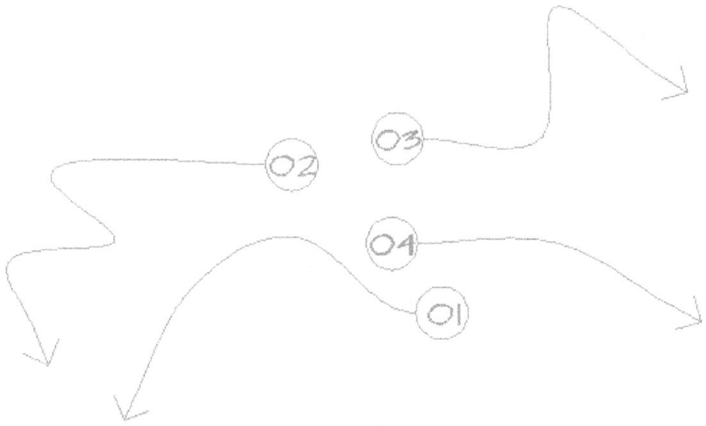

Figure 29–24

1. Open **AEC-Facilities3-AM.dwg** from your practice files folder.
2. In the *Annotate* tab>Leaders panel, click .
3. In the Multileader Style Manager, click **New...**.
4. In the Create New Multileader Style dialog box, name the new multileader **Keynote**. Start with the **Standard** style and make it **Annotative**. Click **Continue**.
5. In the *Leader Format* tab, in the *General* area, set the *Type* to **Spline**. In the *Arrowhead* area, set the *Symbol* to **Oblique**.
6. In the *Leader Structure* tab, clear **Maximum leader points** (this enables you to make as many points on the spline as required).
7. In the *Content* tab, change the *Multileader type* to **Block**. In the *Block options* area, set the *Source block* to **Circle**, set the *Scale* to **30**, and click **OK**.
8. In the Multileader Style Manager, select Keynote and click **Set Current**. Click **Close**.

9. Start the **Multileader** command to test the new multileader style by clicking several points to create a zig zag leader. Press <Enter> to stop selecting points along the spline.

10. In the Edit Attributes dialog box, enter a tag number for the keynote. Click **OK**.

11. Erase the leaders, switch back to Model Space, and save the drawing template.

Chapter Review Questions

1. If you change the font of a text style, what happens to existing text that uses that text style?
   a. The text is moved to a new layer.
   b. The text remains the same.
   c. The text is deleted.
   d. The text updates with the new font.
2. What are dimension sub-styles used for?
   a. To override the dimension style settings for a particular type of dimension, such as angle or radius.
   b. To automatically dimension specific objects, such as rectangles and circles.
   c. To link dimensions to specific layers.
   d. To copy dimension styles between drawings.
3. You have a dimension style that uses decimal units and you want to change it to use fractional units. What do you do?
   a. Modify the *Alternate Units* in the dimension style.
   b. Modify the *Primary Units* in the dimension style.
   c. Edit the text of the dimension and change the value.
   d. Edit the *Fit* settings in the dimension style.
4. What multileader type in the multileader style would prompt users for input, such as sheet number or callout? (Select all that apply.)
   a. Block
   b. Mtext
   c. None
   d. Circle
5. You cannot use custom blocks with Multileader.
   a. True
   b. False

6. When creating a Text Style, Dimension Style, or Multileader Style, you want the size of the text and other objects to scale automatically according to the scale of the viewport in which they are used. In the related Style Manager, which of the following options would you set?

    a. **Text Size**

    b. **Alternate Units**

    c. **Scale Text**

    d. **Annotative**

Command Summary

Button	Command	Location
	**Dimension Style**	• **Ribbon:** *Home* tab>expanded Annotation panel or the panel arrow in the *Annotate* tab>Dimensions panel • **Command Prompt:** dimstyle
	**Multileader Style**	• **Ribbon:** *Home* tab>expanded Annotation panel or the panel arrow in the *Annotate* tab>Leaders panel • **Command Prompt:** mleaderstyle
	**Text Style**	• **Ribbon:** *Home* tab>expanded Annotation panel or *Annotate* tab>Text panel>Text Styles list>Manage Text Styles or the panel arrow in the *Annotate* tab>Text panel • **Command Prompt:** style or ST

Chapter 30

Projects: Drawing Setup and Utilities

This chapter contains practice projects that can be used to gain additional hands-on experience with the topics and commands covered so far in this student guide. These practices are intended to be self-guided and do not include step by step information.

Learning Objectives in this Chapter

- *Mechanical:* Create a template that contains features such as layers, limits, text, and multileader styles to use for electronic schematics or part designs.
- *Civil:* Create a template that contains features such as layers, limits, text, and multileader styles to use for mapping.

30.1 Interiors Project

Estimated time for completion: 30 minutes

In this project you will create a new template drawing for use with Interior Design projects. You will establish units, limits, layers, a text style, and a multileader style, as shown in Figure 30–1.

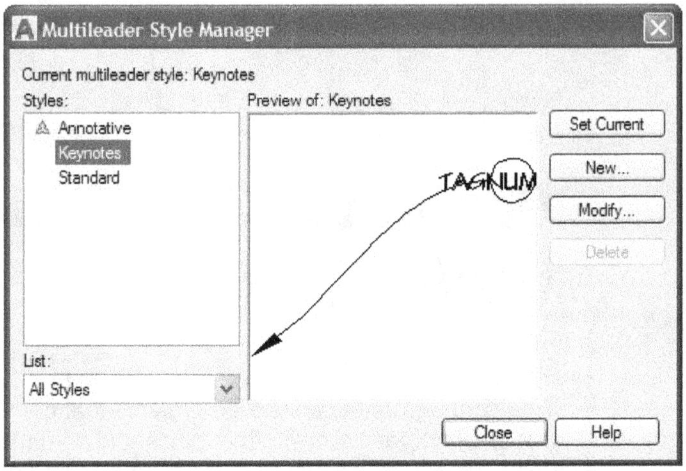

Figure 30–1

1. Start a new drawing based on **AEC-Millimeters.dwt**, which is located in your practice files folder.
2. Verify that the units are **Decimal**. Set the *Limits* to **22800,13700**.
3. Add the following new layers: **Existing**, **New**, and **Demo**.
4. Add a text style named **Room Names**.
5. Create a new multileader style named **Keynotes** using the **Circle** block and any type of leader, as shown in Figure 30–1.
6. Save the drawing as a template named **AEC-Interiors.dwt**. Ensure you save it as a DWT file and add a description as required.
7. Start a new drawing using your template and test some of the settings.

30.2 Mechanical/Schematic Project

Estimated time for completion: 30 minutes

In this project you will create a new template drawing for use with electronic schematic diagrams. You will establish units, limits, layers, a text style, and a multileader style, as shown in Figure 30–2.

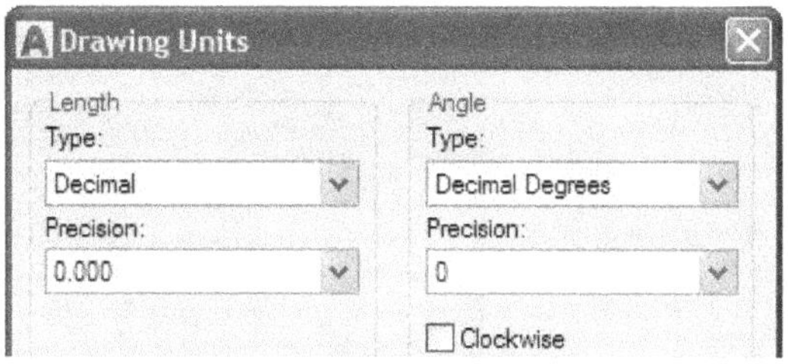

Figure 30–2

1. Start a new drawing based on **Mech-Millimeters.dwt**, which is located in your practice files folder.
2. Verify that the *units* are **Decimal** and set them to **3** decimal places, as shown in Figure 30–2. Set the *Limits* to **900,600**.
3. Toggle on **Snap** and **Grid** and set them to **3**.
4. Add the following new layers: **Resistor**, **Transistor**, and **Capacitor**.
5. Add a text style named **Wiring**.
6. Create a new multileader style named **Keynotes** using the **Circle** block and any type of leader.
7. Save the drawing as a template named **Elec-Metric.dwt**. Save it as a DWT file and add a description as required.
8. Start a new drawing using your template to test some of the settings.

30.3 Civil/Map Project

Estimated time for completion: 30 minutes

In this project you will create a new template drawing for use with mapping. You will establish units, limits, layers, a text style, and a multileader style, as shown in Figure 30–3.

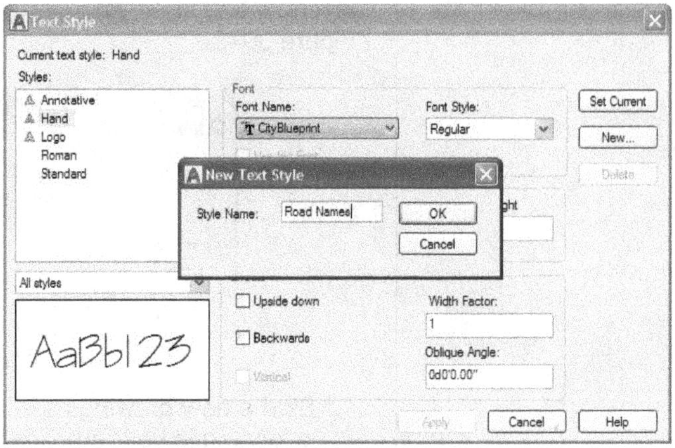

Figure 30–3

1. Start a new drawing based on **Civil-Meters.dwt**, which is located in your practice files folder.
2. Change the *Units* to **Decimal**, with the *Precision* set to **whole units**. This drawing is in decimal feet. Set the *Limits* to **3000,2100**.
3. Add the following new layers: **City Line**, **County Line**, and **District Line**.
4. Add a text style named **Road Names**, as shown in Figure 30–3.
5. Create a new multileader style named **Keynotes** using the **Circle** block and any type of leader.
6. Save the drawing as a template named **Civil-Mapping.dwt**. Ensure you save it as a DWT file and add a description as required.
7. Start a new drawing using your template to test some of the settings you have established.

30.4 Mechanical Project: Dimension Styles

Estimated time for completion: 40 minutes

In this project you will create dimension styles and dimension the part, as shown in Figure 30–4.

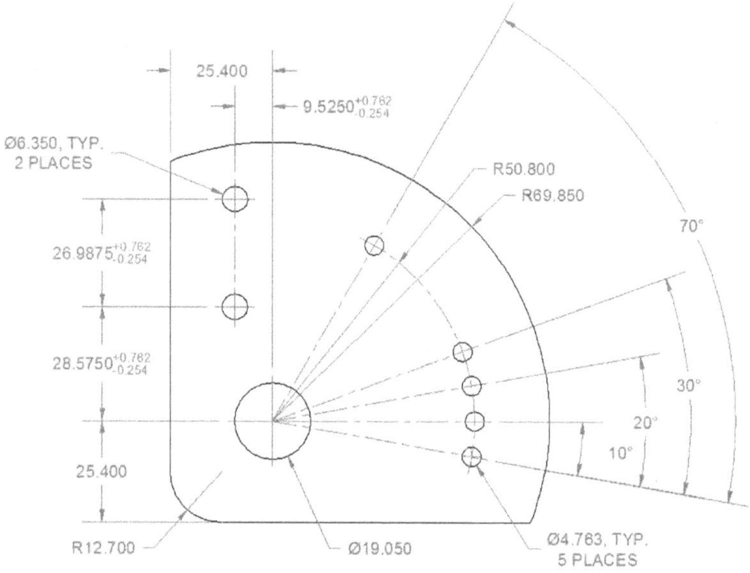

Figure 30–4

1. Open **Dimplate-M.dwg** from your practice files folder.
2. Create two dimension styles: **Normal** and **Tolerance**.

- The **Normal** style should have sub-styles for angular and radial dimensions.

  (Hint: The **Fit** option in the angular dimensions needs to be adjusted to move the text outside the lines first, and set the text placement to be **Over the dimension line, without a leader**. The **Fit** option in the radial dimensions needs to be set to **Draw dim line between ext lines**.)

- The **Tolerance** style, for the toleranced dimensions, uses a deviation style tolerance. Ensure the following values are set:
  - *Precision*: **0.000**
  - *Upper value*: **0.762**
  - *Lower value*: **0.254**
  - *Scaling for tolerance* text height: **0.75** (75% of the other dimension text).

3. Make the layer **Dimensions** current and dimension the part as shown in Figure 30–4. You will need to draw the arc that displays the placement of the five small holes, and the lines from the center of those holes to the large hole.

Chapter 31

External References

In this chapter, you learn how to attach drawing, image, DWF, DGN, and PDF reference files and to open reference files from within a host drawing. You also learn how to detach, unload, and reload reference files, clip reference files, work with drawing reference specific information, edit drawing reference files In-Place, and to bind external references.

Learning Objectives in this Chapter

- Attach image files along with DWF, DGN, and PDF underlays to a drawing.
- Customize the attachment of external reference.
- Open, modify, detach, and unload referenced files.
- Toggle layers and snap to objects on and off in a DWF underlay.
- Clip the referenced file to control the part that is visible.
- Set a drawing reference file to be an attachment or an overlay.
- Copy data of a referenced drawing into the host drawing and then detach it.
- Bind blocks, layers, dimensions styles, etc., from a reference drawing into a host drawing.
- Control how much of a drawing reference file is loaded into the host file.

31.1 Attaching External References

When you insert one drawing into another as a block, the graphics are merged and no link remains between the two files. External References enable you to combine files and retain the link, as shown in Figure 31–1. This serves two main purposes: it controls the file size because objects in the referenced drawing do not become part of the host drawing, and objects modified in the reference file are automatically updated in the host drawing because the files are linked.

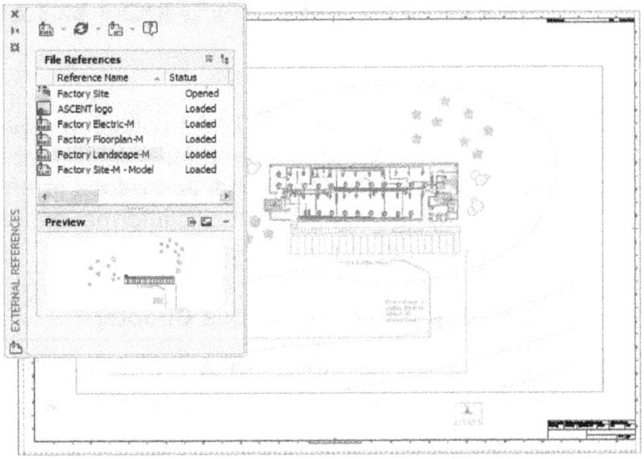

Figure 31–1

- Reference files enable members of a design team to share common source files and still have the most current information.
- External reference files can be managed through the External References palette.

Enhanced in **2018**

- When you open a drawing that contains an external reference file that cannot be found, a References - Not Found Files warning box opens, as shown in Figure 31–2. These files also displays the warning symbol with their file icon and an ! (exclamation mark) besides the file in the External Reference palette.

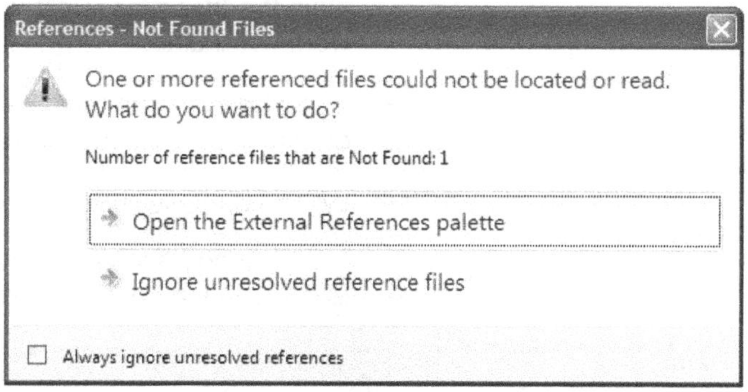

Figure 31–2

Several file formats can be used as external references:

AutoCAD® drawing files	Also known as Xrefs, they are connections to other drawings that you can edit in-place or externally, while retaining the link. You can turn layers on and off in the host drawing.
Raster image files	Various types of graphic files, such as GIF, JPG, and PNG. They can be renderings or scanned images that can be used as a reference as you trace over existing drawings.
DWF underlays	Non-editable files that include vector information that can be displayed in the DWF viewer and incorporated as an underlay in any drawing file.
DGN underlays	Files that come from the MicroStation platform. You can also import and export to DGN files.
PDF Underlays	Attach PDF files as underlays one page at a time.

External References Palette

You can use the External References palette (shown in Figure 31–3) to attach, unload, reload, and detach reference files. You can open a reference file in an appropriate software to make modifications to the original file and can also change the location in which the original file is saved if it is moved.

(Manage Xrefs) does not display in the Status Bar until the drawing contains at least one xref.

The External References palette is similar to other palettes in that it can be either floating or docked and hidden.

- You can open the External References palette by clicking in the *Insert* tab>Reference panel or by typing **Xref** in the Command Line.
- If you have a reference file in the drawing, you can right-click on it and select **External References** to open the palette.
- When you have external references in a drawing, (Manage Xrefs) displays near the right end of the Status Bar. Click it to open the External References palette.

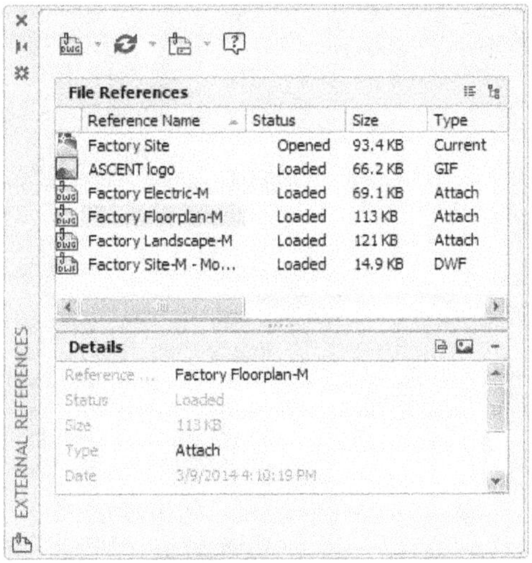

Figure 31–3

The External References palette is divided into two panes.

Top Pane

In the top pane, a list of file references displays as shown in Figure 31–4.

- By selecting the appropriate column heading, you can sort the files in the list according to name, status, size, date, and saved path.

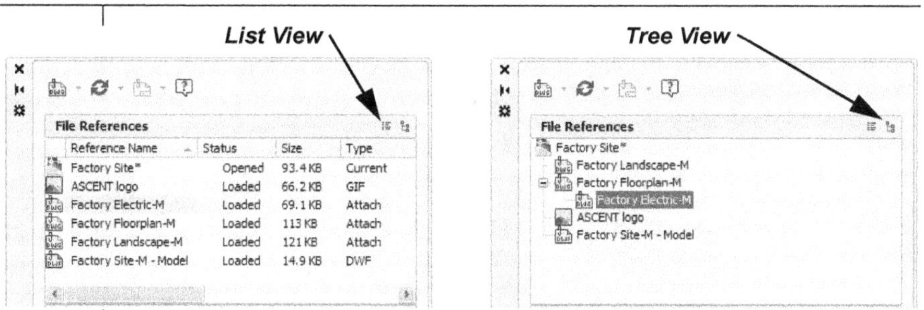

Figure 31–4

- (List View) displays all of the attached external references and detailed information including: size, date, and saved path.

- (Tree View) switches to an hierarchical view that displays nested reference files (i.e., drawings that are attached to referenced drawings). Double-click on a reference filename in Tree View to display or hide the nested reference files below it.

Bottom Pane

In the bottom pane, a list of details about a selected file or a preview of the file displays as shown in Figure 31–5.

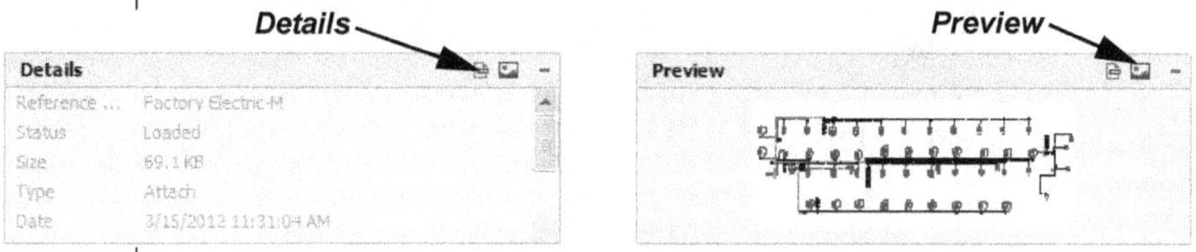

Figure 31–5

- (Details) displays information about a selected file and enables you to modify the name of the reference. If the file is a drawing file, it enables you to modify the type of attachment.

- (Preview) displays a small image of the selected file.

How To: Attach a Reference File

You can also open the External References Palette by clicking the Reference panel arrow in the Insert tab.

1. In the *View* tab>Palettes panel, click (External References Palette).
2. In the External References palette, expand (Attach DWG) as shown in Figure 31–6, and select a file format to attach.

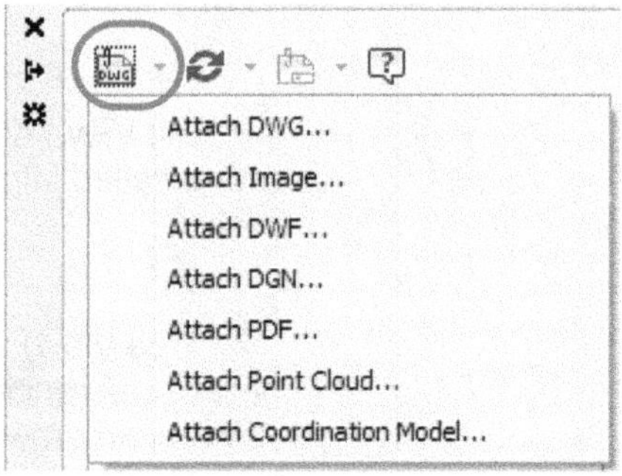

Figure 31–6

3. In the Select Reference File dialog box, select the file that you want to attach and click **Open**.
4. In the Attach External Reference dialog box, set the options as required, as shown in Figure 31–7.

The options and title of the dialog box (External Reference, Image, or Attach DWF Underlay) vary depending on the type of file selected. Several options are used in every situation.

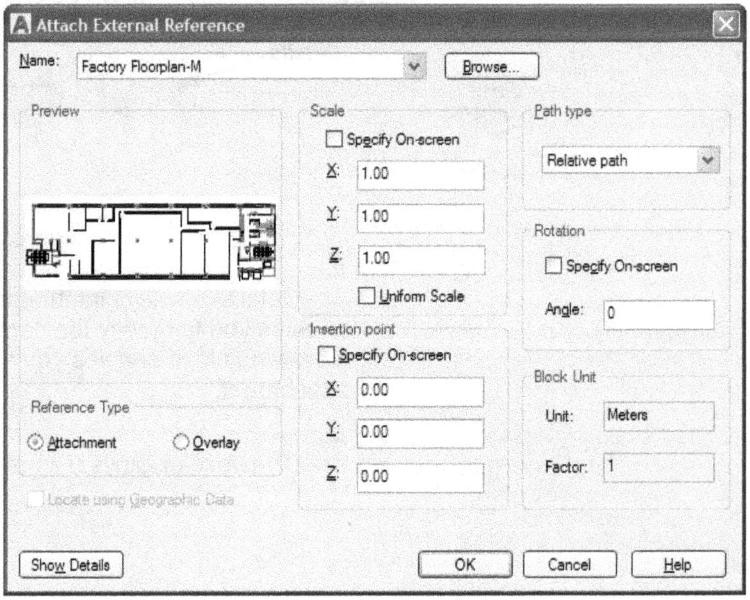

Figure 31–7

5. Click **OK**.
6. If you used the **Specify On-screen** option for *Insertion Point*, *Scale*, and *Rotation* in the dialog box, then specify them in the drawing window.

- You can use the Reference tools in the *Insert* tab> Reference panel to attach or modify various types of externally referenced files, as shown in Figure 31–8.

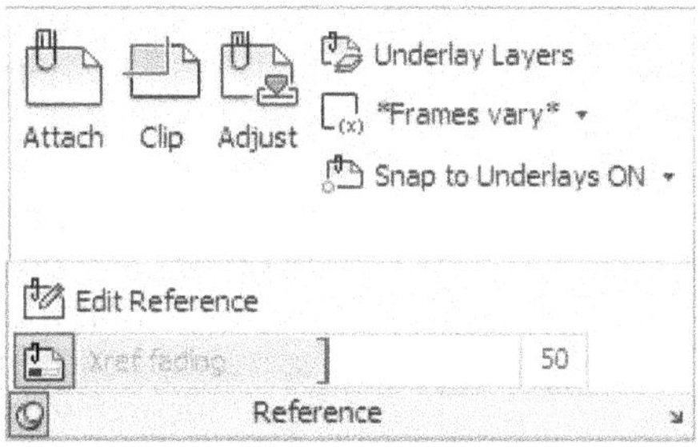

Figure 31–8

General Attachment Options

Enhanced in 2018

Name	Select a name from the list or click **Browse...** and select a different file to attach.
Path type	Controls how the AutoCAD software searches for the reference file to load it. By default, the *Path type* is set to **Relative Path**. It starts from the folder of the host drawing. **Full path** uses the entire path. With **No path**, the AutoCAD software searches in the current folder of the host drawing, and in the project paths, support paths, and *Start-in* folder.
Insertion Point, Scale, and Rotation Angle	These options are similar to the selections for block insertions. The values can be entered in the Attach External Reference dialog box or in the Command Line.

New in **2018**

- When a drawing has an external reference that has been moved and cannot be found, the shortcut menu offers you options to find the file, as shown in Figure 31–9. The **Select New Path** option enables you to fix the missing path by selecting the file from the new location. Once the reference file's new location has been selected, the software prompts you to use the new path for the other missing references or leave the rest of the paths as is. The **Find and Replace** option opens the Find and Replace dialog box, which enables you to find the current path and replace all of its instances with the new path, all at once.

Enhanced in **2018**

- The shortcut menu also provides you with the option of changing the path type by selecting **Change Path Type**. If the path type option of the selected reference file is grayed out and cannot be selected, it indicates that it is the one currently used. Figure 31–10 shows an example of the referenced file using the Relative Path type, which is grayed out to indicate that the path type is currently used.

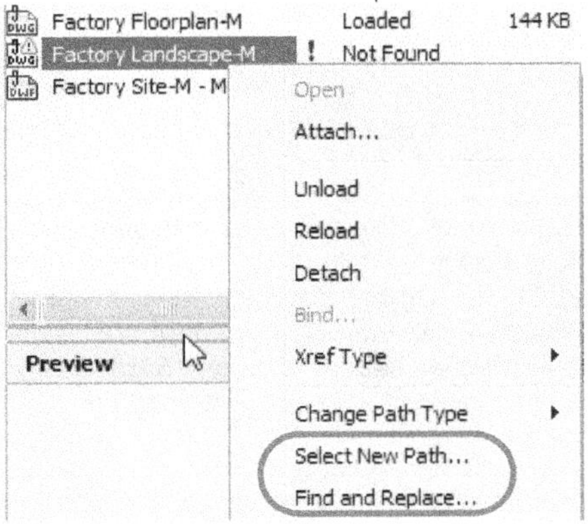

Figure 31–9

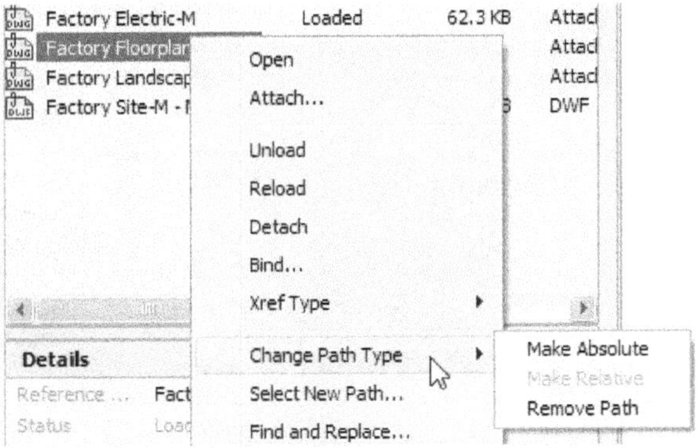

Figure 31–10

Xref Specific Attachment Options

Reference Type	Two types of references are available when one AutoCAD drawing is inserted into another: **Attachment** and **Overlay**.
Block Unit	The Insertion Scale units of the reference file and host drawings (expand Application Menu, expand Drawing Utilities, click 0.0 (Units)) control the automatic scale factor that displays in the *Block Units* area.

Image Specific Attachment Options

You can attach an image as many times as required in the same drawing file. If a raster image by that name already exists in the drawing (even if the extension type is different) a Substitute Image Name dialog box opens in which you can type a new name. This is the name that displays in the External References palette.

DWF Specific Attachment Options

Select one or more sheets	If you are using a multi-sheet DWF file you can select any of the sheets to insert into the host drawing.

- If you set the *scale factor* to **Specify on Screen** then, at the *Specify Scale Factor or [Unit]:* prompt, you have the option to select the units of the existing drawing and have the software automatically scale the DWF file to those units. For example, if you are working in a drawing whose insertion scale units are set to **Meters** and the DWF file is in Architectural units, it automatically scales the DWF file by 0.0254. The default insertion scale unit is set to the current drawing units.
- You can insert multiple copies of a DWF file using the same sheet or different sheets in a multiple sheet file.

DGN Specific Attachment Options

MicroStation DGN file units are set up in *Master units* and *Sub units*. When you insert a DGN as an underlay, you need to specify the units that you want to convert. For example, if you attach a mechanical drawing that is created with *Master units* of millimeters and *Sub units* of thousandths of millimeters you would convert the *Master units*. However, if you are working with a file that has *Master units* of feet and *Sub units* of inches and you want to insert it into an AutoCAD Architectural unit file (which uses inches as its default units) you would convert the *Sub units*.

PDF Specific Attachment Options

Select one or more pages	If you are using a multi-sheet PDF file, you can select any sheet(s) to insert into the host drawing.

- All the supported objects in the PDF file are converted into 2D geometry, raster images, and TrueType text.
- If the PDF file contains SHX fonts, these are converted to separate geometric representations, which can be converted to multiline text objects using the **Recognize SHX Text** tool in the *Insert* tab>Import panel (**PDFSHXTEXT** command).

31.2 Modifying External References

When you have attached external references to your drawing, you can modify the way they function in the drawing.

- You can **Open**, **Unload**, **Reload**, and **Detach** individual references, as shown in Figure 31–11.

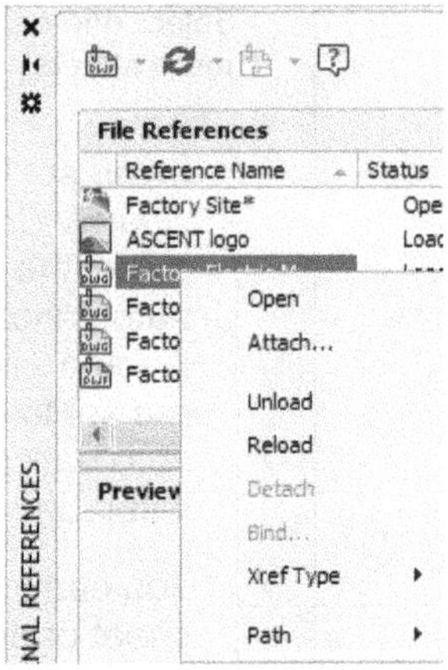

Figure 31–11

- All of the reference file formats can be clipped to display part of the reference. You can make changes to a selected reference in the Properties palette.

- You can use standard AutoCAD® commands, such as **Move**, **Rotate**, and **Scale** on references. Raster images can also be used to trim or extend to another object.

Opening Reference Files

You can modify a reference file in the software in which it was created and then reload it into the drawing. You can open a reference file from within the host drawing. Select the file in the External References palette, right-click, and select **Open**.

- A drawing reference file opens the drawing in the AutoCAD software.

- Image files open the image in the software with which the file format is associated.

- A360 Viewer is a free online file viewer provided by Autodesk® to help you view DWF files. To open it, use https://a360.autodesk.com/viewer/.

- DWF files also open in the Autodesk® Design Review software, if it is installed. DGN files cannot be opened with the AutoCAD software.
- You can also open drawing reference files by picking the reference in the drawing window, right-clicking and selecting **Open Xref**, as shown in Figure 31–12.

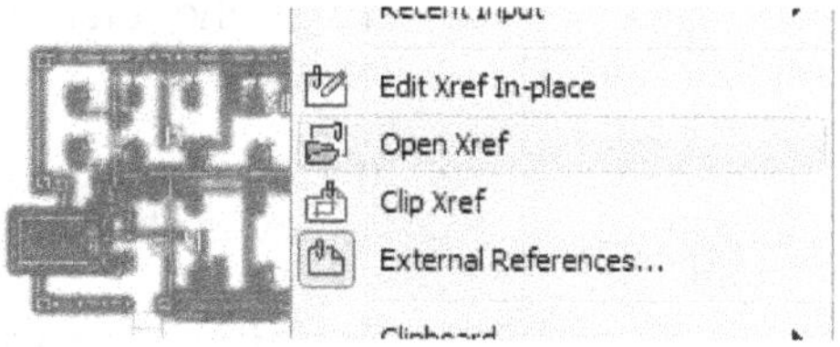

Figure 31–12

- When you return to the host file, an alert balloon opens in the Status Bar indicating that an external reference has changed, as shown in Figure 31–13. Select the link in the balloon to reload the reference. This message also displays when someone else changes a reference while you have the host file open.

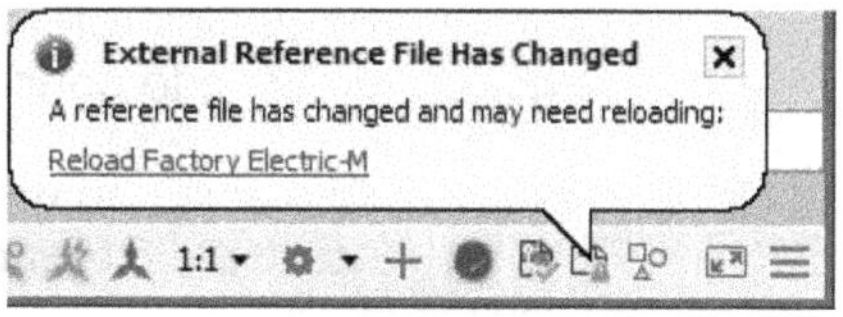

Figure 31–13

Detaching and Unloading Reference Files

There are two ways of removing a reference file from your drawing: **Unload** and **Detach** (as shown in Figure 31–14).

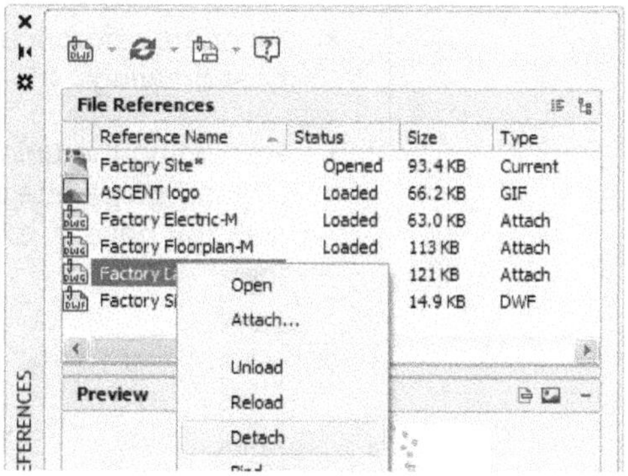

Figure 31–14

Detaching Files

Use **Detach** to permanently remove a reference file from your drawing.

- It severs the link between the current drawing and the external reference drawing.
- To get the reference back after detaching it, you need to re-attach it.
- If you have attached multiple copies of a DWF file, **Detach** removes all of them.

Enhanced in 2018

Unloading and Reloading Files

Use **Unload** to temporarily remove a reference file.

- When you unload a reference file, the AutoCAD software hides the reference geometry. However, it keeps the file in the External References palette list and remembers its insertion point, scale, and other attachment information.
- Unloading references that are not currently required causes a drawing to open and perform faster.
- To display an unloaded reference again, it must be reloaded using the **Reload** option.
- You can use the **Open** option in the shortcut menu to quickly open the unloaded reference file.
- Reloading loads the most recently saved version of the reference.
- All of the references reload automatically when you open the host drawing.
- Renaming the unloaded reference file in the External Reference palette does not automatically reload the renamed file. You have to explicitly reload it, as it remains unloaded till then.

- **Refresh** synchronizes information stored in memory when used with the Autodesk® Vault software.
- **Reload All References** (shown in Figure 31–15) updates all of the references in a drawing so that you are using the most up-to-date versions that have been saved.

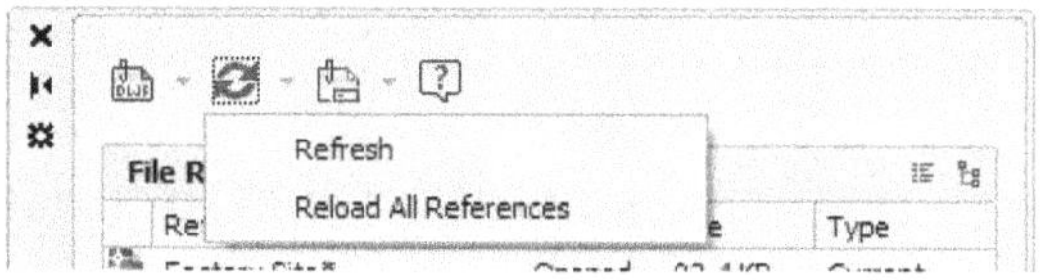

Figure 31–15

Clipping Reference Files

When you attach an external reference to your drawing, the entire reference file displays. However, you might not want the entire file to display, even in Model Space. You can control which part of the referenced file is visible by clipping it, as shown in Figure 31–16.

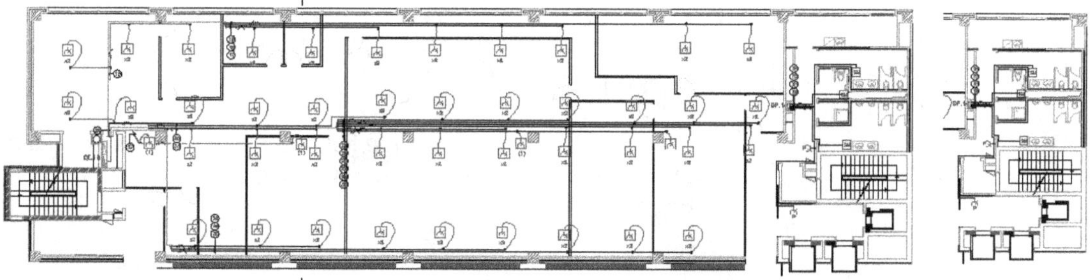

Figure 31–16

How To: Clip a Reference File

If you have selected a drawing file, you have the additional option of selecting an existing polyline as the boundary.

1. In the drawing, select the reference that you want to clip, right-click and select the appropriate **Clip** command for the type of reference selected. (Drawings: **Clip Xref**; Images: **Image>Clip**; DWF files: **DWF Clip**; DGN files: **DGN Clip**.)
2. Enter a **Clipping** option. Press <Enter> to accept the default **New boundary** option.
3. Select the **Rectangular** or **Polygonal** boundary option and draw a boundary.
4. Specify the points or existing polyline. The reference is clipped so the reference information outside the boundary is invisible.

- You can only clip one image, .DWF, or .DGN file at a time but you can clip multiple drawing files.
- Drawing reference files have an additional clip option: **Invert Clip**. Instead of masking everything outside the boundary it covers everything within the boundary. This can be very useful if you are working on a renovation project in which you are moving interior walls but not changing other parts of the building.

Other Clip Options

On/Off	Turns the clip boundary on or off without removing it from the reference. If the boundary is off the entire reference displays.
Clipdepth	Controls the front and back clipping planes in the Z-direction of the clip. Drawing reference files only.
Delete	Removes the clipping boundary from the reference files. You cannot use the **Erase** command to remove the clipping boundary.
Generate Polyline	Creates a polyline at the location of an existing clip boundary. This is a separate entity from the boundary. Drawing reference files only.

- If you run the command on a file that already has a boundary, the AutoCAD software prompts you to delete the current boundary first.
- To modify the clip boundary, start the associated **Clip** command. You can toggle the **Clip Boundary** on or off or delete it.

Clip Frames

The lines around clipped references are called *Clip Frames*. They can be toggled on or off for all of the references in a drawing using system variables that are related to each reference type: **xclipframe** for drawing references, **imageframe**, **dwfframe**, **pdfframe**, and **dgnframe**, as shown in Figure 31–17.

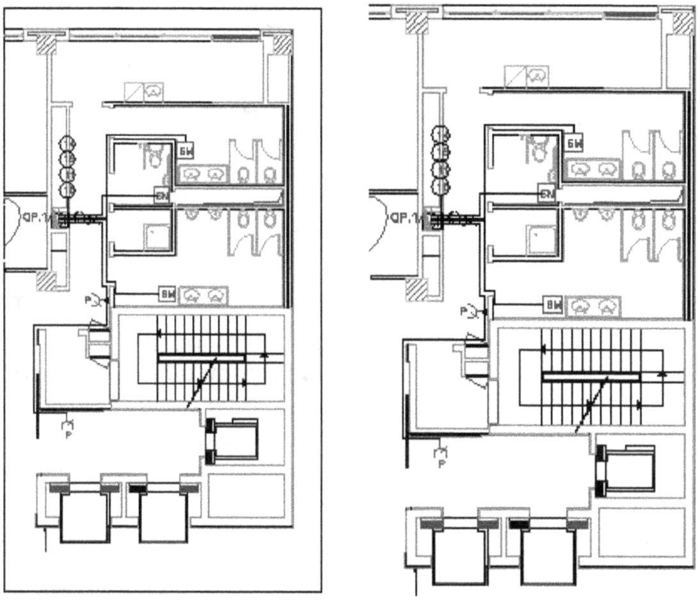

Frame ON *Frame OFF*

Figure 31–17

- **Frame Boundaries** have three options. When set to **0**, the boundary is invisible. When set to **1**, the boundary is visible. When set to **2**, the boundary is visible but does not plot.
- When the boundary is visible, you can select the external reference by selecting the boundary or any visible part of the reference file.

Modifying References

When you select the border of a reference file, a contextual tab displays according to the type of reference file that was selected. A DWF underlay has panels for Adjust, Clipping, Options, and DWF Layers, as shown in Figure 31–18. PDF and DGN underlays are the same.

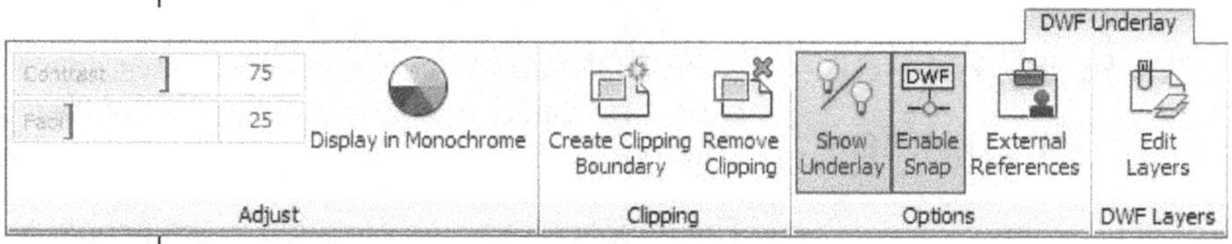

Figure 31–18

Modification options for drawing reference files include editing the reference, clipping, and access to the External References palette, as shown in Figure 31–19.

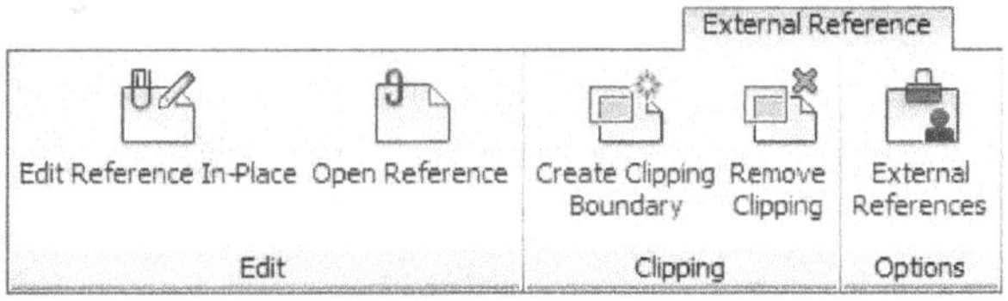

Figure 31–19

Image panels include Adjust and Clipping, and an additional **Transparency** option, as shown in Figure 31–20.

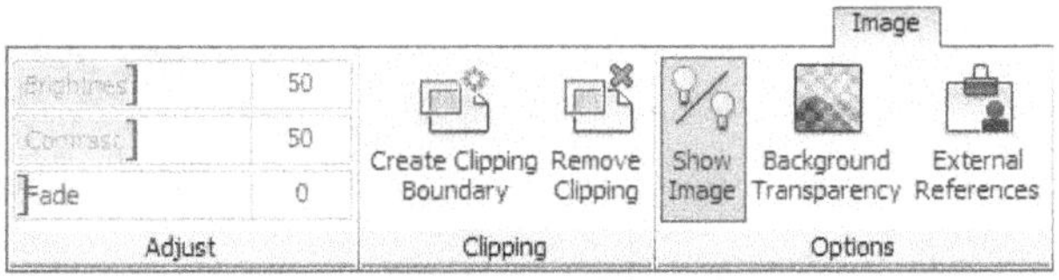

Figure 31–20

- Underlays and image references can only be selected when the frame surrounding them is on. You can change the state of the frames in the *Insert* tab>Reference panel, as shown in Figure 31–21.

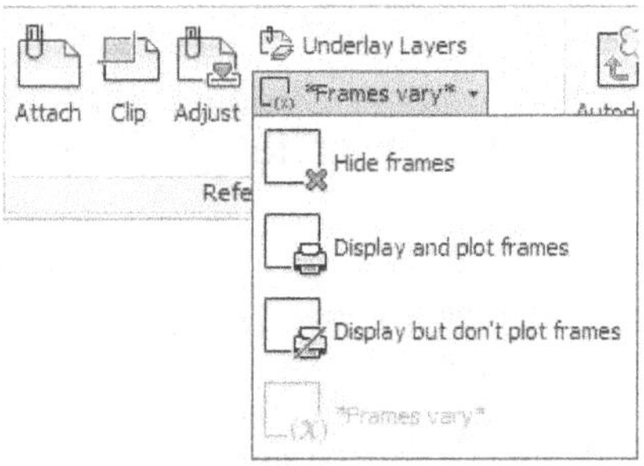

Figure 31–21

Reference File Properties

DWF, DGN, and Image references have several properties that can be modified, including how and what they display in the drawing.

These options can be modified in the Properties palette.

Miscellaneous Options

In the *Misc* area in the Properties palette, you can toggle off DWF or DGN underlays or Images without unloading the files. Set *Show image* to **No**, as shown in Figure 31–22.

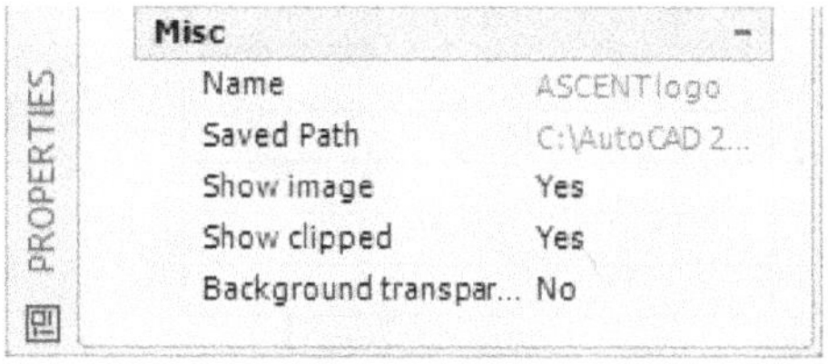

Figure 31–22

- The **Show clipped** option changes the status of displaying whether the object is clipped or not clipped. This is different than displaying the clipping frame.

- Images have the additional **Background Transparency** option. This permits the background of the image to become transparent, so that it matches the general background. However, not all of the file formats enable transparency. You can also access this option in the ribbon and in the shortcut menu under **Image**.

Adjusting Underlays and Images

DWF and DGN underlays and image reference properties can be adjusted.

- With a reference file selected, in the Properties palette, in the *Underlay Adjust* or *Image Adjust* areas, you can specify the amount of *Contrast* and *Fade*, as shown in Figure 31–23. DWF and DGN files can be set to **Monochrome** and Image files have an additional **Brightness** adjustment.

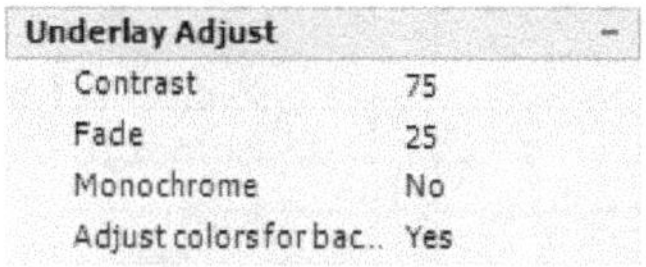

Figure 31–23

- DWF underlays have an option to adjust the colors for the background.

- Click (Adjust) in the *Insert* tab>Reference panel to adjust the *Fade*, *Contrast*, or *Monochrome* settings for underlay and image files.

- Image references can also be adjusted in the *Image Adjust* contextual tab as shown in Figure 31–24. A preview of the changes displays in the drawing window as the modifications are made. The contextual tab is opened by selecting the underlay or image.

Figure 31–24

- The quality of an image can be set to **High** or **Draft** by typing **imagequality** at the Command Line.

Hint: Creating an Image File

In the AutoCAD software, there are several ways of creating a raster file, which can then be used as an image:

- You can copy the contents of the current viewport using **saveimg** at the Command Line. The image can be saved in the .BMP, .PCX, .TGA, .TIF, .JPEG, or .PNG file formats.

- You can render the display to a file (usually done with 3D objects). Rendering can create several different raster formats.

DWF Specific Adjustments

DWF reference files have two additional options because they are created from drawing files: toggling layers on and off and snapping to objects in the DWF underlay.

- Layer visibility can be controlled in DWF underlays (as shown in Figure 31–25), if the DWF file was created with the layers toggled on. When you have selected a DWF underlay, right-click and select **DWF Layers**. Select the layers you want to toggle on or off and click **OK**.

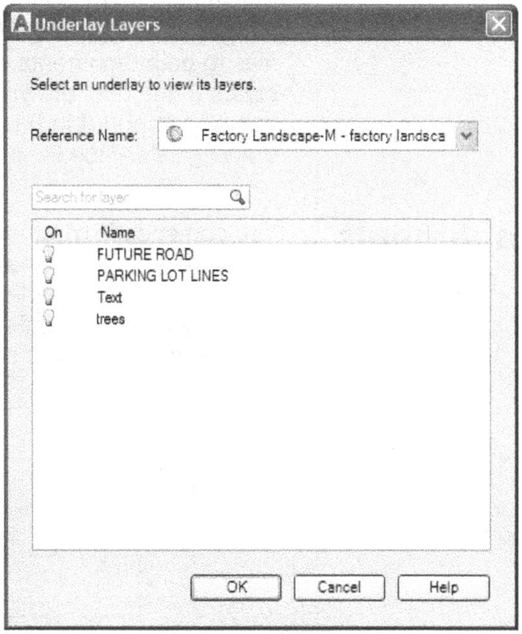

Figure 31–25

- To adjust another reference file's layers, select it in the Reference Name drop-down list.

- If a reference file does not contain layers, this is indicated in the Underlay Layers dialog box. By default, layers are not saved in the **DWF6ePlot.pc3** file supplied with the software.

- You can snap to objects in a DWF underlay. If you do not want object snaps to work with DWF files, select the DWF underlay, right-click and clear **DWF Object Snap**, as shown in Figure 31–26. This impacts all of the DWF underlays in a drawing.

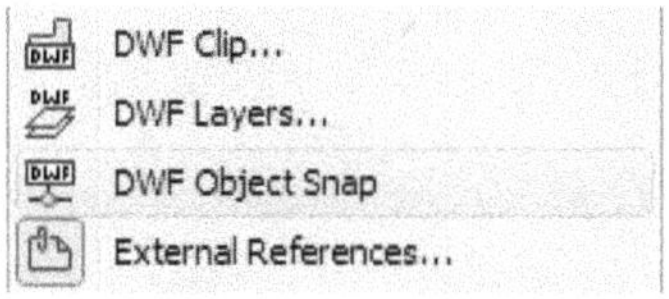

Figure 31–26

31.3 Xref Specific Information

The reference file tools works slightly differently with drawing references (also known as Xrefs). Because drawing reference files contain the same components as the host files, you can manipulate them using methods that cannot be applied to raster images, .DWF, and .DGN files. You can set drawing reference files to be attachments or overlays and can modify Xref layer states in the host drawing without impacting the original file. You can also import (bind) layers and block components of the drawing reference file into your drawing.

Attachments vs. Overlays

You can specify whether a drawing reference file should be an attachment or an overlay when it is originally referenced. Attachments and overlays work in the same way in the host file. You only notice the difference if you reference that host file in another file, as shown in Figure 31–27.

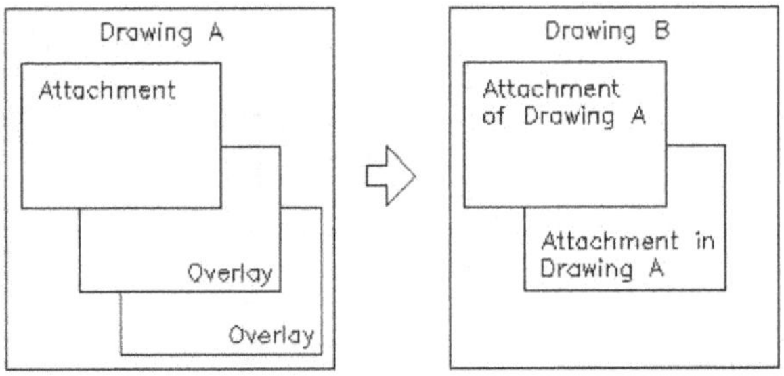

Figure 31–27

Attachment	When a file is referenced as an attachment, it displays with the host file if the host file itself is then referenced in another drawing. Using attachments enables a file to travel along the path with its host. A typical use for this option would be if there were a part referenced inside a subassembly, which is then referenced into a larger assembly.
Overlay	When a file is referenced as an overlay, it does not display in the host file if the host file itself is referenced in another drawing. Using overlays helps to avoid problems of circular references. (Circular references occur when a file references itself, usually indirectly. For example, drawing A references drawing B, which references drawing C, which references drawing A.)

- To change a drawing reference file from an attachment to an overlay, select the reference in the External References palette and modify it in the **Details** pane, as shown in Figure 31–28.

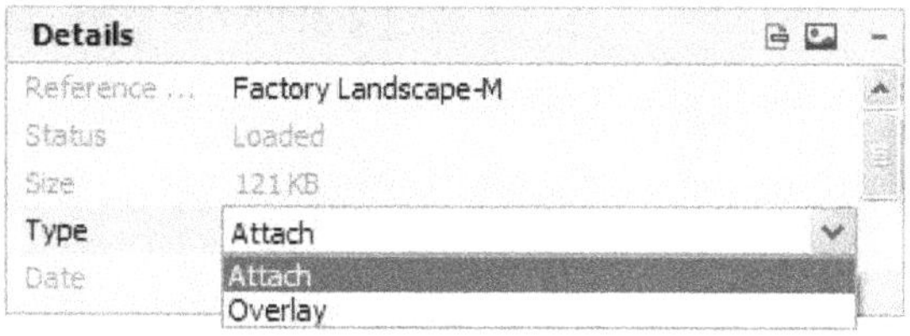

Figure 31–28

- You can also right-click on a filename(s) in the External References palette, expand Xref Type, and select **Overlay**.

Xref Layers

When you attach or overlay a drawing reference file, it brings the drawing objects and its named objects, such as layers and blocks, into the host drawing.

- A special prefix is added to any named objects from the referenced drawing when the names display in the host drawing, as shown in Figure 31–29. It consists of the name of the referenced drawing and a "¦". For example, a layer **Walls** in a reference file named **House5** would display as **House5¦Walls**.

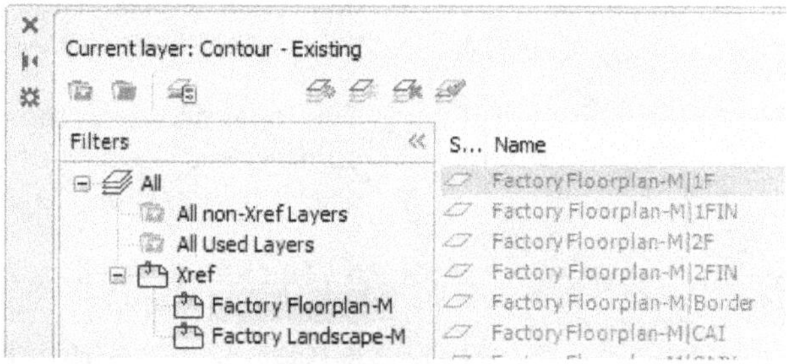

Figure 31–29

- In order to clearly distinguish which layers come from referenced drawings and which layer reside in the active drawing, xref layers are now shown in gray text in the *Home* tab>Layers panel>Layers drop-down list, as shown in Figure 31–30. Additionally, you can only change the visibility of xref layers in the layer panel drop-down.

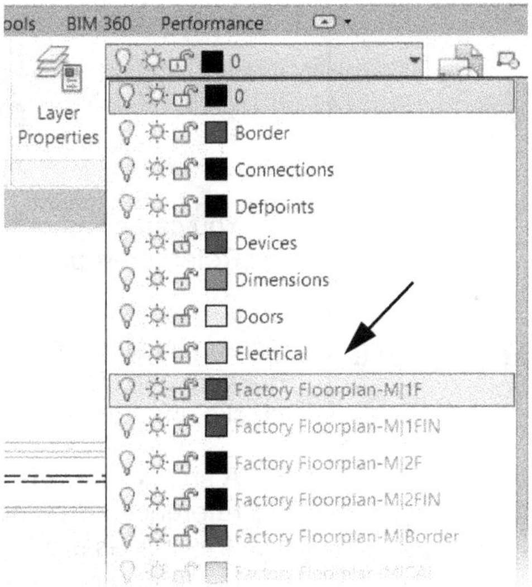

Figure 31–30

- If the Xref layers display in the Layer Control, you can change their state or properties (**Freeze/Thaw**, **Color**, etc.). However, you cannot make an Xref layer current in the host drawing.

- The layer on which the drawing reference file is inserted controls the visibility of the drawing reference file. The drawing reference file is hidden when that layer is frozen.

- If you change the properties of an Xref layer, the change does not affect the referenced drawing. However, the change is retained in the host drawing by default. The default is controlled by the **visretain** system variable. You can also modify it in the Options dialog box, in the *Open and Save* tab, by toggling the **Retain changes to Xref layers** option on or off.

- In Layer Properties Manager you can quickly display all of the layers in a specific drawing reference file by selecting the filter that is automatically created when the drawing reference file is attached. You can then use **Select All** and modify the layers as required.

- You can now control the display of layers for objects in an xref drawing that were not set to "ByLayer" for the layer property updates in the original xref. The new **XREFOVERRIDE** variable enables objects in the reference file to override properties set in the drawing file it is referenced into (host file). Setting the **XREFOVERRIDE** to **1** enables the original file to set the properties. Setting the **XREFOVERRIDE** to **0** enables the drawing in which it is referenced to control the properties.

Binding Drawing Reference Files

The **Bind** option in a drawing reference file copies all of the referenced drawing's data into the current drawing and then detaches the reference. The referenced drawing becomes an inserted block.

How To: Bind a Drawing Reference File

1. Open the External References palette.
2. Right-click on the drawing reference file that you want to bind in the list and select **Bind**.
3. In the *Bind Type* area, select **Bind** or **Insert** (as shown in Figure 31–31) and click **OK**.

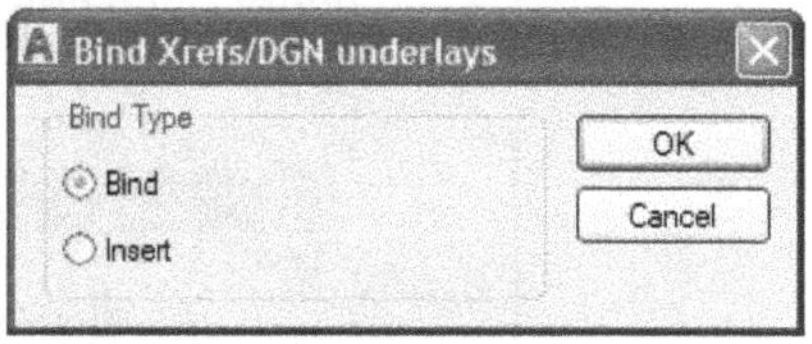

Figure 31–31

When a drawing reference file is bound, it brings all of its layers, blocks, and other named objects into the host drawing. The **Bind Type** controls how these named objects are named in the host drawing.

- When you use the *Bind Type* **Bind**, the object names are prefixed with the name of the reference file (filename0layername). For example, if the layer **Ref¦Floor** (from the drawing **Ref.dwg**) was bound to the current drawing, its name would become **Ref0Floor**. This can result in long names, but keeps the layers that were originally in the drawing reference file separate from the layers that were originally in the host file.

- When a drawing reference file is bound as an **Insert**, the block and layer names are added to the current file without change. For example, the Xref layer **Ref¦Floor** would become **Floor**. If the current file contains a block or layer with the same name, the drawing reference file object is updated to match the definition already in the current drawing.

- Binding a drawing reference file as an **Insert** is equivalent to detaching the reference file and inserting it as a block.

Binding Drawing Reference File Components

Instead of binding the entire drawing reference file, you can bind one or more blocks, layers, linetypes, text styles, and dimension styles. Binding any of these named objects adds their definition to the host drawing so that you can use them in the drawing.

- The **Xbind** command, accessed in the Command Line, enables you to bind specific named objects from a drawing reference file (such as layers or blocks).

- **Xbind** opens the Xbind dialog box (shown in Figure 31–32), in which you can select the drawing reference file from which to bind, the type of object (layer, block, etc.), and the specific named object to bind. Click the **+** sign to display the listings under each category. Select the object and click **Add** to add it for binding.

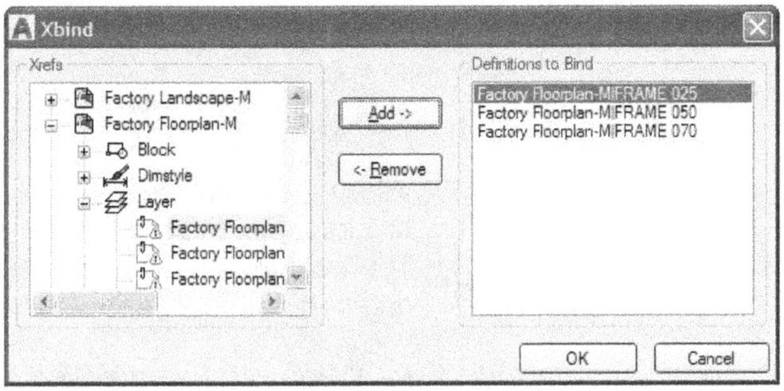

Figure 31–32

- When named objects are bound with **Xbind**, the "¦" in the name is replaced with "0". For example, the block **Office3¦Lamp** becomes **Office3$0$Lamp**. There is no option, such as **Insert**, to add the name without a change. However, you can rename the resulting objects using **Rename**.

- You can use DesignCenter to copy these components into your current drawing without using the long names.

Demand Loading

Demand Loading controls how much of a drawing reference file is loaded. With **Demand Loading** enabled, only the visible parts of the drawing reference file (that are not clipped or on layers that are off or frozen) are loaded. Since it does not have to load the entire drawing reference file, the AutoCAD software responds more quickly.

- **Demand Loading** can be set in the Options dialog box, in the *Open and Save* tab, by selecting the **Demand load Xrefs** options, as shown in Figure 31–33.

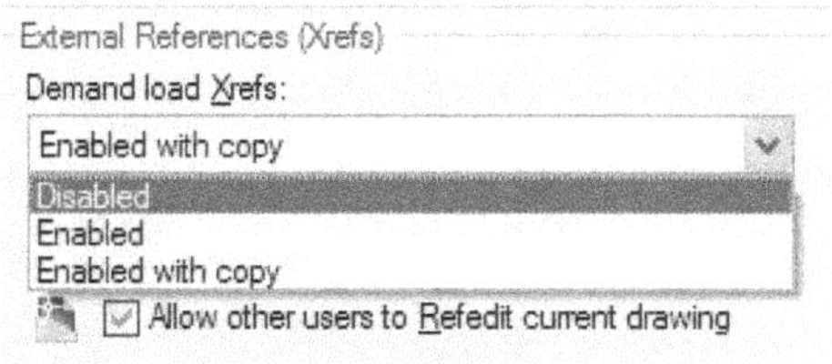

Figure 31–33

- When **Demand Loading** is enabled, others cannot edit the file that is being referenced. To enable others to use the file that is being referenced and take advantage of the improved performance, set *Demand Loading* to **Enabled with copy**. A copy of the file is used in place of the drawing reference file, so that others can use the file.

Practice 31a Attaching External References

Practice Objectives

- Attach and modify external references and overlay drawing references.
- Adjust the layers in a referenced file.
- Bind a reference to a file.

Estimated time for completion: 35 minutes

In this practice, you will attach and modify external references using the External References palette. You will also attach and overlay drawing references and note how they function in another file. You will then adjust layers in a referenced file and bind a reference to a file, as shown in Figure 31–34.

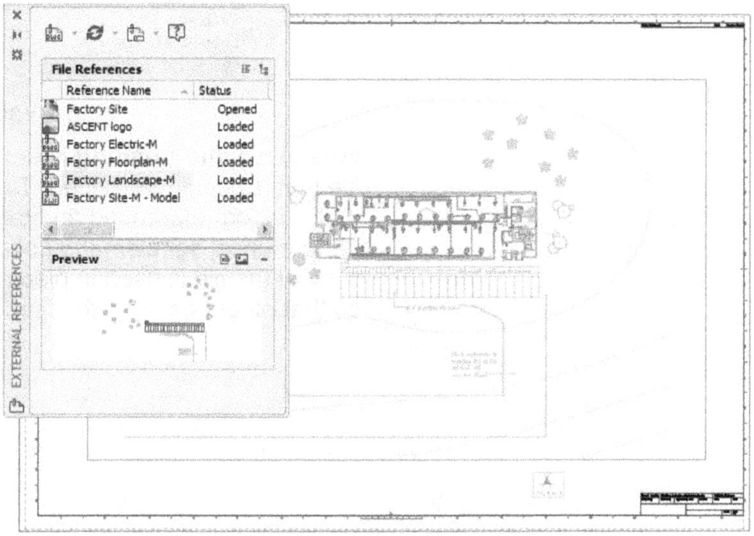

Figure 31–34

Task 1 - Attach external references.

In this task you will explore the features of the External References palette. You will attach a Reference File DWG, Raster Image, and DWF Underlay.

1. Start a new drawing based on **Civil-Meters.dwt**, which is located in your practice files folder and save the drawing as **Factory Site.dwg**.

2. In the *View* tab>Palettes panel, click (External References Palette) to open the External References palette.

3. Near the top of the External References palette, expand (Attach DWG) and select **Attach DWF....**

4. In the Select Reference File dialog box, open **Factory Site-M.dwf** from your practice files folder.

5. In the Attach DWF Underlay dialog box, for *Insertion point*, clear Specify on-screen and verify X,Y,Z values are set as **0,0,0**. Select **Specify on-screen** for the *Scale*. Click **OK** to continue.

6. Right-click and select **Unit**. Verify that **Meter** is selected and press <Enter> to accept the default selection.

7. Press <Enter> to finish placing the DWF underlay.

8. Using the above steps, and using **Attach DWG**, attach **Factory Floorplan-M.dwg** from your practice files folder at **0,0,0** *Insertion point* with the default scale and rotation. Verify that the *Reference Type* is set to **Attachment**.

9. **Zoom Extents** to display **Factory Site-M.dwf** and **Factory Floorplan-M.dwg**.

10. Attach **Factory Landscape-M.dwg** from your practice files folder at any location (*Insertion point*: **Specify On-screen**) at one side of the drawing (you will move it later).

11. Close the External References palette.

12. In the Status Bar, click (Manage Xrefs) to open the External References palette.

13. Select **Factory Landscape-M.dwg** and in the Details pane, click (Preview) to display an image of the landscape reference file.

14. Switch to the **ISO A0** layout. Activate the viewport and **Zoom Extents**.

15. Activate the Paper Space (double-click outside the viewport) and using **Attach Image**, attach **ASCENT logo.gif** from your practice files folder at a scale of **50**. Place it near the left of the title block.

16. Save the file.

Task 2 - Modify external references.

In this task you will move a reference file to a new location, clip a DWF file, open a reference file and make a change to that drawing, close and reload it, and detach and unload it. The completed drawing is shown in Figure 31–35.

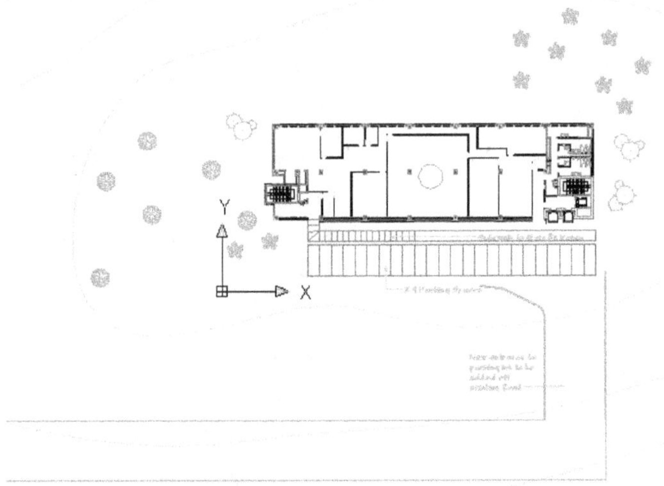

Figure 31–35

1. Switch to the *Model* tab and select **Factory Site-M.dwf** (outer rectangle). Right-click and verify that **DWF Object Snap** is enabled, as shown in Figure 31–36. Press <ESC> to exit selection.

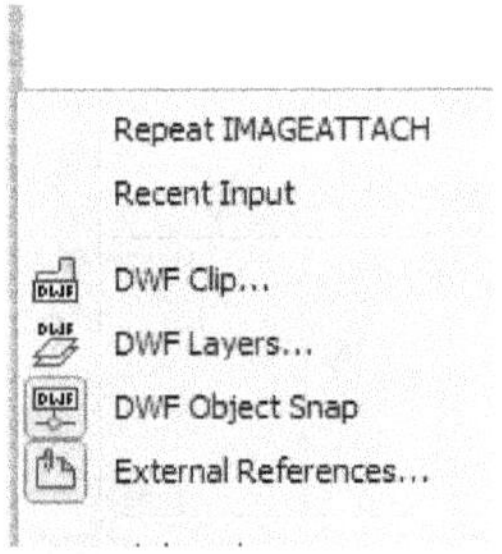

Figure 31–36

2. Move **Factory Landscape-M.dwg** (file with trees) so that the existing road in the DWF file is at the end of the new entrance to the parking lot, as shown in Figure 31–37.

Hint: In the landscape drawing, use the bottom left endpoint of the vertical portion of the road as your base point and move it to the right endpoint of the top horizontal line of the road in the site dwf.

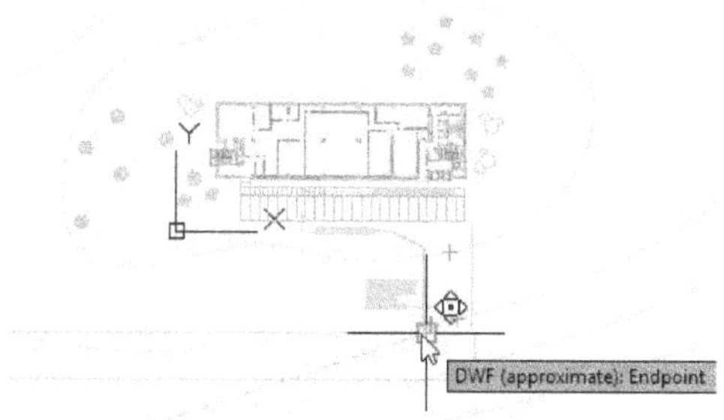

Figure 31–37

3. Select **Factory Site-M.dwf** (outer rectangle), right-click and select **DWF Clip...**. Press <Enter> to accept the **New boundary** option and create a new rectangular boundary close to the landscape elements, building, and road, similar to the area shown in Figure 31–35.
4. Type **dwfframe** and set the *system variable* to **0** to hide the boundary frame.
5. Check the Layer Control, and note that the layers associated with **Factory Floorplan-M.dwg** are listed but they are grayed out.
6. In the External References palette, detach **Factory Floorplan-M.dwg** (Right-click and select **Detach**). The building is removed from the drawing window and the file is removed from the External References palette.
7. Save the drawing.
8. Attach **Factory Floorplan-M.dwg** from your practice files folder to your file at an *Insertion point* of **0,0,0** and a *Rotation* of **0**.
9. In the External References palette, unload **Factory Floorplan-M.dwg** (right-click and select **Unload**). Note that the building is removed from the drawing window but the file is still listed in the palette with a red arrow displayed along with it, as shown in Figure 31–38.

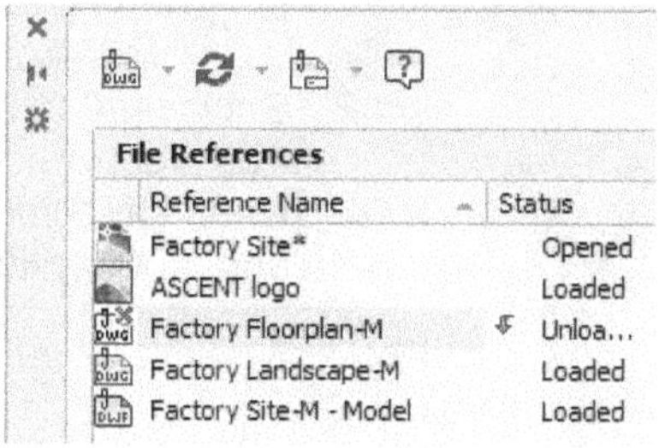

Figure 31–38

10. Reload **Factory Floorplan-M.dwg**. (Right-click and select **Reload**).

11. In the External References palette, select **Factory Floorplan-M.dwg**. Right-click and select **Open**.

12. Set the layer **Equipment** to be current and draw a circle with a *radius* of **2** near the middle of the floorplan.

13. Save and close **Factory Floorplan-M.dwg**.

14. In **Factory Site.dwg**, note that the new circle is not displayed. In the External References palette, reload **Factory Floorplan-M.dwg**. Note that the new circle displays.

15. Save and close the drawing.

Task 3 - Attach and overlay drawing references in another file.

In this task you will attach and overlay drawing references and note how they function in another file. You will then adjust layers in a referenced file and finally bind a reference to a file. The completed drawing is shown in Figure 31–39.

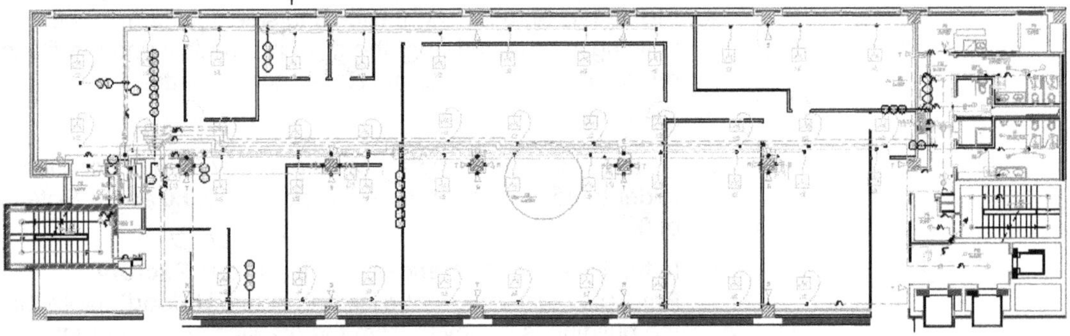

Figure 31–39

1. Open **Factory Floorplan-M.dwg** from your practice files folder.

2. Set layer **0** to be current and attach **Factory Electric-M.dwg** from your practice files folder to the current drawing at **0,0,0** as an attachment. Accept the defaults for the *Scale*, *Rotation*, and other options.

3. Attach **Factory Lighting-M.dwg** from your practice files folder to the current drawing at **0,0,0**. Accept the defaults for the other options.

You can also change it in the Details pane.

4. In the External References palette, right-click on **Factory Lighting-M.dwg**, expand **Xref Type**, and select **Overlay**. Close the palette. The overlay file remains visible in the drawing.

5. Save and close the drawing.

6. Open **Factory Site.dwg** if it is not already open. Note that the attached reference **Factory Electric-M.dwg** displays but the overlaid lighting reference is not.

7. Save and close the drawing.

Task 4 - Work with drawing reference file layers.

1. Open **Factory Floorplan-M.dwg** from your practice files folder.

2. Make a layer other than **0** current (it must be a layer found in the host drawing such as 2FIN) and freeze layer **0**. The other reference files, which were inserted on layer **0**, are hidden, as shown in Figure 31–40.

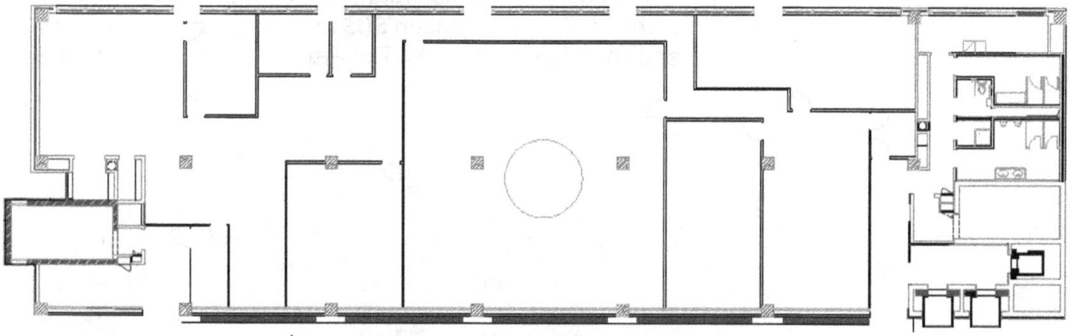

Figure 31–40

3. Thaw layer **0** and make it current again.

4. Expand the Layer Control and note the layers that begin with **Factory Electric-M** and **Factory Lighting-M** are all gray. All of these layers belong to the drawing reference files.

5. Open the Layer Properties Manager.
6. In the left pane, expand the Xref file group and select **Factory Electric-M**. All of the layers in the drawing reference file display in the right pane.
7. In the right pane, right-click and select **Select All**.
8. Select one of the color blocks and change the *color* to **light gray**. The selected layers display in that color in the current drawing. Change the *Layer Filter* back to **All**.
9. Save and close the file.
10. Open **Factory Electric-M.dwg** and verify that the layers retain their original colors. Close the file.
11. Open **Factory Floorplan-M.dwg**. The layers from the **Factory Electric-M.dwg** referenced drawing are still gray.

Task 5 - Bind drawing reference files.

1. Continue working in **Factory Floorplan-M.dwg**.
2. In the External References palette, right-click on **Factory Lighting-M.dwg** and select **Bind...** to bind it to the host file. In the dialog box click **OK**.
3. In the Layer Properties Manager, note that all of the Factory Lighting M layers contain 0 and have turned black, as shown in Figure 31–41. (Tip: Set the *Layer Filter* to **All**.)

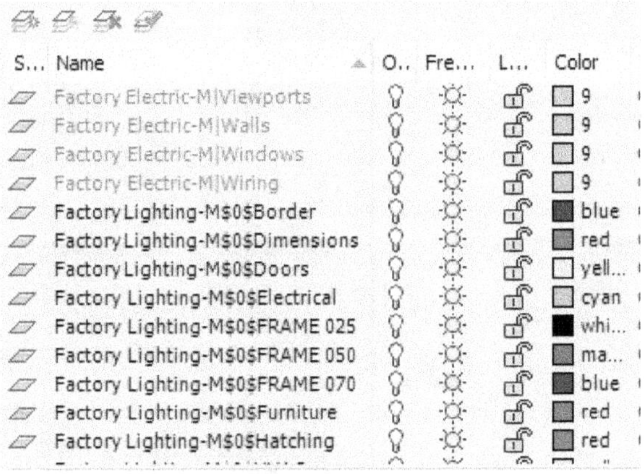

Figure 31–41

4. Undo the **Bind** process.
5. **Bind** the same file again, but this time as an **Insert**.
6. Look at the layers. They are now integrated into the main layer names.
7. Save and close the drawing.
8. Reopen **Factory Site.dwg** and update the change to the reference as required. The Lighting objects now display in the current drawing because they are no longer just an overlay in the referenced file.
9. Save the drawing.

Chapter Review Questions

1. Which of the following describes how External References are different from blocks? An External Reference...
   a. Can contain one or many objects.
   b. Is a link to another file.
   c. Includes layers.
   d. Acts as one object in the drawing.
2. File types that can be used as Eternal References include: AutoCAD drawing files, raster image files, DWF underlay files, DGN underlay files, and PDF underlay files.
   a. True
   b. False
3. What happens when you open a drawing containing a referenced file that cannot be located by the software? (Select all that apply.)
   a. The References - Not Found Files dialog box opens.
   b. An exclamation mark (**!**) displays next to the drawing in the External References palette.
   c. It becomes a block.
   d. It is compressed to take up less memory.
4. Which of the following file formats cannot attach to an AutoCAD drawing as an external reference?
   a. .DWF
   b. .DOC
   c. .DWG
   d. .DGN

5. Drawing A is attached as a drawing reference file to host drawing B and both are then closed.
   Drawing A is then modified.
   Drawing B is opened and displays an image of drawing A.
   What happens to the image of drawing A when drawing B is opened?

   a. It displays a warning message.
   b. It does not change.
   c. It updates to display the changes.
   d. It displays as a blank image.

6. Which command or option enables you to bind one or more blocks, layers, linetypes, text styles, or dimension styles?

   a. **Reload**
   b. **Demand Load**
   c. **Bind**
   d. **Xbind**

Command Summary

Button	Command	Location
	**Adjust**	• **Ribbon:** *Insert* tab>Reference panel • **Command Prompt:** adjust
	**Attach Xref**	• **Ribbon:** *Insert* tab>Reference panel • **Command Prompt:** attach
	**Clip Xref**	• **Ribbon:** *Insert* tab>Reference panel • **Command Prompt:** clip
	**External References**	• **Ribbon:** *View* tab>Palettes panel or *Insert* tab>Reference panel arrow • **Command Prompt:** externalreferences

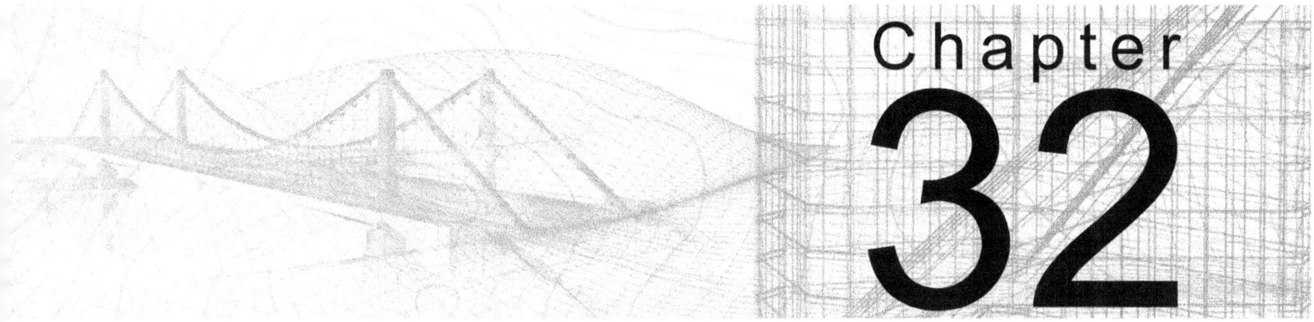

Projects: Drawing

This chapter contains practice projects that can be used to gain additional hands-on experience with the topics and commands covered so far in this student guide. These practices are intended to be self-guided and do not include step by step information.

Learning Objectives in this Chapter

- *All:* Create title blocks that contain borders using rectangles and lines.
- *Mechanical:* Create a drill press base using features such as fillet, offset, trim, hatching and viewports.
- *Architecture:* Create a room layout using features such as hatching, viewports, D-sized block, text and dimensions.
- *P&ID:* Create a piping schematic using features such as viewports, and commands such as move, rotate, and sketch.
- *Civil:* Create a warehouse site using features such as viewports, text, hatching, and dimensions.

32.1 ISO A1 Title Block (36x24)

Estimated time for completion: 15 minutes

In this project you will create a title block. You will add a border using rectangles and lines, and add a logo and permanent text in the title block. This title block (shown in Figure 32–1), works with the DWF6 ePlot plotter with an ISO expand A1 paper size when inserted at 0,0.

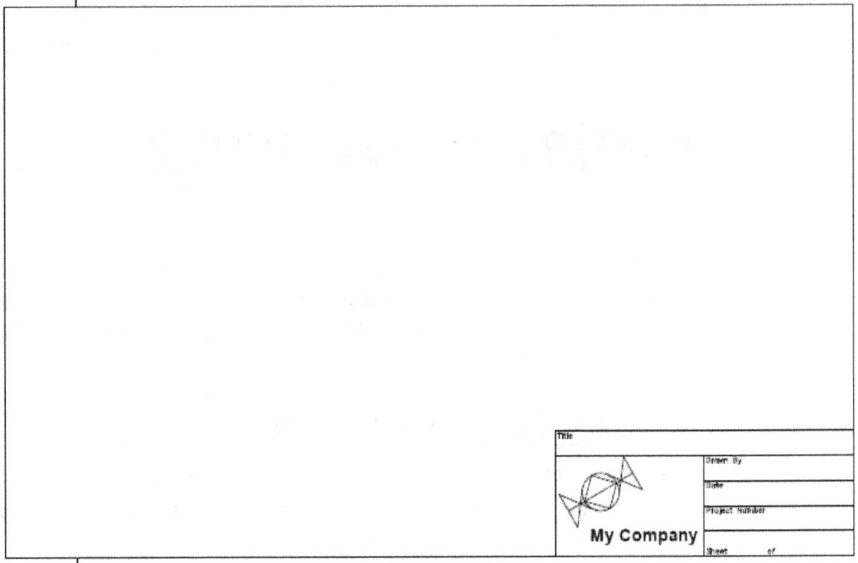

Figure 32–1

1. Start a new drawing based on **Mech-Millimeters.dwt**, which is located in your practice files folder and save it as **Titleblock_ISO_A1.dwg**.
2. Set the current layer to **Border**.
3. Draw a **829 x 572** rectangle, starting with the lower left corner at the point **1.0,0.5** (the border starts at this point so that it fits correctly when inserted into the layout at 0,0). Zoom out to display the entire drawing.

4. Draw the lines for the title block, as shown in Figure 32–2. Place it in the lower right corner of the border.

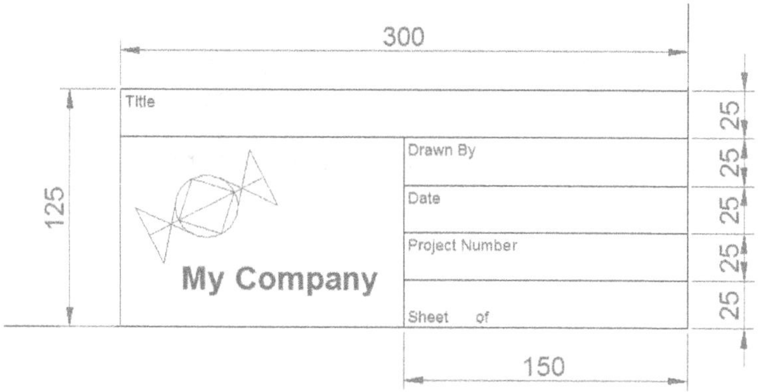

Figure 32–2

5. Change the current layer to **Text**. Draw circles, lines, and rectangles to create a logo in the largest box of the title block.
6. Move, rotate, and/or scale the logo so that it fits inside the box, but with enough room to add text later.
7. Add the text shown in Figure 32–2. All of the small text is **6 units** and uses the **Standard** text style. The text style for the logo is **Title** and you can use any height that fits in the space.
8. Save the drawing.

32.2 Mechanical Project: Drill Press Base

Estimated time for completion: 45 minutes

In this project you will create a mechanical drawing of a drill press base and prepare it for plotting. You will draw the top view, insert a pre-drawn side view, and lay the drawing out for plotting, as shown in Figure 32–3.

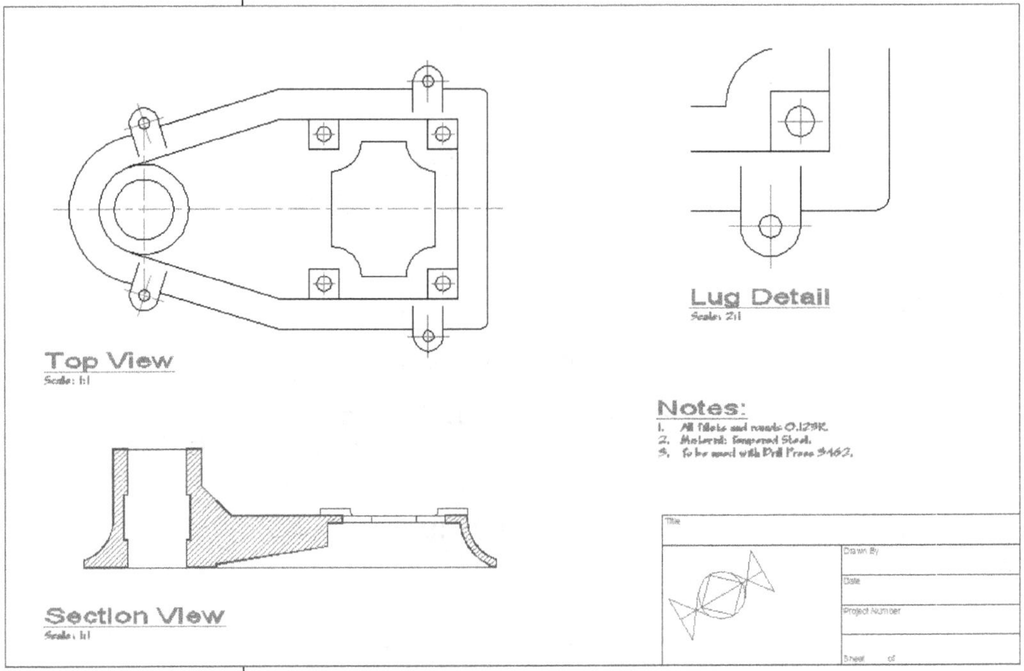

Figure 32–3

Task 1 - Draw the base.

1. Start a new drawing based on **Mech-Millimeters.dwt**, which is located in your practice files folder and save it as **Drill Press Base.dwg**.

2. Draw the objects shown in Figure 32–4 on the layer **Object**. Use **Offset** to help locate the lines correctly. Use **Fillet** or **Trim** to clean up any extra overlapping lines.

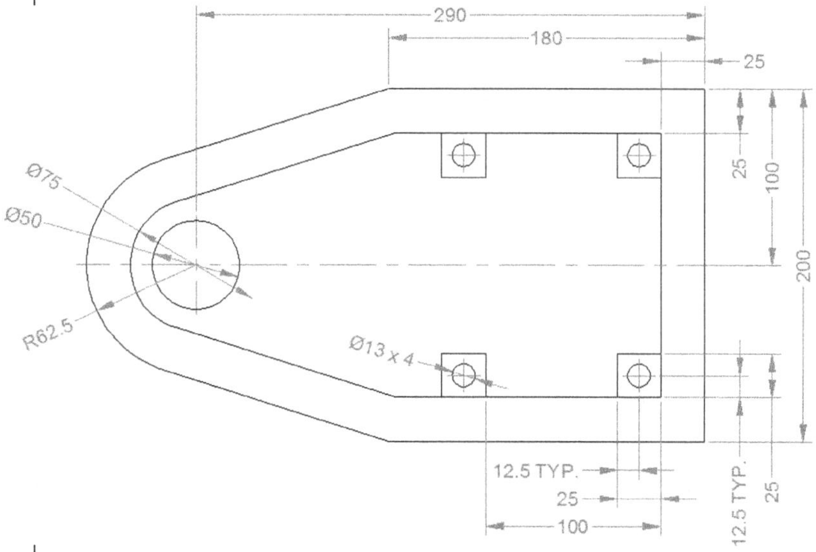

Figure 32–4

3. Fillet the outer corners at a *radius* of **65**.

4. Add the opening shown in Figure 32–5.

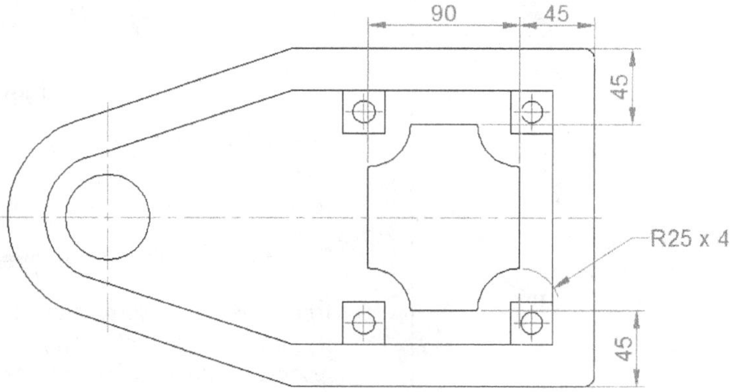

Figure 32–5

5. Save the drawing.

Task 2 - Create a block.

1. Draw one lug in empty space to the side of the part, as shown in Figure 32–6.

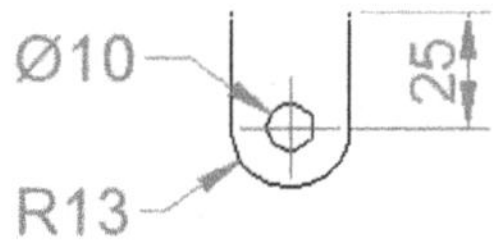

Figure 32–6

2. Make a block called **Lug** from the circle, arc, and lines. Select the center of the circle as the base point, as shown in Figure 32–7.

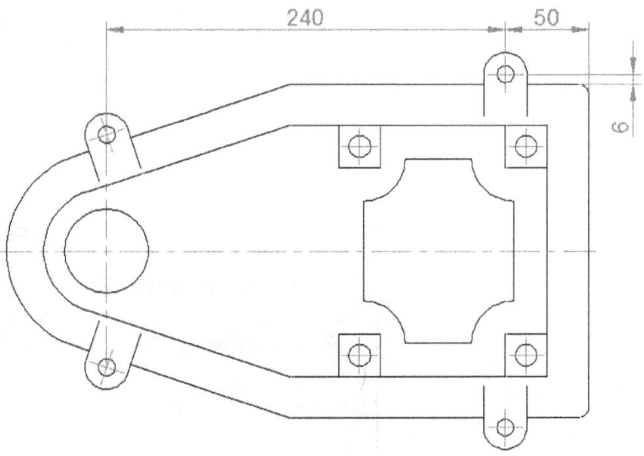

Figure 32–7

3. Insert the four lugs, as shown in Figure 32–7. When you rotate, you can obtain the angles using grips and by snapping to the centerlines used to place the block.
4. Trim the lines that cross over the lugs.
5. Insert **Section-M.dwg** from your practice files folder. Position it above or below the top view of the base. Do not be concerned with its exact position. You can arrange the layout later in Paper Space.
6. Save the drawing.

Task 3 - Set up the drawing for plotting in a layout.

1. In **Drill Press Base.dwg**, create a new layout and rename it **Sheet 1**. Apply a Page Setup to the layout using the plot device **DWF6 ePlot** and the paper size **ISO expand A1 (841.00 x 594.00 MM)**.
2. Set the current layer to **Border** and insert the file **Tblk_A1-M.dwg** (located in your practice files folder) at **0,0**.
3. Erase the existing viewport in the layout.
4. Set the current layer to **Viewports**.
5. Create three new viewports, as shown in Figure 32–8. Scale the *Top View* and *Section View* to **1:1**. Scale the *Lug Detail* to **2:1**.

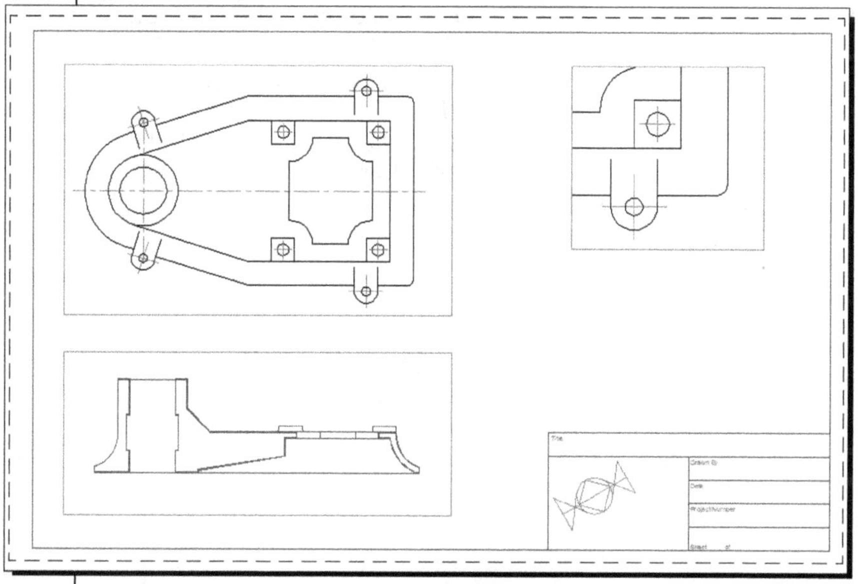

Figure 32–8

6. If the viewport is not big enough, you can return to Paper Space and stretch the viewport using grips.
7. Make the **Section** viewport active.

8. Set the current layer to **Hatching** and hatch the areas of the section view with the **ANSI31** pattern, as shown in Figure 32–9.

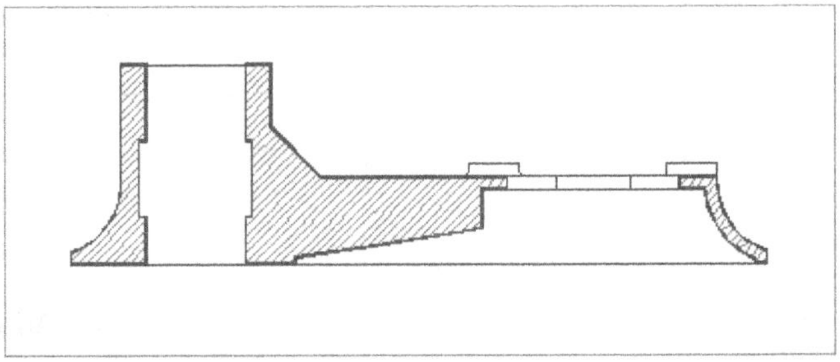

Figure 32–9

9. Save the drawing.

Task 4 - Add text to the layout.

1. Set the current layer to **Text** and toggle off the layer **Viewports**. Add labels to each view using the **Hand** text style with a *height* of **6**. Change the *title part* of the label to the **Arial** font and the *size* to **13**, as shown in Figure 32–10.

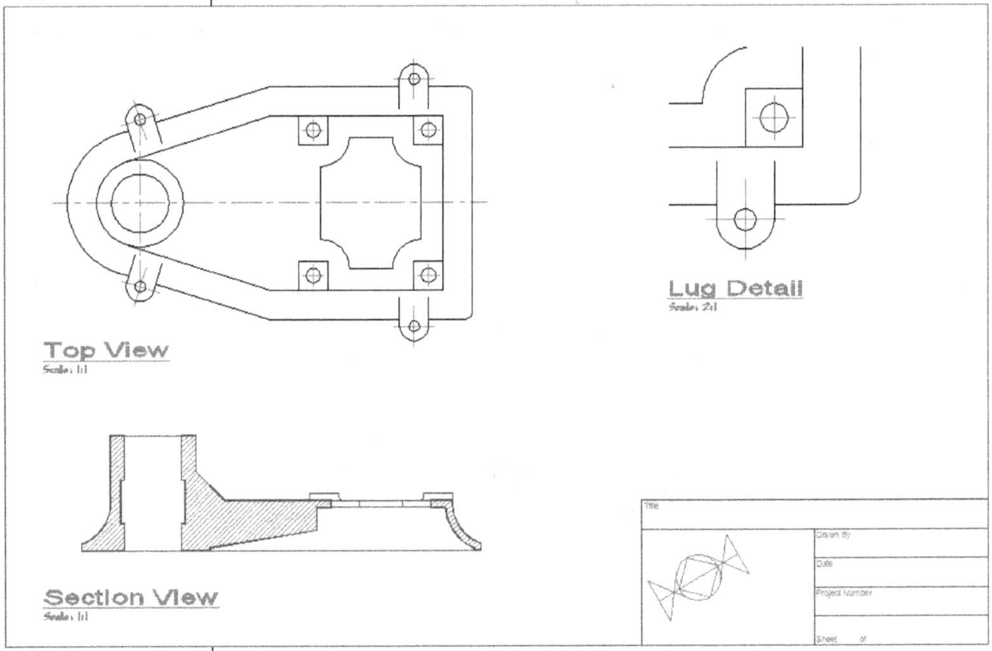

Figure 32–10

2. Fill out the title block with the **Standard** text style and a *height* of **6**.

3. Using multiline text with the **Hand** text style, add the text shown in Figure 32–11 to your drawing. The *text height* is **6**. Change the text **Notes:** to the **Arial** font and make it **13** units tall.

Notes:
1. All fillets and rounds 3R.
2. Material: Tempered Steel.
3. To be used with Drill Press 3462.

Figure 32–11

Task 5 - Add dimensions to the layout.

1. Set the current layer to **Dimensions**.

2. Set the *Dimension Style* to **2places**.

3. Add dimensions in the viewports for the Top View and Lug Detail, as shown in Figure 32–12.

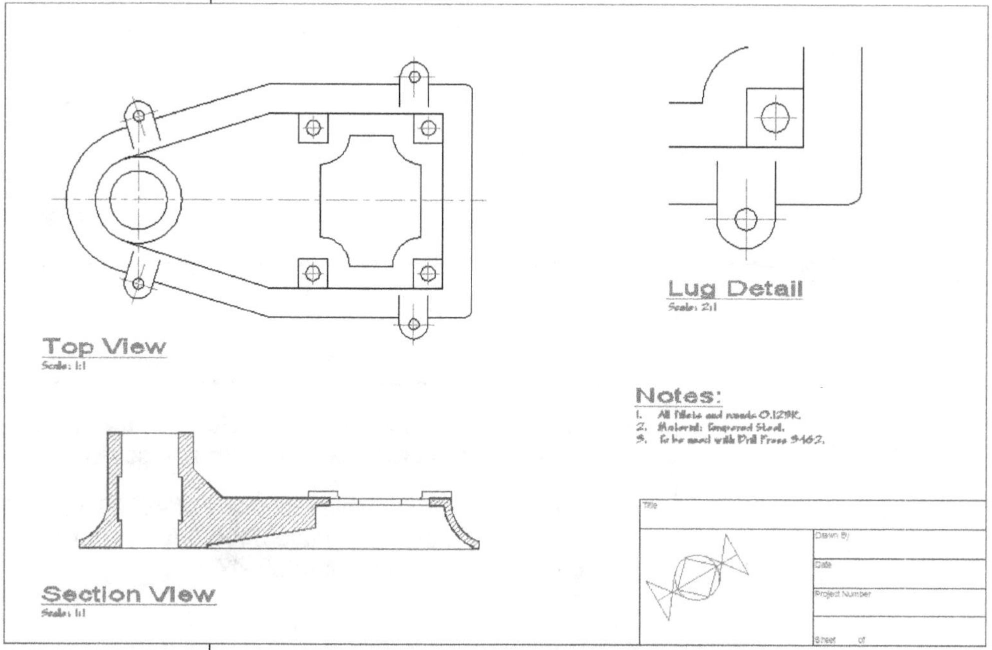

Figure 32–12

4. Save and close the drawing.

32.3 Architectural Project: Office Tower

Estimated time for completion: 45 minutes

In this project you will create an architectural drawing of one floor in an office tower. You will draw the floorplan for the building core, mark the areas for various tenants, and lay the drawing out for plotting, as shown in Figure 32–13.

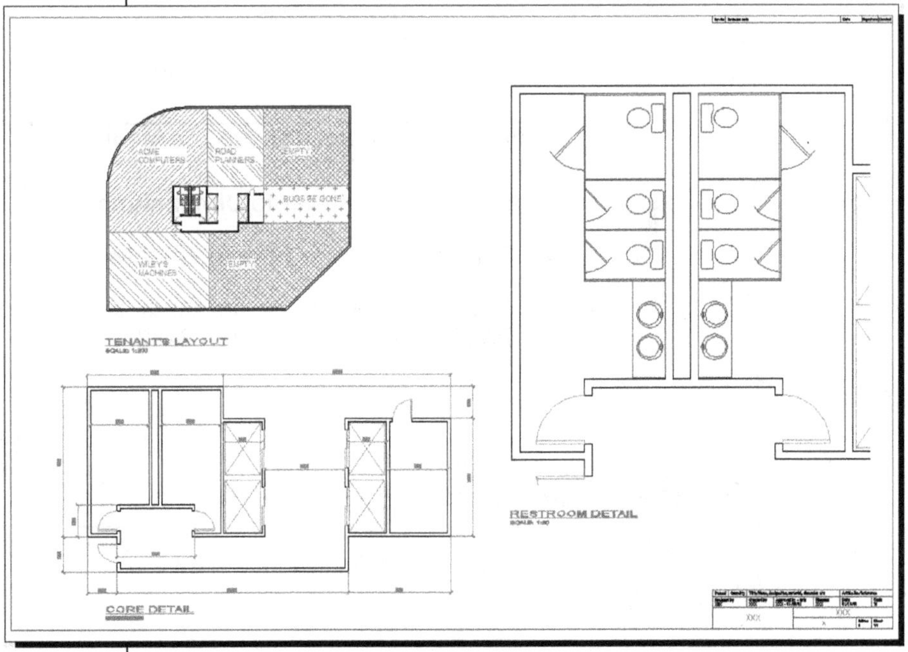

Figure 32–13

Task 1 - Draw the interior and exterior walls and elevators.

1. Start a new drawing based on **AEC-Millimeters.dwt**, which is located in your practice files folder and save it as **Tower.dwg**.
2. Draw a rectangular building outline of **45720 x 38100**, starting with the absolute coordinate **3000,3000** in the lower left corner, as shown in Figure 32–14.

3. Fillet the upper left corner with a *radius* of **15200**, as shown in Figure 32–14.

4. Chamfer the lower right corner with *distances* of **12000**, as shown in Figure 32–14.

5. Use **Offset** to create the walls. The exterior walls are **300** thick, as shown in Figure 32–14.

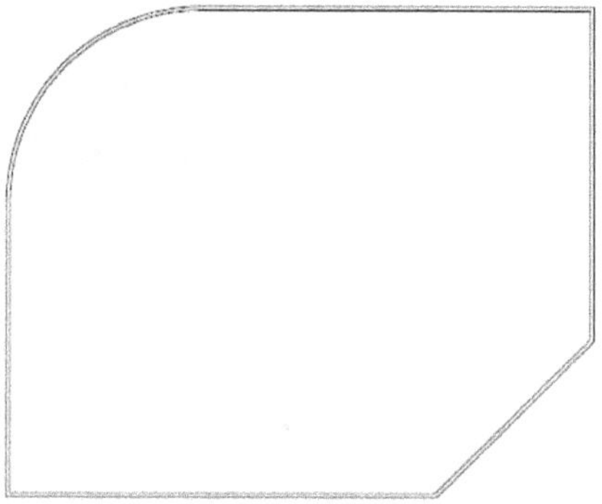

Figure 32–14

6. Draw the interior walls, as shown in Figure 32–15. Start at the absolute coordinate point of **15540,19350** at the intersection of the **1370** and **7000** lines. The interior walls are **150** thick.

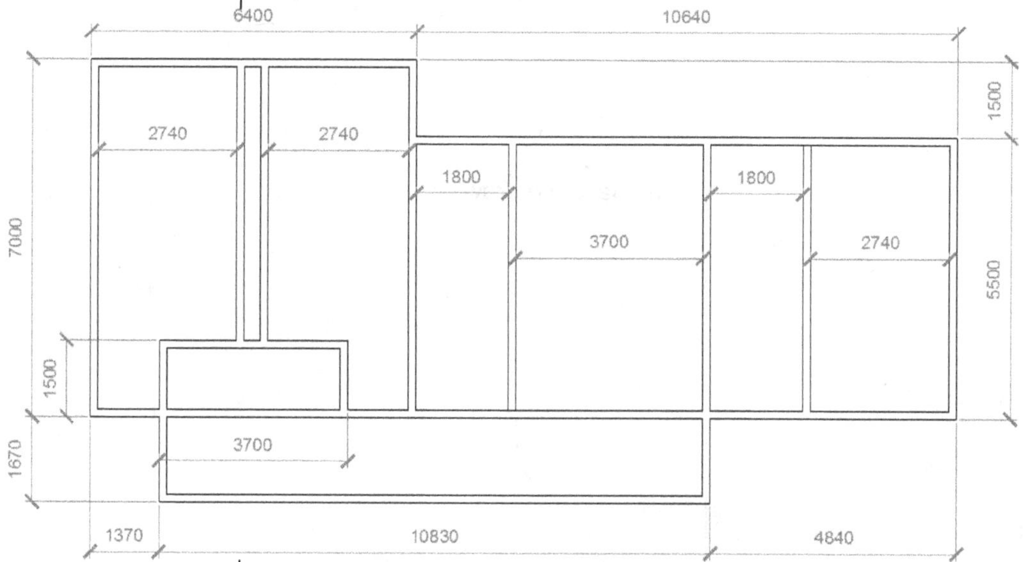

Figure 32–15

7. Use **Trim**, **Extend**, and **Fillet** (with a radius of **0**) as required to clean up the intersections of the walls at the core of the building, as shown in Figure 32–16.
8. Draw a **1670 x 2400** elevator in the bottom left elevator shaft space (the 1800 wide space). There should be **75 units** of clearance between the elevator and the walls (you might want to create an **Elevator** layer).
9. Use **Copy** to create another elevator adjacent to the first one and then use **Mirror** to create the other two elevators. They are centered in the middle of the 3700 wide space, as shown in Figure 32–16.

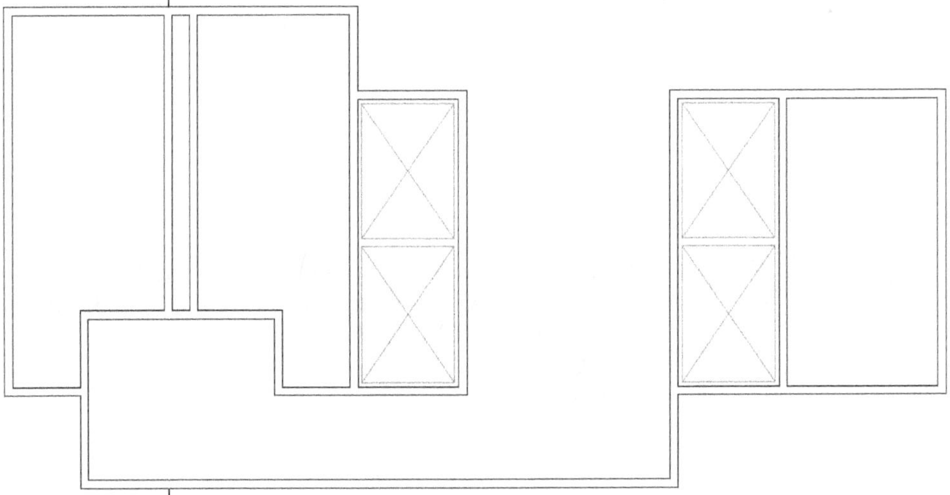

Figure 32–16

10. Save the drawing.

Task 2 - Create doors and insert the bathroom block.

1. Cut the door openings, as shown in Figure 32–17. The elevator openings are **1800**. All of the other doors are **900** wide and either centered on the wall or offset **150** from the closest wall.

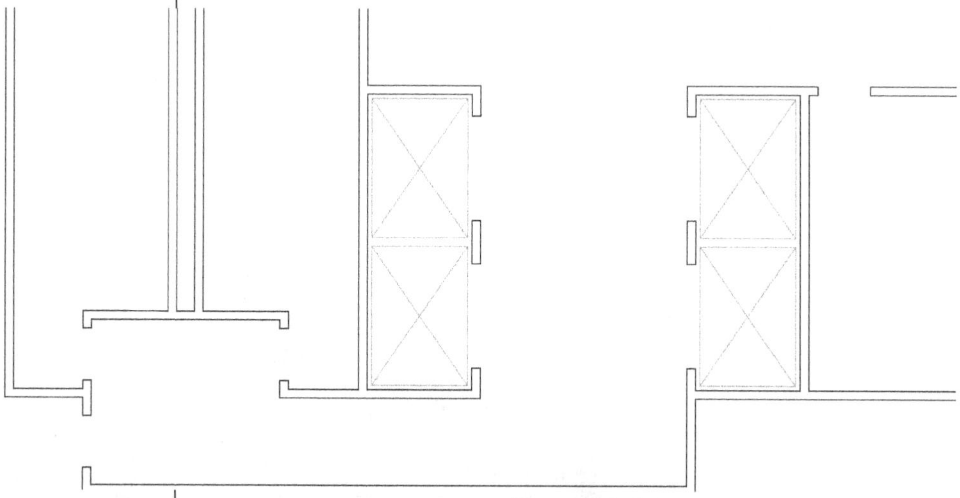

Figure 32–17

2. Set the current layer to **Doors**. Draw the doors shown in Figure 32–18 and create blocks. The door panels are **50** thick. Do not include the dimensions in the blocks.

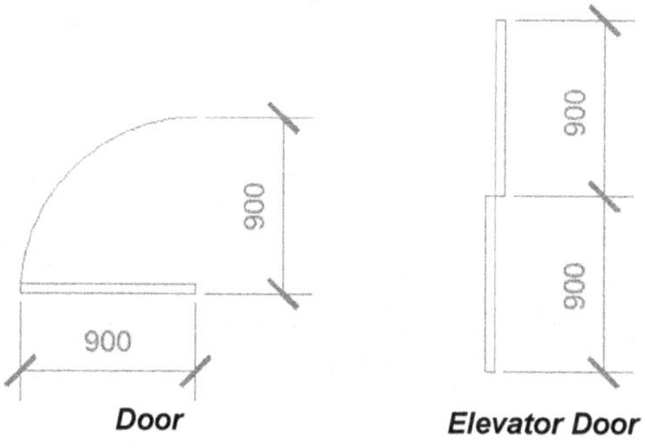

Figure 32–18

3. Insert the door blocks, as shown in Figure 32–19. Insert **Restrooms-AM.dwg** into the restroom areas as well.

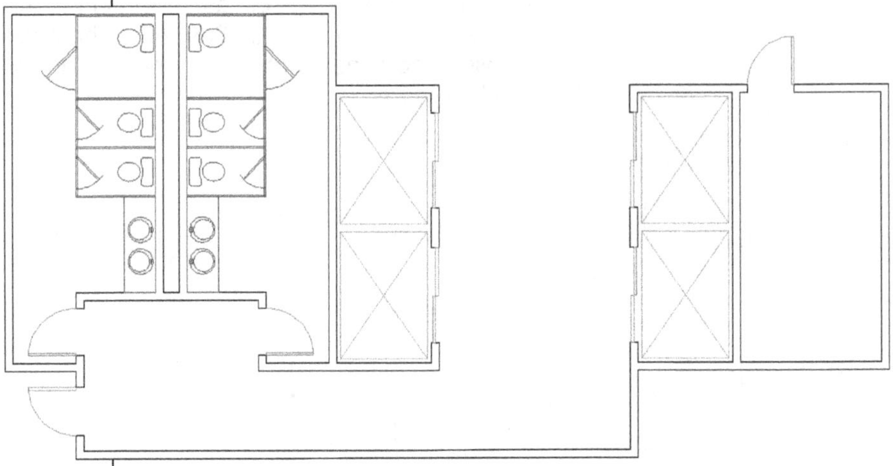

Figure 32–19

4. Save the drawing.

Task 3 - Set up the drawing for plotting in a layout.

1. Switch to the **ISO A1** layout.
2. Set the current layer to **Viewports** and create three viewports, as shown in Figure 32–20.

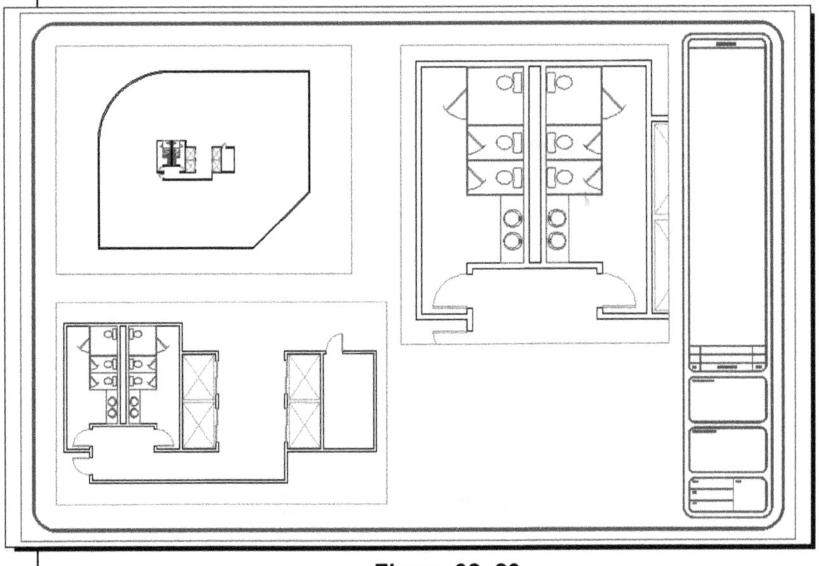

Figure 32–20

3. In one viewport, display the entire drawing scaled at **1:200**.
4. In another viewport, display only the layout of the bathrooms scaled at **1:20**. Freeze the layer **Hatching** in this viewport only.
5. In the third viewport, display the core of the building scaled at **1:50**. Freeze the layers **Hatching** and **Restroom**. You might have to change the sizes of the viewports to fit all of the information once you have applied the scale. You can do this in Paper Space with grips.

Task 4 - Create a tenant layout.

1. Set the current layer to **Hatching**.
2. In the overall viewport, divide the building into several areas, with lines radiating from the core, as shown in Figure 32–21. These are subdivisions for various tenants.

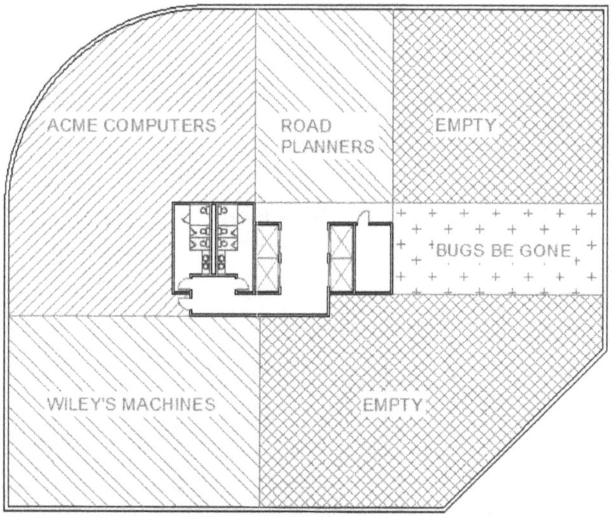

Figure 32–21

3. Set the current layer to **Text**. Add text in each space with the tenant's name.
4. Set the current layer to **Hatching** again. Hatch each tenant's space with a different hatch pattern. Use annotative scales for the hatches.
5. Save the drawing.

Task 5 - Add text and dimensions to the layout.

1. In Paper Space, set the current layer to **Text** and freeze the layer **Viewports**. Use the **Title** text style and add a title for each view, as shown in Figure 32–22. The text size should be **6** for the *title* and **3** for the *scale*.

Figure 32–22

2. Set the current layer to **Dimensions**.

3. Dimension the core, as shown in Figure 32–23. Use the annotative **Architectural-MM** dimension style supplied with the template.

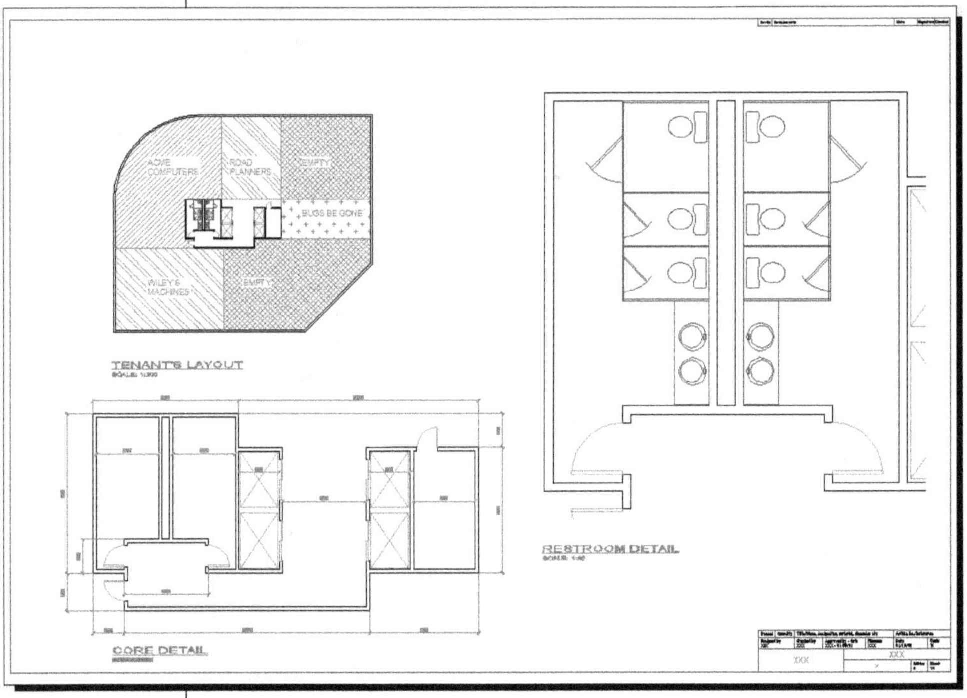

Figure 32–23

4. Save and close the drawing.

32.4 P&ID Project: Oil Lubrication System

Estimated time for completion: 45 minutes

In this project you will create a schematic piping diagram for the oil lubrication system shown in Figure 32–24.

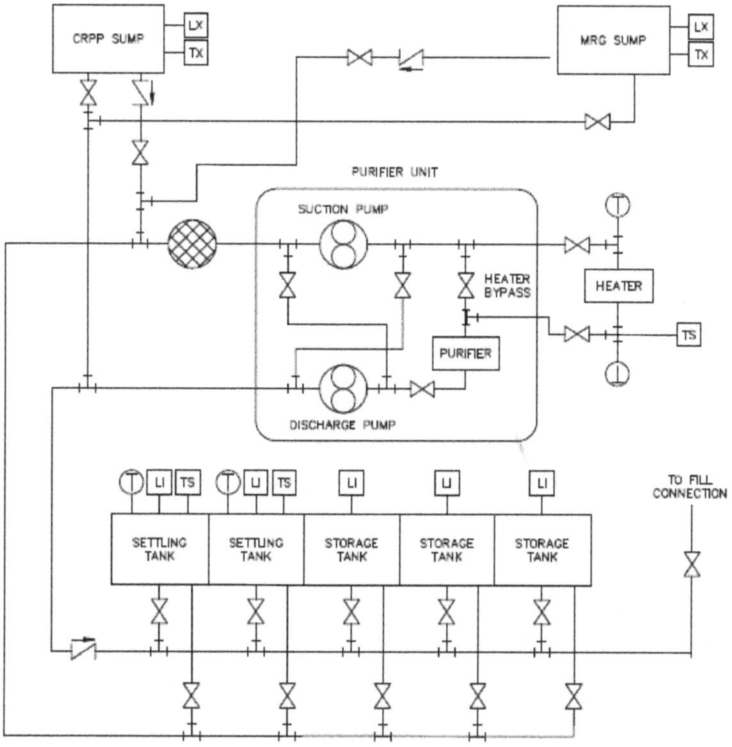

Figure 32–24

Task 1 - Draw the schematic layout.

1. Start a new drawing based on **Mech-Millimeters.dwt**, which is located in your practice files folder and save it as **Lubesys.dwg**.

2. Toggle on (Snap Mode) and (Grid Display). In the Drafting Settings dialog box, set the *Snap type* to **Grid snap**. Set the *Snap spacing* to **1** and the *Grid spacing* to **3**. Zoom in until the grid lines display (the grid is too dense to display at the **Zoom All** magnification).

3. Create the blocks shown in Figure 32–25, snapping to the grid to draw them at the sizes listed below. Study the diagram shown in Figure 32–25 to determine an appropriate insertion point for each block.
   - Gate Valve - 10 X 15
   - Check Valve - 10 x 15
   - Tee - 10 x 4
   - Thermostat - 13 X 6 (Circle 6 x6)
   - Strainer - 14 X 14
   - Pump - 14 X 14
   - Instrument Box - 11 X 5 (Square 5 X 5)

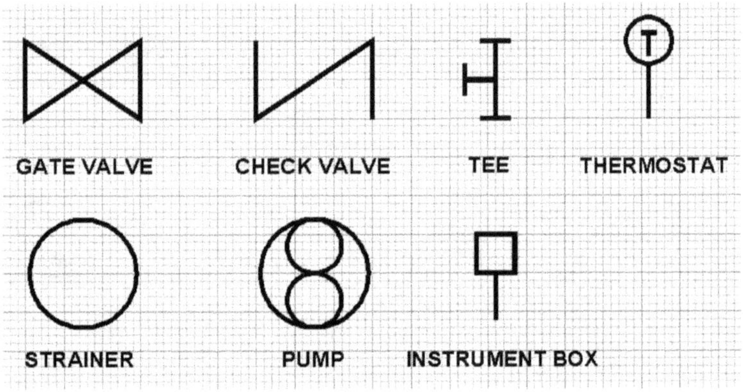

Figure 32–25

   - For the mesh in the Strainer, use the **ANSI37** hatch pattern with the *Scale* set to **1.0**. For the arrow in the Check Valve, use a polyline with the **Width** option.

4. Insert the blocks and draw the other elements to create the diagram.

Tips:

- Exact dimensions are not important because this is a schematic drawing. It might help to start by drawing and positioning some of the large parts (tanks and sumps) and then filling in the connecting pieces.
- Use **Move**, **Rotate**, and **Stretch** as required to arrange the parts correctly. Remember to use Snap or Object Snaps to connect the parts at precise points. Use **Copy** to save time and effort.
- The text should be **3** units high.

Task 2 - Set up the drawing for plotting.

1. Switch to the **ISO A3** layout.
2. Make the viewport active. Set the *scale* to **1:1** and adjust the view in the viewport by panning until the diagram fits the viewport.
3. Switch back to Paper Space and freeze the layer **Viewports** to hide the viewport border.
4. In Paper Space, add a Legend on the right side of the sheet, and include the symbols used in the diagram and their descriptions, as shown in Figure 32–26.

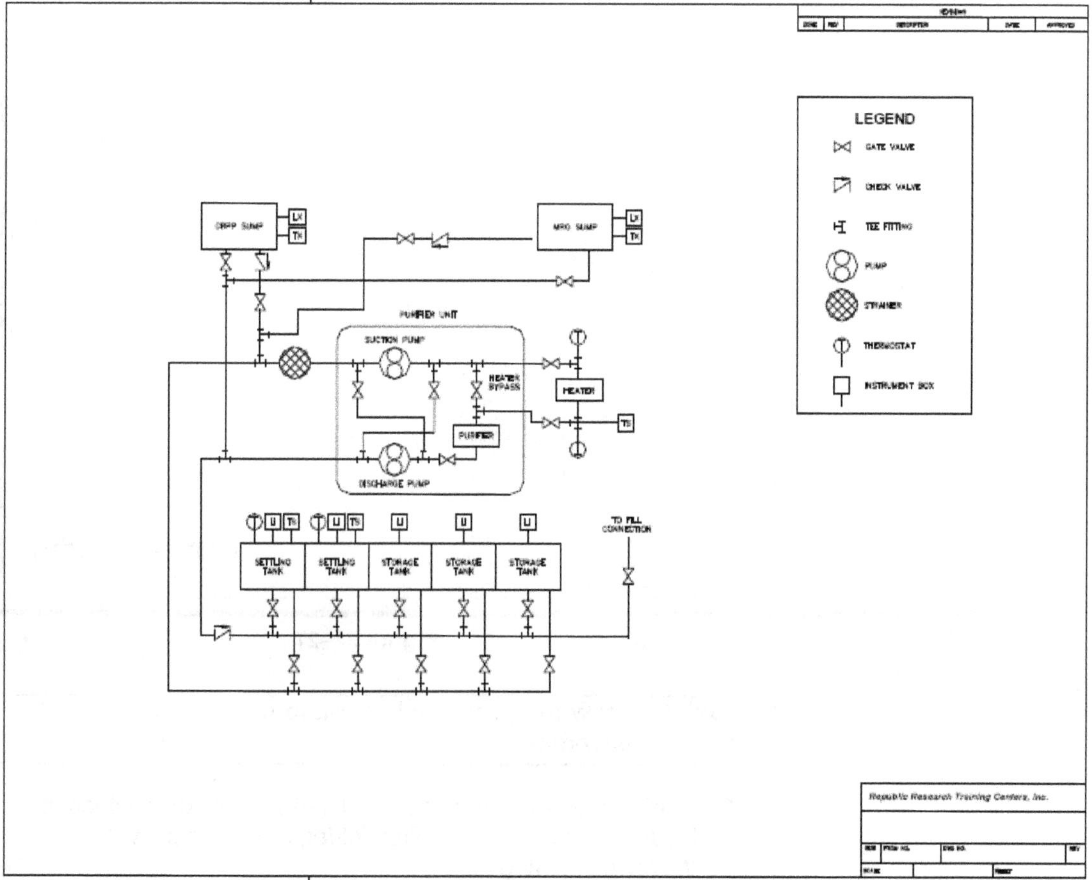

Figure 32–26

5. Save and close the drawing.

32.5 Civil Project: Warehouse Site

Estimated time for completion: 45 minutes

In this project you will create a drawing of a warehouse site. You will draw the property line, and locate the building, parking, driveway, and existing wetlands area. You will then layout the drawing for plotting. Finally, you will dimension, hatch, and add text, as shown in Figure 32–27.

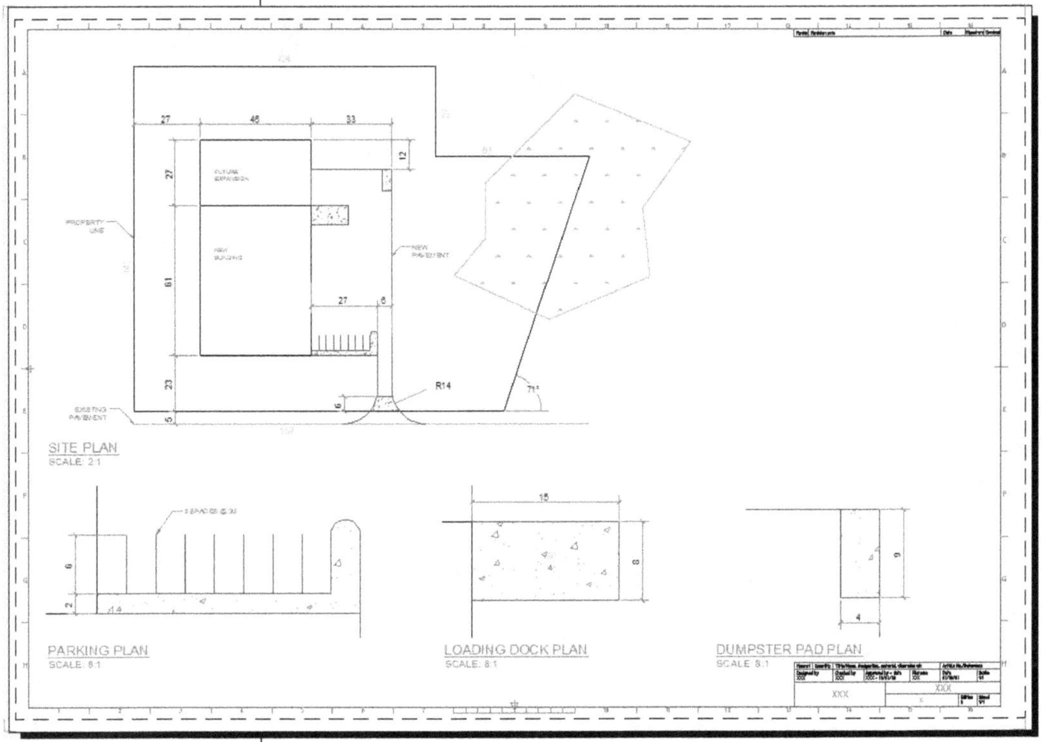

Figure 32–27

Task 1 - Draw the property line, building location, and pavement.

1. Start a new drawing based on **Civil-Meters.dwt**, which is located in your practice files folder, and save it as **Warehouse.dwg**.

2. Draw the property line, building location, existing pavement, and new pavement, as shown in Figure 32–28.

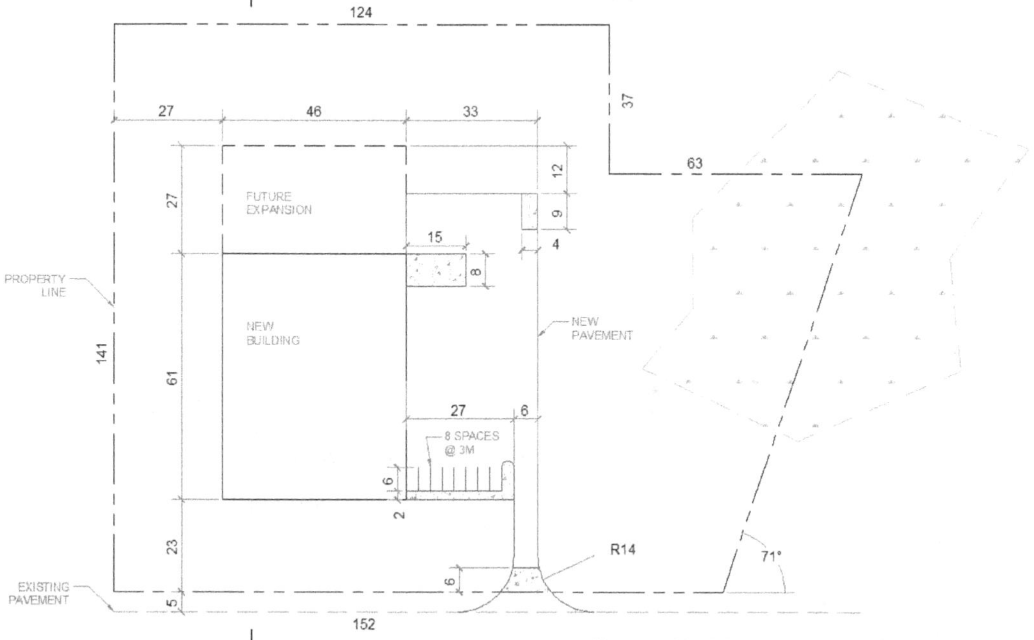

Figure 32–28

3. Add a wetlands area and hatch it with the **Swamp** hatch pattern. You need to use a *hatch scale* of **0.5**.

4. Add the parking area and concrete valley swale to the driveway, as shown in Figure 32–29. Hatch the areas shown in Figure 32–29 on the layer **Pavement Hatching**, using the **AR-Conc** *pattern*, with a *scale* of **0.03**.

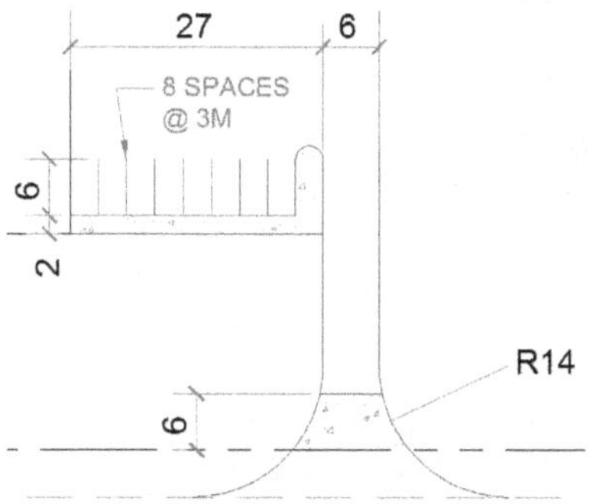

Figure 32–29

5. Add the loading dock pad and dumpster pad, as shown in Figure 32–30. Hatch these areas using the **AR-Conc** *pattern* and a *scale* of **0.03**.

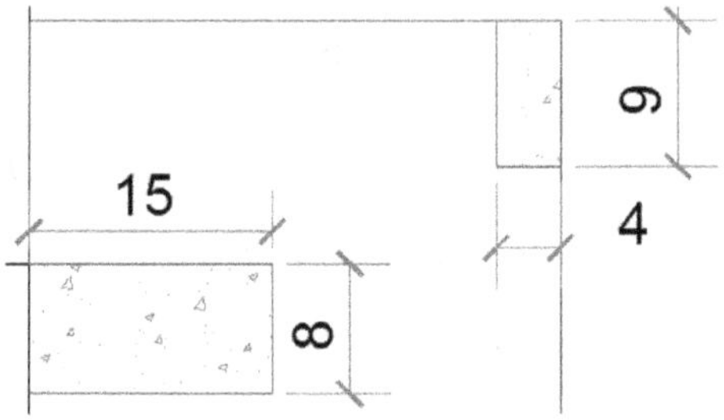

Figure 32–30

Task 2 - Layout the drawing for plotting.

1. Switch to the **D-Sized** layout.
2. Set the current layer to **Viewports** and create four viewports, as shown in Figure 32–31.

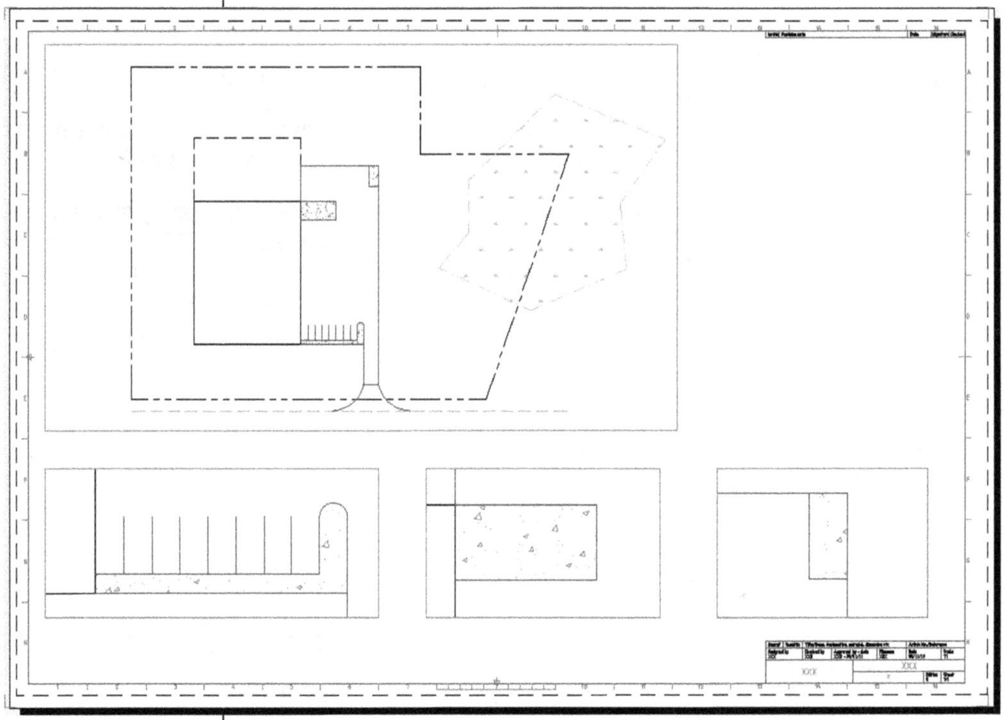

Figure 32–31

3. Switch to Model Space so that you can adjust the view in each viewport. For the larger view, set the *scale* to **2:1**. For the smaller views, set the *scale* to **8:1** and display the parking area in one, the loading dock in the second, and the dumpster pad in the third. You might need to change the sizes of the viewports to fit all of the information once you have scaled them. You can do this in Paper Space using grips.

4. In the Linetype Manager dialog box, in the *Details* area, set the *Global scale factor* to **20** and verify that the **Use Paper Space units for scaling** option is selected. This displays the linetypes correctly in Paper Space.

5. Freeze the layer **Pavement Hatching** in the site plan view only.

Task 3 - Add dimensions and text.

1. Set the current layer to **Dimensions** and add the required dimensions to each viewport, as shown in Figure 32–32. Use the annotative **Civil** dimension style. Use text to input the property line dimension information, as shown in Figure 32–32.

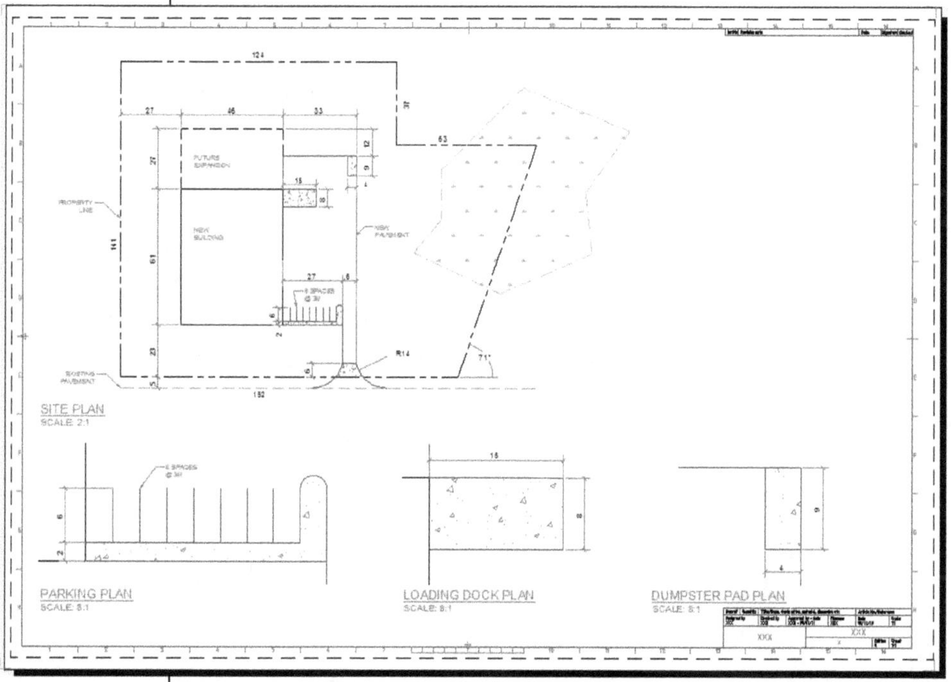

Figure 32–32

2. In the **Text** layer, add titles to label each view and the other text as required. The *text height* for titles is **8** with the **Hand** text style. All of the other text is **6** with the **Standard** text style. The titles of the viewports are as follows:

    - **Viewport 1:** Site Plan, Scale: 2:1
    - **Viewport 2:** Parking Plan, Scale: 8:1
    - **Viewport 3:** Loading Dock Plan, Scale: 8:1
    - **Viewport 4:** Dumpster Pad Plan, Scale: 8:1

3. Freeze the layer **Viewports**.

4. Save and close the drawing.

Appendix B

Optional Topics

In this chapter you learn how to use the calculator to perform standard calculations. You learn to navigate the drawing using some additional zoom commands. You learn to use some additional text and dimensioning tools. You also learn to create boundaries and lengthen objects.

Learning Objectives in this Appendix

- Perform calculations and send the output to the Command Line.
- Create and modify single line text.
- Change the size of multiline text objects and change the justification point (alignment) of selected text objects.
- Make temporary changes to a dimension style and compare various dimension styles.
- Set and compare dimensions styles in a part or assembly.
- Create a closed, complex polyline from existing objects.
- Create a single object that contains an outline and holes.
- Combine regions by adding, subtracting, or intersecting them.
- Change the length of an object or the included angle of an arc.

B.1 Using QuickCalc

The Quickcalc is similar to other palettes in that it can be left floating, docked, or hidden.

QuickCalc is a calculator that is included with the AutoCAD® software (as shown in Figure B–1) and can be used for standard calculations. It sends the output to the Command Line.

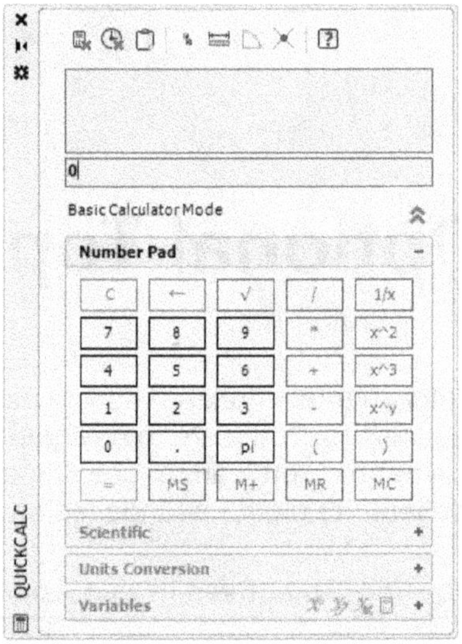

Figure B–1

- To paste a value from the QuickCalc Input box to the Command Line, click  (Paste value to command line) located near the top of the palette.
- In the *Units Conversion* area, you can obtain equivalent values for different units of measurement as shown in Figure B–2. Unit conversions are available for the length, area, volume, and angular values. Based on the unit type selected, you can select a list of units to convert from and a list of units to convert to.

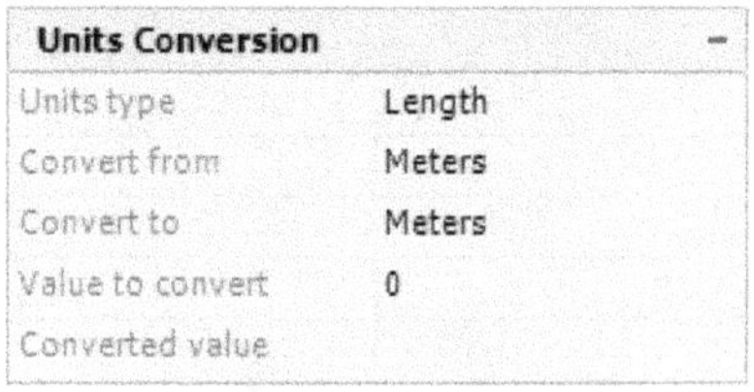

Figure B–2

How To: Convert Units of Measurement with QuickCalc

1. In the *View* tab>Palettes panel or the *Home* tab>Utilities panel, click (Quick Calculator).
2. In the *Units Conversion* area, expand the Units type drop-down list and select a unit category.
3. Expand the Convert from drop-down list and select the type of unit from which you want to convert.
4. Expand the Convert to drop-down list and select the type of unit to which you want to convert.
5. In the *Value to convert* field, enter the value you want to convert. Press <Enter>.
6. The converted value displays in the *Converted value* field.

B.2 Additional Zoom Commands

While these **Zoom** command options are not used frequently, you can access them in the Navigation Bar, as shown in Figure B–3.

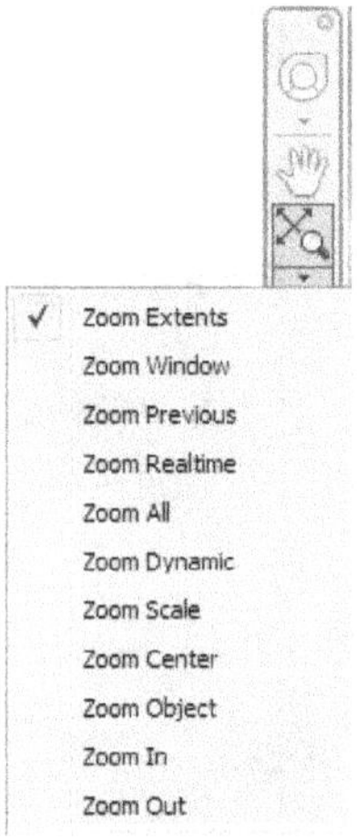

Figure B–3

Dynamic	Enables you to define an area to display using an overall view of the drawing. The screen zooms out to display the full drawing, and a *view box* opens to represents the viewport. Click to resize the view box. Move the box to the location that you want to display and press <Enter> to zoom to that area.
Scale	Changes the scale (magnification) of the display. The scale can be entered as a function of the limits of the drawing and press <Enter>. You can also enter the scale as a function of the size of the active display where you type the scale followed by **X**, and press <Enter>.
Center	Enables you to pick a point to be the new center of the display and to change the scale.
Object	Zooms to fit the object(s) that you select on the screen.
In	Makes the drawing twice as large as the current display (half of the area displays), while keeping the same center.
Out	Makes the drawing half as large as the current display (twice as much area displays), while keeping the same center.

B.3 Additional Text Tools

Several text tools add to the versatility of the AutoCAD software. You can create single line text where multiline text is not required. There are also special tools for scaling and justifying text.

Creating Single Line Text

To make single-line text annotative, set an annotative text style to be current before creating the text or change the existing text in the Properties palette.

Single-line text adds each line of text as a separate object, as shown in Figure B–4. This type of text is quick and easy to use. However, multiline text offers more options in formatting and is better for paragraph editing.

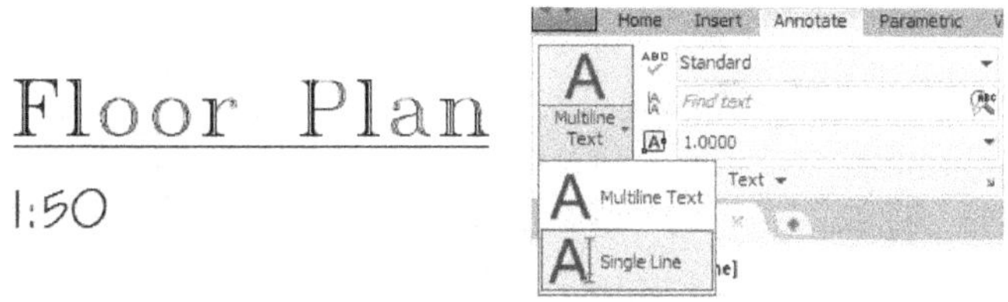

Figure B–4

How To: Create Single Line Text

1. In the *Home* tab>Annotation panel or the *Annotate* tab>Text panel, click (Single Line).
2. Select a start point.
3. Specify the paper height or press <Enter> to accept the default height.
4. Specify the rotation angle or press <Enter> to accept the default angle.
5. Start typing.
6. When you press <Enter> at the end of the line, you are prompted for another line.
7. Press <Enter> at an empty line to finish the command.

- While still in the command, you can select another point to place another line of text. It is a separate text object in the drawing.

Editing Single Line Text

*The **Single Line Text** command enables multiple lines of text to be entered in one sequence. However, each line is a separate text object.*

Double-click on any line of text to edit it. It highlights on the screen and you can make changes as shown in Figure B–5. The *Text Editor* contextual tab and the ruler do not display with a single line text.

This is a line of single-line text.
This is a second separate line.
This is a third separate line.

Figure B–5

- You can change the style, height, justification, and a few other text properties in the Properties palette.

Justify Text

(Justify Text) in the *Annotate* tab>Text panel, changes the justification point (alignment) of selected text objects without changing the location of the text, as shown in Figure B–6. If you use other methods to change the justification, such as **Edit Text** or the Properties palette, the text shifts generally.

Left Justified	Center Justified
New College Art Building Project No: 0125 513 Main Street Alexandria, Virginia	New College Art Building Project No: 0125 513 Main Street Alexandria, Virginia

Figure B–6

The options that can be used with the **Justify Text** command are as follows.

Left	Aligns text to be left-justified against an end point on the left side of the text string.
Align	Aligns text between any two selected points and determines the text height automatically (similar to **Fit**).
Fit	Places text between any two selected points at a user-specified height.
Center	Places text in the drawing, centered above the selected point.
Middle	Places text in the drawing, centered at the top of the selected point. Middle text is convenient for marking callouts and tags.
Right	Aligns text to be right-justified against an end point on the right side of the text string.

- Other alignments are for top, middle, bottom, left, center, or right (TL for Top Left, TC for Top Center, etc.).

- Once a justification has been set, it remains the default each time Single Line Text is used and until it is modified.

- You can also use (Text Align) in the *Annotate* tab>Text panel to align Single Line text. The command also works with Multiline text. First select the text objects that you want to align and then select the text to which you want them to be aligned.

Scale Text

With the regular **Scale** command, scaling several text objects at once changes the location of the text. (Scale Text) in the *Annotate* tab>expanded Text panel, changes the size of multiple text objects without changing their location as shown in Figure B–7.

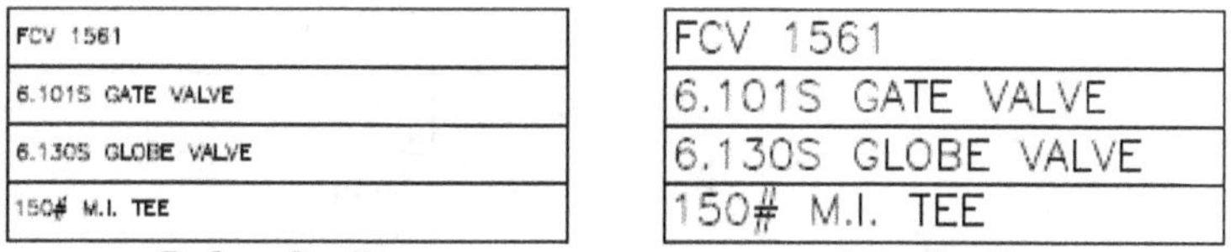

Before Scaling ***After Scaling***

Figure B–7

- You can scale the text around existing base points or specify a different justification base point for scaling (Top Left, Middle Center, etc.).

- The scaling can be specified as a text height, as a scale factor, or to match another text object.

Model Space Text and Paper Space Text

It is recommended that you use Annotation Scaling for most of the text in your drawings. However, text can be placed in either Model Space or Paper Space. In Paper Space, as with an annotative text style, you make the text the required printed height. For example, 3mm text is exactly that height when you print the layout.

For text placed in Model Space without annotation scaling, some calculation is involved for the height, because this text is scaled along with the model when it is printed. For example, room labels in a floor plan would normally be placed directly on the model. If you want the labels to be 3mm on the paper, and you are printing at a scale of 1:100, the labels need to be 300mm high in Model Space. The table displays some of the common values.

Scale	Paper Text Size	Model Text Size
1:100	2mm	230mm
	3mm	300mm
	6mm	600mm
1:50	2mm	115mm
	3mm	150mm
	6mm	300mm
1:25	2mm	57mm
	3mm	75mm
	6mm	150mm

Convert Text to Mtext

Enhanced in 2018

In the *Express Tools* tab>Text panel, use the **Convert to Mtext** tool (shown in Figure B–8) to combine multiple individual text objects to create one multi-line text object.

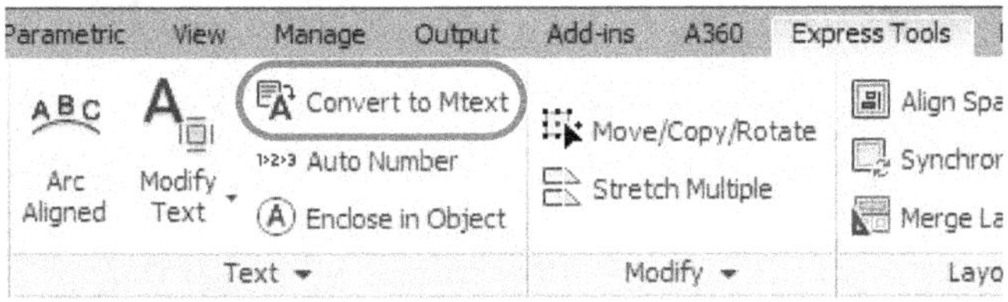

Figure B–8

- When you start this command, you can select the individual single line text objects and then press <Enter>. In the Command Line, it displays the number of Text line objects that were converted to a single multiline object, as shown in Figure B–9.

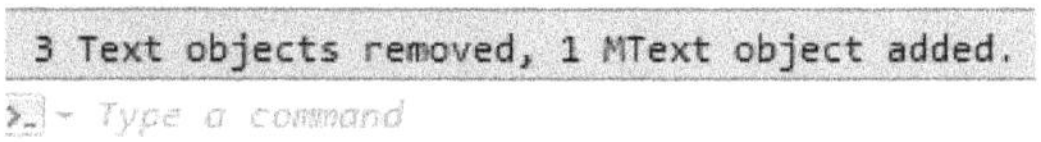

Figure B–9

- Before selecting the individual text lines, you can select the Settings option (<Down Arrow>) which opens the Text to MText Settings dialog box, as shown in Figure B–10. You can use the default **Sort top-down** setting, which sorts the collinear multiple text lines as they are on the same line with a space between them.

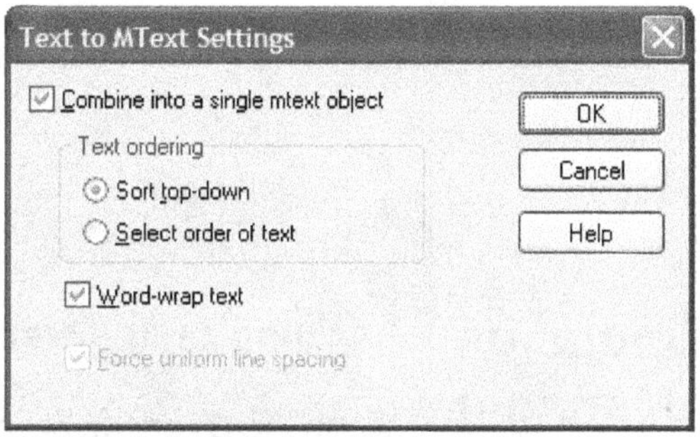

Figure B–10

- If you clear the **Combine into a single mtext object** option, the selected multiple single line text objects are converted to individual multi-line text objects, without combining them into one object.

- The **Force uniform line spacing** option keeps the existing line spacing between the individual text lines.

B.4 Additional Dimensioning Tools

When you work in Dimension Style Manager, advanced tools can be used to override and display the differences between dimension styles as shown in Figure B–11.

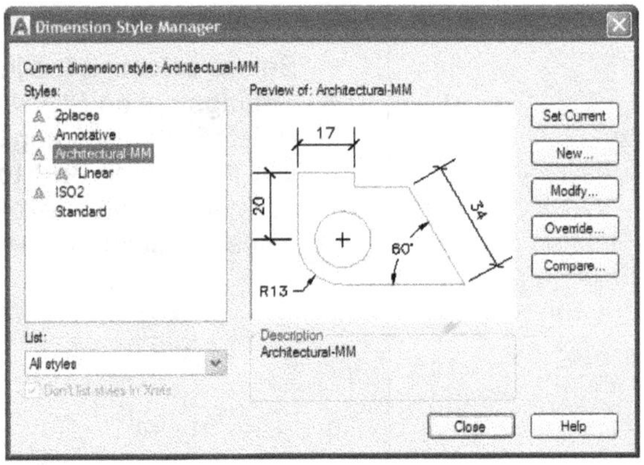

Figure B–11

Dimension Style Manager

Adding Style Overrides

With the **Override** option, you can make temporary changes to a style and add several dimensions with those changes. For example, you might need to add a few dimensions with a different precision or tolerance value from others in the drawing.

How To: Apply a Style Override

To stop using the overrides, set the original style (or any other style) to be current. The override changes are discarded.

1. In the Dimension Style Manager, make the style you want to override current.
2. Click **Override....**
3. In the Override Current Style dialog box, make the required override changes to the style. Click **OK**.
4. Overrides display in the styles list below the style. The *Description* area displays the overrides that you have applied.
5. Click **Close**. In the drawing, add the required dimensions with the overrides.

Comparing Dimension Styles

In the Dimension Style Manager, click **Compare...** to open a table listing the differences between two styles as shown in Figure B–12. You can pick any two styles or sub-styles that have been defined in the current drawing in the *Compare* and *With* lists. The AutoCAD software lists all of the dimension variables that differ and the settings of the variable in each style.

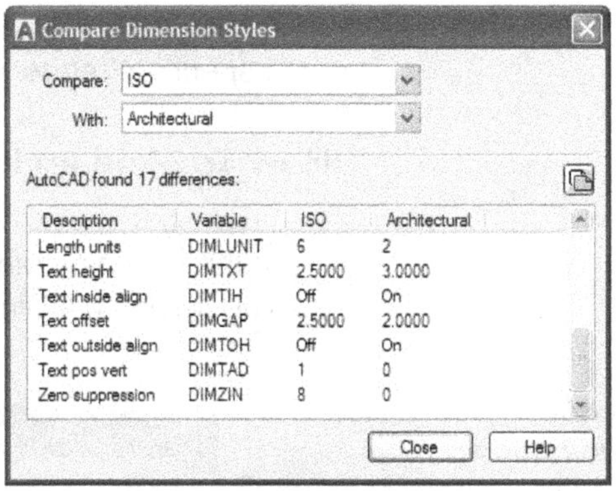

Figure B–12

Inspection Dimensions

The **Inspect (dimension)** command creates special types of dimensions for quality control in mechanical drafting and manufacturing. They are used in Inspection Drawings to indicate dimensions that must be checked for the part or assembly, as shown in Figure B–13. They are useful for companies who out-source parts and must ensure that specific dimensions are met so that the parts fit into an assembly correctly.

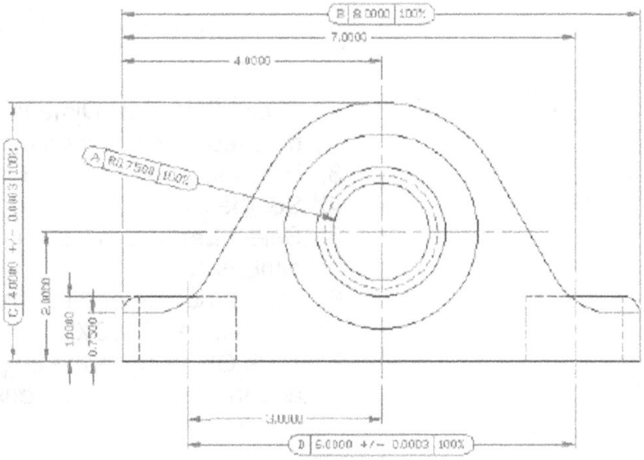

Figure B–13

- You can add Inspection dimensions to any dimension object. Inspection dimensions consist of text and a frame and contain three information fields:

- **Inspection Label:** Located on the left side and used to identify the dimension.

- **Dimension Value:** Located in the middle and containing the original dimension text, tolerances, and prefix and suffix text.

- **Inspection Rate:** Located on the right side, indicates inspection frequency, and is shown as a percentage.

How To: Add an Inspection Dimension

1. In the *Annotate* tab>Dimensions panel, click (Inspect). The Inspection Dimension dialog box opens as shown in Figure B–14.

*Click **Remove Inspection** to remove an inspection dimension from the selected dimension.*

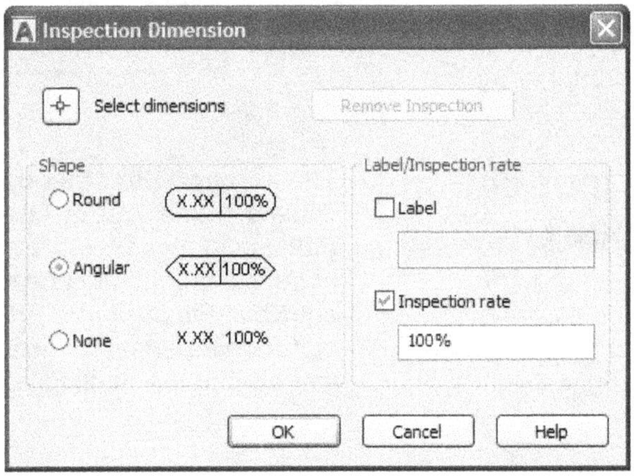

Figure B–14

2. Click (Select Dimensions) and select the dimensions to be used as inspection dimensions.
3. Press <Enter> to return to the dialog box.
4. Set the *Shape* to **Round**, **Angular**, or **None**.
5. Select **Label** and type an identifier for the inspection dimension.
6. Type a percentage for the **Inspection rate** option or accept the default of 100%.
7. Click **OK** to close the Inspection Dimension dialog box and add the inspection dimensions.

B.5 Creating Boundaries and Regions

Creating Boundaries

Sometimes you need to create a complex polyline from several existing objects using the **Boundary** command, as shown in Figure B–15.

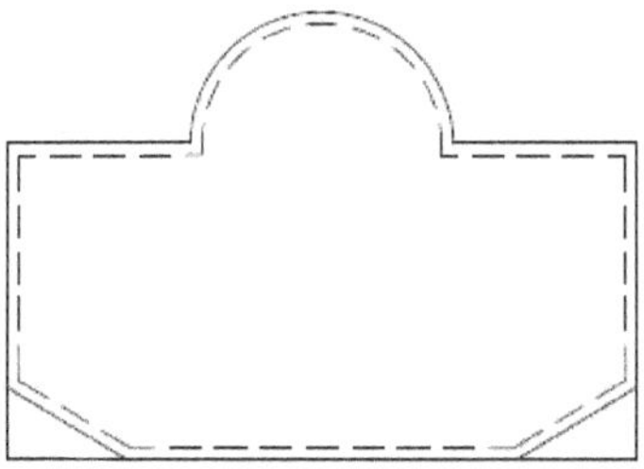

Figure B–15

- The **Boundary** command can also create regions.

How To: Create Boundaries

1. In the *Home* tab>Draw panel, click (Boundary).
2. In the Boundary Creation dialog box, select the required options.
3. Click (Pick Points) or click **OK**.
4. Select a point inside a closed area, as shown in Figure B–16. You can select points in multiple closed areas.

The AutoCAD software creates a closed polyline or region that is defined by the edges of the first objects it detects.

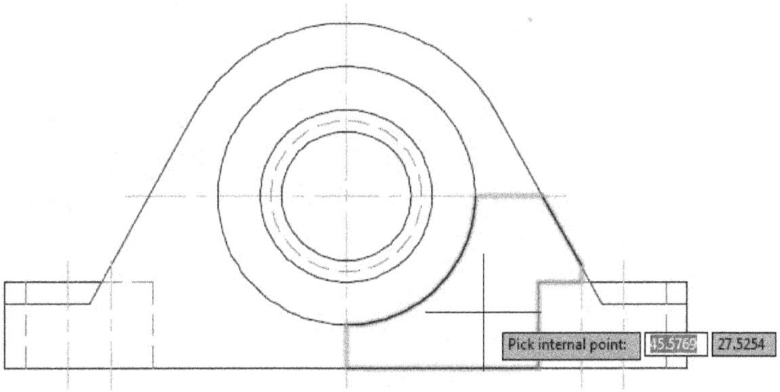

Figure B–16

5. Press <Enter> to create the boundary.

Boundary Options

The new polyline is placed directly on top of the existing boundary lines. It is recommended that you create the boundary on a separate layer from the other objects.

When you create boundaries, you can specify what is included in the boundary area with the options shown in Figure B–17.

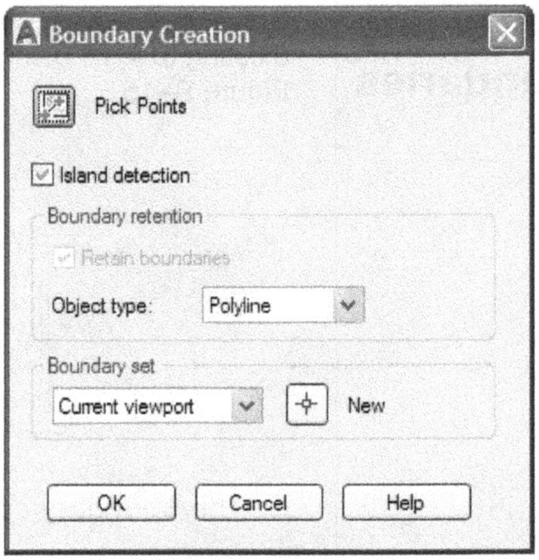

Figure B–17

Island detection	Select this option if you want the **Boundary** command to find any interior objects (*islands*) and create polylines around them, in addition to finding the exterior boundary.
Object type	You can create a polyline or a region. If a boundary set includes ellipses, elliptical arcs, or splines, the **Boundary** command automatically creates a region.
Boundary set	The default option, **Current viewport**, calculates the boundary based on all of the objects that are visible in the current viewport. To select the objects that should be considered when calculating the boundary, click (New - Select new boundary set). This enables you to exclude objects from the boundary calculation and it can make the boundary calculation faster in a complex drawing.

Working with Regions

A polyline is a continuous object. It can be closed, but cannot contain holes. Regions are used to create single objects that contain an outline and holes, as shown in Figure B–18.

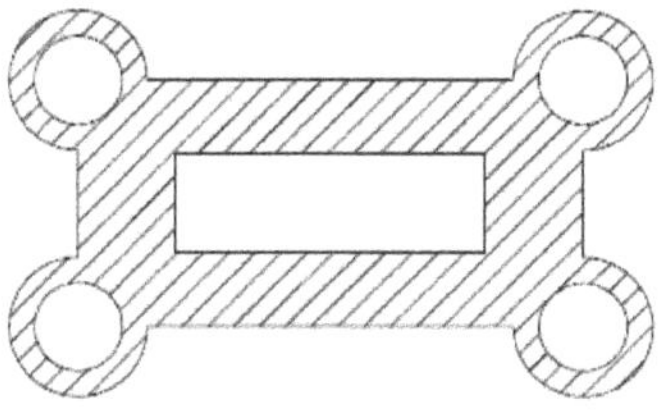

Figure B–18

- A *region* is a 2D solid object or infinitely thin surface. The edges cannot be separated from the shape. Therefore, if you move an edge, the entire surface moves. Typical uses for regions include a plate with holes or a wall with windows.
- You can create objects with holes that are part of the object.
- Regions can be used in many cases to quickly create complex geometry using the **Union**, **Subtract**, and **Intersect** commands.
- The area of a region, even one with holes, can easily be found using the **Area** command with the **Object** option.

How To: Create a Region

1. Draw the closed shape for the region using lines, polylines, etc. The lines must connect precisely end point to end point.
2. In the *Home* tab>expanded Draw panel, click (Region).
3. Select the objects. You can select several closed shapes and convert them all into regions at the same time. In the Command Line, the AutoCAD software reports the number of regions it has created.
   - Regions can be created out of existing closed shapes made of lines, arcs, polylines, circles, etc.
   - If the closed shape consists of separate segments, the segments must connect end point to end point to make a region.
4. The original objects are consumed when you use them to create a region.

- You can **Explode** a region to convert it into lines, arcs, splines, or circles, depending on the shapes involved.

Combining Regions

Regions are useful construction tools because of the ways in which they can be combined. For example, you can create a hole or cutout in a region by subtracting one region from another. You can also add regions and find the intersection of regions as shown in Figure B–19. The addition (union), subtraction, and intersection actions are called *Boolean Operations*.

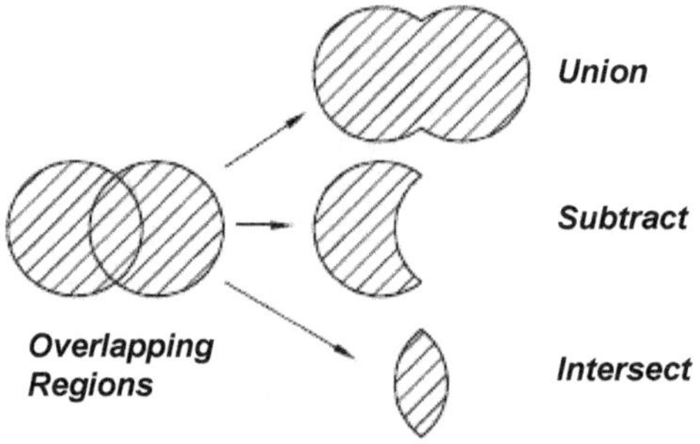

Figure B–19

- You can union, subtract, or intersect two or more regions at a time.
- The regions on which the Boolean Operations are performed do not need to intersect. However, the intersection of two objects that do not overlap erases the regions.
- Regions are considered solid objects and the tools for editing them are located in the *Home* tab>Solid Editing panel (as shown in Figure B–20) when the 3D Modeling workspace is active.

In the AutoCAD LT® software, you cannot combine regions because the Boolean Operations and the 3D Modeling workspace are not available.

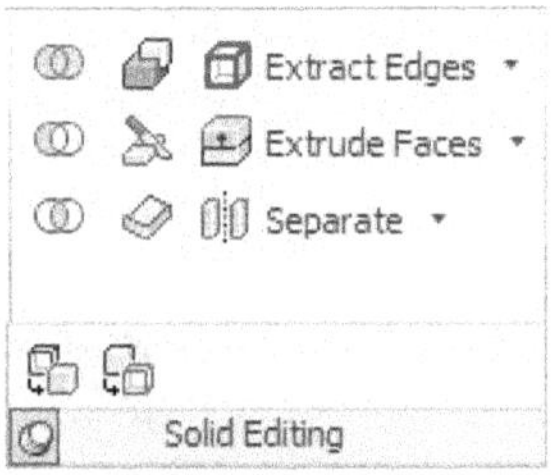

Figure B–20

- You can type the name of the command if you do not want to switch workspaces.

Union

(Union) combines two or more regions into a single region as shown in Figure B–21.

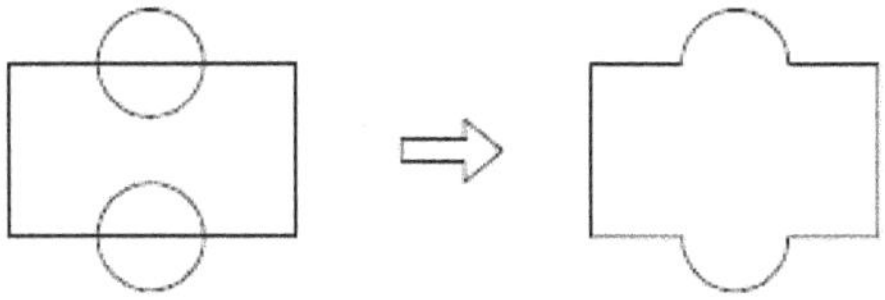

Figure B–21

Subtract

(Subtract) removes the area of one region from another where they overlap as shown in Figure B–22. You can also use **Subtract** to create regions containing holes. By subtracting the holes, you can also find out the area of the closed shape.

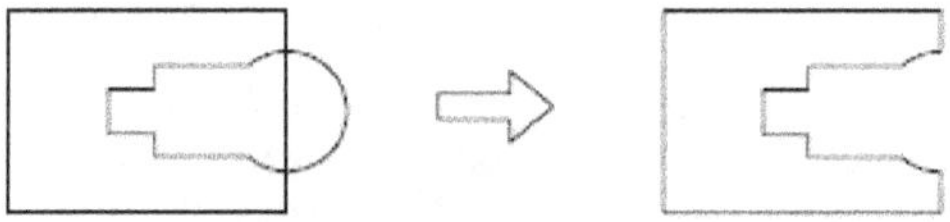

Figure B–22

- Select the region(s) to *subtract from* first. Then select the regions that you want to subtract.

Intersect

(Intersect) finds the common area of two or more regions as shown in Figure B–23. Only the area that is shared by the selected regions remains in the new region.

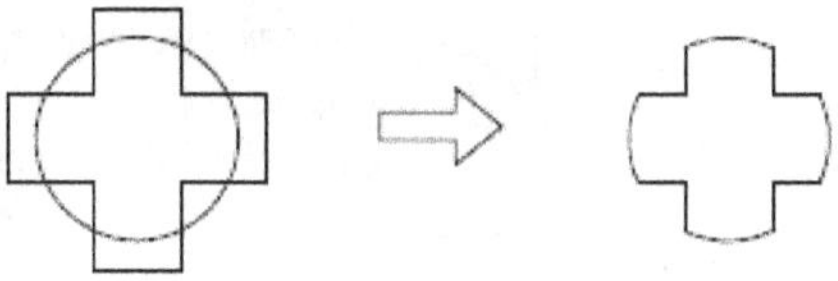

Figure B–23

B.6 Modifying Length

You can use the **Lengthen** command to change the length of an object or the included angle of an arc as shown in Figure B–24. However, you cannot change the length of a closed object.

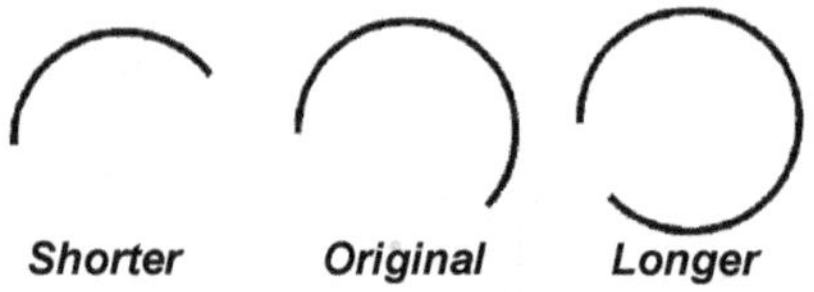

Figure B–24

How To: Lengthen an Object

1. In the *Home* tab>expanded Modify panel, click  (Lengthen).
2. Select the object. Its current length displays in the Command Line.
3. Select an option to modify the object's length:
    - **Delta:** Specify the increments by which the object's length is to be modified. To extend the object, enter a positive value. To shorten it, enter a negative value. The length is always measured from the closest end point to the selection point. Use the same method to change the angle of an arc.
    - **Percent:** Modify the object by a percentage of its length.
    - **Total:** Modify the object's length by a specific amount from a fixed end point. Specify the total required angle to modify the included angle of an arc.
    - **Dynamic:** Toggle on Dynamic Dragging mode. Pick an object's end point and drag it to the required length. The other end point does not change.
4. Hover over the object to preview the changes depending on the selected option and the specified values. Select the object to change it.
5. Press <Enter> to end the command.

Chapter Review Questions

1. You can use the **QuickCalc** command to obtain equivalent values for different units of measurement.
   a. True
   b. False
2. The **Dynamic Zoom** command:
   a. Makes the drawing twice as large as the current display.
   b. Makes the drawing half as large as the current display.
   c. Enables you to define an area to display using an overall view of the drawing.
   d. Zooms to fit the object(s) that you select on the screen.
3. Which one of the following is true of single-line text?
   a. You can only type in one line at a time and then have to start the command again.
   b. There are no options for alignments of single-line text.
   c. You can type in multiple lines, but each line is separate from the last.
   d. You can format the text using the *Text Editor* contextual tab.
4. In which of the following industries are Inspection Dimensions most useful?
   a. Architectural building inspection
   b. Electrical control inspection
   c. Plumbing flow control
   d. Manufacturing quality control
5. When you want to inquire about the area of a closed shape that contains holes, you can create a region and use which of the following Boolean commands?
   a. **Union**
   b. **Remove**
   c. **Intersect**
   d. **Subtract**

6. What does the **Delta** option of the **Lengthen** command do?
    a. Modifies the object's length by specified increments.
    b. Modifies the object by a percentage of its length.
    c. Modifies the object's length by a specific amount from a fixed end point.
    d. Modifies the object's length by dragging its end point to the required length.

Command Summary

Button	Command	Location
	**Boundary**	• **Ribbon:** *Home* tab>Draw panel
	**Inspect**	• **Ribbon:** *Annotate* tab>Dimension panel
	**Intersect**	• **Ribbon:** *Home* tab>Solid Editing panel (*in the 3D Modeling workspace*)
	**Justify Text**	• **Ribbon:** *Annotate* tab>Text panel
	**Lengthen**	• **Ribbon:** *Home* tab>Modify panel
	**QuickCalc**	• **Ribbon:** *View* tab>Palettes panel
	**Region**	• **Ribbon:** *Home* tab>Draw panel
	**Scale Text**	• **Ribbon:** *Annotate* tab>Text panel
	**Single Line Text**	• **Ribbon:** *Home* tab>Annotation Panel or *Annotate* tab>Text panel
	**Subtract**	• **Ribbon:** *Home* tab>Solid Editing panel (*in the 3D Modeling workspace*)
	**Union**	• **Ribbon:** *Home* tab>Solid Editing panel (*in the 3D Modeling workspace*)
	**Zoom Center**	• **Navigation Bar** • **Ribbon:** *Home* tab>Utilities panel
	**Zoom Dynamic**	• **Navigation Bar** • **Ribbon:** *Home* tab>Utilities panel
	**Zoom In**	• **Navigation Bar** • **Ribbon:** *Home* tab>Utilities panel
	**Zoom Object**	• **Navigation Bar** • **Ribbon:** *Home* tab>Utilities panel
	**Zoom Out**	• **Navigation Bar** • **Ribbon:** *Home* tab>Utilities panel
	**Zoom Scale**	• **Navigation Bar** • **Ribbon:** *Home* tab>Utilities panel

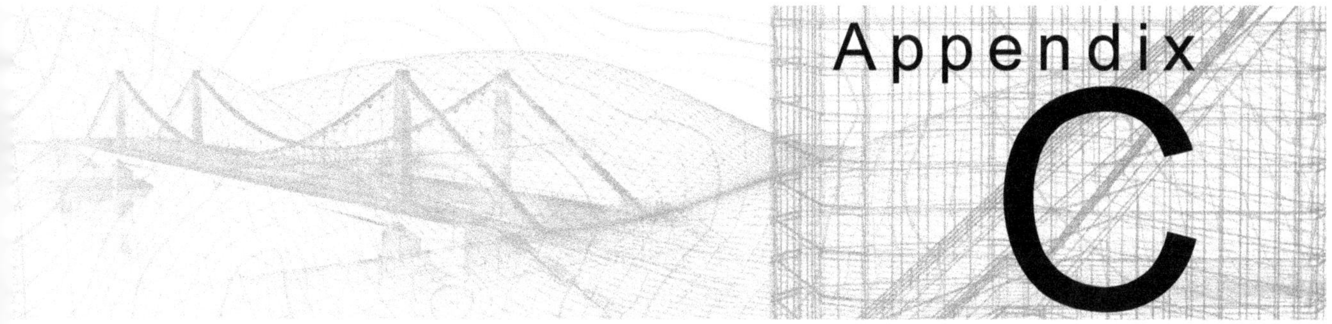

Skills Assessment 2

To test your knowledge on the course material (Chapters 21 to 32), answer the questions that follow. Select the best answer for each question.

1. What does the **Closeall** command do?
   a. Closes all of the open drawings including the *Start* tab.
   b. Closes all of the open drawings except the *Start* tab.
   c. Closes all of the open drawings including the currently active drawing and the *Start* tab.
   d. Closes all of the open drawings except the currently active drawing and the *Start* tab.
2. When defining a block, you specify a base point. Which of the following is true of the base point?
   a. It should always be at the center of the block.
   b. It should always be at the bottom of the block.
   c. It should always be an end point.
   d. It is the handle by which the block is held when being inserted.
3. What technique could you use to draw a circle with its center point 3 units over and 8 units up from the center of an existing circle?
   a. **Temporary Tracking Point**
   b. **Measure**
   c. **Locate Point**
   d. **Array**

4. Settings you can build into a template file include:
    a. Layers
    b. Units
    c. Text and Dimension Styles.
    d. All of the above.
5. How can you add blocks to a tool palette?
    a. Use **Insert Block**.
    b. Use **Make Block**.
    c. Use **Wblock**.
    d. Drag and drop blocks from drawing window onto the palette.
6. Which key enables you to make multiple grips hot?
    a. <Shift>
    b. <Alt>
    c. <Esc>
    d. <Ctrl>
7. Which phrase describes relative coordinates?
    a. They are relative to the current screen display.
    b. They are relative to the object snap.
    c. They are measured from the last point picked.
    d. They are measured from the origin (0,0).
8. What layer properties can you override in viewports?
    a. Color
    b. Freeze
    c. Linetype
    d. All of the above.

9. Which of the following describes the purpose of the **Auto Constrain** command?
   a. It constrains all of the lines in a drawing to be horizontal or vertical.
   b. It constrains all of the objects using basic geometric information in the drawing.
   c. It constrains all of the objects using existing dimensions in the drawing.
   d. It automatically displays all of the constrained objects.

10. Which command converts a local block or selected objects into a separate drawing file?
    a. **Explode**
    b. **Wblock**
    c. **Group**
    d. **Purge**

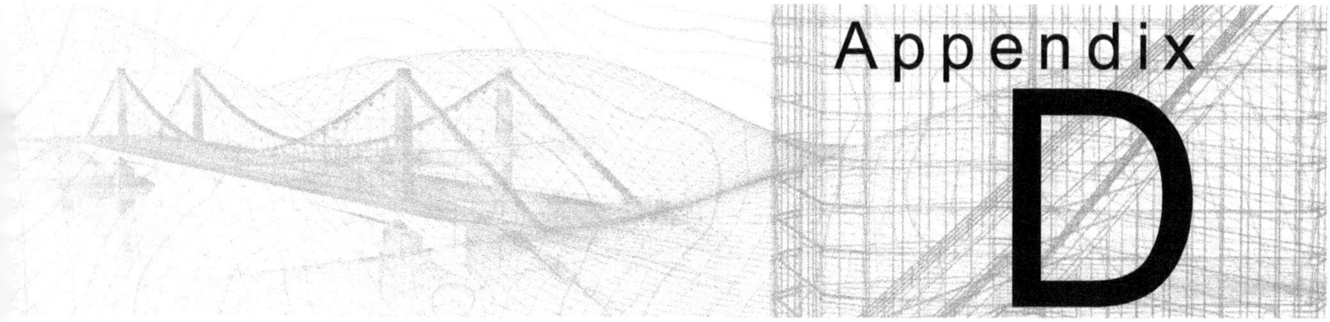

Appendix D

AutoCAD Certification Exam Objectives

The following table will help you to locate the exam objectives in the chapters of the following student guides:

- *AutoCAD®/AutoCAD LT® 2018: Fundamentals*
- *AutoCAD®/AutoCAD LT® 2018: Essentials*
- *AutoCAD®/AutoCAD LT® 2018: Beyond the Basics*
- *AutoCAD® 2018: Advanced*

  NOTE: The content in the *Fundamentals* student guide is identical to the content in the *Essentials* and *Beyond the Basics* student guides. To prepare for the exam, you need either the *Fundamentals* student guide, or both the *Essentials* student guide and the *Beyond the Basics* student guide.

Reviewing these topics and objectives will help you prepare for the AutoCAD Certified Professional exam.

Exam Topic	Exam Objective	Student Guide	Chapter & Section(s)
Draw Objects	Draw lines and rectangles	• AutoCAD Fundamentals	• 2.1, 2.3 & 2.4
		• AutoCAD Essentials	• 2.1, 2.3 & 2.4
	Draw circles, arcs, and polygons	• AutoCAD Fundamentals	• 2.5 • 8.1 & 8.4
		• AutoCAD Essentials	• 2.5 • 8.1 & 8.4

Exam Topic	Exam Objective	Student Guide	Chapter & Section(s)
Draw with Accuracy	Use object-snap tracking	• AutoCAD Fundamentals	• 4.3 & 4.4 • 22.2
		• AutoCAD Essentials	• 4.3 & 4.4
		• AutoCAD Beyond the Basics	• 2.2
	Use coordinate systems	• AutoCAD Fundamentals	• 1.4 • 22.1
		• AutoCAD Essentials	• 1.4
		• AutoCAD Beyond the Basics	• 2.1
	Make isometric drawings	• AutoCAD Fundamentals	• 4.5
		• AutoCAD Essentials	• 4.5
Modify Objects	Move and copy objects	• AutoCAD Fundamentals	• 5.2 & 5.3 • 21.5
		• AutoCAD Essentials	• 5.2 & 5.3
		• AutoCAD Beyond the Basics	• 1.5
	Rotate and scale objects	• AutoCAD Fundamentals	• 5.4 & 5.5
		• AutoCAD Essentials	• 5.4 & 5.5
	Create and use arrays	• AutoCAD Fundamentals	• 11.5
		• AutoCAD Essentials	• 11.5
	Trim and extend objects	• AutoCAD Fundamentals	• 11.1
		• AutoCAD Essentials	• 11.1
	Offset and mirror objects	• AutoCAD Fundamentals	• 5.6 • 11.4
		• AutoCAD Essentials	• 5.6 • 11.4
	Use grip editing	• AutoCAD Fundamentals	• 5.7 • 21.6
		• AutoCAD Essentials	• 5.7
		• AutoCAD Beyond the Basics	• 1.6
	Fillet and chamfer objects	• AutoCAD Fundamentals	• 11.3
		• AutoCAD Essentials	• 11.3
Use Additional Drawing Techniques	Draw and edit polylines	• AutoCAD Fundamentals	• 8.2 & 8.3
		• AutoCAD Essentials	• 8.2 & 8.3
	Blend between objects with splines	• AutoCAD Fundamentals	• 8.3
		• AutoCAD Essentials	• 8.3
	Apply hatches and gradients	• AutoCAD Fundamentals	• 18.1 & 18.2
		• AutoCAD Essentials	• 18.1 & 18.2

Exam Topic	Exam Objective	Student Guide	Chapter & Section(s)
Organize Objects	Change object properties	• AutoCAD Fundamentals	• 9.1
		• AutoCAD Essentials	• 9.1
	Alter layer assignments for objects	• AutoCAD Fundamentals	• 7.4
		• AutoCAD Essentials	• 7.4
	Control layer visibility	• AutoCAD Fundamentals	• 7.3
		• AutoCAD Essentials	• 7.3
		• AutoCAD Advanced	• 14.3
	Assign properties by object or layer	• AutoCAD Fundamentals	• 7.2
		• AutoCAD Essentials	• 7.2
	Manage layer properties	• AutoCAD Fundamentals	• 7.3 • 21.7 • 27.3
		• AutoCAD Essentials	• 7.3
		• AutoCAD Beyond the Basics	• 1.7 • 7.3
		• AutoCAD Advanced	• 14.1
Reuse Existing Content	Work with blocks	• AutoCAD Fundamentals	• 12.1 to 12.5 • 25.1, 25.2, 25.4 & 25.5
		• AutoCAD Essentials	• 12.1 to 12.5
		• AutoCAD Beyond the Basics	• 5.1, 5.2, 5.4 & 5.5
		• AutoCAD Advanced	• 5.1 to 5.4
	Manage block attributes	• AutoCAD Advanced	• 6.1 to 6.5
	Reference external drawings and images	• AutoCAD Fundamentals	• 31.1 to 31.3
		• AutoCAD Beyond the Basics	• 11.1 to 11.3
Annotate Drawings	Add and modify text	• AutoCAD Fundamentals	• 17.2 to 17.4
		• AutoCAD Essentials	• 17.2 to 17.4
	Use dimensions	• AutoCAD Fundamentals	• 19.1 to 19.4
		• AutoCAD Essentials	• 19.1 to 19.4
	Add and modify multileaders	• AutoCAD Fundamentals	• 17.5
		• AutoCAD Essentials	• 17.5
	Create and assign annotative styles	• AutoCAD Fundamentals	• 17.1 • 28.4 • 29.1 to 29.3
		• AutoCAD Essentials	• 17.1
		• AutoCAD Beyond the Basics	• 8.4 • 9.1 to 9.3
		• AutoCAD Advanced	• 2.1

Exam Topic	Exam Objective	Student Guide	Chapter & Section(s)
Annotate Drawings *(continued)*	Use tables	• AutoCAD Fundamentals	• 17.6 & 17.7
		• AutoCAD Essentials	• 17.6 & 17.7
		• AutoCAD Advanced	• 3.1 & 3.2
Layout and Printing	Create layouts	• AutoCAD Fundamentals	• 14.1 & 14.2 • 28.1 & 28.2
		• AutoCAD Essentials	• 14.1 & 14.2
		• AutoCAD Beyond the Basics	• 8.1 & 8.2
	Use viewports	• AutoCAD Fundamentals	• 14.3 • 28.3
		• AutoCAD Essentials	• 14.3
		• AutoCAD Beyond the Basics	• 8.3
	Set printing and plotting options	• AutoCAD Fundamentals	• 15.2 & 15.3
		• AutoCAD Essentials	• 15.2 & 15.3
		• AutoCAD Advanced	• 8.1 & 8.3

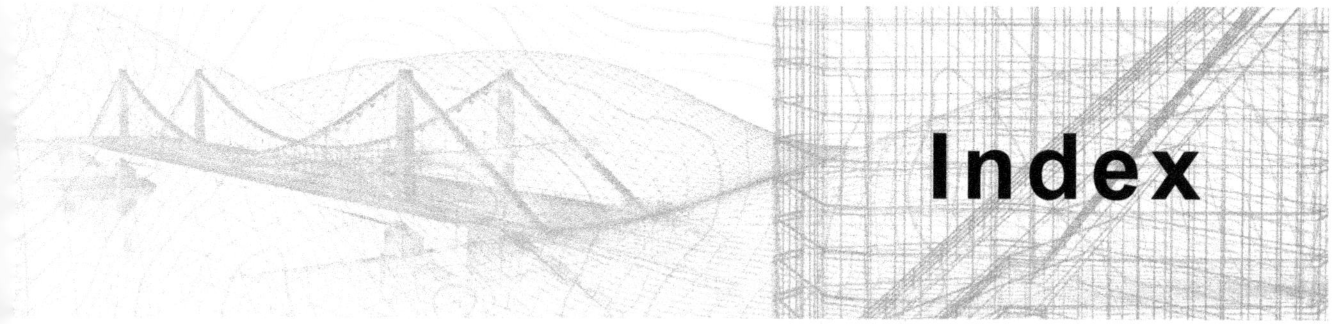

Index

T

U

V

W

X

Z

www.ingramcontent.com/pod-product-compliance
Lightning Source LLC
Chambersburg PA
CBHW080148060326
40689CB00018B/3900